The Power OF A Positive Mom™

2 books in 1

The Power OF A Positive Woman™

W9-AYM-379

Our purpose at Howard Books is to:
- *Increase faith* in the hearts of growing Christians
- *Inspire holiness* in the lives of believers
- *Instill hope* in the hearts of struggling people everywhere

Because He's coming again!

Published by Howard Books, a division of Simon & Schuster, Inc.
1230 Avenue of the Americas, New York, NY 10020
www.howardpublishing.com

The Power of a Positive Mom and The Power of a Positive Woman 2 books in 1
© 2006 by Karol Ladd

10 9 8 7 6 5 4 3 2 1

HOWARD is a registered trademark of Simon & Schuster, Inc.

Manufactured in the United States of America

For information regarding special discounts for bulk purchases, please contact: Simon & Schuster Special Sales at 1-800-456-6798 or business@simonandschuster.com.

Edited by Michele Buckingham
Cover Design by LinDee Loveland
Interior design by Stephanie Denney and John Luke

Karol Ladd

THE Power OF A Positive™ MoM

2 books in 1

THE Power OF A Positive™ Woman

HOWARD BOOKS
A DIVISION OF SIMON & SCHUSTER
New York   London   Toronto   Sydney

About the Author

Karol Ladd has been making a positive impact in the lives of kids for many years. Formerly a teacher, Karol is now a writer and speaker. Most importantly, she is a wife and mother. Karol has written more than ten books that share creative and fresh ideas for families. Her books include *Parties with a Purpose, Party Mix, Summer with a Smile, Scream Savers, Table Talk, Fun House,* and The Glad Scientist series. Her energetic personality and informative ideas make her a popular speaker with numerous women's groups and mothers' organizations. Karol is the cofounder of a character-building club for young girls called USA Sonshine Girls. Karol's rich background also includes working in children's ministry and with Christian camps and serving on the board of several pro-family organizations.

PositiveLifePrinciples.com

THe
P●wer
OF A
P☺sitive
M♥M

Karol Ladd

Dedication

To my precious family, Curt, Grace, and Joy.
Thank you for your faithful love, encouragement, and support.
You are truly God's gift to me.

To my dad, Garry Kinder, whose positive attitude,
example, and leadership influenced me to reach greater heights.

To my faithful prayer warriors, Nancy, Lisa, and Carol.
Your fervent prayers avail much! I truly appreciate your
dedication to this ministry.

And to my supportive friends, Beth, Leslie, Amy, and Tracy.
Thank you for your positive encouragement.

Thank you, Howard Publishing and Philis Boultinghouse,
for your excellence in publishing Christian books.

Most importantly, to our heavenly Father, who gives us the
strength and power to be positive moms each day.

Contents

Contents

Principle #4: The Power of Strong Relationships

Principle #5: The Power of Your Example

Principle #6: The Power of Strong Moral Standards

Principle #7: The Power of Love and Forgiveness

Introduction

You Can Do It!
Making a Positive Difference

The wise woman builds her house.
—Proverbs 14:1

Every child needs a positive push in life. An enthusiastic word, a loving smile, or a prayer of support may be just the encouragement a young person needs to send him or her off in the right direction.

That's where mothers come in. As moms, we have the opportunity every day to boost our children onward and upward. Ours is a highly influential job. Through our affirmative support and loving care, we are in a unique position to help our children reach for their dreams and achieve their God-given potential.

Unfortunately, in the day-to-day struggles of motherhood, our good intentions toward our kids can seem to fly out the window. We may start off the day with a fresh outlook and high expectations, but midway through the second temper tantrum of the morning (theirs, not ours), we somehow lose our handle on the uplifting encouragement we intended to share. How can we be positive when we often feel like the greatest portion of our day is spent correcting, scolding, and trying to avert minor disasters? It doesn't help that we're distracted from

1

our efforts to be affirming by the daily chores of running errands, doing laundry, and putting dinner on the table.

I truly believe that most of us start out as positive mothers when that little newborn baby is first laid in our arms. It is easy to look down at that bundle of precious potential and fill our minds with hopes and dreams of what he or she will one day become (through our guidance and influence, of course). But in the aftermath of those blissful moments we begin to deal with the business of everyday life and child rearing, and we discover that it is more challenging to be a positive parent than we ever dreamed.

This book is written to help every mother rediscover and recapture that spirit of affirmation and encouragement—that sense of great expectation and purpose and possibility we all felt in the beginning—even in the midst of the everyday struggles of raising kids. You can do it! These are four powerful words. Our children need to hear them quite often. But today I want to say them to *you.*

Yes, you can do it! With God's help and with his Holy Spirit living inside you, you can be, as the writer of Proverbs says, "the wise woman [who] builds her house" (Proverbs 14:1). The seven principles I offer in this book are meant to help you recognize the amazing power that God has put in the hands of positive mothers—and to inspire you to become the positive mom you want and need to be. Each chapter is filled with quotes, scriptures, and real-life examples designed to encourage you and spur you on.

At the close of each chapter is a section called "Power Point" with a suggestion for further Bible study, a model prayer, and an activity to reinforce the principles you've just learned. After all, God's power is not in the reading; it's in the *doing!* These Power Point sections lend themselves well to group study with fellow mothers. In fact, studying this book and completing the Power Point steps with other mothers is a great way to find mutual encouragement and support as you seek to become a more positive mom.

Pass It On

I don't know about you, but I was blessed to have been raised by a positive mom and dad. My mother passed away several years ago, but her discipline and godly character were powerful examples in my life. She was a kind woman with a servant's heart who prayed continually for her family and friends. For his part, my dad always taught his kids to look at the positive and not dwell on the negative. Even today he is an encourager—always wearing a smile on his face and ready to speak a good word. I learned a great deal from my parents' positive influence, and part of my desire in writing this book is to pass on to you some of the wisdom they taught me.

Maybe you had positive parents too. Maybe not. Either way, you and I both have the ultimate positive parent: God, our heavenly Father. The principles in this book are powerful and true, not because I had great parents or because I'm an extraordinary mother myself (although I try my best). Rather, they are supremely powerful and absolutely true because they come from God's Word.

I've spoken about these principles in women's meetings for several years, and I've always enjoyed hearing feedback from women who say, " 'The Power of a Positive Mom' has made me a better mother." Interestingly enough, I found myself saying these same words as I searched the Scriptures further and did more research to write this book.

I grew to have a deeper prayer life while writing chapter 6 and studying the faith-filled prayers of George Muller. I became more positive and thankful as I considered the importance of "an attitude of gratitude" while writing chapter 10. I added several time-honored traditions to our family celebrations after working on chapter 16. Throughout the writing of the entire book I learned to encourage my children in more effective ways through my words, actions, and example.

I'm just a fellow journeyman (or should I say journey*mom*) in this adventure of motherhood. The principles in this book have made a strong impact on my parenting abilities, and I believe they will do the same for you. I've written in a "mother-friendly" style, short and to the point, because I realize most moms have only small snippets of spare time to take in a chapter or two. So while the kids are napping or playing happily at your feet, take a moment to relish and reflect on the words of refreshment in the pages that follow. You will find the boost of encouragement you need to make it through the rest of the day.

We live in a rapidly changing world. The values that our mothers and fathers grew up with are no longer being taught in the public arena. We find negative influences and declining moral values every where we look, from television to movies to magazines. Our kids desperately need the positive influence of mothers who love them, who love God, and who know how to tap into the power that only he gives.

The seven principles in this book will help you become not only a positive influence in your home, but also in your community—and possibly in the society at large. As you draw upon the ideas presented in these pages, remember that you can make a positive difference in your world one child at a time. There has never been a more critical time for children to experience the power of a positive mom!

Portrait
of A
Positive
Mom

Adam named his wife Eve,
because she would become the mother of all the living.
—Genesis 3:20

*When Eve was brought unto Adam, he became filled
with the Holy Spirit, and gave her the most sanctified,
the most glorious of appelations. He called her Eva, that is to say,
the Mother of All. He did not style her wife, but simply mother,—
mother of all living creatures. In this consists the glory
and the most precious ornament of woman.*
—Martin Luther

Influence beyond Measure
Never Underestimate the Power of a Mother

She is clothed with strength and dignity; she can laugh at the days to come. She speaks with wisdom, and faithful instruction is on her tongue.... Her children arise and call her blessed.
—Proverbs 31:25–26, 28

Mothers possess a rare form of wisdom. We know important information that others don't—such as the exact location of the rest room in every grocery store in town and the correct color of cough medicine to administer to a child with a dry, hacking cough. The rest of humanity may not know how to cut sandwiches into animal shapes or which fast-food restaurants have the best playgrounds, but mothers know. And moms are keenly aware that a chocolate ice cream cone cannot be consumed by a preschooler without leaving its mark on a freshly cleaned outfit or finely upholstered furniture. Others seem oblivious to that fact (especially dads!).

Obviously, we mothers make up a highly informed segment of society. Some days we may wish we did not possess such experiential knowledge, but the truth is we wouldn't trade this job for the world. It's the toughest job we ever loved!

Motherhood transforms naive, inexperienced young ladies into wise, accomplished women who command respect. Maternal love strengthens us and helps us grow into selfless, thoughtful, and giving adults. I like how author Susan Lapinski describes it: "I guess what I've discovered is the humanizing effect of children in my life, stretching me, humbling me. Maybe my thighs aren't as thin as they used to be; maybe my getaways aren't as glamorous. Still, I like the woman that motherhood has helped me to become."[1]

Yes, being a mom brings out the best in us!

Granted, the work schedule for a mother is a bit challenging: twenty-four hours a day, seven days a week, fifty-two weeks a year, with no weekends or holidays off. Some people would balk at such impossible hours, but not mothers! God has given us an inexplicable strength—a strength beyond our own strength—that allows us to tend to the multiple needs and cares of our precious charges. Like the Energizer bunny, we just keep going and going despite midnight feedings, sleepless slumber parties, twice-a-week soccer practices (plus a game on Saturday), and overdue science projects. It generally requires a doctor's orders for a mom to take "sick leave."

Cathy is a good example. A mother of two preschoolers, she had rarely taken a leave of absence from her job as a mother. But when she found herself restricted to bed rest under a doctor's care, she called her in-laws to come to the rescue. Before her replacements arrived, however, her three-year-old son, Ryan, approached her and said with deep concern, "Mommy what are we going to do? Who is going to feed us and put us to bed and play with us?" Tears filled his little eyes. "I need you!" he cried.

Ryan recognized the truth that when mom is off-duty, things just aren't the same. He was consoled only when he was told that Grandma was on her way. At least his grandmother was an experienced mother!

The Worth of a Mom

A study recently conducted by Edelman Financial Services tried to identify the many occupations that a typical mother might be said to hold over the course of a year. The researchers also examined salary data supplied by the U.S. Bureau of Labor Statistics, trade groups, and human resource and staffing firms. Putting all the information together, Edelman estimated that a mother's worth is approximately $507,000 per year! Here is a breakdown of the various tasks typically performed by a mother and the corresponding median salaries:

Animal Caretaker $17,500

Executive Chef $40,000

Computer Systems Analyst $44,000

Financial Manager $39,000

Food/Beverage Service Worker $20,000

General Office Clerk $19,000

Registered Nurse $35,000

Management Analyst $41,000

Childcare Worker $13,000

Housekeeper $9,000

Psychologist $29,000

Bus Driver $32,400

Elementary School Principal $58,600

Dietitian/Nutritionist $41,600

Property Manager $22,600

Social Worker $30,000

Recreation Worker $15,500

The Edelman study suggested that since a mother wears many hats and is on duty twenty-four hours a day, she deserves a full-time, annual salary for all seventeen positions. And since the retirement, health, and insurance benefits that workers in these positions typically receive were not factored in, the figures should actually be much higher![2]

Quite a flattering list, don't you think? But I noticed that a few items were left out of the calculations. For example:

Kissing a boo-boo . . . . .Priceless

Fixing a favorite meal just the way they like it . . . . .Priceless

Making them feel special on their birthdays . . . . .Priceless

Getting up during the night for feedings or illnesses . . . .Priceless

Adjudicating sibling disputes .Priceless

Searching the entire house for a lost gerbil . . . . .Priceless

Cheering enthusiastically from the sidelines . . . . .Priceless

Scratching their backs while they lie in bed . . . . .Priceless

Baking warm cookies for an after-school snack . . . . .Priceless

Telling stories at bedtime . . . . .Priceless

Holding their hands during vaccinations . . . . .Priceless

Giving a hug, a smile, a word of encouragement . . . . . . .Priceless

There are some things money just can't buy! While Edelman's research may have been on the right track, the truth is a mother's worth is incalculable. Few can duplicate our loving touch. What price tag can be placed on the sense of warmth and comfort we bring to our homes? On the feeling of protection and safety our children enjoy just because we're nearby? On our uncanny ability to sense our children's needs before they even ask?

Recently I asked a small group of mothers, "What makes a mother priceless?" One woman responded, "Nobody but a mom can tell when her child is about to throw up!" Who can calculate the worth of that kind of "mother's intuition"?

Tuning Out Popular Opinion

But the world does not necessarily recognize the unique value of motherhood. In fact, we have to fight hard not to be discouraged by current cultural trends that tend to devalue a mother's role and down-play her influence in the lives of her children. Modern society tells us three myths:

Myth #1: Genetics and Peer Pressure—Not Mothers—Influence Children Most

In her recent book *The Nurture Assumption: Why Children Turn Out the Way They Do* (Free Press, 1998), author Judith Rich Harris argues that nothing parents do or say will make much difference in influencing their children's personality, behavior, values, or intelligence. She concludes that genetics and peer pressure are the main factors con-tributing to the way children turn out. Parents are overrated, in her opinion.

Many experts on children and family issues do not agree with Harris's premise, however. "*The Nurture Assumption* is so disturbing," responds Dr. T. Berry Brazelton, renowned professor of pediatrics at Harvard Medical School. "It devalues what parents are trying to do. To say that they don't matter, it's frightening. Then parents may say, 'If I don't matter, why should I bother?' "[3]

Let me state here unequivocally: Parents do matter! A shifting cul-ture and an increasingly humanistic world-view do not change the fact that a mother has always had—and will continue to have—a powerful impact on the development of her children. Certainly peer groups and genetics play a part in what kind of adults children turn out to be; but it is the parents' involvement that guides their children's interests and influences the direction of their young lives.

We need look no further than the Bible to see that God has given parents the job of training and teaching their children. In Deuteronomy 6:4–7, Moses charges the Israelites to faithfully impress God's commandments on their children's hearts: "Hear, O Israel: The

LORD our God, the LORD is one. Love the LORD your God with all your heart and with all your soul and with all your strength. These commandments I give you today are to be upon your hearts. Impress them on your children. Talk about them when you sit at home and when you walk along the road, when you lie down and when you get up."

Clearly God places in the hands of parents—not peers, not schoolteachers, not government officials, or anyone else—the responsibility for teaching their children to love God and obey his Word. And as parents we have been specially empowered by God to pass on his commandments from generation to generation.

Myth #2: Motherhood Causes Women to Miss Out on the Exciting Things in Life

Modern society is rampant with self-centered philosophies of "self-improvement" and "self-actualization." We are bombarded daily with messages that tell us we should look out for number one and pursue our own interests and goals at any cost. This pervasive thinking, by implying that the selflessness of motherhood is not a worthy investment of our time and effort, often creates feelings of inadequacy in moms.

The underlying myth is that if we endeavor to be attentive mothers, we are missing out in life. Not so! Life *begins* with motherhood. What could be more invigorating, more life-giving, than a house full of energetic teenagers wanting to be fed or a handful of toddlers wanting to play hide and seek or a newborn baby wanting to be held?

Besides, as Jesus said in Matthew 10:39, "Whoever finds his life will lose it, and whoever loses his life for my sake will find it." Committing ourselves to love and care for our children as God commands—even if it means putting their needs above our own time and time again—is the way to a full and abundant life. Motherhood has this kind of selfless love built into the job description. I can assure you, we aren't the ones missing out!

Myth #3: Being a Mother Is a Waste of a Woman's Talents and Abilities

Certain women's movements today deny the significance of motherhood, asserting that our talents and abilities could be put to better use. But the truth is motherhood is not only a good use of our talents and abilities, it actually *increases* and *expands* them.

Being a mother broadens our world-view and opens our hearts to a deeper compassion and love for others. It constantly exposes us to new challenges and stretches us to learn new skills. Where else but in motherhood can a woman learn to effectively juggle five tasks at once? A typical mother can cook dinner, answer the telephone, and help with the homework while feeding the baby and scolding the dog. She can work at the hospital, shop for the household, do a couple of loads of laundry, write the bills, and still show affection for each of her loved ones. Amazing!

And remember Edelman's list of occupational roles filled by a mother over a year's time? Where else could a woman get such extensive on-the-job training?

Still, we often feel put to the challenge when someone asks, "And, what do *you* do?" Unfortunately, because of the way society thinks, it seems shallow to answer, "I'm a mother." Even though we know that motherhood is a high and important calling, we feel as though we must be able to list several substantial interests outside the home to satisfy our inquirers. It used to be that our occupation was spoken of with respect and honor; now it's treated as a mere accessory in the ensemble of life!

For the hand that rocks the cradle is the hand that rules the world. —W. S. Ross ☺

13

Portrait of a Positive Mom

I love the story of the mother who was approached by a young lady conducting a survey in a shopping mall. The interviewer asked the typical question, "What is your occupation?" Feeling a bit bold on this particular day, this astute mom responded, "I'm a manager for human resources and development." The young lady hesitated for a moment, then slowly wrote down the important-sounding title on her clipboard.

"And what exactly does your job entail?" she asked.

The mother's response was priceless: "My job requires continuous research and management both in the office and out in the field *[translation: in the house and out in the backyard]*. Currently, I am busy with three important case studies *[translation: I have two sons and a daughter]*. It is a demanding job, and I often work around the clock to cover all of my responsibilities. Although the monetary compensation is virtually nonexistent, the rewards and satisfaction go far beyond words."

The researcher looked at her with great respect and continued with the rest of the questions. When the survey was finished, the mother smiled down at her three young case studies. Then she led them out of the mall and happily treated them to a power lunch at a local fast-food facility.

Now that's what I call job confidence!

We, too, can be confident in the work we do as moms, knowing that we are making a difference every day in the lives of the children God has placed in our care. Whether we spend a major portion of our day at an office, a school, a hospital, a store, a factory, or at home, we are first and foremost mothers—and we are continuously building values and vision into the lives of our kids.

Sure, it's easy to become overwhelmed and unduly influenced by the expectations of our culture. But don't buy the lies! Hold on to what you know deep within your heart: You are absolutely *essential* in your home and in the lives of your kids. Your job has more than monetary value; it has eternal worth!

Remembering Our Employer

Take a moment now to reflect on the day you first added the word *mother* to your job title. It was on that day that you began a new and unique journey into the unknown. You took on a monumental obligation and trust, agreeing to a lifelong commitment to love and care for that new person God brought into your life. You probably felt inadequate at the time, but day by day you grew in wisdom, strength, and ability to match the challenges of your new role.

The truth is, *mother* describes not only what we do, but who we are. From the moment children were first introduced into our lives, we became new people—women with greater purpose, responsibility, and significance.

But if motherhood is our job, for whom do we work? Do we work to please the people of this world—a society that tells us we're unimportant, even unnecessary? Do we serve only our husband and children? Or are we working to honor our own needs?

Colossians 3:17 gives us the answer. "And whatever you do," the apostle Paul writes, "whether in word or in deed, do it all in the name of the Lord Jesus, giving thanks to God the Father through him." Paul continues in verses 23 and 24: "Whatever you do, work at it with all your heart, as working for the Lord, not for men, since you know that you will receive an inheritance from the Lord as a reward. It is the Lord Christ you are serving."

Our work is for the Lord. It is ultimately God we are pleasing as we devote ourselves to our families. It is God who will reward us one day for our untiring effort. If we were working for people in this world, we would no doubt want recognition or pay for our services. But ours is a higher calling. We are not working for money or accolades on earth; we are working with all our heart for the Lord. In fact, our entire job is done from the heart, rooted in the motherly love God has given us for our children.

Dear friend, you and I can go forward with complete job confidence. After all, we work for the greatest employer in the universe! Our work as mothers does matter—because it matters to God. We can wear the title with humility and honor, recognizing that we have the power to influence and mold our children like the precious pieces of human clay that they are.

Listen to the words of this insightful poem:

I took a piece of plastic clay
And idly fashioned it one day;
And as my fingers pressed it still,
It moved and yielded at my will.

I came again when days were past,
The form I gave it still did last
And as my fingers pressed it still,
I could change that form no more at will.

I took a piece of living clay,
And gently formed it day by day,
And molded with my power and art,
A young child's soft and yielding heart.

I came again when days were gone;
It was a man I looked upon,
He still that early impress bore,
And I could change it never more.[4]

It's true: Every new mother holds in her arms a precious bundle of malleable potential waiting to be molded into flourishing adulthood through her tender, loving care. Our job must never be taken lightly! We have a great responsibility—both to God and to our children. As we understand the impact that our words and actions have on the lives of our kids, we realize the monumental nature of our task. But God never gives us a job he doesn't first equip us to do. As mothers, we have been specially created to influence the lives of the generations that follow.

Consider my friend, Victor Caballero Jr. Victor juggles two demanding jobs. He is a probation officer for a juvenile court during the day and a gymnastics coach in the evenings and on weekends. Victor was one of ten children, raised from his youth by both his mother and grandmother in a household characterized by both strict discipline and unconditional love. He credits these two women with the strength and determination he learned as a young man and which continue to serve him well now.

More than anything else, Victor says, his mother and grandmother taught him the "wisdom of compassion" and how to truly care for others. With great insight, Victor adds, "If anyone understands pain and strength, it is a mother. My mother and grandmother endured much pain in their lives, yet they were incredible pillars of strength mixed with kindness."

Victor is not alone in recognizing the valuable contribution of the women in his life. Men and women throughout history have given their mothers acclaim and credit for the meaningful encouragement and direction they provided.

Abraham Lincoln, for example, was a great and accomplished president who recognized that he owed much to his mother. She not only taught young Abe to read, but she went to great lengths to obtain books for him. She wanted to enlarge his world and encourage him to rise above the poverty his family experienced. Lincoln later praised his mother's influence when he said, "All that I am, or hope to be, I owe to my mother."

The Statue of Liberty offers another magnificent example. Each day hundreds of people visit this great statue to gaze upon the beautiful, feminine figure representing the freedom we experience in this great land. Few realize, however, that they are looking at the image of the sculptor's mother! Yes, Frederic Bartholdi chose his own mother as the model for the Statue of Liberty since she represented a heroic and influential person in his life. Now her image lights the way for all who enter New York Harbor.

You and I may not have statues fashioned after us. But as mothers, we have a similar opportunity to light the way for our children—to help shape them and direct them toward becoming all that God created them to be. Like Lady Liberty, we too can stand tall!

A Humbling Realization

Before we get too puffed up, however, we must realize that the ultimate provider for the needs of our children is not us, but God. There are times when we cannot be present to assist our children through a crisis or challenge. But God is there, ever present and always able to supply the help our children need.

I recently learned this lesson firsthand when I went on a "Mom's Weekend Away" with a couple of old high school buddies. Just as we arrived at our hotel, I received a message that my twelve-year-old daughter, Joy, had fallen and dislocated her elbow. She had been rushed to the emergency room of the local hospital by one of our neighbors, and my husband, Curt, had met her there.

"Everything's under control," Curt said over the phone. "You don't need to come home."

Of course, rushing home was my first instinct. I was only forty minutes away, after all. Surely my baby needed me and would not make it through this crisis without me!

My girlfriends didn't allow me to persist in my motherly arrogance for long. Curt could certainly handle the situation, they said; and besides, it might just be good for both him and Joy. Even Joy insisted that I didn't need to come to her rescue.

"Dad's here," she said simply.

I'll be honest. It was difficult for me not to rush to my daughter's side. But I came to the humbling realization that there are times when our kids can and will make it without us—even *should* make it without us. It is tempting as mothers to step in and solve all of our children's problems, thinking we are the only ones who can. The truth is our children need experiences that teach them to cope without us. If we take care of every need and are present in every situation, how will our children learn dependence on God?

Since the accident I've noticed that Joy and her father now share a new and unique bond. Yes, I could have stepped in and tried to save the day, but I would have denied them a wonderful opportunity to work through this challenge together. Sometimes we "wonder-moms" need to humble ourselves and get out of the way!

Rest assured, our influence lingers on whether we are right there with our kids or not. Consider what Thomas Edison, one of America's greatest inventors, had to say about his mother, a wise woman who passed away when Thomas was quite young:

> I did not have my mother long, but she cast over me an influence which has lasted all my life. The good effects of her early training I can never lose. If it had not been for her appreciation and her faith in me at a critical time in my experience, I should never likely have become an inventor. I was always a careless boy,

19

and with a mother of different mental caliber, I should have turned out badly. But her firmness, her sweetness, her goodness were potent powers to keep me in the right path. My mother was the making of me.[5]

Mothers have one of the most powerful jobs on earth. With God's help, we can influence our children to become world leaders, talented inventors, creative musicians, great athletes, passionate preachers, devoted schoolteachers, committed physicians, and the list goes on. But we must never think pridefully that we are the sole influence in our children's lives! The truth is that while Thomas Edison was greatly influenced by his mother, he somehow made it through most of his life without her. God can use fathers, grandparents, youth leaders, teachers, and friends to assist our children along their journeys. And we should be glad for the assistance!

Someone has said, "God couldn't be everywhere at once, so he created mothers." Not true! God *can* be everywhere at once. He is omnipresent. On the contrary, it is the mother who cannot be there to meet every need and resolve every crisis in her children's lives. Yes, we are highly influential; but let us respectfully and reverently recognize our capabilities and limitations.

God has given each of us the responsibility to train, nurture, develop, prepare, and teach the precious children he has put in our care. Through us—and with his constant guiding presence—he is raising up the next generation. May we be faithful to our high calling! The world may not reward us for our selfless love and diligence. It may never give mothers the credit they are due. But we can still keep going and going— fully assured that one day, in the kingdom that is eternal, we will hear our heavenly Father say, "Well done, good and faithful servant."

POWER POINT

Read: Romans 12. How do these verses encourage you in your role as a mother? Underline or copy the significant verses. Choose one to memorize this week.

Pray: Wonderful Father, thank you for allowing me to participate in the glorious occupation of motherhood. Thank you for being the perfect parent—and the perfect role model! Please help me to remember that my job is significant and eternally important. Help me to glorify you as I work, teach, play, change diapers, and make sandwiches each day. Bless my family with peace and safety as we grow to honor you. In Jesus' name I pray. Amen.

Do: On a large index card, write out your job description. Be creative and include all of your responsibilities. Here's an example:

Investor in Human Resources

Encourages and instructs all clients as to the best use of their time, gifts and talents. Invests love, care, strength, and tears into all clients' accounts. Drives to most locations. Attends all performances and events in which clients are participating. Provides for basic needs of food, clothing, and clean house. Irons occasionally upon request.

Write out Colossians 3:17 on the lower portion of the card, then place the card on your bathroom mirror or in a frame near your kitchen sink. Use it as a constant reminder of your job's significance—and the name of your employer.

The Secret to Your Success
Plugging Into Your Power Source

Of course I'd like to be the ideal mother.
But I'm too busy raising children.
—from the comic strip "The Family Circus" by Bil Keane

Let's be honest. During a typical day in the life of a mother, there are times when it is easy to be a positive person, and there are times when it is not so easy. For me and many of the moms I talk to, the most difficult time to be positive is the hour before dinner. The "killer hour," as many mothers call it, tends to be the time when everyone in the house (including mom) is tired, hungry, and needy. The kids need help with their homework, the baby needs someone to hold her, hubby needs food on the table, and mom needs to figure out some creative way to put together a meal from whatever items happen to be in the pantry or refrigerator. This is the hour that has been known to frazzle even the most positive of moms!

Recently a friend sent me a list of tips on how to be an uplifting wife and mother during the killer hour. Apparently it comes from an old high school home economics book used back in the 1950s. I imagine you will find these guidelines as interesting as I did:

Instructions for Housewives

1. Have dinner ready. Plan ahead, even the night before, to have a delicious meal on the table—on time. This is a way of letting

your husband know that you have been thinking about him and are concerned about his needs.

2. Prepare yourself. Take fifteen minutes to rest so you will be refreshed when your husband arrives. Touch up your makeup, put a ribbon in your hair, and be fresh looking. He has just been with a lot of work-weary people. Be a little gay and a little more interesting. His boring day may need a lift.

3. Clear away the clutter. Make one last trip through the main part of the house just before your husband arrives, gathering up schoolbooks, toys, paper, etc. Then run a dustcloth over the tables. Your husband will feel he has reached a haven of rest and order, and it will give you a lift too.

4. Prepare the children. Take a few minutes to wash the children's hands and faces. If they are small, comb their hair, and if necessary, change their clothes. They are little treasures, and he would like to see them playing the part.

5. Minimize the noise. At the time of his arrival, eliminate all noise of washer, dryer, dishwasher, or vacuum. Try to encourage the children to be quiet. Be happy to see him.

6. Some don'ts: Don't greet him with problems or complaints. Don't complain if he's late for dinner. Count this as minor compared with what he might have gone through during the day.

7. Make him comfortable. Have him lean back in a comfortable chair or suggest he lie down in the bedroom. Have a cool or warm drink ready for him. Arrange his pillow and offer to take off his shoes. Speak in a low, soft, soothing, and pleasant voice. Allow him to relax and unwind.

8. Listen to him. You may have a dozen things to tell him, but the moment of his arrival is not the time. Let him talk first.

9. Make the evening his. Never complain if he does not take you out to dinner or to other places of entertainment; instead, try to understand his world of strain and pressure and his need to be home and relax.

10. The goal: Try to make your home a place of peace and order where your husband can feel refreshed.

A few things have changed in our society since the 1950s, don't you agree? It's safe to assume we'd never find these ten tips in a modern textbook! Of course, the "old-fashioned" instructions are not all bad. When I read them to my husband, Curt, he looked at me with a straight face and said, "So what's so funny? I think these tips are great!"

What husband wouldn't like such treatment? (Hey, I'd like someone to do the same for me!) But the reality of life at the beginning of the twenty-first century is that women have new and different responsibilities than they had a half-century ago. Instead of preparing a wonderful, three-course dinner to place on the table at exactly six o'clock, the modern mom spends the killer hour hurrying home through rush-hour traffic after leaving her own job or picking up the kids from soccer practice and ballet lessons. Greeting her husband at the door with a smile is likely to be replaced by a quick hello on the cell phone as she runs off to her PTA meeting and he stops to pick up burgers and fries for the kids.

But while our world has changed in many ways, I believe it is still possible to be a positive wife and mom. We may not follow the ten textbook tips from the 1950s, but we can learn to be affirming parents and spouses no matter what decade we live in.

No Perfect Moms

What expectations do you have for yourself as a mother? Do you want a spotless house? Perfectly mannered kids? A Martha Stewart image? No doubt, you, like me, have a picture in your mind of what a "supermom" looks like. But is your vision realistic or just a glorified picture of what you think you ought to be?

Being a positive mom doesn't mean you have to be a perfect mom. Quite the contrary; the vocabulary of a positive mom generally does not contain the word *perfect*. A positive mom realizes that neither circumstances nor people are ever perfect. She is realistic in her expectations, recognizing that her husband and children have weaknesses as well as strengths. And most importantly, she humbly acknowledges that she has a fair amount of flaws herself.

The truth is we bring to our families a variety of strengths and weaknesses, talents and faults. As Psalm 139:14 reminds us, we are "fearfully and wonderfully made." God knew just what he was doing when he made each one of us—imperfections and all! In fact, he uses our unique combinations of abilities and disabilities to help build loving and balanced homes. Our success as positive mothers begins as we realize that we are glorious creations—a special blend of strengths and shortcomings that God has put together to create a beautiful work of human art, known to our families as "mom."

Often, however, we are tempted to compare ourselves to other women—even to "perfect" television moms—and we forget that God has created us as unique mothers designed with exacting care to benefit our unique homes and families. Personally, I find comfort in the wisdom of an old Chinese proverb: "Nobody's family can hang out the sign, 'Nothing the Matter Here.'" Other families and other mothers may look like they have it all together, but in reality they, like us, have their good points along with their flaws, their challenges, and their regrets.

One of my glaring flaws, for example, is that I am "time impaired." I always seem to be running late. My tardiness is not necessarily the result of selfishness or rudeness, however, but rather a failure to prioritize. I tend to become engrossed in my work, a conversation with a friend, or an activity with my kids, and I simply forget to look at the clock. God has used my family to help me be more time-conscious; they have to be on time to school, practices, and the like, and I'm the one who has to get them there! But God has also used this particular fault to stretch my family, helping them to understand that there are times when a conversation is more important than a schedule. Sometimes we have to be both flexible and forgiving.

Don't be discouraged by your weaknesses; determine instead to build on your strengths. Rejoice that God is at work in your life. He created you. He is developing you. And he is not finished with you yet! Take encouragement from the words of the apostle Paul: "[I am] confident of this, that he who began a good work in you will carry it on to completion until the day of Christ Jesus" (Philippians 1:6).

One Day at a Time

Schedules are one of those areas in which we often compare ourselves to other moms. "Oh, she accomplishes so much!" we hear people say in admiration of a mother who juggles an overwhelming load of responsibilities. But is it realistic to expect that we can we do it all?

It is tempting to think of filling our schedules with a wide assortment of activities and interests. There's so much for a modern woman to do: find a job, take a class, go to the gym, join a service organization, volunteer at the hospital, host a play group—and the list could go on.

But as ironic as it may seem, a positive mom must learn to sometimes give a negative response. In a society offering such myriad opportunities, it is essential that we learn to sometimes say no.

Usually our decision is not a matter of choosing between good activities and bad ones. For the modern mom, there are many wonderful, bright, intriguing, and fulfilling interests to choose from, and all of them are likely to be equally good.

But as Solomon reminds us in Ecclesiastes 3:1, "There is a time for everything, and a season for every activity under heaven." We don't need to do it all right now! In fact, we must guard against adding too many distractions that will take us away from our main attraction: our relationship with God and our families.

What is on your plate right now? Make a list of all the activities in which you are currently involved. Now add to the list all of your children's activities. (After all, your kids' activities become yours when you drive them to and from practices and classes, attend games and recitals, and volunteer to help out at fund-raisers and concession stands.)

Pretty busy, huh? Is there anything on the list you don't really *have* to be doing? Is there anything on the list you sense God telling you to *stop* doing? You and I must reexamine our activity load on a regular basis, asking ourselves these important questions and making adjustments in our schedules as needed. Although we may think an overflowing plate of activities and interests makes us "well-rounded," the truth is it is more likely to stress us out and make us ineffective in our areas of primary responsibility.

Life always presents us with choices, and some are admittedly hard to make. For many moms it is easier to say yes than it is to say no. But just because you are asked to be president of the women's organization (or the coordinator for the school fund-raiser or the teacher for the five-

Today, I live in the quiet, joyous expectation of good. —Ernest Holmes

28

year-olds at Vacation Bible School) doesn't mean you must accept. Is it best for your family? Will it use or enhance your gifts and talents? What is the time commitment? Is your husband supportive? Have you prayed about it? These are questions you and I should ask ourselves before saying yes to any new activity.

Ultimately, when it comes to our schedules, we need to follow God's direction and "lean not on [our] own understanding" (Proverbs 3:5). After all, only God knows what the future holds.

When my daughter Joy was in the second grade, I was asked to be a room mother. Of course, I wanted to help out in Joy's class in any way I could, so I immediately said yes. At the time, I was already committed to serve on the school's Board of Trustees and co-lead a large troop of Sonshine Girls (an after-school, character-building club). In addition, my girls were involved in a number of other extracurricular sports and interests that kept me hopping.

Then, shortly after the school year began, I got a call from a publisher asking me to write a book based on a proposal I'd submitted. That was an opportunity I had been waiting for! Suddenly my plate was so full that it was overflowing—and I found myself constantly struggling to keep from making a mess. How did I make it through that year? Only by God's grace. But I'm convinced that if I had just sought his direction back at the beginning of the school year, God— who knew that the book project was around the corner—would have guided me into a less harried, more balanced schedule.

A Personal Mission Statement

One of the greatest gifts we can give our families is to stop rushing down the fast lane and start doing what matters most. And what does matter most? Sometimes we have trouble answering that question because our minds are clouded by the "tyranny of the urgent." We think the most important thing is the thing that's screaming the loudest for our attention. As a result we zoom through life as if it were a sprint race instead of slowing down and relishing it as a meaningful journey.

We can learn a valuable lesson from a recent Special Olympics held in Seattle, Washington. In the 100-meter dash the contestants lined up, ready to run. Then, as the race began, they started out at a slow but steady pace—that is, all except one. Back near the starting line, a young boy with Down Syndrome tripped on the asphalt and fell to the ground. The other runners heard him cry out, and one by one they turned to see what had happened to their friend. Forgetting the race, each one went to the fallen boy's aid. One bent down and kissed the boy's knee and said, "It will be okay." Another helped him to his feet. Then all the contestants joined hands and walked across the finish line together! The crowd cheered for several minutes as they realized they'd just witnessed an amazing demonstration of selfless love.

Is our objective to be the mom who accomplished the most when we come to the end of the race of life? In the rush to get ahead and get things done, are we taking time to love and enjoy the people God has placed in our care? What is our goal in life supposed to be?

I believe each woman must answer these questions personally and individually. We must prayerfully consider the purpose God has given us as mothers. I've found it helpful to actually write a statement of purpose—a mission statement—for my life. This is a declaration of what I believe my life should be about, and it is a helpful guide when I lose my bearings in the midst of the whirlwind around me. Perhaps you will want to write your own mission statement. Here's a sample you can adapt for your purposes:

My Personal Statement of Belief and Purpose

I believe Christ died on the cross for my sins and his Holy Spirit dwells within me, helping me to live according to God's will each day. It is my ultimate goal in life to honor him in all I do.

I believe I was created by God with unique gifts, talents, and abilities that he can use to bless and enrich my family and the people around me.

My strengths include _____.

I recognize that I also have weaknesses that I will try to minimize or overcome with God's help.

I believe my purpose in life is to _____.

My hope for my family is _____.

Your personal statement may read differently, but it should reflect what is truly important to you. When you're finished, share it with your husband and children and ask for their encouragement and accountability.

There are actually several reasons for writing out a life purpose. First, when we know where we are going, we can take the right roads to get there. Without direction we tend to wander aimlessly, doing everything that comes along as society pulls us in many different directions.

Second, a mission statement helps us reflect on what truly matters most in the race of life and helps us to pace ourselves for the long run. "Raising children is not unlike a long-distance race in which the contestants must learn to pace themselves," Christian psychologist Dr. James Dobson says. "That is the secret to winning."[1]

Our personal statement also keeps us focused in a positive direction, helping us live our lives with a clear purpose. "The secret of success is constancy in purpose," Benjamin Disraeli once said.[2] With this written reminder of our beliefs, hopes, and dreams, we are better able to focus our strengths toward our life goals and keep our attention off of our weaknesses.

Plugged Into the Power Source

Cell phones used to be a luxury item; now they seem to be a necessity. It's hard to remember how I ever got by without mine! There's only one thing I hate about them: They have to be connected regularly to a power source in order to be recharged. Many times I've had to make an important call only to see the display on the phone blink "low battery." Cell phones may be a great convenience when they are fully charged, but they are useless if they run out of juice!

The same is true for mothers. Our batteries get drained too. We get tired physically and emotionally from the constant effort to discipline, entertain, and care for our kids. There are days when we feel overwhelmed. Most of us can relate to Erma Bombeck, who said, "When my kids become wild and unruly, I use a nice, safe playpen. When they're finished, I climb out."[3] We all need a break, a respite, a safe haven in which we can reenergize from the cares of motherhood.

Wouldn't it be wonderful if we could plug into an outlet and recharge our battery as easily as we juice up our cell phones? But while we may not be able to recharge electrically, we can spiritually. God's Holy Spirit is our power source, and he is "ever-ready" to meet our needs. The Bible tells us the Holy Spirit helps us in our weaknesses (Romans 8:26). He strengthens and encourages us (Acts 9:31). He leads and guides us (John 16:13). He renews us and replenishes us (Isaiah 32:15). As God's Spirit is at work in our lives, he brings forth wonderful fruit—love, joy, peace, patience, kindness, goodness, faithfulness, gentleness, and self control (Galatians 5:22–23).

Have you plugged into the power source? Has the Holy Spirit

come to dwell in your life? The Bible is quite clear that when we believe in Jesus Christ and trust him for salvation, he places his Holy Spirit within us (Ephesians 1:13–14).

God's plan is simple: It starts with faith in Jesus. John 1:12 says, "Yet to all who received him, to those who believed in his name, he gave the right to become children of God." What about you? Do you have a relationship with your heavenly Father, the Living God? If not, perhaps you would like to take a moment right now to examine the Scriptures (I suggest reading the Gospel of John in a modern Bible translation) and discover for yourself God's beautiful message of salvation—the good news.

What do I mean by good news? The good news is that God loves us. Although none of us is completely good and pure, God—who *is* perfectly good—wants to have a relationship with us. Jesus came to offer his life as the price for our sins so we could be clean and forgiven before God. Now we can have a relationship with the heavenly Father simply by believing that Jesus gave his life for us. We can't work our way into heaven; we can't do enough good deeds to make up for our bad ones. We only have to put our faith in Christ.

Here it is in a nutshell: Out of love for you and me, Jesus came to this earth to die on the cross for our sins. He rose from the dead, giving us hope of eternal life. Now that's good news!

When we are connected with Christ through our faith in him, we are automatically plugged into the power of his Holy Spirit. The Bible says that same great power that brought Jesus back from the grave is at work in the life of every believer (Romans 8:11). That power is flowing from his end; we just need to throw open the switch on ours. We do that by abiding in Christ day by day—by acknowledging his supremacy in our lives, following his leading, and obeying his Word.

When we learn to "plug in" daily, we can begin to experience on a

Commit to the LORD whatever you do, and your plans will succeed. —Proverbs 16:3

☺

regular basis the spiritual refreshment that only God can give. We can begin to bear the fruits of "love, joy, peace, patience, kindness, goodness, faithfulness, gentleness and self-control" (Galatians 5:22–23). And that, dear friends, is the *real* secret to our success as positive moms.

POWER POINT

Read: Romans 8 in an easy-to-understand Bible translation. Notice the verses that deal specifically with the Holy Spirit's work in your life. Choose several verses to memorize (I suggest verses 28, 38, and 39).

Pray: Thank you, God, that you have not left me alone to try to live life by myself. Thank you for your Holy Spirit, who lives in me and helps me to be a positive, loving, peaceful, and joyful person each day. Your power—and not my own—is at work in my life, making me the woman you want me to be. Thank you for forgiving my sins and loving me through my weaknesses. Help me to be a positive mom today. In Christ's name, amen.

Do: Prayerfully prepare your own personal mission statement. You may want to refer to the example given earlier in this chapter to help you get started.

Principle #1

THE Power OF Encouragement

Therefore encourage one another and build each other up.
—1 Thessalonians 5:11

Few things in the world are more powerful than a positive push.
A smile. A word of optimism and hope.
A "you can do it" when things are tough.
—Richard M. De Vos

Apples of Gold
The Positive Impact of a Good Word

A word aptly spoken is like apples of gold in settings of silver.
—Proverbs 25:11

A number of years ago, a junior high teacher from Minnesota wrote a letter to "Dear Abby" telling the story of a remarkable life lesson she learned from her students. She began by describing a difficult day in her math class when the kids were particularly cranky with one another and discouraged about the lesson. Frustrated, the teacher told the class to put away their math books and place one sheet of blank paper on their desks. She then instructed them to list the names of their classmates along the left-hand side of the page and write next to each name the nicest thing they could think of to say about each person. The impromptu exercise helped, because as the students turned in their assignments, the teacher noticed that everyone was a little more relaxed and at ease.

Over that weekend, the teacher took the time to write each student's name on a blank page and painstakingly copied the kind thoughts that were expressed about each of the kids. On Monday morning, she handed the students their lists. The room was abuzz with whispers and comments such as, "Wow, really?" "I didn't know anyone liked me that much!" "I never knew that meant anything to anyone."

Then the assignment was put away, and class continued with the students feeling better about themselves and each other.

Years later, the math teacher attended the untimely funeral of one of her students who was killed while serving his country in Vietnam. After the service, the parents of this brave young man approached the teacher and said, "We want to show you something Mark was carrying when he was killed." The father pulled a crumpled piece of paper from his wallet, and as he unfolded it, the teacher recognized her handwriting. It was the paper from that long-ago assignment consisting of all the nice things the young man's classmates had said about him! The parents thanked the teacher, saying that their son had always treasured the encouraging words.

Other former students standing nearby spoke up. One smiled sheepishly, saying he kept his list of compliments in his top desk drawer at home. Another said his sheet had been placed in his wedding album. A third person pulled out his wallet and proudly displayed his folded page as if it were a prized possession. Overwhelmed, the teacher sat down and cried, realizing the full value of that impromptu assignment and the power of encouraging words.

Abby responded to the teacher's letter in her column with a quote from George Herbert: "Good words are worth much and cost little."[1]

There is no greater investment we can make in the lives of our children than giving them generous doses of encouraging words. It costs us so little in time and effort, but the rewards are priceless. When our young people are reminded of their God-given value, they receive deposits of confidence, security, and well-being in their emotional bank accounts. They begin building on their strengths, knowing they have something to contribute to this world. On the other hand, when our children have nothing positive to believe about themselves, their emotional bank accounts can become bankrupt—overdrawn by the negative comments and disappointments that occur every day in the world around them.

The old adage "Sticks and stones can break my bones but words will never hurt me" is certainly *not* true. Think back to when you were a child. Do you remember a taunt or jeer you received from other kids at some point in your growing-up years? Most of us can! No matter how small or insignificant the comment was, the hurt can still linger in our memories. Isn't it amazing that we still remember these incidents, even though many years have come and gone?

Some psychologists say that for every negative comment a person receives, they need to hear ten positive comments to overcome the effects of the negative one. Ten to one—now that's a lot of positive words, especially when you consider all the negative input our kids are likely to encounter during a typical day.

It is easy for any child to become a target for cruel words in today's society. Kids ridicule each other for everything from physical features to clothes to being a "goody-goody." The adolescent years can be especially difficult with its added pressure on young teens to "fit in" and belong to a group. Many of the school shootings reported in the national media in recent years were carried out by kids who were ridiculed by their classmates or treated like outcasts. The hurt that comes from being mocked or ostracized can leave an indelible imprint on a child's impressionable mind.

Even a caring family member, youth leader, or teacher can make a careless statement and unknowingly hurt a child. What may seem to an adult like a slight or simple comment can loom large to a young person. I remember an incident my daughter Grace experienced when she was five years old. Grace is a lovely young lady, and she is blessed with a good many freckles on her face. One day at church, a well-meaning adult commented on her appearance and concluded, "Your nickname should be 'Freckles'!" What seemed like a quaint observation to the woman crushed Grace, who had not realized that her freckles were so noticeable to others. It actually took many more than ten positive comments from mom to overcome this one negative comment that had unintentionally hurt Grace's feelings.

Reckless words and unkind criticism are like a highway demolition crew in our children's hearts. They have the potential to cause great damage and make for a rocky road in life. But as mothers, we have the responsibility and the privilege of filling in the potholes. Do the math. If our kids encounter just two negative comments or put-downs during the course of the day, they need approximately twenty fillings of love and appreciation to plug up the potholes.

How many times during a typical day do you build your child up with encouraging words? Two, maybe three times? Some days, that may not be enough! We need to be deliberate about building up our children's strengths and putting regular deposits in their emotional bank accounts. We need to make sure they're getting a positive picture of who they are.

Not that our children's sense of self-worth should be dependent on the affirmation we give them. This is an important concept to understand and pass on. Our children's self-worth, like our own, must be based on the fact that God made us and loves us. Every person has value as a beautiful and miraculous creation of their heavenly Father. We affirm our kids—and others—not because they are dependent on praise, but because our encouragement can provide them with the strength they need to press on to reach their full potential. In fact, the word *encourage* means "to put courage into, to give strength." We have the responsibility each day to give strength and courage to our children to help them face life's opportunities and challenges.

As part of that process, we need to teach our kids that they are valuable no matter what comments are made about them, good or bad. "If God is for us, who can be against us?" Paul writes in Romans 8:31. From an early age, children need to establish in their hearts and minds that their worth is not wrapped up in what they do or what anyone else thinks about what they do; rather, it is based on who they are in Christ.

Consider the analogy of a luxury car and the fuel we put into it to make it run. The positive affirmation we give our children is the gasoline we put in the tank of their car. The car has value whether we put gas in the tank or not; but if we want the car to go somewhere and stay in good condition, we need to fill it up with quality fuel. Our kids have great value. The more we fill them with the fuel of encouragement, the more energy they will have to reach their goals and follow their dreams.

Are you filling your kids with quality, high-octane fuel? Proverbs 12:25 says, "An anxious heart weighs a man down, but a kind word cheers him up." Our kind words and encouragement have a powerful effect in our children's lives. They're some of the most effective tools available for positive moms.

Be on the Lookout!

Sometimes my kids must think I have an invisible magnifying glass that focuses in on everything they do wrong. I can't blame them. There are definitely days when it seems I'm constantly finding something to correct in their actions or conversation. I'm not totally out of line, of course; it *is* my job as a parent to discipline, train, and help my kids grow into well-behaved young adults.

Most moms, I think, are like me—fairly adept at discovering their children's faults. Somehow it's easier for us to find and focus on our kids' mistakes than it is to be attentive to what they are doing right. But our challenge as positive moms is to identify our children's positive attributes and actions and encourage them in those things.

Unfortunately, no one has invented a magnifying glass powerful enough to uncover the good in our children. We have to make our own observations—and some days that can be difficult!

In the summer of 1998, our family had an exciting opportunity to go to London for a business conference. Imagine our delight when, several months before the trip, my husband decided we should take an extra week to see Paris as well! To prepare for our journey, I immediately began teaching Grace and Joy about the French culture and language. We learned about key points of interest such as the Eiffel Tower, the Arc de Triomphe, the Louvre, the palace at Versailles, and more.

The Eiffel Tower seemed to capture the girls' imagination the most, and as our plane touched down in the French capital, they pressed their noses to the window to search for the famous landmark. Sure enough, they found it! During the taxi drive to the hotel, they found it again. Then they found it from our hotel window. In fact, every place we went in Paris and the surrounding areas, they were on the lookout for the Eiffel Tower—and they found it every time!

Why were they able to find it? Because they were looking for it! We too can find the good qualities in our children. They'll pop out at us from nearly every vantage point if we'll just be on the lookout for them.

What are the Eiffel Towers in our children's lives? We need to be on the lookout for qualities such as kindness, gentleness, joyfulness, gratitude, self-control, patience—attributes the Bible calls "fruit of the Spirit" (see Galatians 5:22–23). We should notice and encourage these qualities as we see them begin to sprout in our children's words and actions. Unique talents and abilities (a good singing voice, a skill in soccer, a mind for math, a way with words, an artistic flair, etc.) offer additional opportunities to encourage our kids to reach for their highest potential. We must simply be determined to find these points of praise! Just as my daughters were bent on finding the Eiffel Tower from every location in Paris, we can be on the lookout for our children's positive gifts and attributes in everything they do from day to day.

How do we identify these pillars of positive potential? We begin by paying attention to our children's interests. Do they enjoy drawing? Odds are we will find an opportunity to give a sincere compliment as we observe their finished artwork or watch them create a new masterpiece. Do they like to swim? We need to take a moment to watch them paddle in the pool and verbally admire their skill. The key is making ourselves available to our kids. How can we comment on a soccer game we didn't see? Or praise a poem we didn't take the time to read? To be positive moms, we need to spend *quantity* as well as *quality* time with our children.

Secondly, until encouragement becomes habit, we need to remind ourselves to fill up our children's emotional fuel tanks with accolades. Unfortunately, our kids don't come with an "affirmation gauge" like the gas gauge in our cars. We don't necessarily get a warning that lets us know they're almost on "empty." We need to stay constantly on the lookout for good and admirable qualities so we can seize the moment and offer encouragement when an opportunity arises.

While shopping recently, I found a pillbox in the shape of the Eiffel Tower. The price was fair, so I purchased it and set it on a bookshelf in my study. Now it serves as a daily reminder to diligently and deliberately search for the good qualities in my daughters and find opportunities to strengthen them through my words. What will help you remember to encourage your kids? Perhaps you can purchase several inexpensive magnifying glasses at a local drugstore and attach a note to the glasses saying, "Have you searched for the good in your child today?" Then you can place the magnifying glasses in strategic places you're sure to see, such as by your purse or in the pantry or in the car. Or you might draw a little gauge on an index card and write yourself a note saying, "Have you put fuel in your kid's emotional tank today?"

I have yet to find the man, however exalted his station, who did not do better work and put forth greater effort under a spirit of approval than under a spirit of criticism. —Charles Schwab

43

Experts say the best way to form a new habit is to deliberately do the action for at least twenty-one consecutive days. Why not begin now to form the habit of speaking positive words to your children? Set a goal of saying at least three encouraging comments to each child each day. As you put them to bed at night, check to see if you have put enough verbal deposits in their emotional bank accounts that day. If you come up short, you can use this bedside time to make up the difference before they doze off.

Be deliberate and persistent for three weeks. Look for those opportune times when you have a quiet moment or two with your child. Besides bedtime, I find the two best times for me to compliment and encourage my daughters are when I take them to school and when I pick them up in the afternoon. It's easy for me to think of good things to say about them as I send them off in the morning, and I can usually find areas for encouragement in our afternoon review of the day's events.

We need to practice this "attitude of accolades" in order to make affirmation and encouragement natural parts of our daily conversation. But the best practice is not done with our kids, our spouse, or any other person. The best practice is to begin each day by praising our heavenly Father. We should, after all, adore him first and foremost in our lives. "I will praise the LORD all my life, I will sing praise to my God as long as I live," the psalmist wrote in Psalm 146:2. As we focus on the praiseworthy qualities of Almighty God and form the habit of praising him, we can't help but become more positive and encouraging—and more likely to have positive comments on the tips of our tongues for our children and others.

Giving Strength through Our Words

When it comes to strengthening and encouraging our kids, there are four guidelines that can help our words have greater power and effectiveness.

1. Be Specific

"You're terrific!" "Wow, you did great!" "Super job!" These are uplifting sentiments that can encourage and inspire our children, and our kids certainly benefit from hearing them. Brief, general phrases like these have their time and their purpose. But if we truly want to give a special gift to our children, we need to offer them specific compliments. Instead of broad statements that could fit almost anyone doing almost anything, "personalized praise" lets our kids know we're really paying attention.

"I think you are a terrific goalie. Very few soccer goalies can stop the side kicks like you can." "I loved the way you painted that picture. You really have an eye for color!" By using specifics, we not only give our children a wonderful gift, we add a beautiful bow and a card that says, "This compliment is meant for you, and only you." Children recognize our sincerity when we use specific details to describe the qualities we appreciate about them.

2. Be Prepared

It may seem insincere to prepare positive comments in advance, but preparation doesn't undermine the sincerity we want to convey to our kids. A public speaker is not deemed insincere simply because she has planned out what she is going to say beforehand. Quite the contrary; she is able to deliver a much better, more thoughtful address when she puts her thoughts together in advance.

The same is true for moms and positive comments. It never hurts to be prepared! If we know we will be attending our daughter's piano recital, for example, we can think of some specific compliments that will fit the situation. "Honey, I am so proud of you," we might say. "It takes a lot of courage to play in front an audience, and you did so well. I especially liked…"

Here are some other comments we can have ready to use when the time and place is right:

- "I love spending time with you. You are a bright spot in my day."

- "I'll never forget the day you were born. You were so beautiful, and you still are."

- "God made you special, and I am so glad he made you a part of this family."

- "You gave it your best effort. That makes me proud of you. You are a hard worker."

- "Your hugs are so special. Can I have one right now?"

- "You did a fantastic job! Your hard work and preparation paid off!"

- "I love the way you _____. I can tell God has given you a special talent."

- "Thank you for _____. You bring joy to our family."

- "I appreciate the way you _____. You are a very thoughtful person."

3. Be Creative

It is helpful to use a variety of ways to express affirmation and encouragement to your family members. Variety is the spice of life, they say—even when it comes to speaking positive words.

Several years ago, the Camp Fire Boys and Girls declared a national "Absolutely Incredible Kid Day." Recognizing the value of affirmative words to children, the organization encouraged parents, teachers, and youth workers to get creative and write special notes of appreciation and praise to the kids in their care. The goal of the Camp Fire effort was to get adults to begin raving about their children's assets—and to promote the best qualities of the next generation.

We don't need a national holiday to write special notes to our children. We can pen a sentence or two on a sticky pad or note card and leave it:

- On their pillow

- In their lunch box

- In their shoes

- On the door to their room

- In their backpack

- Between the pages of a textbook or their Bible

- On the bathroom mirror

For more variety, try e-mailing a note to your child or sending a card through the mail. (It's always fun to receive a letter in the mailbox.) Or write a few sentences of encouragement, fold the paper into a small box, and wrap the box with fancy paper and a bow. Then present the gift at a special moment.

If you want to get even more creative, make an audio or videotape expressing your appreciation for your child. (You can bet that tape will be played over and over again!) If you have a poetic bent, write a poem or song. Or use the letters in your child's name to make an acronym, with each letter standing for some positive trait you see. Then add artwork (if you can) and frame the page.

4. Be Resourceful

There are many good resources that can serve as catalysts for our positive words. Bible verses can be particularly effective in offering godly compliments and building on eternal qualities such as love, joy, and peace. I'll never forget the letter I got from my boyfriend Curt (now my husband!) the summer I served as a camp counselor in East Texas. He quoted from Proverbs 31:29: "Many women do noble things, but you surpass them all." Wow! I walked a little taller that day, knowing that Curt cared enough to compliment me with such a meaningful verse!

We can use Scripture to encourage our children as well. We can compliment them on demonstrating the same kind of loyalty that Ruth showed toward Naomi or being a good friend like Jonathan was to David. Quoting from Psalm 139:13–16, we can assure them that God designed them to be unique and special. Turning to Proverbs 1:7, we can let them know they show wisdom when they reverence the Lord. As we read the Beatitudes from the Sermon on the Mount, we can tell our kids that we see in them a pure heart or a hunger and thirst for righteousness. From 1 Corinthians 13 we can point out the qualities of love we see in their words and actions.

Reading books or watching television or movies with our children can be resources too—offering both good examples for comparison and bad examples for contrast. For instance, as we read *Little House on the Prairie* by Laura Ingalls Wilder or watch reruns of the old television show, we can point out Laura's respect for her parents and say, "I'm grateful that you have the same kind of respect for your dad and me that Laura seems to have for her parents." Later, as we read Mark Twain's *Tom Sawyer* or watch one of the movies adapted from the book, we can point out the heartache that Tom's troublemaking caused Aunt Polly and say, "I'm certainly thankful for the way you behave. Your obedience is a blessing to me." After a comment like that from mom, a child is not going to want to run toward mischief anytime soon!

The Right Kind of Attention

A number of years ago a peculiar man decided to dress up in a silly-looking red Spiderman suit, attach suction cups to his hands and feet, and climb up the side of one of the tallest buildings in the world. When he reached the top, 125 stories up, the crowd that had gathered below broke out in thunderous applause. Both the police and news reporters were on the roof ready to greet the self-made superhero.

"Why did you do it?" they asked.

His reply was simple: "I love to hear the applause."[2]

A man risks his life in a pair of red pajamas—just to hear the applause of people! It is amazing the lengths we will go to receive encouragement and praise. But as William James once said, "The deepest craving of human nature is the need to feel appreciated."[3]

Children are no exception. In fact, I'm convinced kids are born with an invisible sign around their necks that says, "I want to feel important." Too often, however, they must struggle to gain the attention and praise they need from the important people in their lives. Schoolteachers know that children who do not seem to get enough attention for doing the right things are the ones who tend to act up. In the kids' minds, negative attention is better than no attention.

As mothers, we hold the key. There is no better stimulus to motivate young people toward goodness than the knowledge that their best qualities are noticed and appreciated by mom.

Several years ago a friend and I went out to lunch at a delightful little tearoom. It was a popular restaurant and quite crowded during the lunch hour. As we waited in line to be seated, we noticed the people in front of us were rude and impatient with the hostess. So when our turn came to be seated, we were extra-kind to the woman, knowing that she was having a difficult day.

A few moments after we settled in at our table, the hostess returned with a tray of glasses filled with ice water. Among the assortment of plain glasses were two crystal goblets. She took the plain glasses to a nearby table then brought the expensive goblets to us. "You two were nice to me today," she said, "so I brought you the nicest glasses we have in the restaurant. Thank you for your kindness."

Imagine how we felt! Our kind words had seemed so small and insignificant, yet this woman had noticed them. And since we'd made her feel special, she decided to make us feel special. Now, do you think we were going to complain about the food or rush our waitress that day? Not on your life! Our kindness had been rewarded, and we were happy to continue in it.

Our kids will respond the same way when we deliver a compliment to them on a silver platter. They will want to keep up the good work!

Lavina Christensen Fugal, the 1995 Mother of the Year, offers mothers the following advice: "Love your children with all your hearts.... Praise them for important things.... Praise them a lot. They live on it like bread and butter."[4] A few simple words of affirmation and admiration may be just the spark our kids need to try harder and pursue greater dreams. Let's continue to dish out delicious morsels of encouraging words and watch our children's finest qualities strengthen and grow!

POWER POINT

Read: Ephesians 4:29–32; Colossians 3:12–15; and Philippians 4:8. How do these verses help you to become a better encourager to your children? Underline or write out a verse that is especially meaningful.

♡ **Pray:** Wonderful heavenly Father, I praise you for your omnipotent wisdom in creation. I thank you that each and every person was created by design, with flaws and weaknesses as well as strengths and talents. Help me to accentuate the positive with my kids. Help me to see their potential and encourage their best qualities. Help me to be a builder of my family with the words of my mouth, speaking praise for the good things I see in my spouse and children.

☺ **Do:** Write out four specific accolades for each of your family members and deliver one of them each week for the next four weeks. When you see the positive response you get, you may want to make one day a week your note-writing day to regularly express to your family members and friends how special they are.

JESSICA   Kind/sweet/loving
1. Good at being to   to others
2. Works hard at school work
3. Gets up on her own
4. Great singer/dancer/actress

Doug
1. Obedient
2. Kind loving
3. Great soccer player
4. Loves righteousness

Great Expectations
Helping Your Children Discover Their Potential

"For I know the plans I have for you," declares the LORD, "plans to prosper you and not to harm you, plans to give you hope and a future. Then you will call upon me and come and pray to me, and I will listen to you. You will seek me and find me when you seek me with all your heart."
—Jeremiah 29:11–13

Imagine a beautiful sailboat with large, billowing sails, moving across the surface of the wide, blue-green ocean. Strong gusts of wind blow into the sails, filling the broad canvases and propelling the vessel to new and different places—far beyond any port it has ever known.

As mothers, our affirming influence is like that breeze that firmly sends the sailboat of our children's lives across the waters of life. Helping our children reach their destination—to achieve the fullness of their God-given potential—is one of the most rewarding aspects of our job as moms. But we must be careful. It is tempting to impose our own expectations on our children, to try to push them in the direction we want for them rather than the direction God has planned for them since the beginning of time. Our challenge is to learn how to be the wind in their sails without blowing them off the course God has set for their lives.

Olympic swimmer Summer Sanders believes that "champions are raised, not born." In her book by that title, she notes that good parenting can be the key factor in making the experiences of a child's life positive and empowering. Sanders, who swam her way to two gold medals, one silver medal, and one bronze medal in the 1992 Olympics, believes that her parents played a big role in helping her get to that level of world competition. Her mom and dad did not push her or drive her to her success, she says; they simply provided joyful support, positive encouragement, and constant reassurance that they were there for her whether she won or lost. Summer believes her parents gave her what few men and women ever receive: "the infinite satisfaction and self-confidence that comes from getting to do what you do best and knowing you're tapping your potential to the fullest."[1]

How do you unlock the door to *your* child's potential in a healthy and affirming way? The Bible gives us the key when it tells us to "train a child in the way he should go" (Proverbs 22:6). A better translation might be "train a child *according to his bent.*" In other words, our children have been put together by God in a unique way and pointed by him in a unique direction. Our job is to recognize that direction, then encourage and instruct our kids to grow and develop in their God-given way.

In the field of education, we can apply this idea to identify our children's unique learning styles (whether auditory, visual, or kinesthetic). In the area of personalities, we can learn to deal with each child according to his or her particular temperament (whether choleric, sanguine, melancholy, or phlegmatic). When it comes to skills and talents, we can steer our children toward the activities for which they seem to have an aptitude (sports, music, art, drama, academics, and so on.)

Study Your Children Well

Our children are not exactly like anyone else—not us, not our spouse, not their siblings. They are not clones of the other kids in the school or neighborhood. We may see similarities between them and others in appearance, in temperament, or in aptitude; but our children are unique individuals with their own incredible boatloads of potential and possibilities.

Under my own roof dwell four completely peerless individuals (and two rather unique dogs). Each person in our home represents a one-of-a-kind product of the Creator. My husband, Curt, is a confident, hard-working, highly driven businessman. He has a multitude of hobbies and interests ranging from golf to antique shopping. He rarely sits still.

Grace, our fourteen-year-old, is a delightful and bubbly sanguine who loves to sing, act, shop, and decorate. She is involved in a youth group at a large church in our area and enjoys every opportunity to get together with her sweet and equally energetic friends.

Twelve-year-old Joy, meanwhile, relates best to the small youth group at our home church. She has wonderful friends, but she enjoys being at home as much as being with other kids. She is an excellent student and a talented gymnast. She is also kind, thoughtful, and gentle.

Then there is me, Mom. You could characterize me as one of those "creative types." It is easy and enjoyable for me to spend hours at the computer writing ideas for a speech, article, or book. I love to be with my friends, but I also value time alone. Teaching and hospitality are my gifts, so our house is usually buzzing with people and parties.

Clearly God made each one of my family members in a special way, creating a beautiful collage of personalities for our unique home. He has also given my daughters different interests, abilities, and temperaments. Already I can see him leading the girls down separate paths, with a definite plan and a purpose for their individual lives.

Take a moment to think about the unique qualities of your own family members. How would you describe each of your children? To be positive moms, we need to be students of our kids. That may sound funny since we tend to view ourselves as teachers of our children and

If one advances confidently in the direction of his dreams and endeavors to love the life which he has imagined, he will meet with a success unexpected in common hours. —Henry David Thoreau

55

not the other way around. But in order to help them grow and mature to their fullest potential, we must get to know our children, understand them, and recognize their strengths and weaknesses. We must help them discover their unique bents. Then, once they are pointed in the direction God has set for them, we can be the wind in their sails, helping them reach the destination of their own special goals and dreams.

Step #1: See the Potential

In 1882 a precious, nineteen-month-old girl lost her sight and hearing due to an unfortunate illness. As she grew up she became wild and unruly, with seemingly little opportunity to make something of herself. Most people would have looked at her situation in life and given up on her. But one teacher dared to look beyond the surface of her disabilities and see the potential inside of her.

Anne Sullivan, though nearly blind herself, began teaching little Helen Keller how to read, write, and communicate in what seemed to Helen a foreign language. Eventually Helen attended Radcliffe College, where she studied French and Greek and learned to type her papers and assignments using a typewriter with Braille keys. At the age of twenty-one, Helen published her life story and became a well-known public figure. She was compassionate toward the needs of others and maintained an excitement about life that many people who can see and hear never possess.

Living in a dark and silent world did not keep Helen Keller from reaching her God-given potential—mainly because one woman, Anne Sullivan, made the effort to look beyond the limitations and imagine what God could do with the abilities he had given to her young student. How about you? Do you see the abundant potential that your child possesses? Many times our children's worst attributes glare at us. We're so focused on what our children *can't* do that we fail to see what they *can* do. Yet each child is born with certain abilities and gifts to offer to the world. We need to identify these things and build on them. As Helen Keller said, "I thank God for my handicaps, for through them, I have found myself, my work and my God."[2]

Exploring the possibilities, gifts, and treasures within our children can be a wonderful journey of discovery. How do you begin? Start by writing down the potential you see in your children in four key areas of growth: mental, physical, spiritual, and social. The Bible tells us that Jesus developed in each of these areas throughout his boyhood: "And Jesus grew in wisdom and stature, and in favor with God and men" (Luke 2:52). Are your children academically inclined? Do they excel in a particular subject? What physical skills or attributes do they possess? How are they developing in their relationship with God? Are they comfortable around adults? Are they good at making friends?

Examine and observe each of your children, noting those qualities, interests, or aptitudes you see God developing in their lives. Pray over those things as you write them down, asking God to help you understand how they can be developed and used. Share with your children the possibilities you see for their lives. Offer them a vision of their God-given potential.

Be careful, though, not to make your kids feel trapped by your personal wishes or expectations for them. An interest in science may lead your son to become a high school chemistry teacher, not a brain surgeon. An aptitude for the piano may offer your daughter a lifelong outlet for relaxation and pleasure, not a career at Carnegie Hall. Our task is to encourage them in their bent—not to plan out the details.

Step #2: Offer Opportunities for Growth

As your children grow up, it's a good idea to let them try their hand at a variety of things—sports, dance, art, music, and the like. I'm not suggesting, however, that you overload them with organized activities. A heavy schedule of classes, practices, and meetings can lead to burnout—both for the kids and for the frazzled mom-turned-chauffeur. Instead allow your children to test different areas of interest by practicing at home with family and friends first. A bent for art may show up as your son sketches "doggies" or paints flowers on scrap paper at the kitchen table. A skill for soccer may become evident as your daughter kicks a ball around the backyard with the neighborhood kids. As a particular interest or aptitude emerges, you can look for a class or team or meeting where they can develop that skill or talent further.

But don't be in a rush! Today's culture places an unspoken pressure on parents to engage their children in organized activities from a very early age. Our fear is that our children will be left behind if we hold them back while every other kid in the universe starts the activity in preschool. That concern is unfounded, however. In many cases our children will excel in an area at a later age because they've developed a love for the activity and have a natural skill, while kids who were pushed at an early age lose interest and don't progress.

In fact, many great athletes started their sport during adolescence or later. Consider these Olympic examples just for starters:

- Crissy Ahmann, who won a gold and a silver medal swimming in the 1992 Olympics, took up the sport in her college years.

- Matt Biondi, one of the most decorated male Olympic swimmers, favored basketball over pool sports until about age fifteen.

- Justin Huish, winner of the gold medal in archery in 1996, didn't shoot an Olympic-style bow until he was fourteen.

- Bonnie Blair, the world's fastest woman speed skater, grew up being competitive in many sports, including cycling, track, and gymnastics. She was twelve before she realized she wanted to skate more than anything else.[3]

Yes, it's good for us to encourage our children to do their best. But we must also allow them to grow and develop at their own God-given pace.

Step #3: Set Realistic Goals

Can you imagine sitting in an airplane when the pilot makes this announcement over the intercom? "I have some good news and some bad news," he says. "The bad news is we have lost one engine, along with our direction finder. The good news is we have a tailwind, and wherever we are headed, we are getting there at 650 miles per hour!"

Personally, I don't think I'd like to be on a flight headed fast to who-knows-where. And we don't want to send our kids skipping through life without direction, preparation, or purpose either. They need goals—targets to shoot for—as well as strategies for reaching them.

As a former track coach, I used to teach young athletes two important principles: Run your best and keep your eyes on the finish line. The Bible tells us to do the same on the track of life. "Let us run with perseverance the race marked out for us," Hebrews 12:1–2 says. "Let us fix our eyes on Jesus, the author and perfecter of our faith." As we keep our eyes focused on the goal of serving Christ and becoming more like him, we are less distracted in our race by the cares, frustrations, and temptations of the world. Having Jesus as our first and foremost goal keeps us on the right track!

"Goals give you the specific direction to make your dreams come true," says Bob Conklin.[4] This is as important for children as it is for adults. After setting Jesus as their first goal, you can set other goals with your kids on an annual basis once they're mature enough to understand the concept (usually by about eight years old).

Set aside a time each year when you will work with each child to develop his or her specific goals for the next twelve months. My dad taught my sister and me to write out our annual goals every New Year's Day. I've continued this habit throughout my life and have encouraged my daughters to do the same. It is a good idea to write down one goal for each of the four growth areas mentioned earlier—mental, physical, spiritual, and social. Keep in mind that these goals should be realistic, obtainable, yet stretching. They should not be *your* goals for your children; rather, they should be an expression of their goals for themselves.

The goals should also be measurable. "To be a better basketball player" is a nice idea, but it's not something that can be measured objectively. A better goal is something like "I will put the ball up and shoot at least five times in every game." Or "I will score at least thirty points for my team this season." Sometimes it's good to set a minimum and a maximum goal, with the first one being fairly easy to achieve and the second one requiring a greater stretch.

As you work together with your children to plan their goals for the year, talk to them about strategies they could use to reach the desired goals. For instance, if your child has set the "mental" goal of reading two new books per month (in addition to school requirements), you may want to jot down a strategy for accomplishing that feat. Perhaps he or she can read for thirty minutes each afternoon after school and an hour every Saturday.

As your children get older, consider helping them develop a "five-year plan" in which they set a bigger, general goal of where they want to be in five years and talk about how they plan to get there. If your son wants to go to college, what courses must he take in high school—and how good must his grades be? If your daughter wants to draw closer to

Train a child in the way he should go, and when he is old he will not turn from it. —Proverbs 22:6

the Lord, what disciplines of prayer, Bible study, and service does she need to develop?

But even as you set goals with your kids, remember: Change happens. Be open to new possibilities, and help your children understand that the circumstances of life may put a twist in their plans. The important thing is that they adjust to whatever God allows in their lives and look for ways to set new goals in different directions. Case in point: Joni Eareckson Tada was an active teenager who had a wonderful outlook on life and high hopes for the future. But God had other plans for her life, and when an accident left her paralyzed below the neck, she adjusted her goals accordingly. Today she is a wonderfully accomplished artist and author and an inspiration to everyone who knows her.

Because we don't know what the future holds, we must always view our goals with our eyes fixed first on Jesus. Whatever life brings, however our goals change, we can hold on to the assurance that God is at work in our lives "to will and to act according to his good purpose" (Philippians 2:13).

Step #4: Support Their Endeavors

Sometime ago Dr. Donald Clifton of SRI/Gallup Poll conducted a study to see if there was a correlation between an athlete's performance and the presence of family members in the audience. The evidence showed that those athletes who had moms and other family members watching from the sidelines were more likely to perform at a higher level than those who had no one cheering them on.[5]

During my junior year in college, I decided to run a marathon. After months of diligent training for this twenty-six-mile test of endurance, the day of the race finally arrived. My entire family and several friends showed up to cheer me on. My mother actually made signs with encouraging messages—for example, "I can do everything through him who gives me strength" (Philippians 4:13)—and she and the others held them up for me to see at strategic spots along the course. My father and my boyfriend (now my husband, Curt) even jumped into the race and ran a few miles with me just to encourage me.

As you can imagine, it was a grand and glorious moment when I crossed the finish line! Who can say how well I might have fared without the support of my loved ones? I know without a doubt that I gave it my very best because my family and friends were there.

As positive moms, we can support our children by being there—by taking them to their lessons and practices and showing up for their recitals and games. We can encourage them by looking for opportunities to build up their self-confidence and skills. A little research on our part can help. What skills are involved in your child's field of interest? Does your city or county have a league? Are there classes in that skill for his or her age group? Who are the best teachers or coaches? Is the teacher qualified and able to motivate and work well with kids?

Of course, our children will not always succeed at what they do. We need to be there when they win—and also when they lose. Through the tears, heartaches, and disappointments, we need to lend a listening ear and a shoulder to cry on. Our children should know that we are a safe haven for them—that we will love them whether they perform perfectly or mess up. Our support must be unconditional!

We are not lowering our expectations by comforting our children rather than scolding them when they don't perform to the best of their abilities. Everyone has a bad day or an off performance. By our response to their failure, we can either douse their confidence or be the catalyst that helps them want to try harder next time. They may fall, but they'll dig deep for the courage to get up if they know mom is there saying, "I believe in you!"

The apostle Paul said it best: "Brothers, I do not consider myself yet to have taken hold of it. But one thing I do: Forgetting what is behind and straining toward what is ahead, I press on toward the goal to win the prize for which God has called me heavenward in Christ Jesus" (Philippians 3:13–14). What great words for us to pass on to our children! We can say to them, "I know you are not there yet, but you will be. Let's forget what is behind us and press forward to reach the goal God intends for you!"

The Blessing of Encouragement

The story is told of an elderly man who once approached the famous nineteenth-century poet and artist Dante Gabriel Rossetti. Under his arm, the old man carried a number of sketches and drawings he'd recently completed. He asked the great artist to look at his work and tell him if they showed any degree of artistic value or skill.

Rossetti looked over the drawings carefully for a few minutes before concluding that they did not show the least sign of artistic talent. Gently he broke the news to the old man, who seemed disappointed but not surprised.

The man then asked Rossetti to look at just a few more drawings done by a younger art student. Rossetti agreed, and this time he found the work to be quite good. With enthusiasm, he told the old man that this young student showed great potential and should be encouraged to pursue a career as an artist.

The man seemed deeply moved by these words, so Rossetti asked if the drawings were perhaps the work of his son. "No," the man replied sadly. "These are mine also, done forty years ago. If only I had heard your praise then! For you see, I got discouraged and gave up too soon."

Perhaps this unknown artist would be a household name today if someone had taken him under wing and encouraged him to continue

63

to hone his skills and pursue his dream. As a young man, he did not get the affirmation and blessing he needed at a critical time in his life. As positive moms, we can help ensure that our children do not suffer the same fate.

Many books have been written about the importance of parental blessings in a young person's life. Blessings are not a new idea; the great patriarchs of the Bible often spoke blessings to their children, thereby helping to mold and shape their futures. How can you bless your kids? Begin by telling them that God created them unique and special, and he has a great plan for their lives. Read Jeremiah 29:11–13 and Psalm 139:14–16 to them. Pray with them, asking God to bless the good qualities you see in them and to guard and guide them as they go forward with their lives.

Our children are embarking on an exciting adventure. Who knows what the future holds for them? Only God—the one who has built their boat, charted their course, and who now gives us the privilege of being wind in their sails. As positive moms, may our affirmation, encouragement, and unconditional love help them reach their destination!

POWER POINT

Read: The exciting story of Esther in the book of the Bible by that name. Reflect on the potential that Mordecai saw in Esther and what he did to encourage and support her. Notice how God used her life for an important purpose as a result of a pursued dream.

Pray: I praise you, Lord, for having a plan and a purpose for each one of us. You love us, and you know more about us than we know about ourselves. Help me as a mother to see the potential and the possibilities in each of my children. Help me to be faithful to support them in the direction of their bent. Help me to refrain from placing any selfish or unrealistic expectations on them. Help us to set realistic and wise goals and to keep our focus on those goals. Most importantly, help us to keep our eyes fixed on you, the author and finisher of our faith.

Do: Write down the positive qualities and attributes you see in your children in the four key areas of growth: mental, physical, spiritual, and social. Plan a time to sit down with each child (age eight and up) individually and set realistic goals for growth in these areas. Pray with your children as they go to bed at night, asking God to bless the specific plans he has for each one of them.

The Beauty of a Smile
Bringing Son-shine to Others

What sunshine is to flowers, smiles are to humanity.
They are but trifles, to be sure, scattered along life's pathway.
The good they do is inconceivable.
—Joseph Addison

When your children hear the word *mother,* what picture do they get in their mind's eye? Do they imagine a pleasant, encouraging woman with a warm expression and a cheerful disposition? A haggard lady shaking her head from side to side with a disappointed expression on her face? Or maybe an angry woman giving "the look"—you know, that fearful, pointed glare that could stop a raging bull in its tracks?

It's a little scary to speculate on what our children envision when they think of a "mother." We know the portrait we wish they'd have—the one we hope we give them more often than not! But how do we model the "warm and cheerful mom" when we feel more like the "haggard mom" after juggling an unending list of daily chores and responsibilities—or worse, like the "angry mom" after spending the day cleaning up spills, correcting bad attitudes, and disciplining wayward rugrats?

There are days when it can seem too difficult to even lift a smile when our kids come in the door after school or play. But a smile, physically speaking, is not a great burden. After all, it takes fewer facial muscles to create a smile than to produce a frown. And a simple smile, offered on a regular basis, can make a world of difference in the way our children view their days, their lives—and their mothers!

I know, it's hard to smile when we don't feel like it. But as positive moms, we need to recognize that a smile is less the result of a good feeling and more a gift that we give to others. When we give the simple gift of a smile, we lift the spirits of the people around us. We help them get through their day. Doesn't it work that way when someone smiles at you, whether you're at the shopping mall or at church or in your own home? Don't you feel uplifted, encouraged, as if someone likes you and believes in you? Don't you want to do the same for others—especially your kids?

A smile speaks volumes to our children. When a mother smiles at her son from the audience of a school play, she tells him, "I'm proud of you. You're doing a great job." When she smiles as her daughter comes in the door after a difficult day at school, she reassures her, "It's okay. Everything will be all right." When she grins from ear to ear as she picks up her ten-year-old from a week at summer camp, she says, "I missed you so much. I'm glad to see you! You are special to me."

I remember the impact my own mother's smile made on me when I competed on the school gymnastics team as a young girl. Even though I practiced and practiced, I continued to struggle with one particular move on the balance beam: the forward head roll. I seemed to lose my balance and fall off the beam every time!

I still had not mastered that roll by the time the first competition rolled around, so my sweet mother prayed with me before the meet, asking God to help me stay on the beam. Then she went into the stands to watch. Miraculously, when it was my turn to compete, I did the forward head roll without a slip! But as much as that accomplishment is etched in my memory, the moment I will never forget is when I looked up in the stands and saw my mother smiling. Her beaming face told me loud and clear: "I knew you could do it! Praise the Lord!"

Learn to greet your friends with a smile; they carry too many frowns in their own hearts to be bothered with yours. —Mary Allette Ayer

Don't Wait for the Feeling

Every moment of every day we have a choice as to what we will put on our face: a smile or a frown. We don't have to wait to have "happy feelings" before we smile. Think about it. Most of the actions we take in life are not based on a feeling but on a deliberate decision. You don't wait for the feeling to hit you before you do the laundry, do you? I hope not—otherwise you'd have piles of dirty clothes lying around just waiting for you to get a warm, fuzzy feeling about doing the wash. For most of us, I think, those piles would simply keep growing! No, you do the loads because they need to be done. It's not a matter of feeling like it; it's a matter of choosing a course of action. Smiling, too, is something we can choose to do whether we feel like it or not. It's an act of kindness— sometimes a sacrificial one—extended to those around us.

In his book *How to Win Friends and Influence People*, Dale Carnegie tells the story of a man in one of his classes who had a life-changing experience because of the power of a smile. The class had been instructed to smile at everyone they met for an entire week and then report back on the results. Here's Bill's story:

> When you asked me to make a talk about my experience with smiles, I thought I would try it for a week. So the next morning, while combing my hair, I looked at my glum mug in the mirror and said to myself: "Bill, you are going to wipe the scowl off that sour face of yours today. You are going to smile, and you are going to begin right now." As I sat down to breakfast, I greeted my wife with a "good morning, my dear!" And I smiled as I said it.
>
> You warned me that she might be surprised. Well, you underestimated her reaction. She was bewildered. She was shocked. I told her that in the future she could expect this as a regular occurrence, and I kept it up every morning. This changed attitude of mine has

brought more happiness into our home in the two months since I started than there was during the entire last year.

As I leave for my office, I greet the elevator operator in the apartment house with a "good morning," and I smile. I greet the doorman with a smile. I smile at the cashier in the subway booth when I ask for change. As I stand on the floor of the Stock Exchange, I smile at the people who until recently never saw me smile. I soon found that everybody was smiling back at me...

I am a totally different man; a happier man, a richer man, richer in friendships and happiness.[1]

Wow—the power of a smile! Notice Bill didn't wait for a feeling to hit him before he started sharing smiles with others. He just began smiling, and the feelings followed. Make the decision today to be a smiling mom and see what happens. You may want to forewarn your husband of your new objective; we don't want to cause any heart attacks!

The Basis for Smiling

Perhaps you are still not convinced that you can produce a smile when you don't feel like it. Consider what the Bible says about the characteristic of joy. Paul (I call him the "positive apostle") wrote to the early Christians about joy quite often. "Be joyful always," he wrote in 1 Thessalonians 5:16. "Rejoice in the Lord always," he said in Philippians 4:4. Now, this is a pretty amazing command when you consider that the early Christians faced persecution and even death for their faith in Christ! Many had friends and family members who'd already made that ultimate sacrifice—and for all they knew they could be next.

How could Paul expect them to rejoice in such circumstances? For this reason: True, biblical joy is not based on circumstances or feelings, but on something more substantial deep within our hearts.

There is a distinct difference between happiness and joy.

Happiness tends to be based on what happens in our lives. Suppose you get a knock at the door and a florist hands you a box filled with a dozen roses. A note from your spouse is attached, saying, "I'm proud of all you do. Keep up the great work!" No doubt a smile will erupt across your face due to the happiness you feel in that circumstance. Joy is different; it is there whether you get the roses or don't get the roses. It is a consistent attitude of peace, confidence, and satisfaction that resides deep within you because you know a loving God is at work in your life.

The early Christians didn't live in happy circumstances, yet Paul told them to "rejoice always." They could do that because they knew that Jesus Christ paid the penalty for their sins. They knew they were forgiven; they were deeply loved; and they had the assurance of eternal life. That deep sense of joy gave those early Christians a great and abiding strength that enabled them to face their difficult circumstances. The Old Testament hero Nehemiah explained this when he said, "The joy of the LORD is your strength" (Nehemiah 8:10).

Perhaps this kind of joy seems impossible to you. In a sense, it is. In the list of qualities that God produces in our lives through the Holy Spirit (known as the "fruit of the spirit" in Galatians 5:22–23), joy is the second quality named. We are not the producers of joy; God is! He develops joy in us as we get to know him, love him, and trust and obey his Word.

When we have true, godly joy, we experience a fulfilling gladness, deep satisfaction, and great pleasure. We have day-to-day confidence that "in all things God works for the good of those who love him, who have been called according to his purpose" (Romans 8:28). We can rejoice because we know that God is faithful and can be trusted to work through the good and the bad situations in our lives.

The word *joy* or *joyfulness* is mentioned more than 180 times in the

A cheerful heart is good medicine. —Proverbs 17:22

Old and New Testaments. If you still need help rejoicing, take some time to look them up using a Bible concordance. You can consider these two scriptures for a start:

> I delight greatly in the LORD;
>> my soul rejoices in my God.
> For he has clothed me with garments of salvation
>> and arrayed me in a robe of righteousness,
> as a bridegroom adorns his head like a priest
>> and as a bride adorns herself with her jewels.
>> —Isaiah 61:10

> Then will I go to the altar of God,
>> to God, my joy and my delight.
> I will praise you with the harp,
>> O God, my God.
> Why are you downcast, O my soul?
>> Why so disturbed within me?
> Put your hope in God,
>> for I will yet praise him,
>> my Savior and my God.
>> —Psalm 43:4–5

Like the early Christians, our reason to rejoice is our hope in God's salvation. Our wonderful and loving heavenly Father has provided forgiveness of our sins through his son, Jesus. He has given us the hope of eternal life as we put our faith in him. With Isaiah we can rejoice because he has clothed us in the "garments of salvation." With David, we can dispel worry, disappointment, and discouragement by putting our hope in God and choosing to say, "I will yet praise him, my Savior and my God." With Nehemiah, we can affirm that the joy of the Lord is all the strength we need to get through each day with a smile on our face.

Let Your Light Shine

Do you know people who seem to shine? Invariably, these are people who experience joy deep within their hearts. In fact, several references to joy in the Old Testament can be translated "to shine" (Psalm 21:1; Isaiah 9:3; Proverbs 23:24).

A joyful smile helps us to shine. It brightens the day for us and for everyone around us! And a little can go a long way. Think of the way one small, glowing candle can illuminate an entire dark room—that's how our smile can spread "Son-shine" into someone else's dark day. What greater gift can we give our kids than the example of a mom who shines for Christ?

Mother Teresa, the Nobel prize-winning nun who spent her life helping the sick and needy in Calcutta, India, always gave the gift of a smile to the hurting people she met. Listen to some of her thoughts about smiles:

> Peace begins with a smile—smile five times a day at someone you don't really want to smile at at all—do it for peace.

> Smile at one another. It is not always easy. Sometimes I find it hard to smile at my Sister, but then we must pray.[2]

If Mother Teresa could smile in the midst of the suffering and poverty that surrounded her, surely we can offer a smile from the warmth of our kitchens, surrounded by our precious loved ones!

Recently I asked my husband what he would like to have me do for him as he comes home from work each day. Did he want dinner on the table just as he walked in? Did he want a clean house upon his arrival (and if so, which room?) Would he like to hear some of his favorite music playing in the background?

Curt admitted that all the offers sounded good. But then he declined them, saying, "Karol, what I really need to see when I come

73

home from work is a smile on your face. It makes my day when you greet me with a smile."

At first I was relieved that he had not picked one of the more difficult offers. But then I began to think of the downside. After all, I had worked hard to develop that just-right "haggard look" that would make Curt realize how difficult my day had been and cause him to feel sympathy for me as soon as he came in the door! As I thought about it, though, I had to admit "the look" hadn't been working as well as I'd hoped. And a smile, I figured, was an easy gift to give—much easier than dinner on the table on time.

Amazingly, as I made the effort in the days that followed, I found that I could produce a smile for Curt even on days when I wasn't feeling tremendously happy. I could even smile on PMS days! For about a year now I've kept the smiles coming, and you know what? My efforts have been infectious. These days we seem to have a contest to see who can greet Curt at the door first each evening—me, my girls, or the dogs. (I have to admit those faithful pooches beat me most of the time.) Curt enjoys his arrival at home each evening—and so do the rest of us.

I've found that my children also benefit from a smile when they come home after a long day of school or play. I make it a point to greet them with gladness when they emerge from the school building or hop in the car or walk in the door. The blessing I receive in return is to see them smile back!

A cheerful look sends an uplifting message that says, "Whether I feel it or not, there is something to smile about. There is something in our lives for which we can be glad!" Our children and family members need to hear that message—and so do we.

A Time and Place for Everything

Of course, there is a time and a place for everything. A smile is appropriate much of the time—but there *are* times when it is out of

74

place. I'm not suggesting that we smile 100 percent of every day for the rest of our lives. Solomon put it best when he said, "There is a time for everything, and a season for every activity under heaven…a time to weep and a time to laugh, a time to mourn and a time to dance" (Ecclesiastes 3:1, 4).

A positive mom, generally speaking, is a smiling mom. Our kids will become smiling kids as they learn from our example. But we need to be *real* moms as well. When the circumstances of life call for a cry, we must weep out of the depths of our being. When there is reason to mourn, we must mourn thoroughly and completely. Expressing sadness or loss doesn't mean that God's joy has left us; it simply means that we are not afraid to show our emotions and be transparent about our feelings. Joy is deeper, remember? A quiet, joyful peace can still reside within us even as we work through sadness, grief, and pain.

When I was thirty years old, a car tragically killed my mother while she was crossing a street during her routine morning walk. This was a devastating time for me and my family. Everyone loved Grammy. We cried and grieved together—but were never without the peace of knowing that God was at work in our lives. We had the assurance that my mother, a godly woman, was in heaven with the Lord. Did we smile? No, this was not the time for smiling; it was the time for grieving. But when our grieving had run its course, the smiles returned.

The True Worth of a Smile

Several years ago our family took a trip to Florida. In the small but quaint town of Appalachicola, I found a unique item in a little gift shop. It was called "Smile on a Stick" and was actually a cardboard picture of a smile mounted on a craft stick. For the bargain price of $1.75, you could hold it in front of your mouth anytime you wanted to smile!

If you see this little gadget in your own travels, let me encourage you: Don't buy it! You already have a smile. It costs you nothing, but it's worth a million bucks. Start giving your smile away as a gift to the people around you, whether you feel like it or not; you'll find that the feelings will follow, and you will be the richer for it.

Smiles are contagious. Let's infect our family members—and everyone else we meet—with ours. Think how much brighter our lives will be with all those shining faces around us!

After all, with the joy we find only in Christ, we have reason to smile.

POWER POINT

Read: John 3:29; 15:11; 16:20–24; and 17:13. Underline the word *joy* every time you see it. Notice the basis for joy in each of these verses.

Pray: Dear wonderful and loving heavenly Father, I praise you for the salvation I have in you. Thank you that through Jesus my sins are forgiven and I have the hope of eternal life. Thank you that your joy can be my strength through the ups and downs of life. Thank you for the ability to smile. Help me to give this gift of a smile to my family and friends. Help my children to learn to experience joy in life as they watch my example. In Jesus' name, amen.

Do: Choose a day this week to give everyone you come in contact with the gift of a sincere smile. Share with your husband, your children, or a friend how your experience with smiles touched you and touched others.

Principle #2

THe P●wer oF Prayer

The prayer of a righteous man is powerful and effective.
—James 5:16

Prayer is a sincere, sensible, affectionate pouring out of the soul
to God, through Christ, in the strength and assistance of the Spirit,
for such things as God has promised.
—John Bunyan

6

A Positive Mom Is a Praying Mom
How to Effectively Pray for Your Kids

I know not by what methods rare,
But this I know; God answers prayer.
I know not if the blessing sought Will come in just the guise I thought.
I leave my prayer to Him alone Whose will is wiser than my own.
—Eliza M. Hickok

The famous preacher Billy Sunday told the story of a young minister who enjoyed visiting the families in his church during the week. At one home, a child answered the door and politely invited him in. When the minister asked to see her mother, the young girl replied, "You cannot see mother, for she prays from nine to ten." The minister decided to wait.

After forty minutes the woman finally emerged from her "prayer closet." Her face was filled with such a bright glow that the minister knew immediately why this woman's home was such a haven of peace and order, and why her oldest daughter was a missionary and her two sons were in the ministry. Billy Sunday finished the story by saying, "All hell cannot tear a boy or girl away from a praying mother."[1]

Do you want to make a positive impact on the next generation? Become a praying mom! Many men, women, boys, and girls have been kept from falling into sin, foolishness, and destruction because their mothers' knees were bent in prayer. Jesus said, "Ask and it will be given to you; seek and you will find; knock and the door will be opened to you. For everyone who asks receives; he who seeks finds; and to him who knocks, the door will be opened" (Matthew 7:7–8). Are you willing to take God at his word and ask him to help and bless your family?

Why Pray?

Jesus also said, "Your Father knows what you need before you ask him" (Matthew 6:8). If God already knows all of our needs, is it really necessary to tell him in prayer? Perhaps your children have asked you this question—and if they haven't yet, they will. You need the answer for their sake as well as yours. Why do we pray if God knows everything?

1. We Pray Because God Tells Us to Bring All Our Requests to Him

Jesus' statement about God knowing our needs before we verbalize them was not intended to discourage prayer—just to discourage long and showy prayers. We don't need to impress God (or the people around us) with our ability to spout windy, pious-sounding prayers! Prayer, Jesus said, is actually best when kept personal and simple. He followed that statement by teaching his disciples the simple model for prayer we know today as "The Lord's Prayer" (Matthew 6:9–13).

Later, in the Garden of Gethsemane, he instructed his followers to "watch and pray" (Matthew 26:41). He himself prayed—in the garden and throughout his life and ministry. His followers also called people to pray. "You do not have, because you do not ask God," James reminds us (James 4:2). "Do not be anxious about anything, but in everything, by prayer and petition, with thanksgiving, present your requests to God," Paul says in Philippians 4:6.

2. We Pray Because We Need Wisdom from Above to Be Good Mothers

Frankly, we need wisdom to survive this job of motherhood—and the source of all true wisdom is God. "For the LORD gives wisdom, and from his mouth come knowledge and understanding" (Proverbs 2:6). There is no parenting book we can read or family seminar we can attend that will give us the answer to every problem that arises in our children's lives. We need God's help! Fortunately, he promises to give us wisdom if we ask for it: "If any of you lacks wisdom, he should ask God, who gives generously to all without finding fault, and it will be given to him" (James 1:5).

Isn't it inspiring to think that the creator of the universe is willing to give us wisdom if we just ask? But wisdom is not the only thing we need as mothers. We should also pray for patience, strength, peace, perseverance—and the list could go on and on. When we pray, we can be confident that God will give us everything we need. Jesus said in Mark 11:24, "Therefore I tell you, whatever you ask for in prayer, believe that you have received it, and it will be yours."

I remember a particularly challenging time in my life as a young mother when prayer became a solace and a necessity to me. Grace was two years old and Joy was six months old, and I felt out of my league. I had neither the patience to handle a child in the "trying twos" nor the strength to meet the needs of a demanding baby. Day after day I found myself both frazzled and frustrated, often displaying my emotions in tears in front of Curt and the kids. And as if that weren't overwhelming enough, we were in the process of moving our little family into a new house—no small feat under the best of circumstances.

My prayer life, I must admit, had dwindled to little more than a few whispered words as I cleaned up the dinner dishes. After all, who has time to pray when you have a bottle to warm, diapers to change, a toddler to chase, loads of laundry to fold, and boxes to pack and unpack?

Have you ever felt overwhelmed by the circumstances of life? Perhaps my situation seems like a piece of cake compared to what you've gone through. Or maybe you, too, have experienced a number of small frustrations adding up and eating away at your joy and strength. Whatever our situations, we all have times when we feel unable to handle or control our circumstances. Those are the times when we need prayer the most.

During those trying months I began to recognize my true need for help from above. Clearly I didn't have the power within myself to renew my physical or emotional strength. Only God could do that. So I began to pray that God would help me organize my tasks and give me the strength and direction I needed. I even asked him to help me make more time for prayer. And as I gave my cares and anxieties over to him, I began to experience a wonderful new peace and calm in my heart and in my home. The scripture in Isaiah 40:28–31 came alive to me:

> Do you not know? Have you not heard? The LORD is the everlasting God, the Creator of the ends of the earth. He will not grow tired or weary, and his understanding no one can fathom. He gives strength to the weary and increases the power of the weak. Even youths grow tired and weary, and young men stumble and fall; but those who hope in the LORD will renew their strength. They will soar on wings like eagles; they will run and not grow weary, they will walk and not be faint.

3. We Pray Because Our Families Need Our Fervent Prayers

No matter how good we are as mothers, we can't be our children's sole protector and provider. We can't be their around-the-clock bodyguard. No, only God can be in all places at all times; only he has the power to watch over every family member every moment as we scatter in the morning to work, school, or play. We must entrust our precious ones to God daily in prayer, recognizing our dependence on him for their physical and spiritual health and safety.

The Old Testament character Hannah is a wonderful example of a praying mom—a mother who diligently, faithfully, and persistently sought the Lord for her needs and the needs of her family. Unable to have children of her own, she nevertheless prayed earnestly that God would give her a son. She deeply, desperately wanted a child. If God would give her a son, she promised, she would "give him to the LORD for all the days of his life" (1 Samuel 1:11). God heard the prayer of this devoted woman, and eventually a son—Samuel—was born.

True to her promise, Hannah took young Samuel to live with Eli the priest. You would think that a priest's home would be a safe and nurturing place to grow up. But while Eli himself was a good man, his two sons were evil. Imagine Hannah leaving her precious son—her very own answer to prayer—in a household with two wicked brothers! No doubt Hannah continued her petitions to God, praying for her son's protection. As a result, Samuel "continued to grow in stature and in favor with the LORD and with men" (1 Samuel 2:26). Eventually he became God's prophet, a true man of God who led the nation of Israel for many years.

We can sum up Hannah's story—and our own responsibility to pray for our families—with a paraphrase of James 5:16: "The effective, fervent prayer of a righteous mom avails much" (NKJV). Our families need our fervent prayers if they are to become everything God intends for them to be. Their physical health and spiritual growth will not go unnoticed and unchallenged. The Bible tells us, "Your enemy the devil prowls around like a roaring lion looking for someone to devour" (1 Peter 5:8). He would love to sink his teeth into our children and cut them off from the future God has planned for them. For their sakes we must "resist him" (v. 9)—and we can do that best on our knees.

Hannah could not be with Samuel as he grew up. But, fortunately, she was a woman of prayer, and we can gain inspiration and encouragement from her example. Like Hannah, we will not be able to hold our

Be joyful always; pray continually. —1 Thessalonians 5:16–17

83

children's hands every time they face a challenge or hit a bump in the road. But we can pray for them and rest assured that God is with them, watching over them and molding them into the people he wants them to be.

Pray without Ceasing

One of my favorite verses as a child was 1 Thessalonians 5:17: "Never stop praying" (PHILLIPS). I loved this verse because it was short and easy for a ten-year-old to memorize (which meant an easy sticker in Sunday school!) As an adult, and especially as a mother, I still love this verse. Now more than ever I recognize that continual prayer is more than a nice idea; it's an absolute necessity—a moment-by-moment recognition of my dependence on God to meet the numerous responsibilities, decisions, and concerns that arise each day.

But can a person really pray continually, without stopping? Bible scholars say this command can be understood two ways. One interpretation is that we must continually be in an *attitude* of prayer hour by hour and day by day, constantly talking to the Father as we go about our daily work and routine. Mother Teresa was a wonderful model of this attitude of prayer. She once said there was only one reason she was able to minister faithfully day in and day out to the poorest of the poor in Calcutta: "I pray!" She went on to explain, "You should spend at least half an hour in the morning and an hour at night in prayer. You can pray while you work. Work doesn't stop prayer, and prayer doesn't stop work. It requires only that small raising of mind to Him. 'I love You, God, I trust You, I believe in You, I need You now.' Small things like that. They are wonderful prayers."[2]

Perhaps you have found, as I have, that there are many opportunities to turn our thoughts heavenward during a typical day. We can pray as we fold the laundry, lifting up prayers for the recipient of each freshly cleaned item. As we set the table, we can pray for the one who will be seated at each place. We can pray as we cook dinner or wash dishes. We can pray as we drive our children to different practices and events, and we can certainly pray as they perform or participate in those activities. We should pray as we drop them off at school or day care or a friend's home. Never stop praying! A positive mom is a praying mom.

A second interpretation of the command to "pray without ceasing" is that we must never allow our prayer life to fall by the wayside. It is important that we set aside a regular time for prayer and stay devoted to it, never letting it get choked out by the busyness of motherhood and the distractions of our daily routines. We need a time each day to purposefully, lovingly, and deliberately pray—a set time when we praise God for who he is, thank him for what he has done and is doing in our lives, and lay before him our cares, worries, and requests (more on this in the next chapter). "Sometimes we think we are too busy to pray," C. H. Spurgeon once said. "That is a great mistake, for praying is a saving of time."

Jesus, of course, is the best example of someone who never allowed anything to keep him from being a person of prayer. Scripture is full of scenes of Jesus praying to the Father. And if the *Son of God* felt compelled to pray, shouldn't we pray as well?

We read in Mark 1:35, "Very early in the morning, while it was still dark, Jesus got up, left the house and went off to a solitary place, where he prayed." Notice, the scripture says Jesus got up "while it was still dark." Sorry, all you non-morning people, but early in the day does seem to be a particularly good time to lift our cares heavenward! Listen to the words of the psalmist: "In the morning, O LORD, you hear my voice; in the morning I lay my requests before you and wait in expectation" (Psalm 5:3).

Personally, I like to get up early each morning, before anyone else is stirring, and sit down at my kitchen table for a time of prayer and study. There, with a cup of coffee and an open Bible, I meet with God. I relish the quiet stillness of the household at that hour and the wonderful embrace of my heavenly Father in the alone time. As I read the Scriptures each morning, recognizing that they are God's love letters to me, I grow to love him more and more. In prayer, I pour out my requests to him and lay my anxieties at his feet. I praise him for who he is and what he means to my life. Occasionally one of my girls will come into the kitchen and find me with my head bowed over God's Word, but that's okay. I believe my children need to see that prayer is important to me and that I depend on God for each day's strength.

I'm not suggesting that you *must* be an early riser to have a fulfilling prayer life, but first-thing-in-the-morning prayer does have some definite advantages. For mothers especially, the most peaceful time of the day tends to be in the morning, before the other members of the household are up and running. Why not start getting up just a few minutes earlier each day to pray? You will soon find that you enjoy getting up early and beginning your mornings alone with God.

Notice that Mark 1:35 also says that Jesus went to a "solitary place" to pray. If it were only that easy! Finding a solitary place often presents a unique challenge for mothers. Generally speaking, wherever we go—anywhere in the house—*they* will find us. Funny how we can even retreat to the privacy (we think) of the bathroom and not have two minutes of quiet before we hear a knock on the door and see little fingers poking underneath. Yes, it is hard for moms to get away!

The opportunity to find a little solitude is another good reason for praying early in the morning. But sometimes, no matter how early we try to rise, some little tyke will beat us to the breakfast table. If that's what regularly happens to you, don't despair! Instead, choose a small room or large closet in your house and designate it as your special "prayer place." Then instruct the rest of the family to respect your time when you're in that place. You may even want to hang a sign on the door that reads:

```
MIP
Mother in Prayer
Please Do Not Disturb
```

If you have a young baby and feel you cannot physically "get away" for a few minutes, try simply holding your little bundle in your arms while you pray. After all, our children are only that young and cuddly for a short time; go ahead and relish the opportunity to hold and cuddle your baby while you pray! The purpose for finding a solitary place is to minimize the distractions of the household and help us stay focused on our conversation with God. If you can pray with your baby in your arms, go for it.

Think of your prayer time this way: If you were planning to get together with your best friend to chat about the important issues in your lives, would you choose to meet in a room with lots of noise, activity, and constant interruptions? I didn't think so! We need to plan our conversations with God with similar thoughtfulness and care.

Praying with Confidence

Howard Chandler Robbins once said, "The prayers of the Christian are secret, but their effect cannot be hidden."[3] Certainly that was true in the life of Englishman George Muller, considered to be one of the mightiest men of prayer of the nineteenth century. While founding a number of successful orphanages for the children of England, Muller determined to never ask anyone for money to meet his needs or the needs of the orphans. Instead he committed all of those needs to prayer. Amazingly he raised more than eight million dollars (think how much that would be in today's money!) by directing his petitions not to men, but to God. Somehow God always made sure Muller received all the resources he needed.

Muller never prayed for things just because he wanted them, or even because he felt they were needed for God's work. No, before praying, he would search the Scriptures to find if there was a promise in God's Word that covered the circumstance or need in question. Sometimes he would search the Bible for days before presenting his petition to God. What devotion!

When he found the appropriate promise, Muller would then place his finger on that spot in his open Bible and plead with God based on the assurance of God's own Word. As mothers, we can devote ourselves to prayer in the same way. Perhaps you can set aside a Bible in the household for use as your family's "prayer Bible." Highlight the passages and promises you want to pray for you and your family. (You may want to use a different color marker for each family member.)

Here are some passages that contain promises you will certainly want to highlight:

- *Comfort and peace:* Psalm 42; 2 Corinthians 1:3–5; 4:7–12; Philippians 4:6–7

- *Family relationships:* Deuteronomy 6:4–9; Proverbs 22:6; Ephesians 5:21–6:4

- *Faith and character:* Matthew 6:25–34; Galatians 5:16–26; Colossians 1:9–12; 3:13–15

- *Love for others:* Mark 12:30–35; 1 John 4:7–10; Hebrews 10:24; 1 Corinthians 13

- *God's provision:* Matthew 6:25–34; 7:11

- *Strength:* Psalms 9:9; 34:4; 37:23; 69:22; 73:26; 138:7; Ephesians 6:10–18; 2 Timothy 4:16–17

- *Wisdom:* Proverbs 2:6; James 1:5

- *Faith:* Hebrews 11

- *Joy:* Nehemiah 8:10; Isaiah 12; Galatians 5:22

- *Safety:* Psalms 46; 91

Like George Muller, we can pray with confidence when we know our prayers are based on God's unchanging Word. Thomas Watson put it this way: "God's promises are the cork to keep faith from sinking in prayer."[4]

Praying Specifically for Your Children

Prayer is the most powerful force available to us in raising our children. It is not enough that we give our kids food, clothing, shelter, education, or any other benefit. To be positive, godly moms, we need to pray for them—continually. In addition to the general scriptures listed above, there are many Bible verses that deal specifically with the needs of our children and the direction they need to go in order to live godly lives. Here are some prayers and related scriptures to help you get started:

- Pray that they will come to know Christ and follow him (Romans 10:9–11).

- Pray that they will be able to recognize evil and hate it (Psalm 97:10).

- Pray that when they do something wrong, they are caught (Psalm 119:71).

- Pray for their protection against the evil one (John 17:15).

- Pray that they would be kind and forgiving toward others (Ephesians 4:32).

- Pray that they'll have courage to stand up for what is right (Joshua 1:7).

- Pray that they will have respect for authority (Romans 13:1).

- Pray that they choose wise friends (Proverbs 13:20).

- Pray for their future spouse, that they will marry a godly person (2 Corinthians 6:14–17).

- Pray for them to submit to God and resist the devil (James 4:7).

- Pray for a hedge of protection around them (Hosea 2:6).

Don't stop with these verses; search the Scriptures for yourself and find all the wonderful truths and promises you can pray for on behalf of your family. I promise this effort will revolutionize your prayer life. I know it did mine. Not long ago I went to a book resale shop and bought a Bible to use specifically for my prayer time. I don't hesitate to mark it up, and I attach different colors of "sticky notes" to identify scripture promises I want to pray for each of my family members. I pray with confidence for my husband, children, and other loved ones as I point (like George Muller) to God's promises in his Word!

In addition to your prayer Bible, I recommend that you begin to record your prayers—along with the answers you receive—in a notebook or journal. Many moms (and others) have found that the simple act of writing down prayer requests each day provides a tangible reminder that those requests have been turned over to God. We know that we have cast those cares on him. We don't have to worry about them anymore!

And as we record the answers to prayer that God gives us, we find that our faith is strengthened and our desire to pray is increased. We begin approaching our heavenly Father with a greater sense of awe and gratitude. You know, sometimes we need to be reminded to thank the Lord for responding to our prayers! How sad it would be if we were like the nine lepers in Luke 17:11–19 who never returned to thank Jesus after he healed them of their terrible disease. As positive moms, we need to be like the tenth leper who ran to Jesus and fell at his feet, full of gratitude and praise to God.

In the years to come, when you look back over your prayer journal, you will feel as if you're taking a stroll down Memory Lane and a walk through Thanksgiving Park. You will be blessed to see how far God has brought you and what he has done in your life—and in the lives of each family member for whom you have prayed.

Never Give Up

As positive, praying moms, we need to be persistent in our prayers and never give up. Jesus made this point in a parable about a persistent widow in Luke 18:1–8. In this story, the widow went repeatedly to a judge to seek justice for a wrong that had been done to her. But the judge neither feared God nor cared about the people in his jurisdiction, and he sent her away each time. The widow was persistent, however, and she continued to cry out to the judge. Finally he said to himself, "Even though I don't fear God or care about men, yet because this widow keeps bothering me, I will see that she gets justice, so that she won't eventually wear me out with her coming!" (vv. 4–5).

Jesus capped off the parable by saying, "Listen to what the unjust judge says. And will not God bring about justice for his chosen ones, who cry out to him day and night? Will he keep putting them off? I tell you, he will see that they get justice, and quickly" (vv. 6–8).

If the inconsiderate judge finally gave in to the widow's pleas, how much more will our loving heavenly Father hear our persistent requests and respond with kindness toward us? Never stop praying! The saying is true: We are never so high as when we are on our knees in prayer. Begin to reach to new and greater heights. Be a praying mom!

POWER POINT

Read: The story of Hannah in 1 Samuel 1 and her prayer of thanksgiving in 1 Samuel 2:1–10.

Pray: I praise you, most loving and kind Father, for hearing my prayers. It is incredible to think that the God of the universe would want to have a conversation with me! Thank you for allowing me to come to you with my needs and requests. Thank you for loving my family more perfectly and more deeply than I could ever love them. You are truly "our refuge and strength, an ever-present help in trouble" (Psalm 46:1). Help me to be a woman of prayer and a diligent and faithful prayer warrior for my family. In Jesus' name, amen.

Do: Decide on a time that would be best for you to spend in prayer each day, then choose a private place where you can be alone during that interval. Write the time and place in your calendar or day planner. Place a Bible, pen, and prayer journal in your place of prayer so it can be waiting there for you each day.

7

Casting Your Cares
Finding Strength, Hope, and Wisdom for Each Day

Every evening I turn my worries over to God.
He's going to be up all night anyway.
—Mary C. Crowley

About once a year at our house, we overhaul the junk closet. We rummage through the layers of old shoes, broken toys, worn-out backpacks, and other sundry items, and throw out everything that has been outgrown or gone unused. I'm not quite sure how all the stuff accumulates there each year, but it sure feels good to dig in and finally get rid of the excess baggage.

Whether it's a junk closet, a catchall drawer, or an overloaded purse, most of us have a place where we store things that we probably should have thrown out or given away long before. We feel so good when we finally get serious and unload the clutter that we wonder why we didn't do it sooner!

As mothers, we have a tendency to hold on to things we shouldn't—and I'm not just talking about old bowling balls, broken umbrellas, and worn-out tennis shoes. Too often we allow the cares of life to pile up in the closet in our hearts called "worry." Just as we clean out the junk in our home closets on a regular basis, we need to continually cast off the worries that we collect and tuck away in our hearts. And while we might reasonably clean out a junk closet once or twice a year, we should tackle our worries on a daily basis.

Perhaps you are thinking, "What's the big deal? Doesn't everyone worry? What's so bad about savoring some anxieties and enjoying a little apprehension now and then? I'm a mother. I've earned it!"

Well, what does God want us to do with worry: relish it or relinquish it? The apostle Paul is quite clear on this subject. "Do not be anxious about anything, but in everything, by prayer and petition, with thanksgiving, present your requests to God," he writes in Philippians 4:6–7. "And the peace of God, which transcends all understanding, will guard your hearts and your minds in Christ Jesus." Notice, Paul doesn't say, *"Consider* getting rid of anxiety." No, he is quite straightforward: "Do not be anxious."

In the Sermon on the Mount, Jesus also addressed the topic of worry:

Therefore I tell you, do not worry about your life, what you will eat or drink; or about your body, what you will wear. Is not life more important than food, and the body more important than clothes? Look at the birds of the air; they do not sow or reap or store away in barns, and yet your heavenly Father feeds them. Are you not much more valuable than they? Who of you by worrying can add a single hour to his life?

And why do you worry about clothes? See how the lilies of the field grow. They do not labor or spin. Yet I tell you that not even Solomon in all his splendor was dressed like one of these. If that is how God clothes the grass of the field which is here today and tomorrow is thrown into the fire, will he not much more clothe you, O you of little faith? So do not worry, saying, "What shall we eat?" or "What shall we drink?" or "What shall we wear?" For the pagans run after all these things, and your heavenly Father knows that you need them. But seek first his kingdom and his righteousness, and all these things will be given to you as well. Therefore do not worry about tomorrow, for tomorrow will worry about itself. Each day has enough trouble of its own. (Matthew 6:25–34)

Once again we are told in no uncertain terms that we are not supposed to worry. The truth is, when we wallow in worry and give in to our anxious fears, we are actually disobeying the instructions of the Bible! Have you ever thought of worry as disobedience? In our culture, fear, anxiety, and worry have become so commonplace that few people realize that they are disobeying God when they do these things.

Author and motivational speaker Ed Foreman describes worry as "nothing less than the misuse of your imagination."[1] What do you tend to worry about? What makes your mind run off and begin to imagine everything bad that could possibly happen? The list of worry prompters is different for each of us, but we all have areas that we find difficult to release fully to God. Some of us worry about finances; others, our children's safety; others, what people think about us. Some of us worry about all three—and then keep going. Sometimes we can feel as if we're drowning in the imaginary oceans we create with our persistent worrying.

Why do we harbor and savor our worries like that? Could it be that worrying is easy, but faith is difficult?

Worry and faith are mutually exclusive! They're opposites. God doesn't want us to live in fear and anxiety because when we do, we are not practicing faith in his loving care and provision. What we're really saying is, "God, I don't think you will come through for me on this one, so I need to concern myself with this problem."

That's not faith; that's fear—and it's rampant in our society. It's even rampant in our churches! In fact, anxious fear is such a common human problem that the Bible often tells us not to be afraid. The command "be not afraid" appears more than twenty times in the Old Testament alone.

Choosing Faith, Not Fear

Consider the story of Jehoshaphat, one of the ancient kings of Judah, found in 2 Chronicles 20:1–30. This faithful king was under attack by a vast fighting force—the combined armies of three of Israel's worst enemies. Though alarmed by the situation, King Jehoshaphat chose not to pace the floor fretfully and wring his hands in worry. Instead he declared a time of fasting and prayer and sought help from God.

A prophet arrived and gave this word of hope to Jehoshaphat: "This is what the LORD says to you: 'Do not be afraid or discouraged because of this vast army. For the battle is not yours, but God's'" (v. 15). The king then turned to his people as they left for battle and said, "Listen to me, Judah and people of Jerusalem! Have faith in the LORD your God and you will be upheld" (v. 20). And they were! The Lord set ambushes against their enemies, and the three armies that had allied themselves against Israel ended up destroying one other.

Yes, the circumstances were challenging, but God was with the people of Judah as they looked to him for their strength. In fact, drawing strength from God to overcome fear and worry is a recurring theme in Bible history. Long before Jehoshaphat, for example, Joshua was chosen to be Moses' successor to lead the nation of Israel into the Promised Land. Now, how would you feel if you were handed the responsibility for leading millions of grumbling people with no military training through the wilderness and into a land inhabited by fierce armies? A tad bit anxious? But God did not allow Joshua to wallow in worry; instead, he gave him this message of hope: "Have I not commanded you? Be strong and courageous. Do not be terrified; do not be discouraged, for the LORD your God will be with you wherever you go" (Joshua 1:9).

Joshua, like Jehoshaphat, was a person of great faith. In fact, I believe the reason God chose Joshua to be the leader of Israel was because he had proven himself to be a man who lived out his faith in God. Remember when Moses sent Joshua, Caleb, and ten other Hebrews to spy out the Promised Land? Joshua and Caleb returned from their mission with confidence and hope, encouraging Moses to "go for it" because God would surely be with them. "We should go up and take possession of the land, for we can certainly do it," Caleb said (Numbers 13:30). But the other spies worried and fretted, telling Moses that the enemies in the land across the Jordan River were much too great for Israel to tackle. By their worry, the ten showed their lack of faith. They didn't believe God was big enough or dependable enough to help them defeat the opposition! As a result, those fretting spies never made it into the Promised Land.

You may not be leading an army into a foreign country, but you are leading a family into a future mapped out for them by God. To be a positive mom, faith is crucial. "And without faith it is impossible to please God," Hebrews 11:6 says. The way we choose faith—and resist the tendency to be worried and afraid—is to give our cares over to God each day in prayer.

Life with a View

The story is told of an old widow who lived with her two sons in San Francisco. They were immigrants from Asia and depended entirely on the boys' earnings to meet their living expenses. Fortunately, the sons were enterprising young men and had their own small businesses—one selling rain ponchos and the other selling sunglasses. Still, every day the mother wore herself out with fret and worry. If she looked out the window and saw that the day would be sunny, she became filled with anxiety, worrying that no one would purchase her first son's ponchos. If it looked like rain, she would become desperately afraid that no one would buy her second son's sunglasses. No matter how the weather turned out, it seemed this woman always had something to worry about!

With this anxious outlook on life, she was continually glum—until a kind neighbor told her she was looking at it all wrong.

"Instead of being anxious all of the time," the neighbor suggested, "you should be joyful each day. After all, no matter what the weather brings, at least one of your sons will have a successful day!"

From then on, the woman's outlook changed, and she lived out the rest of her years with an abiding sense of happiness and peace. You see, perspective is everything! Are we able to see all of life's circumstances in the hands of a loving Lord who wants the best for us, or do we worry and fret about how we can make things work out for ourselves?

Joseph, the son of Jacob in the Old Testament, had a good perspective on life. Although Joseph was well loved by his father, his eleven brothers hated him—so much so that they threw him in a pit and sold him as a slave. Joseph could have given up on life at that point, thinking God had left him. But Scripture is clear that he continued to have faith that God had a great plan for his life.

Joseph was sold to a man in Egypt named Potiphar and rose to a position of responsibility in that household. Things were definitely looking up—until a false accusation brought an end to Joseph's prosperity and landed him in prison. Amazingly there is nothing in Scripture to indicate that Joseph was worried, despite these new circumstances. Instead he kept looking to God, who showed himself faithful to Joseph over and over.

One day Joseph was brought out of prison and given the opportunity to interpret one of the Pharaoh's ominous dreams. Stepping out on faith, Joseph trusted God to tell him what the dream meant. When Joseph shared the interpretation that God gave him, the Pharoah was so impressed that he elevated the former prisoner to second-in-command in all of Egypt. God continued to bless Joseph with wisdom; and through Joseph's foresight, the Egyptians were able to avoid the ravages of a severe famine that hit the region several years later.

What was Joseph's perspective on life? Faith! We catch a glimpse of his faith in his response to his scoundrel brothers, who begged him for

Prayer puts God's work in his hands—and keeps it there. —E. M. Bounds mercy for their abuse so many years before. "Don't be afraid," Joseph said. "Am I in the place of God? You intended to harm me, but God intended it for good to accomplish what is now being done, the saving of many lives" (Genesis 50:19–20). Joseph acknowledged both the good and the bad in his life. But because of his perspective of faith, he understood that every challenge he encountered was God's way of working toward a bigger picture in his life.

How do you approach the challenges in your life? Do you see them as an opportunity to worry—or an opportunity to trust God?

I believe God works in our lives like a jigsaw puzzle. One piece looks nice; another is ugly. One piece fits in an obvious place; another seems to fit nowhere at all. Some pieces are unidentifiable in themselves; but as they are connected with the rest of the pieces and put in proper perspective, they begin to create a wonderful picture.

We face many different situations in life—some we understand and some we don't; some that are pleasant and others that are just plain awful. Our faith comes in as we trust God with the big picture, recognizing that he has a plan for our lives. We can stand confidently on the words of Romans 8:28: "And we know that in all things God works for the good of those who love him, who have been called according to his purpose."

Some friends of ours are a case in point. Several years ago, they went through a difficult time with their finances. After losing a job, they fell into debt and eventually lost their large, beautiful home. Of course, they never would have asked for such tragedy; but the result was that they became totally dependent on God as they prayed for a new job and for help to meet their daily needs. They talked openly about their struggles and their new journey of faith, encouraging many people in the process. Today they are back on their feet financially, but with new priorities and a new perspective on life. They truly believe that their time of crisis was ultimately a blessing for their family.

Living Day by Day

I find the job of washing dishes downright frustrating, don't you? After you wash all the dishes from a meal, low and behold, you eat another meal and have to wash them all over again! You can't say, "Well, I finished that load. Now I'll never need to wash another dish." It doesn't work that way!

Many or our responsibilities as mothers require that kind of continual, repetitive attention: the laundry, dusting, vacuuming, cooking, even changing diapers (up to a point). Casting our cares on the Lord should be a daily responsibility as well. Funny how old worries tend to sneak back into our hearts and minds, just like the dust that keeps reappearing on the furniture. But rather than be discouraged when a particular worry rears its head again, we can consider its reappearance as an opportunity to once again cast our cares where they belong: in God's hands.

When I was in high school, I made a "God Box." It was pretty simple really; I took a shoebox, wrapped it with construction paper, and put a slit in the top. Then whenever I found that I was worrying about a particular issue in my life, I wrote the concern on an index card and placed it in the God Box. This was a physical, visual way for me to recognize that I was giving that care over to the Lord. Whenever the anxious thought came back to my mind, I would remind myself that I had already placed that worry in God's hands.

Recently I spray-painted a similar shoebox for our family and cut a slit in the top. I'm convinced that with the trails and worries that tend to accompany and complicate the middle school years, my daughters (and I!) will really need a God Box.

It is amazing how much time and energy we can save if we do not spend our days worrying! We can even feel better physically if we make it a habit to cast our cares daily on God. As Dr. Charles Mayo explains, "Worry affects circulation, the heart and the glands, the whole nervous system, and profoundly affects the heart. I have never known a man who died from overwork, but many who died from doubt."[2]

Worry also has a stifling effect on our creativity and ability to live life to the full.

Consider the little clock that worked herself into a frenzy because she began thinking about how often she would have to tick in the coming year. She thought to herself, "I'll have to tick two times per second, which means 120 ticks per minute, 7,200 ticks per hour, and 172,800 ticks each day!" As she continued to calculate the challenges before her, she began to feel a sense of panic. She couldn't possibly complete 1,209,600 ticks every week, which meant nearly 63 million ticks in the coming year! The more she thought about the enormity of her task, the more she worried—until she finally felt so overwhelmed that her little ticker began to go on the blink.

Realizing her need for help, the dismayed clock visited a counselor. "I just don't have what it takes to tick so much in one year," she lamented.

"How many ticks must you tick at one time?" the wise counselor asked.

"Just one at a time," the clock responded.

The counselor smiled, saying, "If you use your energy to tick just one tick at a time, I think you will be just fine."

The little clock left that day with a new outlook, wound herself up, and began to concern herself with just one tick at a time. And as you can imagine, she ticked happily ever after.

Aren't you thankful we can't see into the future of our lives or the lives of our children? We might want to give up if we knew some of the challenges that await us! Instead, because we don't know what the future holds, we must trust God. I think of Corrie Ten Boom, who lovingly trusted her heavenly Father. If she would have known as a young girl that she and her family members would be sent to concentration

Cast all your anxiety on him because he cares for you. —1 Peter 5:7

☺

camps for harboring Jews during World War II, she might have shrunk back in fear from the destiny God had for her. But God gave her—as he gives us—the grace to handle life one day at a time.

Corrie tells the story of a particularly anxious time in her life. Her father sat down on the edge of her bed and said, "Corrie, when you and I go to Amsterdam—when do I give you your ticket?" She sniffed and said, "Why, just before we get on the train." Her father responded, "Exactly. And our wise Father in heaven knows when we're going to need things, too. Don't run out ahead of him, Corrie. When the time comes that some of us will have to die, you will look into your heart and find the strength you need—just in time."[3]

Corrie Ten Boom faced severe persecution in her life, but she experienced great faith, as well. Don't worry about tomorrow; today has enough cares of its own. Take your cares to the One who cares! He will be faithful to give you the grace you need when you need it.

To God Be the Glory

We give God glory—and draw others to him—when we learn to lay our anxieties daily at the feet of Jesus. As we cast our cares on him, God gives us a deep and profound peace that "transcends all understanding" (Philippians 4:7). People can't help but be attracted to God when they see believers living in trust and not despair, despite difficult circumstances. Then, as God answers our prayers and works miracles in our lives, we have the opportunity to honor him, thank him, and tell others about his great faithfulness. If we choose to worry and fret instead of trusting the Lord, who gets the glory?

I know, moms tend to worry. It's hard not to. We wring our hands over many issues that are ultimately out of our control. Will our kids succeed in school? Will they get hurt while they are at camp or running on the playground? What if someone is cruel to them? Will they grow

To you, O Lord, I lift up my soul; in you I trust, O my God. —Psalm 25:1–2

up to be honorable and self-reliant adults? We could go on for days with a list of a mother's possible worries! Certainly we must do our best to keep our children safe and to teach and train them properly. We should never confuse casting our cares on the Lord with sitting back and not doing our job. But once we do all that is in our power as mothers to do to take care of our kids, we must leave them—and our worries about them—in God's hands. He is faithful!

Norwegian Christian author O. Hallesby referred to prayer as the "breath of the soul." He wrote:

> The air which our body requires envelops us on every hand. The air of itself seeks to enter our bodies and, for this reason, exerts pressure upon us…. The air which our souls need also envelops all of us at all times and on all sides. God is round about us in Christ on every hand, with His many-sided and all sufficient grace. All we need to do is to open our hearts. Prayer is the breath of the soul, the organ by which we receive Christ into our parched and withered hearts…. As air enters in quietly when we breathe, and does its normal work in our lungs, so Jesus enters quietly into our hearts and does His blessed work there.[4]

Spiritually speaking, we need to breathe continually every day. As we exhale our worries and fears, we inhale the peace of God, knowing that our lives are in his hands. Then we can say with the psalmist, "When I am afraid, I will trust in you. In God, whose word I praise, in God I trust; I will not be afraid. What can mortal man do to me?" (Psalm 56:3–4). And we can stand on the words of Isaiah: "You [the Lord] will keep in perfect peace him whose mind is steadfast, because he trusts in you. Trust in the LORD forever, for the LORD, the LORD, is the Rock eternal" (Isaiah 26:3–4).

As positive Christian moms, we know that we have a solid Rock on whom we can build our lives, and to whom we can entrust our children's lives. Determine to put your confidence and hope in him—and leave your cares far behind.

POWER POINT

Read: Matthew 6:25–34. Underline every instance of the word *worry* in this passage. What does Jesus have to say about worry, and how can you apply those principles to your present anxieties?

Pray: I praise you, for you are a wonderful and caring God. You know my needs before I present them to you. You love me with an everlasting love! Thank you that you care for the needs of the birds of the air, and you care so much more for the needs of my family. I trust you with the worries of my life. I have faith that you are working all things in my life together for the good. Thank you for your abundant love and kindness. In Jesus' name, amen.

Do: Cover a shoebox with wrapping paper, cut a slit in the top, and call it your family's "God Box." Decorate the box with Bible verses such as Philippians 4:6–7; 1 Peter 5:7; Psalm 56:3; and Isaiah 26:3–4. Keep index cards and a pen nearby. Explain to your family members that anytime they are worried about something, they are to write their care on a card and put it in the box as a reminder that they are casting their cares on God. (Make sure you lead by your example!)

Women of Prayer
Changing Lives through the Power of Prayer

*Everyone is capable of praying, but many have the mistaken idea
that they are not called to prayer. Just as we are called to salvation,
we are called to prayer.... Prayer is nothing more than turning our
heart toward God and receiving in turn His love.*
—Jeanne Guyon

Perhaps you remember the "running craze" of the 1980s. I
was a student at Baylor University at the time, and jogging was
quite popular among many of my friends. I wanted to be a runner,
too, but I wasn't sure how to begin. *How does a college girl with no previous experience in track and field become a strong runner?* I wondered. A
friend of mine, a physical education major, gave me this brief but
sound advice: "Just do it." (Apparently, a Nike executive overheard that
conversation!) My friend encouraged me to begin at a slow, steady pace,
be consistent, and stay at it. And you know what? The advice worked!

Since that time, I've been amazed to find that this simple tip can
apply to more areas in life than just running. Take prayer, for example.
How can a mother become a woman of prayer? Just do it! The best way
to learn is to simply begin. Start slow and steady, dedicating just a few
minutes each day to prayer. Then grow from there. As you stay at it,
you will find that a few minutes is no longer enough time to express all
your thanks and lay all your needs before the Lord. By being consistent
in meeting with God each day, you will develop a habit of daily prayer

in your life that will not easily be broken. In fact, you'll find that your prayer time is the key that gives you the power to be a positive mom.

The Power of a Mother's Prayers

Many great and godly women throughout history were praying moms who saw the power of God work through their prayers. How did they become women of prayer? Probably in much the same way that you and I can—by starting with a slow, steady pace that built up to a consistent, daily prayer walk with the Lord. We can learn and draw great encouragement from their examples.

Consider the mother of the great Christian leader Augustine of Hippo. Augustine was born in A.D. 354 to a devout Christian woman named Monica. Monica dearly loved her firstborn son and wholeheartedly believed that God had a plan for his life. But Augustine's father was a pagan man who had little respect for godly moral values, and much to Monica's dismay, Augustine grew up to follow in his father's footsteps. While attending the university in Carthage—a city known for its corruption, brothels, and pagan temples as much as for its learning and culture—Augustine was introduced to skeptical philosophies and a lifestyle of immorality. He even lived with a woman for many years and fathered a child by her, yet couldn't marry her due to the cultural class restrictions.

As you can imagine, Monica grieved and prayed over her son. At one point, seeing little change in Augustine's life or beliefs, she implored a local bishop to talk to her son and help him come to repentance and faith in Christ. But the bishop recognized his limitations; he knew his words could do little to turn a young man's hardened heart. He encouraged Monica to return home and continue in prayer for Augustine. "Go your way, and God bless you," he said, "for it is not possible that the son of these tears should perish."

Monica held on to the bishop's words and continued to plead with God for the salvation of her beloved son. Eventually Augustine's heart began to soften. During a period of doubt and truth-seeking, he decided to give up his pagan beliefs—but stopped short of accepting Christ. Monica continued to pray. Then one day, as Augustine sat in a garden reading from the letters of Paul in the Bible, Monica's prayers came to full fruition. Augustine suddenly realized that these letters from the apostle were meant for him!

To Monica's great joy, Augustine committed the rest of his life to Christ. His own prayer best expressed his mother's response to his new-found faith: "She was jubilant with triumph and glorified you, who are powerful enough, and more than powerful enough, to carry out your purpose beyond all our hopes and dreams."[1]

A similar story is told of John Newton, the wicked sailor of the mid-eighteenth century who later became John Newton, the sailor-preacher. His Christian mother believed in the power of prayer to reform her wayward son. God answered her faithful prayers by changing Newton's heart and lifestyle. He was converted to Christ, and his subsequent preaching and writing reflected his gratitude for God's wonderful salvation. In fact it was Newton, in 1779, who penned the words to "Amazing Grace"—a song that continues to lead people to Christ to this day.[2]

Never underestimate the power of a praying mom! My own mother, Barbara Kinder, was a devoted prayer warrior. She kept a prayer journal, regularly writing out her heartfelt requests to the Father. She and her prayer partner prayed together often, lifting up to God even the smallest details of both families' lives. She prayed for my tests at college, for my dates and friendships, for my running and races. (Yes, my running in college became more than a fad.) She constantly lifted up the minor and the major decisions of my life, praying fervently for

I have many times been driven to my knees by the utter conviction that I had nowhere else to go. —Abraham Lincoln

my future spouse and my career choice. Although I came to faith in Christ at an early age, I am convinced that her prayers kept me on the right path and away from influences that could have set me on a course for destruction.

Busy Moms, Busy Praying

Unfortunately, praying mothers are somewhat of an endangered species these days. When two moms meet—whether at the grocery store, the school parking lot, or the sideline of the soccer field—the typical conversation goes like this: "Hi, how are things going?" "Good, thanks. I've been really busy…" Busy seems to be the name of the game in these fast-paced times. As mothers, we feel that we must always be doing *something*, whether it's church business, work, shopping, volunteering, shuttling kids to activities, or getting together with friends. We seem to think we have an *obligation* to stay busy!

My friend Lisa, the mother of two elementary-age children, made a conscious decision this year not to "overvolunteer" or take on her typical, overflowing plate of outside interests and responsibilities. Bucking all trends, she determined that she would step out of the fast lane for a full twelve months. She is still busy, mind you. But she is busy *praying*.

Yes, praying. Lisa spends a significant amount of time each day praying for the specific needs of her family. She prays for her friends and for the sick and the hurting. She prays for other issues that are brought to her attention. She stands firmly on the promises of God, believing in the power of prayer. She is serious about being busy with the most important business in life: taking her needs—and the needs of her loved ones—to the Father's throne.

In the process, Lisa has *not* become a recluse from life. She has remained involved in her church and her children's school to an extent. But she has chosen to devote most of her energy this year to praying, not running around like the proverbial chicken with its head cut off. I admire her faith and resolve!

Surely the greatest casualty of our overcommitted, warp-speed society is prayer. Fewer mothers these days feel they have time to pray. I can't help but wonder: How different would our homes, our communities, and our churches be if we as mothers did less running around and more praying? What would our country be like right now if thousands upon thousands of prayer-warrior mothers were regularly, fervently lifting up the youth of this nation?

You and I might not be able to make the kind of commitment Lisa has made, but we can find time—*make time*—to lift up the needs of our family, our community, and our nation to God throughout the day. We're busy, it's true. But as François Fenelon wrote, "Time spent in prayer is never wasted."[3]

Becoming a Woman of Prayer

There is no mystery to becoming a woman of prayer. As we said earlier, you just take the first step, then move slowly, steadily, and consistently forward. You pray a few minutes today, then a few minutes tomorrow, then the next day, and the next. God will help you grow from there.

In chapter 6 we talked about the importance of setting aside a place and a time to pray. But once you're in that place, what do you do? Let me say first of all that prayer cannot be reduced to a formula. Conversations with God are too intimate and personal to be "one size fits all." At the same time, certain frameworks for prayer can be helpful tools for those just starting out. One that I recommend is based on the acrostic ACTS.

A—Adoration

Start your prayer time with adoration and praise. In your own words and ways, worship the Lord. Acknowledge his sovereignty and greatness. Tell him how wonderful you believe he is.

C—Confession

Recognizing and praising God's greatness naturally reminds us of our own sinful nature. Take time to humbly confess your sins to God, knowing that when "we confess our sins, he is faithful and just and will forgive us our sins and purify us from all unrighteousness" (1 John 1:9).

T—Thanksgiving

First Thessalonians 5:18 tells us to "give thanks in all circumstances." Yet we so often forget to actually thank God for the things he has done in our lives! Take a few moments to "count your blessings" (as the old hymn goes), then thank God for the love, grace, and mercy he has poured into your life.

S—Supplication

Supplication is the act of telling God our prayer requests—of sharing our needs and the needs of those we love with a loving heavenly Father. Use this part of your prayer time to place all your worries, concerns, and cares in God's all-sufficient hands.

Many moms have found the ACTS acrostic to be a good guideline to follow in their times of prayer. But even with a guideline, we can often feel overwhelmed by the seemingly endless list of things to pray about—our family members, our friends, our church, our pastor, the missionaries we support, our children's school, our job, our local and national governments, and so on. I've personally found it helpful to organize my prayer topics according to the days of the week. This way, I make sure that I pray each week for the people and issues that are on my heart.

Here is a sample plan you might want to adapt for your own purposes:

- Sunday: Pray for your church, its leaders and teachers, and for church leaders around the world.

- Monday: Pray for missionaries around the world, as well as local or national ministries you and your family support.

- Tuesday: Pray for extended family members and in-laws.

- Wednesday: Pray for our government officials and world leaders.

- Thursday: Pray for schools, colleges, institutions, and organizations in which you and your family are involved.

- Friday: Pray for your friends' personal needs.

- Saturday: Pray for the moral integrity of our society. Pray for our nation to have a heart of repentance and a desire to follow God.

Notice that this schedule doesn't include prayer for your children, your spouse, or your personal needs. That's because you will want to be praying for the needs and concerns of your immediate family on a daily basis; the other prayer topics are in addition to these! But whether you use this plan or come up with one of your own, don't forget to record your prayer requests in a prayer journal—and then document God's responses as they come. That way, when you get to that *T* in ACTS, you'll never be at a loss for reasons to say "thank you"!

Partnering in Prayer

Spending time alone with God in prayer is precious and important. But many mothers have found that praying regularly with a special friend—a "prayer partner"—is a wonderful complement to personal prayer. Jesus said, "For where two or three come together in my name, there am I with them" (Matthew 18:20). There is an added strength, a multiplication of faith, that occurs when you and a friend join together on a regular basis to pray over the needs of your families. If you do not already have a friend with whom you can pray, begin now to ask God to bring the right person into your life. Then use these tips to make your prayer times together effective and enjoyable:

1. Be trustworthy. When choosing a prayer partner, make sure she is someone you can trust, since many times your prayers will include deep needs and sensitive family details that shouldn't be shared with the general public. Of course, your partner will be sharing sensitive prayer requests, too. You need to be as trustworthy as you want her to be!

2. Meet regularly. Make every effort to meet with your prayer partner on a regular, scheduled basis. My friend Carol and I meet once a week for prayer. While we are flexible when we need to be (and moms often need to be!), we try to stay as consistent as possible with our weekly prayer times. And on those weeks when we can't meet together face to face, we at least take time to share our prayer needs over the telephone.

3. Write your prayer requests down before you get together. Unfortunately, many women spend most of their time with their prayer partners talking about their problems and trying to solve them—and very little time actually praying about them. By coming to your prayer time with your requests already written down, you can make sure you spend more time praying and less time chatting about the requests.

4. Set a time limit. Make sure you and your prayer partner set a definite starting and stopping time for your meeting together. In this age of busy schedules, just knowing that your prayer time will last a specific length (say, one hour) makes it easier to keep that appointment. If the meetings are always open-ended and frequently go on for hours, however, you may become disheartened and think that you don't really have time for prayer with your partner.

5. Hold one another accountable. A prayer partner can help encourage you to stay committed to prayer—and you can do the same for her. Your enemy, Satan, would love for you to get out of the habit or prayer or to forget about it completely. He knows that you are never so high as when you are on our knees! Your prayer partner can be that external force that holds you accountable and helps you stay steady in prayer.

Chore or Cherished Time?

Can you relate to this mother's prayer?

> Dear Lord, so far today I am doing pretty well. I haven't screamed at the kids or thrown anything in a burst of anger. I have not grumbled or gossiped or whined. I haven't been greedy or self-centered. I have not yet charged anything to the credit card, and I haven't pigged out on the chocolate cake in the refrigerator. However, in a few minutes I will be getting out of bed, and I am going to need your help to make it through the rest of the day. Amen.

The good thing about this mom is that she recognized her need for God's help to make it through the day! She obviously considered prayer a necessity. What is prayer to you? Is it a burden that you must get done each day so you can check it off your "to do" list, or is it a blessed necessity in your life?

Perhaps the following poem by Ralph S. Cushman will provide meaningful motivation as you grow in the blessing of prayer:

The Secret

I met God in the morning
When the day was at its best,
And His presence came like sunrise
Like a glory within my breast.

All day long the presence lingered,
All day long He stayed with me;
And we sailed in perfect calmness
O'er a very troubled sea.

Other ships were blown and battered,
Other ships were sore distressed;
But the winds that seemed to drive them
Brought to us a peace and rest.

Then I thought of other mornings,
With a keen remorse of mind,
When I too had loosed the moorings,
With His presence left behind,

So I think I know the secret
Learned from many a trouble way,
You must seek God in the morning
If you want Him through the day.[4]

Want to be a positive, joyful mom? Then be a praying mom! Jesus stands at the door of our hearts and beckons us: "Until now you have not asked for anything in my name. Ask and you will receive, and your joy will be complete" (John 16:24). By consistently taking our concerns and requests to our heavenly Father, we open the floodgates of God's blessing and joy in our lives and the lives of our family members.

William Law once said, "He who has learned to pray has learned the greatest secret of a holy and a happy life."[5] A positive mom has learned the secret! Each day she meets with her heavenly Father, praising him for who he is—an awesome and wonderful God. She not only asks for help to make it through the day, but also lifts up the needs of her family, her community, and her world. She does not wring her hands in worry but casts her cares daily on the Lord. And as she consistently meets with God day after day after day, a joyful radiance fills her heart, reflected not only in her countenance but in her every word and deed. May you and I learn that secret, too, and grow to be women of faith and prayer!

Power Point

Read: Daniel 6. Notice Daniel's dedication to prayer, even at the risk of death. If Daniel was willing to lose his life for the opportunity to pray, what are you willing to give up in order to have a time of daily prayer?

Pray: O gracious and loving heavenly Father, what a joy and privilege it is to come to you! You are the great Provider, the solid Rock, my faithful Friend. Thank you for hearing my prayers and answering in your time and in your way. My heart and mind are filled with many burdens and needs. I lay them at your feet this moment, knowing you can do all things. I trust you. In Jesus' name I pray. Amen.

Do: Begin today to be a woman of prayer. Spend some quiet time in prayer using the ACTS acrostic (adoration, confession, thanksgiving, and supplication). Ask God to lead you to a faithful and trustworthy friend with whom you can pray on a regular basis. Remain committed to your time with your prayer partner for at least six weeks to form the habit of praying together.

Principle #3

THe P❀wer of A Good Attitude

Do everything without complaining or arguing.
—Philippians 2:14

Constant complaint is the poorest sort of pay
for all the comforts we enjoy.
—Benjamin Franklin

The Ladies Pity Party
Don't Accept the Invitation

I have learned to be content whatever the circumstances.
I know what it is to be in need, and I know what it is to have plenty.
I have learned the secret of being content in any and every situation,
whether well fed or hungry, whether living in plenty or in want.
I can do everything through him who gives me strength.
—Philippians 4:11–13

As the author of several party books, I am often invited to speak to women's groups on the topic of how to plan memorable parties. Women love parties—birthday parties, baby showers, wedding showers, anniversary parties, holiday parties, all kinds of parties! But the one party that tends to attract the most women, particularly in North America, is the Ladies Pity Party. The invitation goes something like this:

> You are cordially invited to self-indulge in
> A Pity Party
> Place: *At home or at meetings or gatherings with friends*
> Date and Time: *Any time, any day*
> Please Bring: *A spirit of discontentment, complaints*
> *of every kind, a negative attitude, plus a detailed list of*
> *everything that is wrong with your life*
> RSVP: *to your conscience (only if declining)*

Take my advice: Don't accept the invitation! I know life is not always fair. It's not always easy, especially for mothers. But you and I have a choice each day whether to wallow in self-pity or put our trust in God as he works in our lives.

What do moms tend to whine about? For starters, the laundry, the dishes, the clutter. Then we expand our complaining to include our husband's shortcomings and our children's squabbles. Finally we look outside the home to grumble about the neighbors, the teachers at our children's school, and problems at our church. There is never a shortage of subject matter for a good pity party! The question we face day by day, even moment by moment, is whether or not we will attend.

Why do we complain? One reason, I think, is because complaining is easy! It is simple to say what is wrong about a situation; it's more difficult to find what is right and talk about the good points. Another reason is that we tend to find fellowship in common complaints. When we have something negative to converse about, we can talk for hours—why something's bad, how it might get worse, how my bad circumstance compares to your bad circumstance, and so on.

A third reason we complain is to get attention. It's not always popular to sound like a Pollyanna, pointing out the positive. But when we sing that all-too-familiar tune, "Nobody knows the trouble I've seen," our friends rush to our side to give us sympathy for our pain. Of course, they fully expect that sympathy to be reciprocated when it's their turn to whine!

Checking Your Focus

Grumbling is an age-old problem, not just a modern vice. The Israelites, for example, had a real problem with complaining when they left behind their four-hundred-year bondage in Egypt to follow Moses out into the wilderness. They complained about the lack of water, so God provided water. They complained about the food, so God gave them manna from heaven. They wailed about their lack of meat, so

God sent them quail. They continued to grumble and complain about their hardships (poor Moses!)—even saying that they'd be better off back in Egypt as slaves.

Had God left them for a moment? No. Were they starving for lack of provisions? No. The Bible even says that the shoes on their feet did not wear out during their journey in the wilderness! So how did God feel about their groaning? Numbers 11:1–2 gives us a picture:

> Now the people complained about their hardships in the hearing of the LORD, and when he heard them his anger was aroused. Then fire from the LORD burned among them and consumed some of the outskirts of the camp. When the people cried out to Moses, he prayed to the LORD and the fire died down.

Oh my! Apparently, God was not at all pleased with the Israelites' constant complaining. Can we blame him? He had miraculously delivered the Israelites from slavery in Egypt. He was lovingly leading them toward the Promised Land. Along the way, he was providing for all of their needs. Yet they still complained! Granted, their journey was hard, and their wilderness camp was no luxury resort. But instead of focusing on the great miracles God had done on their behalf and his goodness toward them in securing their freedom, they focused on what was bad about the situation.

Aren't you glad God doesn't send down fire on our camps today? Many of our yards would be burning! The truth is every coin has two sides, an upside and a downside. Most circumstances in our lives have two sides as well. Are we able to see God's provision for us? Do we see his hand at work for our good? Or are we so focused on our problems that all we can do is complain?

Perhaps you are saying, "But you don't know how bad my circumstances are." You're right! I don't know what you are going through. But

I do know there are women who are probably in far worse situations, yet they are making it through the tough times without drowning in self-pity. I also know there are women with relatively minimal challenges in their lives who still grumble every step of the way—making life miserable for themselves and for everyone around them.

The question is not "What are you going through?" but "What is your perspective and attitude in the process?" As you may know, the famous author Robert Louis Stevenson was bedridden with tuberculosis for much of his life. One day, he began to hack and cough loudly. His wife said to him, "I suppose you still believe it is a wonderful day." Stevenson turned toward his window where the bright yellow sunshine blazed through and said, "I do! I will never let a row of medicine bottles block my horizon."[1]

Are you looking at the sunshine—or the medicine bottles? Don't let anything block your horizon! The Bible says, "Let us fix our eyes on Jesus, the author and perfecter of our faith, who for the joy set before him endured the cross" (Hebrews 12:2). Jesus was able to endure more than you and I will ever have to—all because he had his eyes focused on the joy of securing our salvation. If we are going to be positive moms, we need to check our focus. Dr. Laura Schlessinger puts it simply: "Stop whining!"

The Secret of Contentment

The story is told of a king who was glum and discontent. No matter what he did, he just couldn't seem to get out of his sad state. Finally, he called his wise men together and asked for help. The men conferred, then approached the king with their remedy.

"O king, if you will wear the shirt of a contented man, you too will be content," they said. So the king immediately sent out search parties from the castle to travel throughout the land, looking for a man who was truly content. For months, the king's representatives traveled far and wide. They looked among the nobility, then among the villagers, then among the commoners. Finally after nearly a year of searching, the announcement came from a far corner of the kingdom: "We have found a contented man!"

The king sent a reply: "Hurry, get me his shirt!"

Sometime later, another message arrived at the castle. "Sire, we have searched the countryside for a contented man, and we have found him," it read. "But alas, he has no shirt!"

The man didn't even have a shirt on his back, yet he was content! How could this be? The truth is, contentment comes from the heart; it is not dependent on material things. Are you waiting on an updated kitchen or new wall-to-wall carpet to be content? Do you think that if your kids get into the best schools you will be happy? Are you waiting for the day when your husband is more sensitive and understanding of your feelings? Why wait? The truth is, our contentment is independent of what we have or who surrounds us.

Contentment is the opposite of self-pity. If our hearts are content because we trust in God as our loving provider, then we'll tend to keep our eyes off our troubles. But if we dwell on our wants or our difficulties (great or small), we will lose sight of the provisions God is granting us.

The Old Testament character Job learned this secret of contentment. Amazingly, after losing everything—his home, his wealth, his family, even his health—he was able to say, "Naked I came from my mother's womb, and naked I will depart. The LORD gave and the LORD has taken away; may the name of the LORD be praised" (Job 1:21). In all of his sorrows, Job continued to believe in God's goodness. He refused to charge God with wrongdoing, even when his complaining wife urged him, "Curse God and die!" (Job 2:9). Job resisted the temptation to be

He is richest who is content with the least. —Charles H. Spurgeon ☺

The real voyage of discovery consists not in seeking new landscapes but in having new eyes. —Marcel Proust

angry with God. He knew his peace and security came not from having a multitude of things, but from knowing beyond a shadow of a doubt that God was faithful.

Our church in North Dallas helps with a wonderful ministry called Voice of Hope that provides an after-school program in a Christian environment for underprivileged kids. Several years ago my family, along with others, agreed to help deliver holiday turkey dinners to some of the families that were being served by Voice of Hope. Our simple task was to deliver the dinners to the people's homes and sing a few Christmas carols.

At virtually every house, we were greeted by wonderfully warm and grateful people. Each visit went the same way: We presented the dinners, sang our songs (even though none of us could carry a tune), then said our good-byes. To my surprise, almost every household asked if they could offer a prayer before we left. Their prayers typically went something like this:

> Dear Lord, you have given us so very much. We do not deserve your rich blessings! Thank you, Lord Jesus. Thank you for your loving-kindness, your forgiveness, and your mercy. Thank you most of all for your son, Jesus, in whom we have abundant life. Thank you also for these kind people who have brought us a bountiful turkey dinner. We are so grateful! In your wonderful son's name we pray. Amen.

These were contented people! They had very little in the way of possessions, but they were rich with peace and joyfulness. My family and the other volunteers learned an incredible lesson that day as we got back in our SUVs and returned to overindulgent, discontent North Dallas. We learned that contentment is not based on what you have; it is based on how you choose to view life. It is an issue of the heart.

Paul's Potential Pity Party

Consider the apostle Paul for a moment. Now, here was a man who deserved a pity party! He was thrown into a Roman prison not for committing a terrible crime, but for sharing the gospel of Jesus throughout Asia Minor. Certainly he could have whined, shaken his fist at God, and cried, "It's not fair!" We wouldn't have blamed him, would we? Haven't we all said those words at some time in our lives?

Many situations in life are not fair, especially for mothers. We work hard serving our families and the needs of our homes, and we don't get enough appreciation for all we do. It's not fair! Paul could have said the same thing. "I've given my all to tell others about Jesus, and what has it gotten me? A jail cell!" Paul could have grumbled and complained and given up on the mission God had called him to. But he didn't.

Instead, Paul faced this challenging situation by choosing to look up and not down. He did not focus on how bad the circumstances were but on what could God do through the circumstances. And what did God do? For one, he opened up many opportunities for Paul to minister to the prison guards, the officials who tried him, and the visitors who came to see him each day. Second, he made sure Paul had some ink and some papyrus and prompted him to begin writing. Today we can open our New Testaments and refer to the letters Paul wrote to the early churches from his prison cell. We can see—and benefit from—the awesome work that God did through Paul in prison.

Paul was able to write these words during his time in jail: "I have learned to be content whatever the circumstances" (Philippians 4:11). Now if Paul could say this from his prison cell, I wonder if we could say it from our laundry room? The good news is that Paul did not leave any confusion as to how he was able to be content. In the next two verses he gives us the key that unlocks the prison door of self-pity: "I know what it is to be in need, and I know what it is to have plenty. I have learned the secret of being content in any and every situation, whether well fed or hungry, whether living in plenty or in want. *I can do everything through him who gives me strength"* (vv. 12–13, emphasis added).

Perhaps you have heard that last phrase before. You may have even memorized it in another translation: "I can do all things through Christ who strengthens me" (NKJV). It is truly a wonderful—but often misused—verse. Did you realize that Paul was talking about contentment when he wrote it? He was giving us the key to unlocking our prison of self-pity: believing that with God's strength, we can get through whatever life brings.

Can we still be content if our child doesn't get the best teacher in the first grade? If our friend disappoints us? If our husband won't agree to new carpet for the living room? Through all the stressful and challenging situations of life, we can still find contentment when we fix our eyes and place our hope in God—the only one who can give us strength to make it through.

Heading Off Bitterness and Anger

When we forget that key to contentment, we can spend all of our time dwelling on the negative in situations—and that's dangerous. When we continue to rehearse our discontented thoughts and attitudes over and over, anger and bitterness set in, threatening and sometimes destroying the relationships we hold most dear.

Recently our family took a cruise to the Caribbean. We enjoyed visiting many wonderful tropical islands and seeing the sights as our large ship sailed from port to port. Standing on the deck one afternoon, we watched in awe as smoke billowed out of a mountain on the nearby island of Montserrat. We realized we were looking at an active volcano. What an impressive sight!

That volcano comes to mind as I think about the danger of anger in relationships. As it rumbles within us and heats up over time, anger can erupt and overflow. And just as the hot lava of a volcano destroys everything in its path, so our outbursts of anger, rooted in resentment, bitterness, and self-pity, can destroy the people around us.

I think about Suzette, who married a wonderful man but was discontent from the moment she returned from the honeymoon. She didn't feel that her husband's job provided her with the income she desired. The home he could afford wasn't in the "right" neighborhood. He never seemed to help out enough around the house and with the kids. And he certainly wasn't sensitive to her feelings!

Over time, the bitterness and anger festered and grew inside of her. What began as a spirit of discontent led Suzette to begin looking for greener grass—and eventually to an affair with her husband's best friend, Rick. The devastation and heartache caused to both families has been incalculable. If only Suzette's discontentment had been checked at the door of her heart before she began each day, perhaps this picture would have turned out differently!

How do you keep anger from overtaking your heart? You cut it off at the pass! Here are three simple steps you can follow daily:

1. Recognize who the enemy is. This is the first step in any successful battle plan. Your real enemy is Satan, who would like nothing more than for you to get your eyes off God and onto your problems. What are the areas about which you tend to complain? These are the places where Satan will try to get a foothold. Make a mental boundary around these areas and put up a sign that says "No Self-Pity Allowed."

2. Change your perspective. Consider what is good about your situation. Write it down. In every situation there are positives, although they

Happiness is a habit—cultivate it. —Elbert Hubbard

may be hard to see. If you cannot see any positives, then hold on to this one fact: God loves you and will be with you through the difficulties.

3. Ask God to give you strength. Pray to God for strength based on Philippians 4:11–13. Ask him to dismantle your discontented spirit and replace it with a peace that "transcends all understanding" (Philippians 4:7). Thank God for his provisions for you and your family.

Rising above the Fray

Imagine a wonderful day you have planned for your kids. You feed them a nutritious breakfast, complete with eggs, ham, whole-wheat pancakes, and fresh-squeezed orange juice. They respond by complaining about the temperature of the eggs, the texture of "those healthy pancakes," and the orange pulp on the sides of their glasses. Next you take them out to their favorite park. They whine because you won't let them play in the creek and get soaked. Afterward, you go to the library for story time, but the kids frown and grumble and refuse to sit still. Finally, you drop by the grocery store to pick up their favorite food for dinner, and they cry, "We don't want to go in! We want to go home! It's not fair!"

By dinnertime, you are no doubt exhausted! Here you are, trying to do what is best for your children from sunup to sundown, and all they do is complain!

Believe me, God understands. His children frequently complain and grumble and whine, oblivious to all the good he is doing in their lives. May you and I not be those kinds of kids!

Instead, as positive moms with children of our own, let's determine to decline the daily invitation to the Ladies Pity Party. Yes, situations may not always go as we would like. Life may throw us some curves. But through it all we know that we have a loving heavenly Father, and we can rest assured that he is providing for all our needs.

POWER POINT

Read: Philippians 4. Which verses help you to be a more positive person? Memorize verse 8 as an invitation to a Positive Party and not a Pity Party.

Pray: I praise you, wonderful Father, for you are able to provide for all of my needs. Thank you that you are the Good Shepherd. You lovingly tend me and my family as a good shepherd would take care of his sheep. Thank you not only for the green pastures in my life, but the deserts I must journey through as well. I am confident you will never leave me. Help me to be a positive woman, looking for the good in every situation you allow in my life. Help me to decline the opportunity to feel sorry for myself. Give me strength to live this life abundantly and victoriously. In Jesus' name, amen.

Do: Hang a wall calendar in your kitchen. On the square with today's date, write one thing that you can think of that is good about this day. Then with each passing day, write a new entry in the appropriate square. At the end of the month you will have a calendar full of good perspectives and positive thoughts gleaned from the month. Make it a daily habit to find what is good about the day!

10

Attitude of Gratitude
Creating a Thankful Environment

Come let us sing for joy to the LORD: let us shout
aloud to the Rock of our salvation.
Let us come before him with thanksgiving
and extol him with music and song.
—Psalm 95:1–2

Few activities are more delightful than watching children, wide-eyed with excitement and wonder, opening brightly wrapped gifts on Christmas morning. Two types of children generally emerge under the Christmas tree. First there are the grateful ones—those kids who react with gratitude as they open every package, even if they don't like the present or already have two of the same thing. Then there are the difficult-to-please ones—those kids who respond with a less-than-enthusiastic "oh, thanks" as they open each box with thinly veiled disappointment. Even when kids in this second group get something they want, it never seems to be quite right! "Uh, nice wagon. Didn't they have a red one?" "I wanted a new dress…this one looks a little big."

Now, which of these two types of children do you think enjoy their Christmas most? Surely the first group! It's amazing how attitude makes all the difference—and not just on Christmas morning. This scene around the Christmas tree is but a brief snapshot of the big picture of life. Some people view life through the eyes of thankfulness; others dwell on the negatives. Of the two groups, thankful people are happier people.

I know a woman—let's call her Brenda—who always has a smile on her face. She is a bright light to everyone around her! Many people would be disappointed and angry if they had been given her lot in life, but not Brenda; she is a thankful person. After trying to have children for years, Brenda finally received a phone call informing her that the test results were positive. She was pregnant! But her excitement was mixed with concern about how her husband would receive this information. Their marriage was already shaky, and when she broke the news, her husband was less than thrilled. They divorced soon after the baby was born.

Brenda was faced with the prospect of raising a son on her own. Her ex-husband refused to pay child support, making her situation even more difficult. Brenda knew she had a choice: Would she become angry and bitter, or would she look for the good in the situation? Brenda decided to be a thankful person. She gave thanks to God for the gift of her wonderful son. She gave thanks for her God-given talents that enabled her to earn money to support her little family. She thanked the Lord for her parents, who moved close by to help. With a thankful heart, she chose to look for the loving hand of God in the situation and refused to allow angry and bitter thoughts to fester.

Several years later, Brenda received the terrible news that her brother had suddenly died of an undetected heart problem. Her entire family, which had always been very close, was devastated. But even through this sad and difficult time, Brenda had peace, knowing that her brother was in heaven and God was with them both. She was able to give thanks for the years she had been blessed to spend with her brother.

That event actually became something of a turning point for Brenda. Realizing that time is precious, she began to reexamine her schedule, consider her priorities, and change her life accordingly. She

A grateful mind is both a great and happy mind. —William Secker

wasn't thankful for her brother's death, of course, but she was thankful for what God was able to do through the situation. Today Brenda is a positive mom because she is a thankful mom. She continues to choose to view life's challenges through gratitude-colored glasses.

What glasses do you use to view the world? Are they rosy, gratitude-colored glasses that help you look at your circumstances through the eyes of faith, trusting that God will see you through? Or are they dark-shaded glasses that block out your view of the Son, allowing you to see only what is wrong with a situation?

Ultimately the quality of your life and mine depends on the way we view it. Bible teacher Chuck Swindoll puts it this way:

> The longer I live, the more I realize the impact of attitude on life. Attitude, to me, is more important than facts. It is more important than the past, than money, than circumstances, than failures, than success, than what other people think or say or do. It is more important than appearance, giftedness or skill. It will make or break a company...a church...a home, or an individual. The remarkable thing is we have a choice every day regarding the attitude we will embrace for that day. We cannot change our past...we cannot change the fact that people will act in a certain way. We cannot change the inevitable. The only thing we can do is play on the one string we have, and that is our attitude. I am convinced that life is ten percent what happens to me and ninety percent how I react to it. And so it is with you...we are in charge of our attitudes.[1]

Each day Brenda chooses to have an attitude of gratitude, impacting not only her own life but the lives of her family members and friends. She is a beacon of blessing and joy to everyone she knows. Would someone say the same about you and me?

Giving Thanks in Everything

I know it's not always easy to be thankful. Sometimes we have to look long and hard for the smallest spark of something to be thankful for. At times we must simply trust God, knowing that every circumstance that comes into our lives was first filtered through his loving hands. The essence of faith is being able to say, "Thank you, God," in every situation, even when we don't see anything good about it.

The apostle Paul (writing from the confines of a prison cell) tells us to "give thanks in all circumstances" (1 Thessalonians 5:18). How can we do this? Only by putting our faith in the goodness of God's character and trusting in his love for us. We can give thanks in everything, Paul says, "for this is God's will for you in Christ Jesus" (v. 18). It's hard to believe that the difficult times are a part of God's loving will. But the Bible is clear: Even through life's difficulties, "God works for the good of those who love him, who have been called according to his purpose" (Romans 8:28). There is always something to be thankful for!

As moms, we have many reasons to give thanks—if we will just open our eyes and see them. That's the message behind this prayer of gratitude written by my friend Anne:

A Mother's Thankful Heart

I come before You Father
To thank You for this life
The blessings You have given me
As a mother and a wife

I'm thankful for my children
As I watch them grow and play

Knowing that each moment
Will live for just today

I'm thankful for the laundry
For the dust to wipe away
I'm thankful for the problems
That make me stop and pray

I'm thankful for my husband's job
The roof above our heads
I'm thankful for our daily food
For the comfort of our beds

I'm thankful for the errands
The phone that always rings
I'm thankful for the tears we cry
For the joy that laughter brings

I'm thankful for our family's love
The way we sit and talk
The simple games we often play
The picnics and the walks

I'm thankful for the little things
That make up every day
For therein lies Your love, Lord
And the wonder of Your ways

I'm thankful for the memories
That life has brought my way
I count it as Your blessing
To be a mother every day[2]

Have you ever stopped in the midst of your daily routine just to offer a prayer of thanksgiving? Let's try an experiment. Stop reading, put this book down, and take a moment to thank the Lord for at least three blessings in your life. There now, doesn't that feel good? I bet you didn't stop at three things!

Unfortunately, many people forget to express their gratitude—even when their blessings are more obvious than a sink full of dirty dishes. The story of the ten lepers in Luke 17 is a perfect example. The Bible says that ten men, suffering from the dreadful, disfiguring disease of leprosy, approached Jesus and asked for healing. In his compassion, Jesus told them to go show themselves to the priests. As they obediently walked on their way, they found they had been miraculously healed!

Yet, amazingly, only one of the healed men came back to say, "Thank you." Jesus asked him, "Were not all ten cleansed? Where are the other nine? Was no one found to return and give praise to God?" (v. 17). Only one out of ten made the effort to express gratitude!

As positive moms, we must never become like those nine ungrateful people who received a life-changing gift from God but forgot to return and say, "Thank you." Instead, we must take time each day to give thanks for all of God's blessings. For me, that time is often when I lay my head on my pillow at night and think over the events and the blessings of the day. I find that when I put my mind to it, I begin to see all sorts of reasons to give thanks that I never saw before. Try it yourself tonight. It's a wonderful way to go to sleep—with a grateful heart!

Gratitude Is Contagious

We can give our children no greater gift than a positive, consistent attitude of gratitude. Attitudes are contagious! If we are discontented, our kids know it and begin to reflect it. If we are grateful, they pick up on that too. What attitudes are our kids catching from us? If we are making the effort to develop a habit of giving thanks, our kids will grow up to be thankful as well.

I've found that the dinner table is a great place to begin teaching children about thankfulness. As you offer thanks for the meal, go ahead and mention several other things for which you and you family can be thankful. Later, as you put your kids to bed at night, take another opportunity to thank God, spotlighting in prayer the good things he is doing in their lives and yours.

You might also want to start a "Grateful Poster" in your kids' rooms to help them reflect on God's loving-kindness toward them. Have your children help you decorate a poster board using stickers and markers. Add some sequins and glitter for an extra flair. Then work with your kids to come up with a small sentence each day that thanks God for his blessings, both great and small. Older kids can decorate a bulletin board and tack up notes of thanks to God. These visual reminders will help keep your children's thoughts in a thankful direction and hopefully instill a habit of thankfulness in their lives.

In the utility room in our house, we have a large chalkboard that is seen by every family member at one time or another during the day. I write funny quotes, interesting sayings, and important messages to my family on this board. Now and then I simply write at the top "I am thankful for…" and leave the rest of the board blank. I encourage Curt and the girls to fill in the blank in different colors of chalk. It is always fun and informative to see what everyone has written by the end of the day.

Pollyanna Was Right

Perhaps you are familiar with the story of Pollyanna, which was made into a wonderful movie by that name back in 1960. The main character, played by a young Hayley Mills, was a delightful little girl who came to live with her rich but dour Aunt Polly following the death of her missionary parents. Pollyanna ended up bringing joy and happiness to Aunt Polly's otherwise gloomy household.

Give thanks in all circumstances, for this is God's will for you in Christ Jesus. —1 Thessalonians 5:18 ☺

Principle #3: The Power of a **Good Attitude**

Little Pollyanna played a game that gave her a unique outlook on life: the Glad Game. Whenever she was feeling down, she would try to think of something to be glad about. She explained that the game was first started by her parents on the foreign mission field. Pollyanna had been anxiously waiting for a special doll that was supposed to come in a large missionary shipment. But when the barrel arrived from overseas, there was no doll—only a pair of child-sized crutches with a note attached explaining, "There hadn't been any dolls come in, but the little crutches had." The note went on to suggest that perhaps some poor child could use them.

To help Pollyanna deal with her disappointment, her father instituted the Glad Game at that moment. He encouraged his daughter to find something to be glad about in the situation. Pollyanna finally realized that she could be glad simply because she didn't have to use the crutches![3]

Some people get annoyed when others consistently respond to complaints or grumpiness with positive, rosy comments—but not our heavenly Father. He wants us to practice an attitude of gratitude, giving thanks in everything. He knows a thankful attitude is good for us and for the people around us. And as is often the case, science is now catching up with God. Doctors and researchers are beginning to recognize the clear health benefits of focusing on the good. The prestigious Stanford Health Care Center has even begun offering a workshop with the title "Happiness: Pollyanna Was Right!"[4]

We can play the Glad Game as positive mothers in our homes. When the milk spills, we can be glad the glass didn't break. When it's raining and the kids can't play outside, we can be glad to have a day to snuggle with them and read or play an indoor game. When a child brings home a bad grade on a math test, we can be glad there will be another chance to do better. It's not always easy to come up with something to be glad about, but playing the Glad Game forces us to have a positive outlook on life.

Of course, we must be sensitive to sad feelings. If a child is truly upset about something, that may not be the best moment to point out a reason to be glad. Remember what Romans 12:15 tells us: "Rejoice with those who rejoice; mourn with those who mourn." There are times when the Glad Game doesn't fit the circumstances. But more often than not, making the effort to think positive thoughts will help us avoid frustration and embrace thankfulness, even in difficult situations.

The story is told of a little boy named Tommy who tried out for a part in the school play. He had his heart so set on being in the program that his mother, quite aware of his lack of acting talent, feared that he would be crushed when he wasn't chosen. On the day the roles were announced, Tommy's mother made sure she was first in the carpool line so she'd be able to console him right away if he was upset. To her surprise, Tommy came rushing out of school toward her car, his face beaming. "Mommy, mommy!" he shouted. "I have been chosen to clap and cheer!"

When it comes to being thankful, perspective is everything. Let's be positive moms and show our families the blessing of having an attitude of gratitude.

POWER POINT

Read: Three women's songs of thanks to God: Hannah's (1 Samuel 2:1–10), Deborah's (Judges 5:1–31), and Mary's (Luke 1:46–55). Notice how these women recognized God's handiwork in their lives and took the time to offer thanks.

Pray: Thank you, Father, for your mercy, your forgiveness, and your loving care for me. Thank you for my family—for every good and not-so-good quality in each member. Thank you for the privilege of being a mother! Thank you for the circumstances in my life this very moment; help me to see your hand at work. In Jesus' name, amen.

☺ **Do:**   Start a Thanksgiving Journal. Using a blank notebook, begin recording your prayers of thanks to God. Make it a habit to write in the journal on a regular basis, whether once a day, once a week, or once a month. Now and then reflect on past prayers of thanks, remembering what God has done in your life. You may even want to read some of the prayers to your kids, especially the prayers that concern them.

The Challenges of Life
Learning to Grow through Difficult Circumstances

For every hill I've had to climb, For every stone that bruised my feet,
For all the blood and sweat and grime,
For blinking storms and burning heat,
My heart sings but a grateful song—
These were the things that made me strong!
—Anonymous

Wilma Rudolph was born prematurely and faced numerous complications. She developed double pneumonia (twice) and scarlet fever, and later had a bout with polio that left her with a crooked leg and a foot that twisted inward. As a result, Wilma endured her childhood with her legs in braces—an adversity that built a determined spirit within her. At the age of eleven she began slipping the braces off and secretly attempting to walk without them. Finally the doctor gave his consent to allow Wilma to remove the braces at times. This, to Wilma, meant never putting them on again.

At the age of thirteen, with much hard work and perseverance, Wilma made her school basketball and track teams. At sixteen, she reached the semifinals in the 200-meter dash in the 1956 Olympic Games. She came home with a bronze metal as a member of the 400-meter relay team.

Wilma committed herself to returning to the 1960 Olympics for a gold medal and immediately began a rigorous and disciplined training program. While putting in numerous hours at the track, she also paid her way through Tennessee State University, maintaining the B average that was required to stay on the track team. Her hard work was rewarded. At the 1960 Olympics, she came through victoriously with three gold medals—the first American woman to win three gold medals in track and field in a single Olympics.[1]

Challenges? Yes, Wilma Rudolph had many challenges in life; but instead of letting them get her down, she was determined to overcome them. Difficulties in life are inevitable for all of us. The question is, what will we do with them?

If Only…

Just as a precious stone can only be polished with friction, so our lives are perfected through the trials and challenges that come our way. If we had our choice, we'd probably choose to go through life without any struggles. Who wouldn't want life to be easier? But like it or not, our struggles actually serve a purpose. They help us grow and develop into stronger, wiser, and more faithful people.

How would you fill in the following blank? "Life would be more enjoyable if only _____." What is the problem or difficulty, great or small, that you'd most like to see go away? If only…

…we didn't live in this neighborhood.

…my husband had a better job or made more money or worked harder.

…I didn't have all this laundry to do.

…my child was more compliant.

…my house was bigger.

…the kids wouldn't fight.

…my child had a better teacher.

…my parents lived nearby.

…his parents lived out of town.

What did you put in the blank? Whatever it was, stop right now and take a few moments to ask God to help you make it through that circumstance. Ask him to help you find something to be thankful for in the situation. Then promise that you will never say "if only" again, for those words only serve to send your heart and mind reeling in a negative direction. "If only" makes you look backward with regret, focusing your thoughts on things you can not change, rather than looking forward to what God can do in and through the struggle. A friend of mine puts it this way: "Every time I face a challenge, whether great or small, I look at it as an opportunity to trust God."

Moses was a man who refused to say "if only." He faced many setbacks in his life, any one of which could have been the "final straw" that would have rendered him helpless. Yet for Moses, each challenge turned into a new opportunity to allow God to work through him as the leader of the Israelites. From being saved as a baby from the murderous pharaoh, to fleeing Egypt and living in the desert for forty years, to leading millions of people across the dry bed of the Red Sea, Moses was a man who faced many challenges. But instead of regretting what he couldn't change, Moses looked at the difficulties as opportunities to see God's hand at work.

As we peer through the portholes of time we find numerous examples of heroes, leaders, writers, composers, and inventors who overcame great hurdles in their lives and were better men and women as a result. Take, for example, Ludwig van Beethoven (1770–1827). By the age of thirty, Beethoven was stone deaf, yet he was still able to compose his greatest work. Beethoven's *Ninth Symphony*, which many consider to be his greatest, combined instruments and voices in a majestic expression of glorious sound. Perhaps you have heard the touching story of the first performance of the *Ninth Symphony* in Vienna, Austria, in 1824. Beethoven was unaware of the thunderous applause he was given by the audience until the soloist came down from the stage and turned him around to see the cheering.[2]

Have courage for the great sorrows of life and patience for the small ones. And when you have finished your daily task, go to sleep in peace. God is awake. —Victor Hugo

Fanny Crosby (1820–1915) is another example. Blinded at a young age due to improper medical treatment, she received her education from the New York School for the Blind and served as a teacher there. In 1858 she married Alexander Van Alstyne, a blind musician and one of the school's music teachers. She began writing verses for secular songs but turned to writing gospel lyrics in her early forties. She never wrote lyrics for a hymn without first kneeling in prayer and asking for God's guidance. Over the course of her lifetime, she wrote more than eight thousand songs, including "Blessed Assurance," "Rescue the Perishing," and "All the Way My Savior Leads Me."[3]

What are the challenges you face in your life? Whatever comes your way, you can be sure that God is with you—even through the lowest points. I love this passage from Isaiah 43:1–2:

Fear not, for I have redeemed you;

I have summoned you by name; you are mine.

When you pass through the waters, I will be with you;

And when you pass through the rivers, they will not sweep over you.

When you walk through the fire, you will not be burned; the

flames will not set you ablaze.

For I am the LORD, your God,

The Holy One of Israel, your Savior.

Sooner or later we will all face a crisis. We will all experience our own personal fire or flood. "In this world you will have trouble," Jesus said in John 16:33—not as a promise but as a reality check. Your crisis may be a life-changing event; it may be a minor blip on the big screen of life. You may feel like you're drowning at this very moment. But whatever difficulty you face, you can have faith that God is there with you. You can trust that he will use the struggle to help you grow stronger, both as a woman and as a mother.

Strength in the Struggle

The story is told of an old man who discovered a caterpillar. He decided to keep the small creature and watch its transformation into a butterfly. Sure enough, within days the fuzzy worm began spinning its cocoon. The man watched with fascination as the entire encasement was meticulously completed. Then he waited. And waited.

Finally, after several weeks, the old man noticed that the butterfly was beginning to emerge from its woven shell. His interest turned to concern, however, as he watched the little creature struggling hard to free itself. Feeling compassion, he decided to help. With a small knife he clipped away part of the cocoon, enabling the butterfly to get out quickly and easily. But the man's initial delight turned to sorrow as he saw the beautiful creature now struggle to fly. You see, butterflies strengthen their wings through the process of pushing and struggling against the cocoon walls. As they emerge, fluid is pushed from their bodies into their wings, giving them the necessary elements to fly. In cutting away the cocoon, the man had denied the butterfly the opportunity it needed to persevere and grow strong on its own.

Sometimes we, as mothers, treat our children like that old man treated the butterfly. We do everything we can to help them avoid struggle. We shield them from sadness, disappointment, and the challenges of life. No mother wants to see her children sad or disappointed, of course; but the truth is, it is neither healthy nor beneficial to prevent our kids from going through challenges. How else will they grow strong? How else will they develop the faith they'll need to survive the inevitable storms of life? How else will they learn to approach God as their "refuge and strength, an ever-present help in trouble" (Psalm 46:1)?

At my children's school I've noticed that there are three types of mothers. Some mothers hover like helicopters over their children, trying to make sure their kids get the best teachers, the best grades, the best roles in the school play, even the best seats in the lunchroom. Others say (in actions, if not words), "I don't care what you do, kids. You are on your own"—and they keep their distance from most school activities. Then there are those mothers who walk in faith, assisting their children when it's appropriate but allowing them to experience struggle and disappointment too.

Several years ago a particular teacher at school—I'll call her Mrs. Tobin—had a reputation for being difficult and not always kind to her students. Few parents would choose to have their child in her class. Of course, the helicopter moms met with the principal before the school year started to ensure that their children would not be in this woman's classroom. Other parents didn't care. Still others simply trusted God and the school officials to do what was best for their kids.

When my daughter reached Mrs. Tobin's grade level, I decided not to approach the principal. To that point, I had made it a personal policy not to interfere with the choice of my children's teachers. I knew that the administrators and teachers carefully and prayerfully considered the placement of the students each year. And as you can probably guess, my daughter ended up in *her* class.

At the beginning of the school year, my daughter was less than thrilled to have Mrs. Tobin as her teacher. But as we talked about the situation, I encouraged her to see it as an opportunity to trust God and to learn to understand and work with "difficult people." While some kids were being shielded from that struggle, I explained, the students in Mrs. Tobin's class would learn to deal with challenges—and grow and mature in the process. They would learn that they didn't have to fear difficult situations, because God was able to give them the grace and the help they needed to make it through.

One day my daughter came home from school and told me that

Mrs. Tobin had shared some of her personal struggles with the class that day. She had confessed to the students that her attitude had been less than loving, and she was now asking God to help her be a kinder and gentler person. What a great lesson that turned out to be! Mrs. Tobin's students not only were given the opportunity to watch and experience the grace of God working in their teacher's life; they were allowed to see an example of an open, honest woman who was willing to be vulnerable enough to share her struggles with others. And if God could do a miracle in Mrs. Tobin's life, then surely he could do miracles in their lives too!

I'm glad I didn't try to shield my daughter from her initial discomfort and cause her to miss that lesson and many others she learned that year in Mrs. Tobin's class.

We hurt our children and block God's work when we protect them from difficulties and disappointments in life. The truth is, life will not always go the way we want it to. And if we aren't willing to persevere, adjust, and grow, we might just miss some special blessings that God has prepared for us. As the old saying goes, if you want to see a rainbow, you must first experience some rain!

I like the approach to adversity that Emily Perl Kingsley takes in her story "Welcome to Holland," which was published in the book *Chicken Soup for the Mother's Soul:*

I am often asked to describe the experience of raising a child with a disability—to try to help people who have not shared that unique experience to understand it, to imagine how it would feel. It's like this...

When you're going to have a baby, it's like planning a fabulous vacation trip—to Italy. You buy a bunch of guidebooks and make wonderful plans. The Colosseum. The Michelangelo *David.* The gondolas in Venice. You may learn some handy phrases in Italian. It's all very exciting.

After months of eager anticipation, the day finally arrives. You pack your bags and off you go. Several hours later, the plane lands. The stewardess comes in and says, "Welcome to Holland."

"Holland??!" you say. "What do you mean, Holland?? I signed up for Italy! I'm supposed to be in Italy. All my life I've dreamed of going to Italy."

But there's been a change in the flight plan. They've landed in Holland and there you must stay. The important thing is that they haven't taken you to a horrible, disgusting, filthy place, full of pestilence, famine and disease. It's just a different place.

So you must go out and buy new guidebooks. And you must learn a whole new language. And you will meet a whole new group of people you would never have met.

It's just a different place. It's slower paced than Italy, less flashy than Italy. But after you've been there for a while you catch your breath, you look around…and you begin to notice that Holland has windmills…and Holland has tulips. Holland even has Rembrandts.

But everyone you know is busy coming and going from Italy…and they're all bragging about what a wonderful time they had there. And for the rest of your life, you will say, "Yes, that's where I was supposed to go. That's what I had planned."

And the pain of that will never, ever, ever, ever go away…. Because the loss of that dream is a very, very significant loss.

But…if you spend your life mourning the fact that you didn't get to Italy, you may never be free to enjoy the very special, the very lovely things…about Holland.[4]

A Balanced Outlook

When retail tycoon J. C. Penney was asked the secret to his success, he replied, "Adversity. I would never have amounted to anything had I not been forced to come up the hard way." Of course, there is a balance. We don't want to *invite* pain into our children's lives! But when it does come, we must teach them how to handle it properly. A positive mom doesn't take away her children's troubles; she teaches them how to look for the hand of God in the midst of them. She teaches them how to think, react, and develop through the tough times.

If your son doesn't make a certain athletic team at school, what should you do? Allow him to grieve, then point him in the direction of a new sport or opportunity. If he makes a bad grade, use it as an opportunity to teach him a better way to study for the next test, or encourage him to ask the teacher for help. If your daughter's best friend moves away, allow her to cry, then provide opportunities for her to build new friendships. Remember, it is not the situation but the *reaction* to the situation that matters most.

I recently heard of a teenage girl who didn't make the cheerleading squad in high school. Her mother didn't want her to be sad, so she bought the girl a new car and let her miss a day of school so she could go to a local spa for a massage, a facial—the works. I couldn't help but wonder: What will this girl do in the future when she doesn't have her mother to buy away her sorrows? If she is never allowed to feel disappointment or pain, if she is never taught how to respond and grow through adversity, how will she get through life? Some people choose to avoid pain through drugs, alcohol, binge eating, shopping, sex, or some other escape.

As positive moms, let's give our children a balanced outlook on life. Yes, there is pain in this world. There is disappointment. There is struggle. But there is also God. And according to his Word, "he will never leave you nor forsake you" (Deuteronomy 31:6). He is working out "all things...for the good of those who love him" (Romans 8:28).

We can read countless stories in the Bible of people who experienced at least as many struggles as victories in their lives—from Adam to Noah to King David to John the Baptist. Even God's own Son suffered and died; yet without his willingness to experience tribulation, we would not have the forgiveness of our sins. Thank the Lord that he brings redemption from heartache and healing from sorrow!

If you are struggling with a situation in your life right now, don't be discouraged. Spiritual growth always comes through struggle. Allow God to use this circumstance to polish you, to perfect you, to complete the work he started in your life. Take encouragement from these words of Paul in 2 Corinthians 4:16–18: "Therefore we do not lose heart. Though outwardly we are wasting away, yet inwardly we are being renewed day by day. For our light and momentary troubles are achieving for us an eternal glory that far outweighs them all. So we fix our eyes not on what is seen, but on what is unseen. For what is seen is temporary, but what is unseen is eternal."

Ordered Steps

We never know when life will throw us a curve ball. Adversity can come upon us in an instant. But while we might be surprised by the turn of events, God never is.

Just ask my friend Leslie and her nine-year-old daughter, Amanda. This precious pair was driving to a special tea hosted by one of Amanda's friends on Valentine's Day 2000. With every mile, their anticipation and excitement rose. Finally they had only one more intersection ahead of them. But just as they were crossing the six lanes of traffic, a pickup truck rammed into the passenger side of the vehicle, flipping the car and landing it upside down. After the car came to rest, Leslie's maternal survival instinct took over. She managed to unbuckle her seat belt and carefully slide over to Amanda, who was still buckled in and hanging upside down. She released her daughter's seat belt, and together they crawled out through a shattered window and walked to safety. Leslie escaped with three cracked ribs and a partially collapsed lung; Amanda had a swollen right eye. It was a miracle that their injuries were not more serious!

Of course, Leslie and Amanda had not planned to spend the day in the emergency room, deal with a totaled automobile (it was a new car, by the way!), and devote the next few weeks to doctors' appointments and rehabilitation. But God allows certain unplanned adventures in our lives for reasons we may never know.

He also provides the help we need to make it through. At the time of the accident, a paramedic was on her way to work at a nearby hospital. She was the first one on the scene to help Leslie and Amanda through their ordeal. Then friends who were also on their way to the tea arrived one by one at the intersection. Within minutes, Amanda and Leslie were surrounded by medical help and supportive friends! As they will tell you, the hand of God was clearly covering them in the midst of their unexpected challenge.

Several days after the accident, Leslie discovered Psalm 37:23–24: "The steps of a good man are ordered by the LORD, and He delights in his way. Though he fall, he shall not be utterly cast down; for the LORD upholds him with His hand" (NKJV). Like Leslie, you and I have a wonderful heavenly Father who is watching over us, ordering our steps. He knows what we need to grow as strong, positive moms.

Yes, the winds will blow. The rains will come. The fires will burn. But God promises to be with us—"our refuge and strength, an ever-present help in trouble" (Psalm 46:1). He will give us all the grace we need to make it through.

POWER POINT

Read: The story of Ruth in the Bible (found in the Old Testament book of Ruth). List the difficulties she faced in her life, then write down the blessings God brought to her as well.

Pray: Oh Lord, my comfort and my strength, thank you for always being with me. Thank you for holding my hand. Thank you that although I may stumble, I will not fall, for you are there to hold me up. I trust that whatever happens to me and my family is filtered first through your loving hands. Strengthen me through the tough times. Help my children to grow through their own times of sadness, frustration, and disappointment. Help us to trust and honor you through all the circumstances and challenges in life.

Do: Make a "Life Map" to illustrate the significant events in your life—both the wonderful times and the difficult times. Set it up as a time line, and, if you want to get creative, include photos or illustrations. When you have finished, share your Life Map with your family. Talk about how God has brought something positive out of the good times and the bad times in your life.

Principle #4

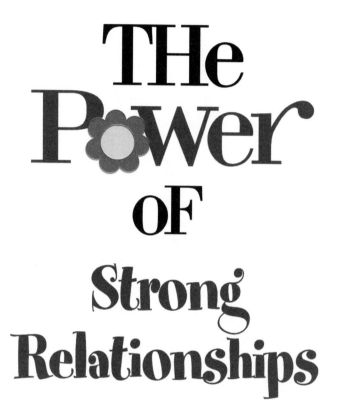

THe Power OF Strong Relationships

As iron sharpens iron, so one man sharpens another.
—Proverbs 27:17

Jesus made it clear that the most important thing in the world is our relationship to God and to others. When we achieve that, everything good will follow.
—Norman Vincent Peale

Harmony with Hubby
Keep Fanning the Flame

It is the man and woman united that make the complete human being. Separate, she wants his force of body and strength of reason; he, her softness, sensibility and acute discernment. Together, they are most likely to succeed in the world.
—Benjamin Franklin

One winter several years ago we made a novel purchase: We bought a fire pit. It's nothing spectacular, but it allows our little suburban family living on the outskirts of Dallas to build a fire and roast marshmallows in our own backyard. We love sitting and talking around the fire while enjoying the rustic smell and the wonderful night breeze.

We have found that the firelight works as a sort of truth serum. People tend to relax, unwind, and share personal stories while sitting together around a roaring blaze. But eventually the fire dies down. If we want to keep the fire going—and extend that pleasant time of intimacy and sharing—we have to get up, poke the ashes, and add a few more logs.

Marriages are like fires; they both need constant tending. We can't sit back at any point and say, "There now, my marriage is fine. I don't have to give to it anymore." This philosophy doesn't work for a campfire, and it doesn't work for the home fire either. We must continue to be attentive to our relationships with our husbands in order to keep the flames alive.

One of the cornerstones for building a strong family is a good marriage. Notice I did not say a *perfect* marriage. Everyone has his or her imperfections. We must have realistic expectations as to what a marriage between two imperfect people ought to be.

At the same time, we must recognize that a positive husband-wife team has an invaluable impact on the family. Truly one of the best things we can do for our children is to pursue harmony with our hubbies, doing our part to strengthen our marriages. Of course, our husbands have their part too. It takes two to make a marriage. But as positive moms, we want to make sure we're doing everything we can to keep the marriage flame glowing and growing. Let's examine several logs we can put on the fire to keep our marriages strong.

Fire Builder #1: Love Your Husband

You wouldn't think we would need to be told to love our spouses. Didn't we commit to love them the day we married them? Even so, many marriages break up because spouses claim they just don't love their marriage partners anymore. They say they have fallen out of love—as if love is something a person can fall in and out of.

Since love is the key basis for our marriage commitment, we ought to have a better understanding of what it is. Think back. When you started dating the man who would become your spouse, you probably got those warm, fuzzy feelings that often come with the building of a new relationship. Those feelings were wonderful. They *are* wonderful. But ultimately, they cannot be the sole basis for love and commitment in marriage.

The roots of love run much deeper than just the surface foliage of sweet, romantic feelings and likable moments. Rather, love is a choice— a deliberate act of compassion based on our will, not just our emotions. It is not based necessarily on finding the right person (although marriage is one of the most important decisions in our lives and must be considered carefully and prayerfully). Rather, it is based on a commitment that we will continually accept the one to whom we've pledged our life, for better or worse.

True love is not easy. It requires devotion, forgiveness, loyalty, and selflessness. When we commit to marry someone, we make the choice to love that person through his weaknesses and strengths, his failures and successes. We make a decision to put down roots in our new life together.

We can even *learn* to love a person—whether or not we like him at that moment. We simply need to make the deliberate choice to love, then follow up that decision with action. If we truly love someone, what will we do for him? What actions will we take? Write him a note? Help him with a project? Cook his favorite meal? Give him a smile when he comes in the door?

In his book *The Five Languages of Love: How to Express Heartfelt Commitment to Your Mate*, author Gary Chapman describes the various ways different individuals give and receive love.[1] We're not all the same. What makes you feel loved might not be what will make your spouse feel loved. (In fact, you can probably count on it!) This evening, ask your husband what you can do to make him feel loved, and then begin to do the actions day by day. When you do the actions of love, the feelings will follow.

One of those all-important love-actions is forgiveness. God's love, of course, includes forgiveness. He forgives us even when we don't deserve it. In the same way, the Bible says, we are to forgive others: "Be kind and compassionate to one another, forgiving each other, just as in Christ God forgave you" (Ephesians 4:32). What are you holding over your spouse's head? Do you need to forgive him? Remember, God has forgiven you of all your faults; how can you withhold forgiveness from someone else?

As an imperfect wife, I am thankful for the forgiveness Curt has shown me through the years. The error in my checkbook, the dent in the car (and the damage to the fence by the driveway), the mess that

A successful marriage is an edifice that must be rebuilt every day. —Andre Maurois

157

occurred when I let the dog in with muddy feet—these situations (and many more) were opportunities for me to receive forgiveness when I really needed it. I appreciate that Curt forgives my shortcomings, and I try to extend that same forgiveness to him, recognizing that each one of us is imperfect in many ways. Who isn't?

Of course, in a physically abusive relationship or one riddled with infidelity, forgiveness does not mean allowing your spouse to continue his destructive behavior. You can forgive in your heart yet maintain boundaries and limits. True compassion and forgiveness mean helping your spouse stop his destructive lifestyle by showing tough love. If you are in a situation like this, I recommend seeking wise counsel and reading the book *Love Must Be Tough: Proven Hope for Families in Crisis* by James Dobson.[2]

Fire Builder #2: Respect Him

What do men need most? Many husbands agree that respect is high on their list of needs. God already knew this, of course, and wrote it into his directions for marriage: "Each one of you [husbands] must love his wife as he loves himself, and the wife must respect her husband" (Ephesians 5:33).

Respecting one another is paramount in keeping a marriage strong and positive. Often the bottom line in a divorce is the wife's loss of respect for her partner. But what exactly is respect, and how do you show it?

To respect a spouse is to reverence, honor, and esteem him. When a wife does that, she finds that her husband lives up to the honor more often than not. In fact, husbands can go farther and higher in their God-given pursuits when they know that their wives believe in them and are backing them. As Proverbs 12:4 says, "A wife of noble character is her husband's crown." Make him feel like a king, and you'll be the queen reigning by his side!

But respect isn't always easy. In marriage, there may be times when our husbands disappoint us, bother us, or even disgust us. Consider Susan, who met her husband, Rick, in college where he was a star football player. As far as she was concerned, Rick hung the moon. But real life is different than the thrill of the university years, and now Rick just can't seem to find the right job. After years of jumping from business opportunity to business opportunity, they remain in debt to both parents and numerous credit-card companies. What once was a blissful dream has come to be a real-life nightmare. Susan has lost all respect for Rick. "He isn't a hard worker, he can't hold a job, and he certainly can't provide for his family!" she tells her friends.

Does Susan's story sound familiar? The details may be different, but many women find themselves in a relationship where respect has been lost. The sad thing about a wife who disrespects her husband is that she tends to see only what is wrong with her spouse. Her eyes, heart, and mind dwell only on the problems. She tends to forget two important truths: Although her husband has some glaringly bad qualities, he also has some good qualities (probably the ones for which she married him); and while it might seem impossible for her spouse to get his act together, "with God all things are possible" (Matthew 19:26).

Whenever we accentuate the positive qualities in other people, the negative qualities begin to dwindle. In Susan's case, she needs to remember that Rick is both a good family man and a spiritual leader in their home. If she could begin to focus on these positives, she could help her husband grow in confidence and overcome some of his weaknesses. Instead of verbally beating him up, she could praise him for what he does right and encourage him to find a job where his gifts and talents are best used. What a difference that change of focus would make in her home!

If you are struggling with a loss of respect for your husband, decide

A wife of noble character is her husband's crown, but a disgraceful wife is like decay in his bones. —Proverbs 12:4

☺

today that you will stop focusing on his bad qualities. Honor your husband when he is not around by guarding your tongue and not tearing him down in front of others. If you can't say anything nice about him, remember what you learned in kindergarten: Don't say anything at all.

Begin praying now, not only for your spouse, but for your response to him. Spend time each day thanking God for the good qualities in your husband and for the way God has made him. Pray that God would continue to develop your husband to grow according to God's plan for his life. Your husband needs your prayer support more than he needs your pressure or condemnation. Be patient and allow the Lord to work in his timing. Ask God to help you be a supportive wife, honoring and respecting your mate through the process.

On a daily basis, show your respect for your husband through your choice of words. Are you communicating respect in your message and your tone of voice? It can be so easy for us to speak our minds and lash out with our words; it is much harder to hold our tongues and treat our husbands with esteem! You can also show respect through such love-actions as:

- Sending a quick note to his office that says "I believe in you because…"
- Getting up early to fix him a good breakfast before the big presentation.
- Complimenting him in front of the kids and others.
- Listening to his point of view when he is up against a challenge.

Our children need to see our respect for our spouses. They need to know that we revere our husbands as the authority in the household who must answer to God for their leadership. What our kids see modeled by us will affect the kind of spouses they will grow up to be. It will also affect their view of God, since the marriage relationship is a picture of Christ and the church: "For the husband is the head of the wife as Christ is the head of the church.... Husbands, love your wives, just as Christ loved the church and gave himself up for her" (Ephesians 5:23, 25).

Fire Builder #3: Enjoy Him

Here's a log that is fun to throw on the fire: Enjoy your husband! Laugh together! Do fun things with each other! Enjoy your relationship! Life is too short to take it seriously 100 percent of the time. Unfortunately our busy schedules, career pressures, and family cares seem to keep our minds occupied to the point of eliminating any time for fun. You have to wonder: Is it possible in today's world to simply enjoy one another and create memorable moments outside of the normal routine? The answer is yes—but it takes a strong dose of both will power and creativity.

To get you started, here are a few ideas to help you add a little fun and flair to your marriage:

In the Home

Plan a romantic dinner. Now and then, put the kids to bed a little early and have a candlelight dinner. Prepare your husband's favorite meal, dim the lights, light the candles, and play his favorite CD.

Watch a video. After the kids are in bed, snuggle up on the couch and watch a movie together. Laugh together, cry together, enjoy one another.

Read a book. If you both enjoy reading, read a book together. Start a fire in the fireplace and turn on some soft background music to help you relax. If the kids are awake, encourage them to read or watch a video while you and Daddy read together.

Cook together. Pick a challenging recipe that you think both of you will enjoy. Split up the chopping, mixing, and sautéing duties and cook the meal together.

Have a romantic rendezvous. Prepare the environment with low lights, scented candles, and quiet music. Wear something fun and new. Be adventurous!

Outside the Home

Visit the local bookstore/coffee shop. Go together to a local coffee shop or bookstore (often these can be found under the same roof). Curt and I love to get a cup of coffee at our favorite bookstore around the corner and look at different books or sample new CDs together.

Make a date. What is something special and entertaining that you both like to do? Do you like to go to the movies, the ball game, the amusement park, the theater, the symphony? Save your money, make a date, and go out on a regular basis.

Do something for someone else. Serve dinner at a homeless shelter, help a friend move, visit a lonely relative. As you and your spouse join together to help someone else, your own bond grows stronger.

Take a trip. I know it is hard to leave the children, but every couple needs a little time to themselves. Even a short weekend away can help you focus on each other and learn to enjoy one another once again. If you don't have family in town to help you watch the kids, consider hiring a single person or a couple from your church or even one of your kids' schoolteachers.

Do something spontaneous. Although there are times when it's fun to plan ahead for a special event, last-minute surprises can be great too. Be spontaneous! Call a friend this afternoon and tell her you'll watch her kids one night if she'll watch yours tonight. Then surprise your husband with a special night out or a romantic evening at home.

Make a tradition. Choose a holiday tradition that only you and your husband will do together—without the kids. After the children are grown, you will have many holidays when it is just the two of you.

Establish a fun tradition now that you will enjoy every year for the rest of your life together.

Exercise together. Choose a sport or activity that you both enjoy and start working out together. Since our daughters are old enough to be home alone, Curt and I enjoy taking evening walks—just the two of us. These have become our special times to talk, discuss the issues we're facing, or share the joys of our day. Our walks are reminiscent of our dating relationship in college, when we would run together and train for distance races. Now, in deference to our aging knee joints, we walk instead of run—but we enjoy the pleasure of being exercise companions once again.

The Essential Ingredient

Of all the ingredients necessary to keep a fire burning, one ingredient is invisible but absolutely essential: oxygen. In our marriages, that critical but invisible ingredient is God. Even Christian couples are often guilty of not making the Lord an essential part of their marriage. But it is God's example of love that encourages us to love. It is his example of forgiveness that prompts us to forgive. It is his Spirit within us that helps us to love in a way that often surpasses human ability or understanding. Hebrews 12:29 describes God as "a consuming fire," and it is his flame that can ignite the barely glowing embers of struggling marriages, renewing the fire of love we have for our mates.

How do we bring God into our marriages? One of the best ways is to pray with our spouses on a regular basis. From the first day of our marriage, Curt and I began to form the habit of praying together each night before going to sleep. Eighteen years later, we are still praying. Those nightly prayer times remind us of the source of our strength and help, and turn our eyes together toward God's faithfulness and love.

Some husbands and wives read the Scriptures together; others attend a couples' Bible study at their church. However you choose to draw closer together spiritually, the important thing is that you and your husband make your relationship with God the central element of your marriage. Through the difficulties as well as in the blessed times, turn to God together for strength and direction. He is your all in all, in marriage as in all of life. May his undying love be the glue that seals your hearts together!

POWER POINT

Read: The entire book of Song of Solomon. Notice the love, respect, and enjoyment this couple has for one another.

Pray: O wonderful Father in heaven, I praise you, for you are love. You love me so perfectly and completely! Thank you. Fill me with your loving-kindness and forgiveness, especially toward my husband. Help me to love my husband as you love me. Help me to respect my spouse, honoring him and holding him in high esteem. Help me to overlook his faults and focus on his strengths. Help me to be an encourager. Give me the will power and the creativity to keep the flame strong in our marriage. Please bless and keep our marriage so we may glorify you in our union, knowing we are a picture of Christ and the church. Thank you for putting such a high value on marriage, and may we magnify you together! In Jesus' name, amen.

Do: Choose one of the ideas in this chapter for enjoying your spouse. Set a date, make plans, and carry them through!

13

Affirming Friendships
The Value of a Wise Companion

If a man does not make new acquaintances as he advances
through life, he will soon find himself left alone; one should
keep his friendships in constant repair.
—Samuel Johnson

Connie and Sandra enjoy meeting at the park or the local McDonald's at least once a week. It is a ritual they formed over the years, since the time their children were toddlers. As the kids play, the two moms talk about every topic under the sun, from preschools to potty training. Frequently during the week they help each other out by watching each other's children, running errands, and sharing information about a hot sale at the grocery store. Most importantly, they care for one another and offer a shoulder to cry on when one has a child who is struggling or the other has a husband who "just doesn't understand." One can hardly put a price on a friendship such as Connie and Sandra's!

Sadly our busy lives, overloaded with the responsibilities of modern motherhood, tend to make it difficult to develop and deepen new and abiding relationships. Many moms today wonder: Is it possible to develop lifelong, heart-to-heart friendships in such a "hurry-up, rush-around" world?

Let's consider for a moment how a relationship develops. Most of us have many acquaintances in our everyday lives. If we were to count,

165

the number might run in the dozens, or even the hundreds. These are people we know, but not well. They go to church with us; their children go to school with our children; they're at the same Little League games; they shop at the same stores we do; they work in the same building as we do. We may know their names; we may not. But we run into them with some regularity due to the places we go and the activities we participate in each week.

An acquaintance is someone with whom we carry on the typical surface conversation. You know the lingo:

"Hello, how are you?"

"Fine, how are you?"

"Fine."

"Glad to hear it. Well, talk to you later."

"Okay, 'bye."

" 'Bye."

Sometimes we may step out of the normal boundaries and talk about the weather or how cute the kids were in the musical, but generally we keep the conversation quite safe and shallow. Every once in a while, however, we find someone from this pool of acquaintances with whom we seem to connect on a deeper level. We find a potential friend.

Friendship tends to happen out of the blue. In one of those "aha!" moments, we realize that the other person shares a connection with us, whether it is a common viewpoint, a similar idea, or children with the same interests—and a companionship is born. The word *companion* means someone who walks with us in the same direction; it denotes someone with whom we can relate and with whom we can begin to build trust. Even Jesus needed companionship in his life on earth, and the four Gospels tell how he drew twelve companions from among his large pool of acquaintances and followers.

If we make that connection into companionship with someone we've known on the acquaintance level, then eventually, through nurturing and growth, that relationship has the potential to grow into a deep and lasting friendship. We might say we have a "soul mate." We can count ourselves fortunate if we develop two or three soul mates in a lifetime. A true heart-friend of this nature is one with whom we can share our lives on a deep level, revealing our hopes and fears, disappointments and dreams. Such friends love us unconditionally and understand us without having to say a word. They are with us for the long haul. Even when we're separated from a soul mate for months or even years, we can always pick right up where we left off without skipping a beat.

Of course, your husband should fit into the soul-mate category of your life. If he doesn't, you need to reread the previous chapter! But for now, I want us to focus mainly on friends outside of our family circles. Jesus had three especially close friends: Peter, James, and John. These friends, drawn from his larger circle of twelve companions, accompanied Christ to the Mount of Transfiguration and saw him revealed in all his glory. They were the ones he asked to stay nearby while he travailed in prayer in the Garden of Gethsemane.

Close friendships like these are much like a garden of beautiful flowers. Just as flowers need water, sunshine, and the proper nutrients in order to bloom and grow, friendships need love, care, and attention to develop and deepen. What can we do to nurture our lovely garden of growing relationships? Let's look at three keys:

Key #1: Make Friendship a Priority

In his book *The Friendship Factor*, Alan Loy McGinnis states that the main reason people do not experience deep and abiding relationships is because they do not make them a priority in their lives.[1] How important are friendships to you? As a busy mother, you certainly have a few other things to think about! Your husband and kids need you first, of course. Next you are probably focused on work or volunteer duties at the school, the church, and in the community. Friendships may fall dead last in your order of priorities!

As we consider the priorities in our lives, it is always good to reflect on God's priorities. Clearly relationships are important in the Bible. Think back to the Garden of Eden and the Creation account in Genesis 1 and 2. After God finished creating the whole world, he saw that everything was good—that is, *almost* everything. "It is not good for the man to be alone," God said in Genesis 2:18. Adam had everything he could possibly want. He was living in paradise, walking in a wonderful relationship with his creator. Still, something was missing. He needed a companion, someone with whom he could relate.

We know that God created Eve at that point to be Adam's helpmate. But other friendships are also important to both men and women. Wise King Solomon recognized the importance of friends when he said, "As iron sharpens iron, so one man sharpens another" (Proverbs 27:17). The friends God puts in our lives challenge us and sharpen us, helping us become better people. Do you have a knife drawer in your kitchen? I do, but I tend to use only about half of the knives in the drawer. Why? Because the other half have grown dull, and I have not taken the time to get the blades sharpened. They just sit in the drawer, not useful for anything. Without friends, we can become like those dull knives; but through good friendships, we are continuously sharpened and made useful in God's kingdom.

While not talking about friendships specifically, Jesus explained how important it was to love others when he was asked, "Teacher, which is the greatest commandment in the Law?" (Matthew 22:36). Jesus answered, "Love the Lord your God with all your heart and with

And let us consider how we may spur one another on toward love and good deeds. —Hebrew 10:24

all your soul and with all your mind. This is the first and greatest commandment. And the second is like it: Love your neighbor as yourself" (vv. 37–39). According to Jesus, second only to relating well to God is the importance of relating well to other people!

Jesus lived this love for others in his own life. Clearly, he devoted himself to his friends. We only need to read his prayer for his disciples in John 17:6–19 to see how much he loved them! Following in the Lord's footsteps, the apostle Paul also gave priority to relationships: "Be devoted to one another in brotherly love. Honor one another above yourselves," he wrote in Romans 12:10.

I believe that mothers especially need one another as friends. We need the companionship, the camaraderie, and the understanding that another woman can give. We need to help each other. Sometimes we need to be picked up and pointed in a positive direction, and an affirming friend can be just the one to do that. Truly a friend is a gift from God, given to us to share our joys as well as to help us get through life's challenges.

So how do we make friendships a priority in the midst of our admittedly crowded lives? By first recognizing those friendships that are important to us and then being a good friend. As Emerson said, "The only way to have a friend is to be one."[2]

To maintain the friendships that are important to me, I've made it a point to set aside certain times during the month to get together. I have one friend with whom I keep a standing lunch date on the second Tuesday of every month. With another friend, I get together on a weekly basis to pray. I meet with two other friends (we make a delightful threesome!) every other Thursday to chat, laugh, and pray. One of my dearest friends and I talk on the phone several times a week and get together for lunch when we can. I've found it helpful to put regular meetings with my friends on the calendar so that the "tyranny of the urgent" doesn't cause me to miss out on the relationships I hold dear.

Being a friend doesn't necessarily have to take a lot of time; it just takes a little kindness, a little thoughtfulness, a little compassion toward others—and a little planning. It also takes obedience to the Word of God. As we begin to live out the principles of Christian love found in Scripture, we will begin to find ourselves becoming better friends to one another.

Key #2: Build on a Common Interest

Put any two mothers next to each other in a doctor's waiting room, and within minutes they can be deep in conversation on any of a number of topics ranging from childhood diseases to favorite children's books. As mothers, we have a basic camaraderie born out of similar experience. And as we learn to build on these common interests, we can begin to see strong relationships blossom.

The good news is that building a friendship doesn't necessarily take time away from family responsibilities. In fact, a good friendship can grow even while we keep our husbands and children a priority. Want to take the kids to the park for the afternoon? Call an acquaintance with kids the same age as yours and ask them to join you. The children will grow in their social skills as they play with one another, and you will have the opportunity to develop a friendship yourself. Need to go to the farmers market or a wholesale store? Invite a friend to go with you and split the bulk-quantity items. Taking the kids to the newest G-rated movie in town? Don't go alone. Invite an acquaintance and her children and build a budding friendship as you all experience the silver screen together. Then go for ice cream or hot chocolate afterward.

Organize a playgroup with acquaintances who have kids the same age as yours. Or join one of the many wonderful mothers organizations in your area, such as MOPS (Mothers of Preschoolers), Early Childhood PTA, Preschool PTA, or Moms Club. (Check for listings in the newspaper or a local parent publication for groups in your area.) Many churches have regular moms' groups as well. If you can't find one, maybe you can start one! Friendships are just waiting to be born and developed from these wonderful circles of shared experiences.

Of course, I'm not suggesting that we spend all of our time in mothers groups or that we call a friend every time we go somewhere. We do need time alone with our families. But we should try to take advantage of friend-making opportunities when it is appropriate. Just be balanced! We don't want to grow dependent upon having company in everything we do, and we don't want our kids to think that we must have someone with us every second. But while we all need some guarded family time, we also need some blessed friendship time. Our kids need to see us making the effort to reach out to others in friend-ship. They'll learn to do the same by watching our example.

In chapter 8, we talked about the blessing of finding a prayer part-ner. Certainly, one of the deepest bonds we can have with a friend is the bond that forms when we pray together. Four years ago, my friend Carol and I began to realize that we had a common devotion to prayer for our families. We decided that we should try to meet together once a week to pray for the specific needs of our four daughters. (Each of us has two girls.) The depth of our friendship continues to deepen because of those precious prayer times. Today Carol and I can share anything with each other. We have an abiding trust and love that has been built over the years on our common interest in prayer.

Have you found something in common with an acquaintance? Similar hobbies, kids the same age, a common enthusiasm for sports? Do you love to shop at the same stores? Read the same books? Whatever your common interest, build on it! You will find a natural relationship beginning to form. Then, as trust develops over time, you will find yourself sharing at ever-deepening levels of honesty and openness. One word of caution: Make sure you know your friend is a loyal person before you begin to really open up. Few things hurt more than having a confidence betrayed by someone you thought you could trust. But once trust is built, be open, honest, and real—and enjoy the blessing of your God-given friendship.

Key #3: Encourage One Another

Beth is a positive friend. Whenever I am down, whenever I feel as though I have messed up as a mother, Beth is there to give me a good word and assure me that everything will be okay. She points me to God and to Scripture. Sometimes I am asked to talk about my books on local radio talk shows, and after I've gone off the air I can depend on Beth to call me up afterward and say, "You were great! I'm proud you're my friend!"

Beth is one of those rare treasures: a true encourager. She never engages in putting people down. She takes no pleasure in watching someone's demise. She always tries to see the good in every situation. If I have a disagreement with my husband and begin to complain, she tells me how lucky I am to have Curt and reminds me of his finer qualities (which far outweigh his negatives).

I am definitely a better person because of Beth! Everyone needs an affirming friend just like her. People who grumble and complain are a dime a dozen, but a friend who gives strength through encouragement is worth her weight in gold.

A number of years ago, I had a friend who was the exact opposite of Beth. She put down everything in my life, including my husband. "Oh, he just doesn't understand you," she'd say. "I'll pray for him—he needs it!" She put down everything and everyone in my life, from my children's school to people in our Bible study.

Surely we contend with enough negative influences in our world today without being bombarded by them in our friendships! I eventually recognized that I needed to discontinue this relationship because I was beginning to be influenced in a negative way toward my family. Instead of helping me see the blessings in my life, this friend was leading me to focus on the few things that were wrong.

Remember the story of the Israelites grumbling in the wilderness? God miraculously arranged their escape from slavery in Egypt and took care of their every need. He gave them a great leader in Moses. Yet they lost their focus on what God was going to do in and through them and worked themselves into believing that life would be better if they were back in Egypt as slaves! How do you think they became such complainers? It probably started with a few grumblers, who spread their negative thoughts to others, who complained to still others, and before they knew it, discouragement had seeped into the hearts of almost everyone. Poor Moses! At least he had two positive friends, Caleb and Joshua, who didn't focus on what was wrong with the situation but focused on what God could do in the midst of it.

What kind of friends do you have? Are they Calebs and Joshuas, or are they grumblers and complainers? Remember, positive friendships make a difference in your life, but so do negative ones. I know of a number of situations in which negative friendships have led to frustration, discontentment, and even divorce. Are your friendships making you better, or bitter? Pray that God will lead you to women who can help you see things from a godly perspective and not a self-centered, earthly one. Surround yourself with friends who are uplifters and not downtrodders—and remember to be that positive influence in your friends' lives in return.

Friendships with other women make our lives incredibly rich. You and I don't need a lot of money to be wealthy. We just need a few good friends!

A friend loves at all times. —Proverbs 17:17

POWER POINT

Read: 1 Samuel 20. Notice that Jonathan and David had a profound and positive friendship, despite many obstacles. Also read Colossians 3:1–17, which provides a wonderful picture of the qualities of a positive friend.

Pray: Most holy and wonderful Lord, you are the perfect friend. You are always there for me. You meet my every need. Thank you for the friends you have brought into my life. Help me to be attentive to these friendships. Help me to be a better friend. Help me to see the new, potential friends you put in my path each day. In Jesus' name, amen.

Do: In a notebook or prayer journal, make three lists: Acquaintances, Companions, and Soul Mates. Fill it in with names of people who are currently in your life. Pray about working to deepen some of these relationships. Pray for each friend by name.

14

Mentor Moms
Building Relationships with Seasoned Mothers

*As she supplies the affection and care that make a contented home,
each mother is strengthening the individuals within her
own circle as well as in the nation.*
—Earl E. Chanley

As the Director of Women's Ministries at a large Bible church in Dallas, Vickie Kraft wanted to find a way to draw out the gifts that God had given to each of the women in her congregation. She also wanted to meet their various needs as best she could. Eventually she found a way to do both at the same time. The more mature women, she realized, possessed wisdom and experience that could be shared with the younger women. Using Paul's instructions in Titus 2:3–4 as her basis—"the older women…can train the younger women"—she organized a program that she called Heart to Heart, pairing mature women with younger women in mentoring relationships.

After Vickie was interviewed on the popular *Focus on the Family* radio program with Dr. James Dobson, the Heart to Heart ministry quickly spread to congregations worldwide. Today Vickie is the author of several books on mentoring and speaks to women's groups across the nation and around the world, teaching them how to connect women to women in this dynamic program.

Why did Vickie's idea spread like wildfire? Clearly, it has a sound biblical basis, and God has given younger women—especially young mothers—a great desire for wise and seasoned mentors in their lives. Many young mothers in today's society don't have the benefit of living in the same community with the elder women in their families. Mothers, grandmothers, and other matriarchal figures are spread all over the globe, and younger women often must forge new territory on their own.

Meanwhile many older women have a desire to give of themselves and make an impact on the younger generation. Their own children are grown and often live far away. Still, they know that they have wisdom and gifts to share, and they often jump at the opportunity to share them with the younger women that come into their lives.

A mentoring relationship doesn't take the place of peers. Friendship with other women our own age and at the same level of experience is special; as we go through similar life experiences, we enjoy a wonderful camaraderie. But a relationship with a "mentor mom" is special too. Not only do we find caring companionship in a mentor, but we benefit from the wisdom and counsel of someone who's "been there." As we learn from our mentor's experience, we gain a more balanced perspective on life. What a relief it can be to hear such words of assurance as "Don't worry; it's just a phase" or "This too shall pass" or "Honey, I felt the same way when I was your age."

Nor can a mentor replace our own mothers or other family matriarchs. Still, a seasoned mother-friend can give advice to a new mother in ways that a family member sometimes cannot. Many times we don't receive advice well from people in our own families because of emotional ties or baggage from the past. In such cases, a wise woman speaking from outside the family circle can be a breath of fresh air!

Making the Connection

Whether there is a Heart to Heart ministry in your area or not, you can still begin to follow Paul's direction and seek to connect your life with a more seasoned mother. But how do you find the right mentor mom? Certainly you cannot force someone to be your mentor, but there are ways to easily and naturally grow into a mentoring relationship. Let's look at three steps that can lead to that special bond:

1. Pray

Begin now to pray that God would prepare the heart of a mature woman to be your mentor mom. Ask him to match you with someone who can encourage your strengths and help you grow through your weaknesses.

2. Inquire

Inquire at your church about women who may have an interest in being mentors. You may want to ask the leader in an older adult Sunday school class, or check with the person in charge of the women's ministry. Tell them you would like to connect with a spiritually mature, older mother who has the desire to influence or guide a younger mother.

3. Initiate

Don't wait for someone to come to you. Many times an older woman will feel awkward offering herself as a mentor; she may feel this implies that she has it all together. Once you discover a person with whom you feel you could connect, ask her to pray and consider being your mentor mom. Assure her that she doesn't need to be perfect, just willing to lend an ear, give some advice, and be a friend.

Of course, while you can't expect perfection in a mentor, you should look for certain qualities. The Bible tells us important attributes that a woman who leads or teaches others should have. In Titus 2:3 Paul writes, "Likewise, teach the older women to be reverent in the way they live, not to be slanderers or addicted to much wine, but to teach what is good." From this description we can see that a good mentor is a woman who lives a godly life. She is neither a heavy drinker nor a gossip, but one who lives and teaches biblical principles. Apparently Paul recognized that women whose families have left the nest can be tempted to idle away their time in gossip or selfish pursuits. His command is that older women use their time in a far more worthy way, by teaching younger women how to live for the Lord. When you identify a potential mentor, ask yourself: Does this person display a godly character and lifestyle? Your intent is to follow the instruction in Titus 2; make sure hers is too.

Building a Bond

Once you have established an association with your mentor mom, how do you begin forming a relationship and create closeness? Initially you simply need to make an effort to get to know each other. Ask your new friend to tell you about her children. Are they grown? Do they live in the area? Does she have grandchildren? Find out about her childhood and what life was like growing up in her family. Ask her how she met her husband. How did she become a Christian? Tell her about your life too. Share more than just the facts; allow her to see your feelings and emotions. As you open up with each other, you will begin to form a trust and an understanding between you.

Once you feel comfortable with one another, what do you do next? Titus 2:4–5 holds the key: "[The older women] can train the younger women to love their husbands and children, to be self-controlled and pure, to be busy at home, to be kind and to be subject to their husbands, so that no one will malign the word of God." Basically, mentor moms are called to impact the lives of young mothers by imparting spiritual encouragement and practical advice born of experience. This can be done informally by talking and spending time together, or more formally by going through a particular Bible study together. Many study guides are available to help. Perhaps a trip to the local Christian bookstore with your mentor can help you find the perfect study to interest you both.

Most importantly, you and your mentor mom can begin to pray with one another and for one another. Women with grown families often have more time to spend in faithful and diligent prayer. How wonderful to share your prayer requests with someone you know will take the time to pray! Remember to keep a journal of your prayer requests, and don't forget to record how God answers them in his perfect timing.

Planning Your Time

As mothers, we have many wonderful opportunities available to us; but if we do not guard our time, we will end up spending too much time away from our top priority, our family. Since time is precious and limited, it is important to consider the amount of time you want to spend with your mentor. I recommend beginning by meeting just once a month, with a set starting and stopping time. Having clear boundaries will help you and your mentor feel more comfortable about getting together again. If, after several months, you can both see your way clear to meet more than once a month, you might agree to spend some additional time together. Many times meeting once a month in person and talking once a month on the phone can be a good mix.

It helps to set a specific meeting day—say, the second Tuesday of every month. This helps you stay consistent; you won't be likely to schedule a dentist appointment on that day by mistake. Your telephone conversation can be scheduled the same way. Perhaps there is a time during the day when the kids are taking a nap or watching a favorite show, giving you a window of opportunity to have an uninterrupted phone conversation. Again, set a time limit. Twenty minutes is plenty of time to update one another and share prayer requests.

Where should you meet? A local park makes a good meeting place, weather permitting. This allows the kids to get exercise and fresh air while you keep watch over them and visit with your mentor. After my mother passed away, one of her good friends met my children and me regularly at the park for picnics and conversation. It was a delightful place to make memories together!

If the kids are at school or can be dropped off at a friend's house, you can meet your mentor at a restaurant over lunch. Visiting over a good meal is always fun, although a restaurant setting does lack the privacy you may want if you are doing a Bible study together. And, of course, you can always meet at your home so you can chat while the baby is napping or the kids are playing nearby.

Throughout the seasons of my life, God has brought several mentor moms into my life. With some, I met regularly and deliberately; with others, I met just a few times or on a sporadic basis. But each woman made a strong impact on my life. Barbara was there for me just after my mother passed away. Norma encouraged me during the challenging years of raising preschoolers. Anne was a godly prayer warrior who helped me during the formative years of my speaking and writing ministry. Jan, Donna, and Doris were (and still are) great blessings to my family and me. My life has been made richer through my relationships with these wonderful mentors.

On the Other Side

I always considered myself to be the one on the younger side of the mentor couplet. But at some point, unbeknownst to me, I became qualified for the more mature side. Amazing how it happened so

Likewise, teach the older women to be reverent in the way they live.... Then they can train the younger women. —Titus 2:3–4

quickly! Now it's my turn to pour into a younger mother some of the wisdom and experience I've gained over the years. And I love it! As the saying goes, "When you hold a torch to light another's path, you brighten your own." What a blessing it is to walk alongside the younger women God brings into my life, helping them to love their husbands, care for their kids, and build their homes!

As mentors (yes, if you aren't there already, you will be), we can allow God to work through us, not only to teach and encourage others, but also to serve. If time allows, we can offer to help a younger friend by watching her children while she runs errands or cooking dinner for her family when she's sick in bed. We can send cards or write notes of encouragement, helping her smile when she feels tired or overwhelmed. We can stay on the lookout for ways to assist her as she raises her family to love and serve the Lord.

Perhaps you are not mature in years, but you are mature in the faith and have grown through the experiences and circumstances God has brought into your life. Age is not the sole qualifier for being a mentor. You, too, have much to share with women who are younger in their walk with God. We should always be ready to share whatever God has given us with the women he sends our way.

I want to close this chapter by telling you about Kaye and Lydia. These two women taught the two-year-olds' Sunday school class together at their church. Kaye was a young, single woman; Lydia was married with two preteen daughters. They became fast friends, despite the difference in their ages. When Lydia's daughters went through the assorted challenges of the preteen years, Kaye was able to offer a "big sister" kind of help. When Kaye met Robert at the singles ministry, Lydia was there to encourage her in the new relationship. Later Lydia helped Kaye make wedding plans. Now Kaye has preteen daughters of her own, and guess who she goes to for counsel and advice?

These two women are a blessing to each other because they were willing, years ago, to reach out and build a bond. Their special mentoring relationship continues to have a positive impact on both of their lives to this day. May we all be as blessed as Kaye and Lydia!

POWER POINT

Read: Colossians 3. How can this passage be applied to a mentoring relationship?

Pray: Wonderful Father, thank you for the privilege of being a mother. Thank you for the help you give me along the way. Thank you for the seasoned mothers you've brought into my life to help me and encourage me to honor you in my home. Lead me to mentors who can share their wisdom and experience with me. Open up opportunities to build friendships. Show me when it is my turn to mentor others and help me to be a godly example to those around me. In Jesus' name, amen.

Do: If you are a young mother, begin praying that God would lead you to a mature woman with whom you can connect in a mentoring relationship. Actively inquire about women in your church who may be willing to build a relationship. If you are a mature mother, ask God to give you opportunities to minister to others.

Principle #5

THe
POwer
OF
Your
Example

In the same way, let your light shine before men, that they may see
your good deeds and praise your Father in heaven.
—Matthew 5:16

The first great gift we can bestow on others is a good example.
—Morell

Living Lesson Books
Your Actions Speak Louder Than Words

The foundations of character are built not by lecture,
but by bricks of good example, laid day by day.
—Leo B. Blessing

The Never Ending Story is a children's movie about a young boy named Bastian who loved to read. One day Bastian wandered into an antique bookstore and discovered a very odd storybook. He took it home, and, as he began to read, he found that he had entered the story and become part of the drama! He experienced incredible adventures in his quest to save the book's heroine, a beautiful, young princess. In the process, he grew in courage and bravery.

Near the end of the movie, Bastian's father began searching for him but could not find him. Finally the father picked up the old storybook and began to scan the pages. To his great astonishment, he found that he was reading about his own son! As the final chapter unfolded, the princess was restored to her throne, and Bastian returned from the pages of the book into his father's arms. Everyone, of course, lived happily ever after.[1]

Wouldn't it be incredible to actually jump into the pages of a book and live out the adventure in the text? In a way, our lives do represent the pages in a book. The title of the book is *Life's Living Lessons*. Our children read this book every day; they see our actions on the pages. It

185

is possibly the most influential book they will ever read, with the exception of the Bible. In fact, reading it is guaranteed to be life changing!

What are some of the chapters in our *Living Lessons* saga? Hopefully, the Table of Contents reads something like this:

Chapter One: Maintaining Self-Control Even When You're Tired and Frustrated

Chapter Two: Showing Patience in Traffic Jams and Grocery Store Lines

Chapter Three: Saying Kind Things about Others

Chapter Four: Telling the Truth, Even about the Little Things

Chapter Five: Helping Others When They Need a Hand

Chapter Six: Grumbling Less, Complimenting More

Chapter Seven: Using Table Manners and Other Forms of Good Etiquette

Chapter Eight: Obeying Traffic Rules and Laws

Chapter Nine: Praying about All Things, Worrying about Nothing

Unfortunately, many of our texts read a little differently. Can you relate to the following chapter titles?

Chapter One: Losing My Temper in a Frazzled Moment in Time

Chapter Two: Frustration and Anger in the Checkout Line

Chapter Three: Telling Juicy Stories about Friends and Foes

Chapter Four: A Few White Lies Go a Long Way

Chapter Five: No Time to Care, I Have Enough Challenges of My Own

Chapter Six: Grumbling without Regret

Chapter Seven: Good Manners out the Window

Chapter Eight: Traffic Rules Were Made to Be Broken

Chapter Nine: Worry Now, Pray Later

Like it or not, our life is an open book, continually read by the little eyes in our homes. The lessons we deliver to our children verbally may be wise and good, but lasting lessons are caught, not taught. It is rather sobering to realize that all the "right stuff" that comes out of our mouths can be made null and void if our kids do not see good character qualities lived out in our day-to-day lives. An old Chinese proverb says, "Not the cry, but the flight of the wild duck, leads the flock to fly and follow." Where are we leading our little flock by our example? How can we become better living lesson books for our children?

Heaven Help Us

It's hard to be a good example. In fact, at times it seems downright impossible. The apostle Paul spoke about this common struggle of knowing what we should do, yet doing what we know we shouldn't. In Romans 7:18–25 he admitted, "For I have the desire to do what is good, but I cannot carry it out. For what I do is not the good I want to do; no, the evil I do not want to do—this I keep on doing. Now if I do what I do not want to do, it is no longer I who do it, but it is sin living in me that does it.... What a wretched man I am! Who will rescue me from this body of death? Thanks be to God—through Jesus Christ our Lord!"

Paul knew that apart from Christ, we are hopeless. But with Christ, all things are possible. Jesus gave his followers hope when he said, "I am the vine; you are the branches. If a man remains in me and I in him, he will bear much fruit; apart from me you can do nothing" (John 15:5). Trying to be a good example in our own power leads to eventual failure, but abiding in Christ brings fruitfulness and hope.

The analogy of the vine and the branches is a beautiful picture of Christ and his followers. Is it the branch's job to create the fruit and make it grow? No, the branch simply stays attached to the vine and receives the nourishment the vine brings. Detached from the vine, the branch cannot bear fruit. But as it stays connected to the vine day by day, the fruit begins to grow naturally.

How can you live as a good example in your home? Stay attached to the vine! Abide in Christ. Continue in him; keep following him; remain in him. Stay close. Live with him, just as a homeowner might say to a new tenant, "Come into my house and abide here."

Is Christ dwelling in you? Is he just an acquaintance, or is he an important part of your day to day life? Remember, without him you can do nothing!

Examples Speak Loud and Clear

There once were two mothers who lived next-door to one another. Both had children the same age, and both were, at the same moment, looking at the mess in their playrooms. The first mother called her children together and, getting down on her hands and knees, began demonstrating how to tidy up the room. Her children followed her lead, and they all finished cleaning up together. The second mother scolded her children, demanding that they get right to work and "do their part" to keep the house clean. With scowling faces and lead feet, the children put a few books back on the shelf then pushed the rest of the toys under the sofa.

The first mother showed by her example how to get the job done; the second used her mouth but not her hands. As you can imagine, the first mother made a positive impact on her children because she led by selfless example; the second mother simply engendered a growing bitterness in her children. Both mothers, whether they realized it or not, were teaching much more than just how to clean a playroom.

Taking the time to show our children how to do certain tasks speaks volumes to them. It says, "My mother cares enough to show me how it is done." Certainly it is much easier to tell a son that he needs to clean the windows or a daughter that she must mop the kitchen floor. But they will learn how to do it right if we take the time to demonstrate. Being an example not only takes character; it takes time. In our busy society, time is a precious commodity—which makes it even more valuable when we hand it to our children and say, "Here, honey, let me show you how to do that." From demonstrating the backstroke to teaching our children how to pray, our example lights the pathway to our children's own accomplishments.

We are all familiar with the old adage, "Give a man a fish, and he has food for a day. Teach a man how to fish and you have fed him for life." The story is told of a time when Saint Francis of Assisi asked a young monk to accompany him on a trip to a small village in order to preach the gospel. The monk was honored to be invited by such a great master and readily accepted the invitation. The two men spent the day walking the streets, byways, and alleys of the village, caring for the needs of the helpless and poor they met along the way. They ministered to hundreds of people in that one day. As nightfall approached, the two headed back home, and the young monk realized that Francis had not once gathered the crowds to preach the gospel message. Disappointed, he said, "I thought we were going to preach the gospel today." The master replied profoundly, "We did preach. We were preaching while we were walking. We were watched by many, and our behavior was closely observed. It is of no use to walk anywhere to preach unless we preach everywhere as we walk!"[2]

As a young girl, I often took walks with my grandfather in his hometown of Pekin, Illinois. Pekin is a small town with very little traffic; yet whenever we crossed a street, Grandpa would reach down and gently take my hand without saying a word. I got the message. It couldn't have been more loud and clear: "I love you. You are precious to

Set an example for the believers in speech, in life, in love, in faith and in purity. —1 Timothy 4:12 ☺

189

me, and I don't want anything to happen to you." I miss those walks with Grandpa. But now, every time I take a walk with my daughters in our little neighborhood, I reach down and take their hands when we cross a street. Call it a habit; I call it a message of love that I learned from my grandfather's example.

Nobody's Perfect

Bil Keane's "The Family Circus" is one of my favorite comic strips. One segment in particular illustrates the powerful influence our example plays in the lives of our children. The first of two frames shows little Jeffy riding his tricycle around the house shouting, "Move over!" "Stoopid!" "Make up yer mind!" The next frame shows his mother, wearing a concerned expression, asking Jeffy what he is doing. The little boy's proud reply: "Drivin' like Daddy!"[3] What would your children do if they imitated your actions on the road, at the checkout counter, in the kitchen after a long day? Stop and think for a moment. A little scary, isn't it? Now ask yourself: What kind of example would you like your children to be imitating?

In my own home, I'm beginning to see more and more of my reflection as I look at my teenage daughters. Thankfully I see some good traits; but I also see some of my negative traits popping up from time to time. It is a highly convicting moment when I hear my own child using the exact same whining words of complaint that I used in my last gripe session with Curt!

Of course, nobody's perfect. We have all done things that we regret. I think of Peter who denied that he even knew Jesus—not once, not twice, but three times. No doubt Peter felt like a total failure. How could God possibly use Peter to build the church when he displayed such obvious weakness? Peter learned—as we should—that God is a forgiving God. He "redeems [our] life from the pit and crowns [us] with love and compassion" (Psalm 103:4). He forgives us, renews us, and still uses us, despite our mistakes.

After Jesus was resurrected, he came to Peter and asked three times, "Peter, do you love me?" (Perhaps he asked the question three times as a balance to the three times the disciple had denied him.) Peter answered, "Lord, you know all things; you know that I love you." And Jesus told him, "Feed my sheep" (John 21:17). Peter had messed up, but God still had a great plan for Peter's life! Peter would become the leader of the first century church, feeding the precious followers who would soon come to know Christ as their Savior.

We, too, are bound to mess up from time to time. But thank the Lord, "If we confess our sins, he is faithful and just and will forgive us our sins and purify us from all unrighteousness" (1 John 1:9). God forgives us, and he can still use us! In fact, when we make a mistake, God can use us to teach our children by example how to humbly come before him, repent, and accept his wonderful mercy and love.

Our lives can be the best sermon our children ever hear. I love how this poem, attributed to Edgar Guest, puts it:

I'd rather see a sermon, than hear one any day.

I'd rather one would walk with me—than merely show the way.

The eye's a better pupil—more willing than the ear,

Fine counsel is confusing, but example's always clear.

And the best of all the people are the ones who live their creed,

For to see the good in action is what everybody needs.

I can soon learn how to do it if you'll let me see it done.

I can watch your hands in action, but your tongue too fast may

    run.

The lectures you deliver may be very wise and true—

But I'd rather get my lesson by observing what you do.

Example is not the main thing in life—it is the only thing. —Albert Schweitzer

For I may misunderstand you, and the high advice you give,
But there's no misunderstanding how you act and how you live.[4]

Our examples should be like a beacon of light, leading our kids down the road of godly living. Jesus tells us, "In the same way, let your light shine before men, that they may see your good deeds and praise your Father in heaven" (Matthew 5:16). As our lights shine for Christ, may our children see our good deeds and praise the Lord—with their words and with their lives.

POWER POINT

Read: 1 Corinthians 4:16–17 and 10:31–11:1. What kind of example did Paul set for those who followed him? Can you confidently proclaim with him, "Follow my example, as I follow the example of Christ"?

Pray: Blessed Lord, you are the perfect example of righteousness. I love you and want to live for you as an example of goodness and godliness in my home. I recognize that I need you. I cannot live an exemplary life on my own. Help me each day, by the power of your Spirit within me, to honor you with my actions and words. Thank you for your help, your loving kindness, and your forgiveness. In Jesus' name I pray. Amen.

Do: Write a one-paragraph description of the example you want to set for your family. You may want to use Galatians 5:22–23 or Colossians 3:12–14 as references. Put this paragraph by your prayer journal and ask God to help you live out this description of a good role model.

Making Marvelous Memories
Creating Lasting Traditions in Your Family

Make a memory with your children,
Spend some time to show you care;
Toys and trinkets can't replace those
Precious moments that you share.
—Elaine Hardt

Before you begin this chapter, I want you to get comfortable. Make yourself a cup of tea. Sink down deep into that chair. Adjust the pillows. Put your feet up.

Now think back to some of your fondest childhood memories. Go ahead, take as much time as you want. Which recollections bring a smile to your face and a warm feeling to your heart? For some women, the best memories are of family vacations and other adventures embarked upon with parents and siblings. For others, the best memories are of holiday celebrations or special birthday parties. Still others would say their most precious memories are of sitting around the dinner table in the evenings, enjoying family meals and interesting conversation.

Special times such as these have woven a tapestry of unforgettable moments into our lives, and we are the richer for it. Now we are the parents, and it is our turn to create memorable moments for *our* kids. What we do with our children over the next few years—the fun that we have and the memories we make—will broaden their horizons, enrich their lives, and prepare them to pass on special traditions to their families for generations to come.

Of course, as we seek to make memories for our children, we mustn't try *too* hard. Sometimes we can become so focused on our efforts to create memories for the future that we fail to enjoy the present! A family tradition can't be forced. In fact, we can ruin a potential family memory by our overzealous efforts to make sure everything is "just right."

Consider one mother—we'll call her Sheila—who came up with what she thought would be a great family tradition. Each spring she ferried her kids to the mall to have their pictures taken on the special Easter train on display in the center court. When the children were toddlers, the "Kodak moment" was great fun for all, and Sheila determined that she would continue the tradition. Her plan was to have a complete collection of framed photos of the kids on the train from ages one to eighteen.

The idea went well while the children were young and easy to manage; but as they grew into preadolescence, they began to balk. What if one of their friends saw them sitting on a kiddie ride? From that point on, a battle erupted each spring when Sheila planned the trip to the mall. Finally she dropped the idea altogether. She realized she was making a memory—but it wasn't the positive one she had anticipated!

Fond memories are born out of pleasant experiences. As we explore ways to build traditions within our families, we must always remember that our goal is to leave wonderful impressions on the minds of our children. If our attempt to create a memory feels forced, it is not likely to have the desired impact.

I'm reminded of a particular woman who was preparing for a dinner party. She was so distracted by the cooking, cleaning, and other preparations that she was unable to give attention to her guests, including the guest of honor. Perhaps you recognize this woman as Martha in the New Testament. She missed the point of having everyone in her home—which was to enjoy the company of good friends. Her sister

Mary, however, seized the moment and enjoyed the relationships. Similarly, we can easily miss the point of creating memorable moments if we are focused on the wrong objective. If we build on our relationships and celebrate the times we have together; wonderful memories will overflow as a result.

In this chapter, I want to share with you some practical ways to celebrate life as it happens. Allow these ideas to spur your own creativity as you think of more ways to develop meaningful family traditions. Happy living!

Unforgettable Birthdays

Once a year each of our children have their special day—their birthday. Birthdays are a time for them to be honored and to feel that they are not only important, they are extraordinary! We can assist our kids in having an unforgettable day by being a little creative. For example:

The Plate of Honor. Buy a bright red plate, or make a special plate with supplies from a craft store. In the middle, write something like "You're Special!" or "It's Your Day!" Then store it away, only bringing it out on a family member's birthday. Serve all of their meals that day on the Plate of Honor. Then put the plate back in the cupboard until the next family birthday.

Favorite Meals. Several days before a birthday, ask the birthday child what he or she would like to have for breakfast, lunch, and dinner. Then go the extra mile to provide those favorite meals on that special day.

Birthday Parties. Creative parties can make wonderful, lifelong memories. You may want to do a party every year or every other year (depending on your sanity level). But planning a party is not as difficult as you might think. Start by coming up with a theme—something that corresponds with your child's interests. You can build a theme around anything your child loves—baseball, fire trucks, teddy bears, you name it! Look in craft stores and party books for ideas for age-appropriate games, crafts, and activities. Allow the birthday child to be a part of the planning process as he or she gets to be a little older. You will find great joy in planning an event together. My kids continue to remember and talk about their favorite parties throughout the years.

Spiritual Birthdays. Just as you celebrate a physical birthday, you can also celebrate a spiritual birthday. The event of spiritual rebirth is described by Jesus in John 3:3–15 as a time when we decide to put our faith in Jesus Christ as God's son and our savior. What a wonderful day to remember and celebrate year after year! Rejoice together as a family as you bring out the Plate of Honor and perhaps present a special, heartfelt gift to the honoree.

Heavenly Holidays

Holidays offer a multitude of opportunities to carry on old traditions and begin new ones. As each holiday approaches, take time to deliberately introduce at least one new tradition. If it is well accepted and everyone has fun, write it down and plan to continue it in the years to come. A "Holiday Traditions Journal" is a splendid way for you to record your ideas and help you remember the best ones from year to year. Later the journal can be copied and passed down from generation to generation. Include in the journal your family's favorite holiday recipes as well as traditions you have carried on from years past.

Here are a few fun suggestions for the holidays, from January through December:

New Year's Day

- Eat black-eyed peas and corn bread as you watch football together. Choose different teams for each of you to cheer on.

Keep tally of the scores, and award a funny prize to the family member who racks up the most points during the day.

- Pray together for the New Year and for each individual in the family.

- Have everyone write goals or resolutions and share them with the rest of the family.

- Make popcorn and watch a movie, or play a board game together.

- Write a "Here's Hoping" list. Ask each family member to contribute one idea of something fun he or she would like to do during the coming year. Try to set some dates for when these ideas could be carried out.

Valentine's Day

- Cut heart shapes from red or pink paper and ask your family members to write kind, appreciative notes to each of the other people in the family. Deliver the notes at the dinner table.

- Read a love story together or retell the story of how you and your husband met. Pull out your wedding album and tell your children about each of the pictures.

- Make heart sandwiches for lunch using heart-shaped cookie cutters to cut out the bread.

- Have the whole family wear red or pink all day.

- Get together with your kids to cook Dad's favorite dessert.

- Think of one way your family could show God's love to others in the community. Make a plan to carry it out together.

St. Patrick's Day

- Give your child a green bracelet or ring to wear each year only on St. Patrick's Day. Keep it in a special green box that you bring out on that morning.

- Serve green food and drinks. A little food coloring can go a long way to make green eggs, green cookies, green biscuits, and much more.

- Read the story about St. Patrick together.

- Eat green lollipops and have a contest to see who has the greenest tongue.

- Hunt for four-leaf clovers. Talk about God's plan for each of your children's lives, and explain why trusting God is different than believing in luck.

Easter

- Read the Easter story in Luke 24 in the Bible. Talk with your children about the hope we have in Jesus.

- Take communion together as a family and explain the symbolism of each element.

- Hard boil and decorate eggs together. Explain that the eggs symbolize new life, and that's what we're celebrating at Easter—our new life in Christ. If you want to go further, you can also note that the egg has three parts, reminding us of the Trinity: the hard outer shell (God, our refuge); the egg white (Jesus, our purifier); and the yolk (the Holy Spirit, our nourishment).

- Make Easter cookies together, then take them to someone you and the kids want to tell about Jesus.

- Attend a sunrise service together at a local church.

- Prepare an Easter egg hunt using plastic eggs that open at the middle. Fill them with coins, candy, or notes that tell some part of the Easter story. Encourage the kids to try to find enough eggs to put together the whole account.

Fourth of July

- Plan a neighborhood parade. Encourage everyone to decorate their bikes, trikes, and strollers and march together through the neighborhood. Use a boom box to provide patriotic music and serve refreshments when the parade is done.

- Invite several families over for hot dogs on the grill and to watch fireworks. Try to include the same families every year.

- Read a short biographical sketch about one of our nation's founding fathers. Read several famous quotes by this person too.

- Fly your flag and make a ceremony of putting it up and taking it down. Have the kids set small flags in the ground to "decorate" your yard.

Thanksgiving

- Allow each child to pick one favorite recipe for the Thanksgiving meal and have him or her assist you in making it. Proudly tell the guests who helped make each dish.

- Decorate the dinner table together with the kids. Use colorful leaves and acorns from your yard to accent the centerpiece on the table.

- Make a "Gratitude" poster or tablecloth. Write the words "I am thankful for..." across the top of a large poster board and ask everyone to add their thoughts. Read them out loud at the end of the Thanksgiving meal. Or purchase a white cotton tablecloth and allow your guests to sign it, adding their thoughts of gratitude and the date. Bring out the tablecloth year after year.

- Read the story of the first Thanksgiving, or read the Thanksgiving Proclamation given by George Washington or Abraham Lincoln.

- Set five kernels of corn at each place setting. Tell the story of how the Pilgrims did the same thing at the first Thanksgiving in remembrance and gratitude for how God brought them through a terrible winter—a season so bad that for a few days they had only a day's ration of five corn kernels to eat.

Christmas

- Have a caroling party with all the kids in the neighborhood.

- Help a family in need by visiting them, giving them gifts, and praying with them.

- Read about the Christmas traditions from the land of your heritage. Choose one you may want to start in your own family.

- Decorate the house and the Christmas tree together. Make sure everyone pitches in! Play your favorite Christmas music and serve hot cocoa.

- Set out a small box and put thin strips of paper beside it. Tell your family members that every time they notice someone in the family doing a kind deed for another person, they are to write it down on a strip of paper and put it in the box. Hopefully, by Christmas day the box will be full. Explain that the box represents Christ's manger, and the kind deeds are the straw laid in preparation for his arrival.

- Set aside one day as a baking day, and have the kids help with the stirring, the mixing, and the licking of spoons. Together, take the cookies, breads, cakes, and pies as gifts to the neighbors.

- Choose one night to drive around and look at the Christmas lights on the houses in your community. Eat Christmas cookies as you go.

- After the Christmas Eve service, invite one family over for tamales and chili.

- Give the kids a new pair of Christmas pajamas on Christmas Eve.

- Give only three gifts to your children, just as Jesus received three gifts.

- Read the Christmas story from Luke 2 and talk about God's gift to the world before you begin to open gifts on Christmas morning.

- Have a green and red breakfast. At our house, we traditionally have green eggs and ham, plus a cherry coffeecake. My family insists on it every year now!

Therefore, brethren, stand fast and hold the traditions which you were taught, whether by word or our epistle. —2 Thessalonians 2:15 NKJV

Two More Significant Days

If your children are school-age, there are two special days which are fun to recognize. They don't fall in the "holiday" category, but they are significant just the same: the beginning of summer vacation and the first day of school. These days loom large to all students, whether they are home-schooled or attend a public or private school. Here are some thoughts on making these days memorable:

Beginning of Summer

- Throw a family party on the first day of summer vacation. Decorate the house with balloons, provide your kids' favorite junk food, and celebrate their achievements from the year.

- Make a summer planning poster. Write across the top "Summer 2001" (or whatever year it is). Then make a list of fun activities you and kids want to do over the next two months. Also include some summer rules, such as how much television time will be allowed, what chores will be required, and how late is too late to sleep in.

- Make a "Boredom Busters" can. Cover a coffee can with construction paper and decorate it with stickers and the words "Boredom Busters." Sit down with the kids and talk about activities they can do when they feel bored. Remind them that "boredom is in the eyes of the beholder" and there is always something to do if they will use their imaginations. Have them each contribute five ideas to the can. If they say they're bored in the weeks that follow, tell them to reach into the can and pull out a "boredom buster."

- Plan several one-day field trips together—to the park, the beach, the zoo, the museum, or other places of interest.

- Provide one interesting workbook for them to do to keep mentally alert. You might want to have an incentive system to motivate them. Or provide an incentive for them to read a good book or two. A new computer program may also be a hit.

- Appeal to their creative bent by providing a new sketch pad, paint set, or musical instrument to take up during the summer.

First Day of School

- Take a picture of the kids at the front door of your home with schoolbooks in hand.

- Make each child's favorite lunch to take to school. Tuck in a special note telling them how proud you are of them.

- Set a scholastic goal for the coming year, such as a certain grade point average or all As and Bs.

- Plan a special snack for after school—or maybe a trip to the ice-cream shop.

- Establish a new work area and study schedule to fit your child's needs. Buy new pens, pencils, and paper for the work area.

- Pray together about the school year. Start a prayer journal or prayer calendar for the year, keeping a record of prayer requests and answers to prayer.

- At dinner, ask each child to tell one thing they like about their new teacher. Encourage them to talk about their day and their friends.

Travel Traditions

Several years ago our family took a short trip to the hill country of Texas. We decided to go exploring down the country roads in our car and came upon a small mountain called Enchanted Rock—a large, granite mount with smooth sides situated in the middle of a state park. Venturing into the park, we noticed that people were climbing up the mountain, so we decided to get out of the car and try the climb too. When we reached the top with only a minimal struggle, we felt victorious. We could see for miles around in every direction, and we were awestruck by the natural beauty of the area.

We got the camera out and took pictures, then decided to descend the rock by a different route. Oops! Trying to find a safe passage down was a bigger challenge than we expected. At times my husband, Curt, had to help the girls and me leap across small crevasses and slide down steep inclines. When we finally managed to make it to the bottom, we rejoiced, knowing that we had succeeded together in a difficult task. We still remember that climb to this day—what a challenge it was and how we helped and encouraged each other along the way. We didn't spend a lot of money to make this memory, nor did we plan for it to happen. But we experienced a special bond, and none of us will ever forget it.

That's what family trips do—they bond family members together and provide opportunities for unforgettable moments. How can you make the most of these traveling adventures? Consider incorporating some of the following traditions into your next travel plan:

Goodie Bag. Put together a small goodie bag for each child with age-appropriate activities, plus snacks and drinks. Books, markers, paper, and small games make good items for the bag. Wait to give the child his or her goodie bag until just before you get on the plane or into the car. My kids look forward to the start of every trip because they love their special bags.

Family Photographer. Designate one family member as the photographer for the trip. Older kids will take great pride in this job. Explain that these will be the photos that will go into the family photo album. When you return, create your photo album quickly so that the task doesn't hang over your head. Get the kids to help. Leave the photo album on the coffee table for several weeks so that everyone can look at it and reflect on the trip.

Travel Video. Designate another family member to create a video record of the trip as you go along. At the end of the vacation, interview each family member on tape and ask them to name their five best memories of the trip. Choose one night to eat popcorn and watch the video.

Mystery Game Bag. Put several small travel games or puzzles in a pillowcase (one for each evening you are on the trip). Before dinner each night, allow one family member to blindly pick one item out of the bag. That game or puzzle can then be played while waiting for your meal at a restaurant or after dinner in the hotel room. Save the games for future trips.

On-the-Way-Home Poem. Coming home from a great getaway can be a downer for everyone. Why not use the travel time to reflect on your journey? Ask each person in the family to list some of their favorite moments. Then, working together, create a family poem about the trip. It can be silly or serious! When you get home, type up the poem and frame it with a photograph from the getaway. Begin a "Wall of Memories" in a hallway in your house.

Passing It On

Passing on traditions from generation to generation is not just great fun; it is important. In the Old Testament, God often instructed his people to pass their traditions from one generation to the next in the form of special feasts. The Passover feast, for example, represents the Israelites' exodus from Egypt, when the angel of death "passed over" those Jewish homes that had the blood of a lamb sprinkled on their doorposts. To this day, Jewish families observe this feast and remember God's faithfulness and redemption. The Passover—and other great feasts and celebrations proscribed in the Bible—not only continue to bring families together in unity and worship, they illustrate spiritual truths and point ultimately to the Messiah.

We, too, are blessed by the traditions and celebrations we pass down through our families. Our children learn to celebrate life and appreciate God's faithfulness through the celebrations and traditions we teach them while they're young. It is not enough to tell them how life should be lived; we must live it abundantly ourselves each day, passing on our ideas, hopes, and dreams. We must teach our kids how to celebrate life through our own example.

This year holds incredible potential for making memories with your family! As a positive mom, start today to celebrate life—and watch with joy as your children celebrate with you.

POWER POINT

Read: Leviticus 23, where God describes the various feasts that the Israelites were to observe. Notice the traditions God set forth for his people and consider the memories he intended to establish.

Pray: Mighty and awesome God, thank you for your loving care over my family. Thank you for your son, Jesus, whom we should celebrate every day. Help me to be faithful to pass on traditions and celebrations that honor you and celebrate life. Help me to build positive memories in the lives of my children—especially ones that help them reflect on your constant love and faithfulness. Help me to live life abundantly in you. In Jesus' name I pray. Amen.

Do: Begin a "Family Traditions Journal" using a blank notebook. Record old and new traditions for each holiday. Add recipes and other ideas you collect over the years. (One day, as a wedding present to your children, make a copy of the book so that they have some family traditions to pass on to their own kids.)

Principle #6

THe Pwer OF Strong Moral Standards

The intergenerational poverty that troubles us so much today is predominantly a poverty of values.
—Dan Quayle

Whoever would love life
and see good days
must keep his tongue from evil
and his lips from deceitful speech.
He must turn from evil and do good;
he must seek peace and pursue it.
For the eyes of the Lord are on the righteous
and his ears are attentive to their prayer,
but the face of the Lord is against those who do evil.
—1 Peter 3:10–12

Living by the Book
Anchoring Your Children in God's Word

In regard to this Great Book, I have but to say, I believe the Bible is the best gift God has given to man. All the good Savior gave to the world was communicated through this Book. But for this Book we could not know right from wrong. All things most desirable for man's welfare, here and hereafter, are to be found portrayed in it.
—Abraham Lincoln

In October 1998 the Guadalupe River in South Texas swelled far beyond its banks and grew into a massive torrent of rushing water, carrying away every object in its path. Susan Foster, one of the survivors of the flood, describes her experience:

About forty feet of water swept over our entire seven acres like a tidal wave. All that remains looks like a war zone—no windows or doors. Even the cedar logs (one foot in diameter and fourteen feet long) which were buried three feet into the ground with concrete were either snapped off or pulled out. Thankfully the first floor is made of cast-in-place bridge concrete pillars. Otherwise our house would have vanished like so many others.... Washing machines and refrigerators made hasty exits through walls and windows, as did all of the furniture.... I did find one chair about one-half mile down the river, although it was thirty feet up in a tree! One man's engraved bowling ball was found over one hundred miles down stream.[1]

Clearly, the powerful current of a raging river can be overwhelmingly destructive. As we see from Susan's account, only those things that are firmly anchored have a chance of withstanding such forceful turbulence. My heart truly goes out to families in the wake of a flood!

But while a flood like the one Susan described will make headline news for days, another flood that continues to destroy lives every day never seems to make it into the mainstream press. I'm talking about our society's destructive moral current that is flowing rapidly downstream. These raging waters quickly and easily sweep over young and impressionable hearts and minds. Only those children who are properly anchored have a chance of surviving such a strong, dominating current.

From the Internet to Hollywood to magazines at the checkout stands, immoral images and corrupting information swirl around our families. Gone are the days when purity was valued, human life was respected, and God was almost unanimously reverenced. The tide has shifted to a sexually open and perverse society that devalues human life through violence and abortion and makes God and his followers the object of derision. Although years ago the name of God was honored and revered even by unbelievers, now Christians are the subjects of jokes, and God himself is portrayed as a goofy cartoon character on prime time television!

Christian apologist Josh McDowell describes the seriousness of our moral decline this way: "I believe that one of the prime reasons this generation is setting new records for dishonesty, disrespect, sexual promiscuity, violence, suicide and other pathologies is because they have lost their moral underpinnings; their foundational belief in morality and truth has been eroded."[2] How true! The pervasive mind-set today is "Whatever you think is right, is right." No absolutes. Just make your own rules for life. If it feels good, do it. With this kind of philosophy, a young person is little more than a house of cards in the path of the floodwaters; he or she will be carried off easily by the thoughts and ideas of this world—and will likely meet destruction along the way.

As positive moms, we can protect our kids from some influences, but we can't control everything that goes into their minds. We can't insulate them completely from the world's way of thinking. If they are school age, they are away from us a good part of most days. Even if they are home-schooled, they are likely to see or hear things at times that we wish they didn't. But while we might not be able to prevent every worldly thought from getting into their impressionable heads, we can give them a foundation of moral truth on which to stand—a solid rock that will not only keep their heads above the water but will give them the strength and courage to stem the tide.

That foundation is the Word of God. The Bible offers timeless truths for us to pass on to our children. The standards set forth in Scripture are not just a set of rules and regulations, but instructions for a joyful and fulfilling life. If we will faithfully teach the truths of the Bible and assist our kids in living out these precepts, they will have an anchor in the flood and a sure foundation. Jesus used a parable to illustrate this concept in Luke 6:47–49:

> I will show you what he is like who comes to me and hears my words and puts them into practice. He is like a man building a house who dug down deep and laid the foundation on rock. When a flood came, the torrent struck that house but could not shake it, because it was well built. But the one who hears my words and does not put them into practice is like a man who built a house on the ground without a foundation. The moment the torrent struck that house, it collapsed, and its destruction was complete.

Perhaps you are familiar with the children's song using this parable. If you could hear the sound of my voice, I'd sing it to you: "The foolish man built his house on the sand. When the rains came down and the floods came up, the house on the sand went *SMASH!*" Point well taken! How are we building the houses of our lives? Are we laying a sure foundation by hearing and doing God's Word? What about the foundation we're laying for our kids? Are we raising them on the solid rock of the Scriptures so they are anchored to withstand the current trends of a rapidly declining morality?

Taming the Barbarian

Dr. Albert Siegel said in the *Stanford Observer,* "When it comes to rearing children, every society is only twenty years away from barbarism. Twenty years is all we have to accomplish the task of civilizing the infants who are born into our midst each year. These savages know nothing of our language, our culture, our religion, our values, our customs of interpersonal relations…. The barbarian must be tamed if civilization is to survive."[3] Now, we may not consider our children barbarians or savages (well, there are times!), but we can't argue that they need direction, training, and discipline. As positive moms, we must take the initiative to teach God's principles to our kids. Civilization may very well be at stake!

How do we effectively teach God's Word? In chapter 15 we discussed the importance of setting a good example with our actions and words. Setting an example of devotion to Scripture is part of that responsibility. Our young observers need to see us pouring over God's Word, enjoying its blessings and applying its truths in our lives. Remember, kids are copycats! But modeling a love for the Bible is not enough. We must also have a deliberate plan of instruction. We must set aside a time and a place to teach our children about the Bible. Taking them to church is helpful, but we should not depend on one hour a week in Sunday school for their entire biblical upbringing.

Parents, after all, have the main responsibility to pass on God's foundational truths to their kids. God tells his people in Deuteronomy 6:6–8, "These commandments that I give you today are to be upon our hearts. Impress them on your children. Talk about them when you sit at home and when you walk along the road, when you lie down and when you get up. Tie them as symbols on your hands and bind them on your foreheads. Write them on the doorframes of your houses and on your gates."

The point is we should always be looking for opportunities to teach our kids the Word of God! We can talk about the Bible:

- Around the breakfast table
- In the car, on the way to school or activities
- In the car, on the way home from school or activities
- During dinner
- Over dessert
- At bedtime

Anytime is a good time to teach the principles of God's Word. Decide what is best for your family, then do it!

How do you start? Perhaps your family would enjoy reading together some of the Psalms or Proverbs, or perhaps one of the Gospels. You might want to purchase one of the many excellent, age-appropriate devotional books available at Christian bookstores. Whatever you choose, begin the habit of reading and enjoying God's Word together as soon as possible, preferably while your kids are young. Set the example early.

As your children grow and mature (say, by about the age of eight or ten), encourage them to begin developing their own personal devotional time. Invest in a youth Bible or other easy-to-read translation. Give them a blank journal, a special highlighter pen, and an age-appropriate devotional plan. Help them to establish a time each day when they can read the Bible and pray. Ask them about some of the truths they are learning; use open-ended questions such as "Can anyone share a miracle they read about this week in God's Word?"

In our home, the dinner hour has become an important time to talk about current events, social issues, and biblical truths. Now and then I like to bring out an interesting devotional book—like *Sticky Situations* by Betsy Schmitt (Tyndale House) or *Courageous Christians* by Joyce Vollmer Brown (Moody)—to help get the family talking. My personal favorite (because I wrote it!) is *Table Talk* (Broadman & Holman Publishers), which includes discussion questions for young and old alike along with correlating Bible verses. Another good discussion starter I found recently is *God—Seen through the Eyes of the Greatest Minds* (Howard Publishing). This book provides interesting quotes about God from renowned scientists, philosophers, artists, musicians, and writers throughout history.

Another good idea is to memorize scripture verses together as a family. Write the memory verse on a poster, chalkboard, or white board for all family members to see. Set a time limit for memorizing the verse and offer a reward for everyone who achieves the goal. Write notes to your kids, encouraging them with Bible verses to help them see how God's Word can be applied day to day. You will find that as your family works together to memorize Scripture and apply it to daily life, your kids' interest in the great Instruction Book for Life will deepen and grow.

A Great American Example

George Washington stands out in history as one of America's greatest heroes. His integrity and leadership led this nation through its challenging formative years. Certainly God's hand was upon our nation's first president, but George Washington also credits another important

How can a young man keep his way pure? By living according to your word. I seek you with all my heart; do not let me stray from your commands. —Psalm 119:9–10

person in his life for his success. Consider what he had to say about his mother: "My mother was the most beautiful woman I ever saw. All that I am I owe to my mother. I attribute all my success in life to the moral, intellectual, and physical education I received from her."[4] What made Mary Ball Washington so influential in the life of her son?

Widowed when George was only eleven years old, Mary was a devoted Christian who earnestly desired to glorify God in the way she raised her children. One historian writes, "In addition to instruction in the Bible and Prayer Book, which were her daily companions, it was Mrs. Washington's custom to read some helpful books to her children at home, and in this way they received much valuable instruction."[5]

One of the books she read to her children was *Contemplations, Moral and Divine* by Sir Matthew Hale, which contained devotional writings that taught biblical principles and gave advice on living a moral and godly life. It is no wonder that as we read George's own writings, we see a man of sincere faith and humble, godly leadership. In his personal prayer book, consisting of twenty-four handwritten prayers, we catch a glimpse of this mighty man's genuine heart:

MONDAY MORNING... O eternal and everlasting God, I presume to present myself this morning before Thy Divine Majesty, beseeching Thee to accept of my humble and hearty thanks.... Direct my thoughts, words and work, wash away my sins in the immaculate Blood of the Lamb, and purge my heart by Thy Holy Spirit.... Daily frame me more and more into the likeness of Thy Son, Jesus Christ, that living in Thy fear, and dying in Thy favor, I may in Thy appointed time attain the resurrection of the just unto eternal life. Bless my family, friends and kindred, and unite us all in praising and glorifying Thee in all our works.[6]

Are you as inspired as I am by Mary Ball Washington's example of faithful, fervent, and diligent teaching of God's Word? I know that as I read her son's prayer, I am motivated to elevate the teaching of the Scriptures to my children to the top priority it deserves.

Passing the Baton

In my first few years as a teacher, I served as the assistant track coach. One of my favorite events at the track meets was the 4 x 100-meter relay. This race is quick and competitive, but running is only a part. Victory rides on the proper handoff of the baton from one runner to the next. If the handoff is not right, the baton is dropped, and the race is lost! In nearly every meet I attended, I saw at least one team drop the baton and fall behind the rest of the pack. I made sure our runners practiced the handoff over and over again so they wouldn't make a mistake when it really counted.

As positive moms, we have a baton to hand off to the next generation in the form of strong moral standards. It is our job to practice the handoff over and over again so that when it really counts, the transition is seamless, and victory is achieved in our children's lives.

I believe four elements are crucial in the makeup of that moral baton. The first is found in Matthew 22:37–40: "Love the Lord your God with all your heart and with all your soul and with all your mind. This is the first and greatest commandment. And the second is like it; Love your neighbor as yourself. All the Law and the Prophets hang on these two commandments." Memorize these verses with your children, then show them how to live them out each day.

Second, teach your kids the Ten Commandments. While these represented God's moral standards for the Israelites in the Old Testament, they are still important precepts for godly living today. You will find them in Exodus 20.

From there, move on to other passages in Scripture that teach how to relate to the world and the people around us—for example, Romans 12, Colossians 3, and Matthew 5, 6, and 7 (known as the Sermon on the Mount). Of course, God's character and principles for living are revealed throughout the Scriptures, so don't limit yourself to these passages.

Finally, teach your children courage by studying the lives of biblical heroes. Courage is a key character trait our kids will definitely need to live godly, moral lives in an immoral world. Courage to stand alone. Courage to stand up for what is right. Courage to do what is right when everyone else is doing wrong.

When my husband was in college (a Christian university, in fact), his biology professor opened the first class with the question, "Is there anyone here who does not believe in evolution?" Curt was the only student who stood up and said, "I believe in the creation/intelligent design plan presented in the Book of Genesis." Perhaps other students in that classroom agreed with Curt, but none had the courage to stand up and be counted.

In today's schools, it can be even harder for Christian students to stand up for what they believe. Fortunately the Bible is full of stories of courageous men and women who faced difficult odds but relied on God's strength to see them through—people like Deborah, Moses, Joshua, Esther, David, Daniel, Peter, and Paul. Help your kids to learn and be inspired by their examples. Memorize Joshua 1:9 with them: "Have I not commanded you? Be strong and courageous. Do not be terrified; do not be discouraged, for the LORD your God will be with you wherever you go."

I am so thankful for God's Word, aren't you? The Bible is a strong and steady anchor for life—the only sure foundation in a world that's teetering on shifting sand. We need that foundation. Our children need that foundation. The world, whether it knows it or not, needs us to have that foundation! Today let's commit to faithfully pass the baton of the knowledge of God and his Word to the next generation. As we do, we'll show the world the power of a positive mom.

POWER POINT

Read: Psalm 119. Notice David's love and devotion to God's Word. Memorize a verse from this psalm that is particularly meaningful to you.

Pray: Mighty and majestic God of the universe, I praise your name. You are powerful, faithful, and just! Help me to honor you with my life and in my home. Help me to be faithful to teach my children the principles of righteous living that you have given in your Word. Show me how to teach effectively. Help me to reach the next generation for you and glorify you through everything I do as a mother. In Jesus' name, amen.

Do: Visit a Christian bookstore and purchase a children's devotional that fits the needs of your family. Then prayerfully plan a time each day when you will teach your children truths from God's Word. Be consistent, but don't get frustrated if you miss a time now and then. Keep everything age-appropriate, upbeat, and relatively brief so that your kids will look forward to your teaching times together and grow to love and understand God's Word.

Legacies in Literature
Teaching Character through History and the Classics

With the loss of tradition we have lost the thread which safely guided us through the vast realms of the past, but this thread was also the chain fettering each successive generation to a predetermined aspect of the past. It could be that only now will the past open up to us with unexpected freshness and tell us things that no one as yet had ears to hear.
—Hannah Arendt

Recently I purchased a book entitled *How to Think like Leonardo da Vinci* by Michael J. Gelb. I have always been fascinated by da Vinci and jumped at the chance to explore this legendary man's thought processes. I'm thankful for people like him who provide wonderful examples of courage and creativity to us all.

We need not look far to find heroes in history and in literature who teach us about life through their mistakes as well as their achievements. As positive moms, we can reach back in time and grab these stories, fables, tales, and biographies to share with our children, teaching them important lessons for their lives and their futures. As we help them develop a love for history and literature, we open up to them new worlds of opportunity to learn and grow and be enriched. They gain so much—and we do too—when we open this door of wisdom into the hearts and minds of those who went before us.

With good books as their guide, our children can explore exotic islands, parched deserts, busy subways, dark jungles, and raging rapids. They can learn how to live lives of spiritual passion and courage from the examples they see in books of brave men, resourceful women, daring adventurers, enthusiastic children, and compassionate friends. They can even learn how *not* to live from the bad examples they see of cruel teachers, unwise leaders, lazy workers, and disobedient kids.

Good resources are plentiful—you just need to know where to find them. So how and where do we start? What books are best for kids of different ages? How do we motivate our kids to read?

I'm reminded of the young mother who once asked a minister, "At what age should I begin the education of my child?"

"Madam," came the reply, "from the very first smile that gleans over an infant's cheeks, your opportunity begins."[1]

We can begin to read to our children from the moment they are born; in fact, some experts say we should begin reading to them *before* they are born since they can hear their mother's voice in the womb! Although they may not understand what the words mean, by beginning the practice of lovingly reading to our children even in infancy, we establish a routine and an interest in their impressionable minds. Soon they will recognize the rhythm and flow of poetry and nursery rhymes. They will want stories repeated over and over as they enjoy the warm embrace of our voices and the familiarity of the tales. Then, in their preschool years, we can begin to focus on establishing a pattern of reading and listening, helping our children learn to love and be attentive to stories and poems.

Gleaning from the Greats

Familiarity with classics in literature allows our children to expand their understanding of everyday communication. When young people hear the term "cry wolf," they will understand the meaning only if they've read or heard of the classic Aesop's fable. Only after reading or listening to the story of King Midas will they understand that the

"Midas touch" describes someone who has the ability to turn everything he or she touches into gold or success.

More importantly, with a knowledge and understanding of literature comes the opportunity for our kids to learn lessons from the characters in the stories. For example, the story of "The Ugly Duckling" presents a wonderful lesson about accepting people for who they are and not rejecting them on the basis of their appearance. Charles Dickens's *A Christmas Carol* shows the power of repentance and the importance of caring for others. The tales of King Arthur and the knights of the Round Table teach bravery, courage, chivalry, and devotion to God. *The Swiss Family Robinson* by Yohann Rudolf Wyss demonstrates the strength of a family working together to overcome difficult odds.

William J. Bennett, in his book *The Educated Child*, puts it this way: "Never underestimate the power of literature to teach good character. Stories and poems can help children see what virtues and vices look like. They offer heroes to emulate. Their moral lessons lodge in the heart and stay there."[2] The books we read to our kids can act as a confirmation of the values we are teaching them from God's Word.

To get the most from a good book, however, we need to do more than just read. It is important to sum up the reading time with questions such as "Was Peter obedient to his parents? What were the consequences of his disobedience? Why do you think he acted the way he did?" By drawing a conclusion to what was just read, we help our kids learn to think with discernment and clarity. With younger children, we can finish up by summarizing the main point of the story for them; with older children, we can ask them to give a summary in their own words.

Linda Karges-Bone, assistant professor of education at Charleston Southern University, says that parents can begin to introduce stories rich in value and content when their kids are about seven years old. She

My son, preserve sound judgment and discernment; do not let them out of your sight; they will be life for you, an ornament to grace your neck. —Proverbs 3:21–22

encourages parents to ask themselves the following ten questions when evaluating the worth of a book for their children (my paraphrase):

1. Has the author's work stood the test of time?

2. Did a reputable company publish the book?

3. Does the description on the book cover indicate a story with a purpose or message?

4. Do words such as "wholesome, values, or thought-provoking" appear on the book jacket or author notes?

5. Has the book won an award, such as the Caldecott Medal or Newberry Award?

6. What does the cover art portray?

7. Is the book written at or just above your child's reading age? It is good to challenge your kids without selecting something that will become drudgery for them.

8. Is the story's theme appropriate for your child? Sensitive topics such as the Holocaust have value but may be difficult for a young child to handle.

9. Do the characters have Christian mind-sets? Many suitable stories show characters behaving in "good ways" without a clear connection to God. Balance these stories with Christian literature, and take the time to discuss each story.

10. Did you preview the book? The extra time is worth the effort.[3]

Here's a list of some of the time-honored favorites to read to your kids or allow them to read when they are ready:

For Preschool and Primary Grades

Aesop for Children, Aesop

Book of Nursery and Mother Goose Rhymes, Marguerite de Angeli

Hans Christian Anderson's Fairy Tales, Hans Christian Anderson

Madeline and other books in the Madeline series, Ludwig Bemelmans

Mike Mulligan and His Steam Shovel and *The Little House,* Virginia Burton

The Courage of Sarah Noble, Alice Dalgleish

John Henry: An American Legend and *The Snowy Day,* Ezra Jack Keats

Pecos Bill, Steven Kellog

Just So Stories, Rudyard Kipling

Frog and Toad Together, Arnold Lobel

Mrs. Piggle-Wiggle, Betty MacDonald

Make Way for Ducklings and *Blueberries for Sal,* Robert McCloskey

Amelia Bedelia, Peggy Parish

Cinderella, Charles Perrault

The Tale of Peter Rabbit, Beatrix Potter

Curious George and other books in the Curious George series, H. A. Rey

A Child's Garden of Verses, Robert Louis Stevenson

The Trumpet of the Swan, E. B. White

The Velveteen Rabbit, Margery Williams

For Intermediate Grades

Little Women, Louisa May Alcott

Sounder, William H. Armstrong

Mr. Popper's Penguins, Richard Atwater

Peter Pan, J. M. Barrie

The Secret Garden, Frances Hodgson Burnett

Johnny Tremain, Esther Forbes

Selections from Poor Richard's Almanack, Benjamin Franklin

The Wind in the Willows, Kenneth Grahame

The Jungle Book and *Captains Courageous*, Rudyard Kipling

The Chronicles of Narnia series, C. S. Lewis

Tales from Shakespeare, Charles and Mary Lamb

A Wrinkle in Time, Madeleine L'Engle

Sarah, Plain and Tall, Patricia Maclachlan

The Borrowers, Mary Norton

Black Beauty, Anna Sewell

Call It Courage, Armstrong Sperry

Heidi, Johanna Spyri

Treasure Island, Robert Louis Stevenson

Charlotte's Web and *Stuart Little*, E. B. White

Little House on the Prairie, Laura Ingalls Wilder

Swiss Family Robinson, Johann Rudolf Wyss

For Older Readers (Age 12 to Young Adult)

Anna Karenina, Leo Tolstoy

Anne Frank: The Diary of a Young Girl, Anne Frank

David Copperfield and *Oliver Twist,* Charles Dickens

Gulliver's Travels, Jonathan Swift

The Illiad and *The Odyssey,* Homer

Jane Eyre, Charlotte Brontë

Kidnapped, Robert Louis Stevenson

The Lord of the Rings trilogy, J. R. R. Tolkien

The Merry Adventures of Robin Hood, Howard Pyle (editor)

Moby Dick, Herman Melville

The Old Man and the Sea, Ernest Hemingway

The Prince and the Pauper, Mark Twain

The Red Badge of Courage, Stephen Crane

Robinson Crusoe, Daniel Defoe

The Scarlet Letter, Nathaniel Hawthorne

The Story of King Arthur and His Knights, Howard Pyle (editor)

20,000 Leagues under the Sea, Jules Verne

The Yearling, Marjorie Kinnan Rawlings

History's Heroes

Like literature, history is a great teacher. "For in history you have a record of the infinite variety of human experience plainly set out for all to see," wrote the Roman historian Livy, "and in that record you can find for yourself and your country both examples and warnings: fine things to take as models, base things, rotten through and through, to avoid."[4] History is rich with pictures of humanity at its best and its worst, and our children grow from the lessons of both. They recognize villains who illustrate bad character as well as heroes who accomplish noble feats. Most importantly, they find that certain truths stand throughout all generations and cultures. They see for themselves that the presence of faith and godly standards help preserve nations and people.

Unfortunately, most modern textbooks downplay or ignore many historical truths that are rooted in biblical faith, replacing them with a revised, "politically correct" record that is both inaccurate and unfriendly to God. As a result, we often must go back to older writings in order to glean from the great lessons history has to offer us. Personally, I enjoy searching for old printed treasures in antique shops. While my husband looks for deals on furniture, I look at the old books! I have found many dated and out-of-print gems that offer delightful and dramatic retellings of history—books such as *When They Were Children: Stories about the Childhood of Great Men and Women* by Amy Steedman, which includes wonderful lessons on faith, courage, perseverance, and character building that we can share with our kids.

Even old textbooks and school readers give us a peek at a history too easily forgotten. As I began to read *McGuffey's Fifth Reader* (the 1879 edition) to my family, I stopped and wept over the beautiful devotion to God expressed in its pages. Our children need to know that our early American forefathers grew up and developed character based on the teaching of God's Word in their classrooms.

Barnes's Elementary History of the United States was a reader used in American schools about a century ago. In the following excerpt about Abraham Lincoln, we are not only reminded of Lincoln's insatiable love for reading, but we see that he aspired to greatness after reading about a hero from history:

> One book that made a great impression on Abe was *Weems's Life of Washington*. He read the story many times. He carried it with him to the field and read it in the intervals of work. Washington was his ideal hero, the one great man whom he admired above all others. Why could not he model his own life after that of the Father of his Country? Why could not he also be a doer of noble deeds and a benefactor of mankind? He might never be President, but he could make himself worthy of that great honor.[5]

Think about it. Abraham Lincoln's reading of history spurred him on to want to be like George Washington! If reading about one of history's heroes could so inspire a young man who lived a simple life in a log cabin, what could it do for our children?

One of my favorite books is *The Light and the Glory* by Peter Marshall and David Manuel. It tells the wonderful, true story of America's godly heritage. I encourage you to read it to your kids, or purchase the children's version so they can read for themselves about the patriotism and faith of our Founding Fathers. *The Book of Virtues* compiled by William J. Bennett is another wonderful resource of literature and history for your entire family to enjoy.

The writings by Washington, Lincoln, and Ben Franklin are interesting family reading, as are good biographies. Again, I prefer to find old biographies from used or antique bookshops because I know they have not been touched by revisionist history.

Providing the Motivation

One lesson we learn from history and experience is that men and women work best when they are properly motivated. When it comes to kids and reading, we would do well to apply this truth in our homes. How can we motivate our children to read some of the marvelous books we bring to them? Try some of the following ideas or mix and match the requirements with different rewards:

- If they read for a certain number of hours during the week, take them out for their favorite meal at a local restaurant or offer some other special activity. Keep a tally of their hours on a chart or chalkboard.

- If they read a certain number of books or pages over a set period of time, provide a monetary reward.

- Allow them to earn television or video game minutes by writing a brief summary about the book they've read.

- For younger kids, adjust the requirement to *listening* to a certain number of books in order to earn their reward—perhaps a trip to their favorite store, reaching into grab bag of goodies, or having a friend over.

Use a chart that you post in the pantry or closet to tally your children's accomplishments. I've found that for school-age kids, this motivation system works best in the summertime, since they are sometimes too busy with their homework during the school year to do extra reading. Still, you can use the time you spend in the car going to and from activities to listen to great literary classics read aloud on tape.

Your efforts, I promise, will be well worth it! In the April 1999 Focus on the Family newsletter, Dr. James Dobson noted six key principles that God has provided as a value system for mankind. They are:

1. Devotion to God

2. Love for others

3. Respect for authority

4. Obedience to divine commandments

5. Self-discipline and self-control

6. Humbleness of spirit

As positive moms, we need to teach our children God's value system using all the resources available to us. The first and foremost resource, of course, is the Bible. But in addition to God's Word, we can supplement our children's education and help them work godly principles into their lives by reading great literature and learning from history. Don't hesitate to start reading to and with your kids. A world of adventure, excitement, and inspiration awaits!

POWER POINT

Read: Proverbs 4. Notice the value Solomon places on listening to instruction and holding on to wisdom. Stories from history and literature bring us wisdom from generations past. Underline all the verses that refer to listening and learning.

Pray: Holy and wonderful Lord, all wisdom and understanding come from you. You are the Creator of all men and women throughout history. Thank you for the opportunity to walk forward into the future having learned from the experiences of others before me. Thank you for the wonderful literature you have provided through the pens of men and women you've inspired. Help me to pass on great truths—your truths—to my children. Help me to raise heroes in the faith within my own family, and thank you for lovingly guiding me in the process. In Jesus' name, amen.

☺ **Do:** Locate some of the books mentioned in this chapter and begin reading them with your children. Talk about the lessons learned from the stories.

Visit an antique shop and search for old books which tell the stories of great men and women of faith. A book resale shop can also provide a multitude of treasures for your family.

Principle #7

THE
POWER
OF
Love and
Forgiveness

Love is an act of endless forgiveness,
a tender look which becomes a habit.
—Peter Ustinov

*A mother's love is like a circle; it has no beginning and no ending.
It keeps going around and around, always expanding,
touching everyone who comes in contact with it.*
—Art Urban

*Bear with each other and forgive whatever grievances you may have
against one another. Forgive as the Lord forgave you. And over all these
virtues put on love, which binds them all together in perfect unity.*
—Colossians 3:13–14

A House of Compassion
How to Sincerely Express Love

Where does love begin? It begins at home. Let us learn to love in our family. In our own family we may have very poor people, and we do not notice them. We have no time to smile, no time to talk to each other. Let us bring that love, that tenderness into our own home and you will see the difference.
—Mother Teresa

At first glance you might think you don't need to read this chapter. Loving your family comes easily to you. It's natural. You're a mother, and love is what mothers do, right?

We are all very familiar with that warm sense of motherly love anchored deep in our hearts for each of our children. But how does that love show itself in our homes? Is it evident in how we treat and speak to our loved ones? It is one thing to proclaim our love for our families and feel it inside; it is another thing to live it out in our daily lives. There are times when we know deep inside that we love our children; but when we are tired and we have just weathered another sibling battle and cleaned up yet another cup of spilled milk, our words and actions may not show it.

I remember a Christmas many years ago when I hired a baby-sitter to play with the kids (then ages three-and-a-half and two) while I went upstairs to a spare bedroom to wrap Christmas presents. It took hours to get all of the packages wrapped just the way I wanted them. When I paid the baby-sitter, I figured it was money well spent.

Several days later, I found myself cooking in the kitchen while the girls played happily upstairs. Suddenly I realized I had heard neither an argument nor a cry for more than forty-five minutes. I hurried up the stairs and noticed small giggles coming from the spare room. You guessed it—my sweet dumplings had gleefully torn the paper off of every present I had so painstakingly wrapped! I must admit my response at that moment was less than loving. In a split second my holiday cheerfulness turned into a winter storm. I wouldn't have wanted anyone to gauge my motherly love based on my words and actions at that moment!

For some mothers, "action" is not the problem. We go through all the motions of what we think is expected of us, day in and day out. But if we're honest with ourselves, we'll admit that we're operating out of duty or guilt or peer pressure or something else. And if our actions are not motivated and accompanied by love, we are spinning our wheels.

Love and action go hand in hand. First Corinthians 13 is considered the "Love Chapter" of the Bible, and in verses 1–3, Paul emphasized the importance of love being evident in our actions:

> If I speak in the tongues of men and of angels, but have not love, I am only a resounding gong or a clanging cymbal. If I have the gift of prophecy and can fathom all mysteries and all knowledge, and if I have a faith that can move mountains, but have not love, I am nothing. If I give all I possess to the poor and surrender my body to the flames, but have not love, I gain nothing.

Romans 12:9 says it another way: "Love must be sincere." What does sincere love look like in word and in deed? In 1 Corinthians 13, Paul provides a description. Read verses 4–7 and see if your love passes the sincerity test. Every time you see the word *love* or *it*, insert your first name:

234

Love is patient, love is kind. It does not envy, it does not boast, it is not proud. It is not rude, it is not self-seeking, it is not easily angered, it keeps no record of wrongs. Love does not delight in evil but rejoices with the truth. It always protects, always trusts, always hopes, always perseveres.

Now are you convinced that this chapter is worth reading? We all could use a little help, hope, and encouragement in pursuing sincere love for our families. Consider the following personalized version of 1 Corinthians 13:1–7:

1 Corinthians 13 (A Mother's Version)

If I correct your manners at the dinner table, but do not have love, I am only a clanging dinner bell. If I take you for your annual doctor's visit and to story time at the library, and if I stop off at the mall to buy you new shoes, but I have not love, I am nothing. If I give you clean laundry every day and keep the house perfectly straight, but have not love, I gain nothing.

Love kisses the boo-boo before scolding about running in the house. Love encourages creativity instead of worrying about the possible mess. Love carefully disciplines and always forgives. Love doesn't sweat the small stuff. Love smiles and hugs. Love takes the time to look you in the eyes and listen to your side of the story.

Sometimes a mother's love is proclaimed to be unconditional and all-encompassing, closer to God's love for his children than any other love on earth. But love is difficult, even for mothers. A mother's love is much more than that warm feeling that welled up inside of us when we held our babies for the first time. It requires selflessness, patience, and self-control—and a day-in, day-out commitment to demonstrating the sincerity of our love through our actions. No doubt we could all use a few pointers!

What Love Is Not

Before we go any further in our discussion of how to truly love our families, let's establish three things that love is *not:*

1. Love is not letting our kids get away with anything they want to do. As we will learn in the next chapter, if we love our children, we will discipline them. Saying yes to everything a child wants to do is sometimes the easiest course, but it does not show love. On the contrary, we show our kids true love when we set limits and give them boundaries. It takes selfless discipline and strong love to say no when we know what is best for our kids.

2. Love is not giving our children everything they want. In our affluent, fast-paced society, many busy moms feel guilty for not spending enough time with their kids, so they buy them things to make up for their lack of commitment. Other mothers shower their kids with gifts whenever they fly off the handle or lose their tempers, as if presents were apologies. Some divorced moms buy gifts in exchange for being named the "favorite parent." But love does not equal material gifts!

3. Love is also not being a doormat for our children. Some mothers seem to believe that if they truly love, they will allow their kids to take advantage of their selfless actions. No, allowing young people to abuse our selflessness is not a healthy love! There are important boundaries to draw if we want to serve our families with sincere love and also help our children to grow into balanced, self-sufficient adults.

Kerri was a single mom who felt guilty about her divorce and about not spending as much time as she used to with her son, Joey. So when she was home she did everything for Joey, thinking this was a way to show him love. If he was watching TV and said he wanted some ice cream, Kerri would get it. If he didn't like the way his shirt was ironed, she would iron it again. If he wasn't happy with his Christmas gifts, she would take them back and get him exactly what he wanted. Kerri thought that she was loving her son, but instead she was creating a self-centered monster who knew just how to take advantage of his mother!

The Power to Love

Unfortunately, you and I are not capable of producing sincere love in our own strength. We can't demonstrate 1 Corinthians 13 by trying to stir up happy thoughts or warm, fuzzy feelings. We need help. And fortunately, that help is ready and waiting. The Bible says:

> Dear friends, let us love one another, for love comes from God. Everyone who loves has been born of God and knows God. Whoever does not love does not know God, because God is love. This is how God showed his love among us: He sent his one and only Son into the world that we might live through him. This is love: not that we loved God, but that he loved us and sent his Son as an atoning sacrifice for our sins. Dear friends, since God so loved us, we also ought to love one another. No one has ever seen God; but if we love one another, God lives in us and his love is made complete in us. (1 John 4:7–12)

This Scripture passage explains why it is so important for us, as positive moms, to demonstrate sincere love and compassion toward our families: *because this is how they begin to get a glimpse of God's love for them.* No one has seen God. But if we love one another, then the people around us—our families most of all—see a portion of what God's love is like.

These verses also explain how we find the power to love. Sincere love doesn't come from inside us. The Bible tells us that love comes from God, because God is love. The source of love, the essence of love, is not that we loved God, but that he first loved us and sent his son, Jesus, to purchase our salvation through his death on the cross. Now that's love in action! Jesus himself said, "Greater love has no one than this, that he lay down his life for his friends" (John 15:13). God showed us—and continues to show us—the true nature of sincere love.

This is the type of love we are to have for our children. It's a sacrificial love, a love that looks past mistakes and sin and loves even when love isn't deserved. As positive moms, we need to ask God to help us on a daily basis to love our families as he loves—with sincerity, compassion, and mercy. The greatest gift we can give our kids is sincere love that reflects the Father's love for his own children.

Forgive Because You Are Forgiven

Forgiveness is one of the major characteristics of God's love that's absolutely crucial in our homes. Forgiveness does not mean overlooking wrongs that are done, but rather not holding a wrong continually over a family member's head. Remember the story of my kids unwrapping all of the Christmas presents? Can you imagine what that Christmas would have been like in our household if I had continued to grumble and complain and remind the girls of their huge error?

We all know the sense of relief we feel when we are forgiven. Not long ago I was driving to a speaking engagement in Dallas. I was running a bit late (as usual) and not watching my speedometer. Sure enough, just as I was about to pull into the parking lot of the church where I was to speak, I looked in my rearview mirror and saw a policeman on a motorcycle waving at me. I was quite sure he was not just saying hello! I pulled over and rolled down my window.

"Officer, I am so sorry," I said. "I was not paying attention to how fast I was going. I am on my way to speak at that church over there, and I'm running late." Then I added, "By the way, how fast was I going?"

The policeman smiled and assured me that I was going well over the posted speed limit. Then he asked to see my driver's license and proof of insurance (expired of course, since I always forget to put the updated card in the car). He looked up at me and then at the church.

"Okay, go on," he said. "But don't do it again."

A surge of relief ran through my veins. "Thank you, officer," I exclaimed as he walked back to his police car. "I will certainly try!"

That policeman forgave me, even though I didn't deserve it. He offered me mercy when what I deserved was a ticket. We all need mercy, don't we? We all mess up, we disobey, and we live for ourselves. I'm so thankful our heavenly Father forgives us and shows us mercy when we least deserve it!

Forgiveness is a big part of true, sincere love. Psalm 103:8–14 is a beautiful account of God's love, mercy, and forgiveness toward his people:

> The LORD is compassionate and gracious, slow to anger, abounding in love. He will not always accuse, nor will he harbor his anger forever; he does not treat us as our sins deserve or repay us according to our iniquities. For as high as the heavens are above the earth, so great is his love for those who fear him; as far as the east is from the west, so far has he removed our transgressions from us. As a father has compassion on his children, so the LORD has compassion on those who fear him; for he knows how we are formed, he remembers that we are dust.

There are times when our children need mercy, and there are times when our children need punishment. As wise, loving mothers, we must exercise discernment in every situation. If our children deliberately disobey, they must be disciplined in order to learn to be obedient. But if our kids make foolish errors, what they may need is a healthy dose of forgiveness— as I received from the police officer. Let's say my daughter forgets to take

Dear children, let us not love with words or tongue but with actions and in truth. —1 John 3:18

☺

out the garbage because she has been up most of the night studying for a history final. She doesn't deserve mercy, but she needs it! If you and I will be generous with forgiveness toward our children, we will be presenting them with the godly compassion expressed in Psalm 103.

If our children's actions do require punishment, however, we must still follow up that punishment with forgiveness. We can't hold grudges against our kids. Why? Because God forgives us of all of our sins, and we ought to forgive others also. This principle is stated and restated in Scripture numerous times (for example, in Ephesians 4:32 and Colossians 3:13).

Our forgiveness needs to be tempered with loving wisdom, however. Even as we forgive our children, we may need to use caution, withhold a privilege, or follow through with appropriate consequences so that they learn from the experience. Take, for example, a young teenage boy who spends the night at a certain friend's house and is caught sneaking out at night. After punishment and forgiveness, his parents would be wise to employ a healthy caution before allowing him to spend the night at that friend's house again.

Reflecting the Love of God

I love to look at a full moon on a clear night, don't you? Many weary travelers have found their way home by the light of the moon; many lost wanderers have found their path illuminated by its glow. But while a full moon gives off great light, it does not produce the light itself. No, the moon's humble, dusty surface simply reflects the light of the sun. The sun's light is so powerful that even its reflection offers light to all who simply look up!

A mother's love is like the moonlight. The love that pours from her is actually a reflection of the incredible love of our heavenly Father. Do you relish and enjoy his love? Spend some time each day reading his love letter to you—the Bible. As you ponder God's incredible, everlasting love for you, you will begin to shine with his love in your home.

God is love; you and I are simply humble reflectors of love's ultimate source. And just as the moon acts as an instrument of the powerful light of the sun, so we are instruments of God's love to our families. What a privilege! May our loved ones see the continual glow of the Father through us each day!

POWER POINT

Read: Romans 5:1–11. Reflect on the awesome love of God that is poured into our hearts. Memorize Romans 5:8 as a constant reminder of God's demonstration of love to us.

Pray: Great and Holy God, God of love and mercy, I praise you for being the ultimate source of love. Thank you for loving me first and sending your son to purchase my salvation. You show me what sincere love is! Help me to reflect that love in my home, and help my children to learn about your love as they see it reflected in my life. I love you! In Jesus' name I pray. Amen.

Do: Spend some quiet time alone reflecting on God's abundant love for you. Play soft praise music in the background as you read scriptures that remind you of God's love. (You can start with the passages used in this chapter.) Write down a prayer of thanks for his love, mercy, and compassion toward you.

Affirmative Training
Disciplining Your Children with Love

My son, do not despise the LORD's discipline and do not resent his rebuke, because the LORD disciplines those he loves, as a father the son he delights in.
—Proverbs 3:11–12

My first year as a teacher was an education—for me as much as for my students. I was a seventh-grade math teacher in a public school with a minimum of classroom experience under my belt. My greatest challenge: how to maintain discipline while teaching pre-algebra to students who had little interest in the subject.

Generally speaking, new teachers fall into one of two categories when it comes to discipline. The Drill Sergeants start off the year using overly strict measures in order to maintain stern and impersonal control over the students. On the opposite end of the spectrum, the Popularity Contestants start off with a minimum of discipline, trying to be liked by their students and hoping that respectful relationships will result. Seasoned teachers, of course, have learned to find a wise and practical balance between these two extremes.

Finding the right approach to discipline can be equally challenging to us as positive moms. Depending on our personalities, we each tend to implement slightly different philosophies in the training of our children. Even happily married spouses can differ as to the best form of correction to use with their kids. But despite the variety of viewpoints that exist, we can still identify several key principles for disciplining our children with love—I call it "affirmative training"—that can apply in every home.

Discipline should be a positive experience. Of course, it may not seem positive for the recipient at the time! But in the long run, if discipline is handled with love, it can effectively teach and train our kids to live effective, self-controlled, fulfilled lives. Now that's positive! Hebrews 12:11 says, "No discipline seems pleasant at the time, but painful. Later on, however, it produces a harvest of righteousness and peace for those who have been trained by it." Our goal in affirmative training is not to make discipline a *pleasant* experience for our children, but to teach and train them to live lives that honor God in a positive way.

Disciplining the Three *D*s

Wouldn't it be great to have a flow chart that could lead us through the issues of parenting and discipline? If our child does A, then we punish with B. If our child says this, then we respond with that. But there are no quick or easy methods. Godly discipline requires wisdom, discernment, and strong love in each new situation.

Fortunately the Bible has a great deal to say about our responsibility as parents to discipline our children, and God—our heavenly Father—provides us with a perfect example to follow. The Bible draws a clear comparison between God's discipline and the discipline we need to show to our own children:

> My son, do not make light of the Lord's discipline, and do not lose heart when he rebukes you, because the Lord disciplines those he loves, and he punishes everyone he accepts as a son.
>
> Endure hardships as discipline; God is treating you as sons. For what son is not disciplined by his father? If you are not disciplined

(and everyone undergoes discipline), then you are illegitimate children and not true sons.... Our fathers disciplined us for a little while as they thought best; but God disciplines us for our good, that we may share in his holiness. (Hebrews 12:5–10)

God, our wonderful heavenly Father, loves us—and therefore he disciplines us. He prods us and leads us for our own good. He disciplines us with a loving hand. I'm so thankful that God doesn't treat each one of us exactly the same, aren't you? He knows us individually. He understands the unique aspects of our sinful nature and lovingly disciplines us, using methods tailor-made for us.

We, too, can train our children with love, not anger or frustration. Affirmative training and discipline is based on the fact that we discipline those whom we love. Our children can rest in the assurance of our love when we show them that we care enough to take the time to lead them and correct them.

Getting to the Heart of the Matter

A large part of disciplining our children with love involves resisting the temptation to focus solely on correcting negative behavior. Instead, we must realize that our children's actions are an outgrowth of what is in their heart. Jesus said, "For from within, out of men's hearts, come evil thoughts, sexual immorality, theft, murder, adultery, greed, malice, deceit, lewdness, envy, slander, arrogance and folly" (Mark 7:21–22). He also said, "The good man brings good things out of the good stored up in his heart, and the evil man brings evil things out of the evil stored up in his heart. For out of the overflow of his heart his mouth speaks" (Luke 6:45).

Dealing with behavior only is like trying to put a bandage on the hurting arm of a man who is having a heart attack. The pain in the arm is a result of the heart problem, and a bandage won't fix the problem. As we lovingly discipline our children, we need to tend to their heart problem first.

In his book *Shepherding a Child's Heart,* Dr. Tedd Tripp encourages parents to learn to work back from a child's behavior to the heart issue—to expose the heart struggles involved in a certain behavior and help the child see that he or she has been created for a relationship with God.[1] Doing so requires effort, however, and a commitment to communicate with our children. Often, dealing with a behavior or a simple surface issue seems like the easier, quicker route. It's especially tempting when we're tired, angry, busy, or all three. But good communication— the kind that expends both time and effort to find out what is truly going on inside the hearts of our children—goes hand in hand with positive discipline.

Take the situation of an eleven-year-old daughter on a Sunday morning who is crying and begging not to go to church. The quick and easy response would be "Stop crying and get in the car. We are going to church whether you like it or not. Hurry up, because you are making us late."

But good communication that gets to the heart might sound more like this:

Mom: "Why are you crying?"

Daughter: "Because I'm having a bad hair day, and I don't want to go to church."

Mom: "I think your hair looks great. Does it really matter if your hair is not perfect?"

Daughter: "Yes! The seventh-grade girls in Sunday school make fun of us sixth graders. I don't want them to laugh at me because my hair is funny."

Mom: "So it's not that you don't want to go to church; you just don't want to face those girls with your less-than-perfect hair. Let's go on to church, because whether your hair looks perfect or not, we still need to go, right? Now let's talk about how you can have confidence with those seventh graders...."

Do you see how this mother is beginning to expose the heart issue here? She is following an important biblical principle: "Everyone should be quick to listen, slow to speak and slow to become angry, for man's anger does not bring about the righteous life that God desires" (James 1:19–20). Because she has made the extra effort to find out what is motivating her daughter's Sunday morning tantrum, this mom can now go on to encourage her daughter about feeling confident despite what others think or say. She can talk about the reason we go to church in the first place. She is still going to make her daughter go to church, but no doubt the girl will go with a much lighter heart than she would have under the first scenario. Both mother and daughter have learned something because they took the time to really communicate.

If our children are still toddlers, of course, we may not be able to get to the heart of a particular behavior through in-depth conversation. Still, we can take a moment to examine a situation and consider the possible underlying issues before rushing in and dealing only with the negative actions. Even at this early age, communication should go hand in hand with the discipline we apply. Younger children can be taught to understand the importance of choosing God's ways instead of their own way through loving, affirmative training.

Discipline for the Three *D*s

The word used for discipline in the Bible refers to the chastening, training, or instructing of our children. It is not to be confused with the

Parents must get across the idea that "I love you always, but sometimes I do not love your behavior." —Amy Vanderbilt

word for punishment. As we instruct and chasten our children, however, we may need to make use of punishment, particularly when it comes to three important areas of negative behavior. They are easily remembered as the three *D*s: disobedience, disrespect, and dishonesty. Children must learn at an early age that negative consequences will follow any of the three *D*s.

The Bible confirms the effectiveness of punishment in such cases. Proverbs 22:15 says, "Folly is bound up in the heart of a child, but the rod of discipline will drive it far from him." Some people, citing this verse, believe in using an actual rod (or wooden spoon or paddle) to administer punishment, while others believe the "rod of discipline" refers to punishment in general. Either way, one thing is clear: punishment needs to hurt in order to be effective in stopping negative behavior. Remember the passage from Hebrews 12 that we cited earlier? Discipline is not pleasant; it's painful. But the end result is "righteousness and peace for those who have been trained by it" (v. 11).

Six-year-old Susan had an attitude of disrespect for her mother, disobeying and talking back to her on a regular basis. Susan's mom tried to stay on top of the situation, using what she thought was loving discipline with each infraction. If Susan spoke disrespectfully, her mom would respond, "Off to your room for another ten minute time-out!" But over time Susan's behavior did not improve; in fact, it got worse. Why? Because Susan loved to go to her room and play with her dolls and toys. Not only did her punishment not hurt, she enjoyed it!

We must carefully consider the form of punishment we use with our children. If a particular penalty doesn't seem to bother the recipient, we need to come up with something else. We need to ask, "What motivates this child—and what will hurt enough to provoke a positive change?"

Even children within the same family may require different forms of punishment. In my home, one of my daughters is money-motivated. I have learned that an effective punishment for her is to take away some of her allowance. She will feel it painfully! My other daughter, however, could care less if I took away her allowance. For her, real pain is to miss out on one of her favorite television shows. Knowing their differences in interest and motivation helps me administer punishment that works.

Whatever form of punishment you choose, however, you can enhance its effectiveness by following three steps.

1. Communicate with your children. Make sure they understand why they are being punished. Have them repeat to you, "I am being punished because _____." This not only helps them understand the purpose of the punishment, it also allows them an opportunity to confess their guilt. Make an effort to examine the heart issue behind the negative behavior and search out some scriptures that can be applied to the situation.

2. Punish immediately and without anger. The punishment for the behavior should be meted out as soon after the offense as possible. Set a limit—say, "ten minutes in time-out" or "no telephone for the weekend." Then follow through and be consistent. Ephesians 6:4 reminds us, "Do not exasperate you children; instead, bring them up in the training and instruction of the Lord." Many parents make the mistake of handing down a lengthy or open-ended punishment that they will either forget about or not be able to follow through on. A long, drawn-out punishment loses its effectiveness. Make the penalty short, immediate, and effective.

3. Renew the relationship. Once the punishment has been administered, it is important to make sure your children know they are loved and forgiven. This does not detract from the punishment, but rather reminds them that although you love them, you don't approve of their behavior. They need to know your love is not performance-based, just as God's love is not performance-based. Pray together, asking God to help them to overcome the temptation to repeat the wrong behavior.

Positive Motivation

According to some schools of thought, parents should never use negative discipline; we should use only positive reinforcement to train our children. But as we have already seen, that is not God's philosophy. In addition to the Scripture passages we've already mentioned, the Book of Proverbs talks often about using "the rod of discipline" (for example, in Proverbs 10:13; 22:15; and 23:13–14).

Still, there are times when positive reinforcement can be used to motivate children in a certain direction. We might, for example, offer them a reward for good grades or for keeping their room straight all week. If we overuse positive reinforcement, however, our kids can become programmed to expect a prize for everything they do. This approach encourages selfish tendencies and a mentality that says, "I will only do it if there is something in it for me." We need to teach our children from an early age that many acts of service in life should be done just because we ought to be givers, not takers.

I know. You don't want to be known as a "mean" mom. Me either. Our kids will not always agree with the discipline we use; but trust me, they will come to appreciate it in time! As evidence, read the following essay, published October 28, 1999, on CNSNews.com. The author is unknown:

We had the meanest mother in the whole world!

While other kids ate candy for breakfast, we had to have cereal, eggs, and toast. When others had a Pepsi and a Twinkie for lunch, we had to eat sandwiches. And you can guess our mother fixed us a dinner that was different from what other kids had too.

Mother insisted on knowing where we were at all times. You'd think we were convicts in a prison. She had to know who our friends were and what we were doing with them. She insisted that if we said we would be gone for an hour, we would be gone for an hour or less.

We were ashamed to admit it, but she had the nerve to break the Child Labor Laws by making us work. WE had to wash the dishes, make the beds, learn to cook, vacuum the floor, do laundry, and all sorts of cruel jobs. I think she would lie awake at night thinking of more things for us to do.

She always insisted on us telling the truth, the whole truth, and nothing but the truth. By the time we were teenagers, she could read our minds.

Then, life was really tough! Mother wouldn't let our friends just honk the horn when they drove up. They had to come up to the door so she could meet them. While everyone else could date when they were 12 or 13, we had to wait until we were 16.

Because of our mother we missed out on lots of things other kids experienced. None of us have ever been caught shoplifting, vandalizing other's property, or ever arrested for any crime. It was all her fault.

Now that we have left home, we are all God-fearing, educated, honest adults. We are doing our best to be mean parents just like mom was. I think that's what's wrong with the world today. It just doesn't have enough mean moms anymore.

What about you? Are you a mean mom? If we're going by the definition above, I hope so! A positive mom lovingly disciplines her children.

She examines the heart issues and trains her kids to live obedient lives that glorify God. She uses punishment with wisdom and discernment. She uses positive reinforcement carefully. The results are not guaranteed, but the potential for blessing and fulfillment is enormous. As Proverbs 6:23 says, "For these commands are a lamp, this teaching is a light, and the corrections of discipline are the way to life."

POWER POINT

Read: Genesis 3, the story of Adam and Eve as they disobeyed God. Notice how God handled the situation through communication, punishment, and forgiveness.

Pray: How wonderful you are, Almighty God! You are the perfect Father. Help me to learn to discipline through your example. Help me to be wise and discerning as I train my children, and may their hearts be drawn to you in the process. Give me the courage and the love to discipline, even when it's not popular to do so. May my children grow to honor you with their lives. In Jesus' name, amen.

Do: Set aside a time with each child in which you talk about God's love and his guidelines for living. Help them to understand that when they disobey or show disrespect or dishonesty, they are stepping out of God's plan, and consequences will follow. Read Psalm 25 together.

Conclusion

Upward Bound
Continuing to Grow in the Schoolroom of Life

For the LORD *gives wisdom, and from his mouth come knowledge and understanding. He holds victory in store for the upright, he is a shield to those whose walk is blameless, for he guards the course of the just and protects the way of his faithful ones.*
—Proverbs 2:6–8

"No fair. *You* don't have to go to school." I hear these words from my kids quite often these days. I remember saying them to *my* mom, too, especially during those challenging junior high years when it seemed as though school would never end. But the truth is, I am still in a classroom. You are too. It may not look like the classrooms we remember, with desks, chairs, and blackboards. But life is its own kind of classroom, and we are in the continuing education course called Motherhood 101.

Each day we take in new knowledge, building on the lessons we've learned from both our mistakes and our victories. Experience is one of our teachers, but there are others. Our friends, family members, and mentor moms are excellent teaching assistants, and we learn from their wisdom and example. Books on parenting—ranging in topic matter from effective discipline to potty training—also help. Then there are the two important instructors God provides: his Word and his Holy Spirit. These represent two sources of powerful wisdom for our daily lives.

Do the classes ever stop? No. The curriculum may change, but we will never arrive at the point where we can say, "Now I know it all." We may move on to courses such as Empty Nest 101 and Grandmotherhood 101, but we are still assimilating new information and experiences. When we're faced with new challenges, we need to tell ourselves the same thing we tell our kids when they face difficult times in their studies: "Don't give up! Don't be discouraged when you make a mistake! Grow from it, learn from it, and become better because of it!"

In the introduction you read a Bible verse that is my theme scripture as a positive mom: "A wise woman builds her house" (Proverbs 14:1). As this verse indicates, you and I are builders. We are shapers of our children's world. We set the attitude and atmosphere in our homes. Yes, we make mistakes along the way, but we can use our failures as opportunities to learn and grow and become better, more positive moms.

How does a positive woman build her home? One brick at a time! She uses bricks of support and encouragement, of positive discipline, of loving forgiveness. She uses bricks formed from her positive example in word and deed. To these, she adds bricks of strong moral conviction based on the foundation of God's Word. She never forgets the important bricks of daily prayer. And, of course, she sets the Lord Jesus Christ as the cornerstone for the whole building.

The wise woman who builds her house is not the only woman mentioned in Proverbs 14:1, however. Solomon, the writer of Proverbs, also describes the foolish woman: "With her own hands the foolish one tears [her house] down." How does a foolish woman tear down her home? Whining and complaining are two destructive influences that come to mind off the bat. Anger and bitterness are another two that have the potential to destroy a marriage and a home. Then there are the negative influences that a foolish woman allows to enter her home through the media or through friends, chipping away at the foundation of God's moral standards. A foolish woman does not use discernment in limiting her children's exposure to these destructive influences.

A foolish mother's example is reckless and harmful, leading to faithlessness and moral decay among her family members. She is too busy to pray. In fact, she is too busy for many things. A foolish woman tends to overload her schedule with activities and interests that make her tired, frazzled, and irritable. She continually screams her demands at her children instead of gently prodding them and training them in the way they should go.

A foolish woman has forgotten her power source. She relies on her own strength instead of leaning on God's abiding love and help.

No Regrets

We all have regrets as mothers. We know what we could have done differently or what could have been said with a more even temper. But recognizing that we all make mistakes, we must forgive ourselves and move on. God has forgiven us through Christ; how can we do less? "Regret is an appalling waste of energy; you can't build on it; it's only good for wallowing in," says Katherine Mansfield.[1] Instead of wallowing in regret, we must learn from our mistakes, commit to doing better, and keep moving forward.

Of course, we don't use the fact that we are forgiven as an excuse to continue in mistakes or wrongdoing. True repentance means that we turn from our sin 180 degrees and go in the other direction. But once we turn in that opposite direction, we start walking. The apostle Paul was a man who had many reasons for regret. Before he became a believer, he persecuted Christians and even helped put some to death. Paul could have spent the rest of his life wallowing in sorrow for what he had done, crushed under the overwhelming weight of guilt and remorse. Most likely, he did grieve over what he had done—but then he moved on. He was confident that God had a plan for his life, and he made himself available for that purpose.

In Philippians 3:12–14 we find Paul's famous statement about moving forward and not looking back. He declared that he wasn't perfect—just faithful in following God's direction for his life. Can you relate Paul's message to your personal calling as a mother?

> Not that I have already obtained all this, or have already been made perfect, but I press on to take hold of that for which Christ Jesus took hold of me. Brothers, I do not consider myself yet to have taken hold of it. But one thing I do: Forgetting what is behind and straining toward what is ahead, I press on toward the goal to win the prize for which God has called me heavenward in Christ Jesus.

God has given us a high calling as mothers that can be summed up this way: *Our calling is to honor Christ in raising our families and building our homes.* This brief sentence encompasses the many roles we have in life—wife, mother, nurturer, teacher, disciplinarian, and so much more. Notice our job is to honor Christ, not to create perfect kids. The results of our efforts are not up to us, they are up to God. As we stay connected to him as our power source and employ the principles he sets forth in his Word, the Bible, we will become the positive moms we want to be.

As we come to the end of this book, my prayer is that the seven principles I've shared with you will give you the encouragement and direction you need to continue on your journey of positive mother-hood. Think of this book as a midday snack—an energy bar or power shake. It's not your main course or primary source of nutrition. Rather, it's a supplement—a healthy one, I hope—to your daily intake of God's nourishing Word.

Perhaps you are in the early years of parenting and need a positive "shot in the arm" to help you through these beginning stages. Perhaps you are midway through the mothering years, or even approaching the end, and you need an extra boost of encouragement to make it to the finish line. Whatever your circumstances, you can continue onward and upward by applying these seven power-packed principles of a positive mom:

1. Seize every opportunity to give encouragement.

2. Stay in prayer.

3. Stop whining and keep a positive attitude.

4. Strengthen your relationships with family, friends, and mentors.

5. Set a good example.

6. Seek God's standards in life.

7. Send a message of love and forgiveness.

May the Lord bless you and give you wisdom and strength as you build your house. And may your children, your family members, your friends, and all those around you see in your life the power of a positive mom!

POWER POINT

⚙**Read:** Philippians 2–4. What positive encouragement does Paul give you? What warnings does he mention? How does this scripture passage help you to be a better mother?

♡**Pray:** Wonderful heavenly Father, you are the king of heaven, the Alpha and Omega, the creator of the universe. How wonderful to know that you are willing to help me in my home! Help me to be a positive mother. Forgive me for my past mistakes and sins. Thank you for your forgiveness through Jesus. Help me to press on in a positive direction, blessing and building my home and family. Thank you for being my power source and never leaving me. Thank you for helping me in this incredible journey of motherhood. In Jesus' name I pray. Amen.

☺ **Do:** Skim back through the pages of this book, highlighting the points you especially need to remember. Ask God to specifically help you in applying these principles to your life. Commit to reading the most important instruction book (the Bible) every day.

Notes

Chapter 1: Influence beyond Measure

1. Susan Lapinski, *God Can Handle It for Mothers* (Nashville, Tenn.: Brighton Books, 1998), 23.

2. Information courtesy of Ric Edelman, author of the national bestsellers *The Truth about Money* and *The New Rules of Money*. Edelman also hosts a weekly radio show and a live call-in television show in the Washington, D.C., area. His firm, Edelman Financial Services, Inc., is located in Fairfax, Virginia. For additional information, see his Web site at www.ricedelman.com.

3. Thomas Huang and Karen M. Thomas, "Do Parents Rule?" *Dallas Morning News,* 7 September 1998, 1C.

4. As reprinted in *God's Little Devotional Book for Moms* (Tulsa, Okla.: Honor Books, 1995), 113. First published in *The Bible Friend*. The poem's author is unknown.

5. Mabel Bartlett and Sophia Baker, *Mothers—Makers of Men* (New York: Exposition Press, 1952), 92.

Chapter 2: The Secret to Your Success

1. Edyth Draper, *Draper's Book of Quotations for the Christian World* (Wheaton, Ill.: Tyndale House, 1992), entry #3884.

2. *The Laurel Instant Quotation Dictionary* (Mundelein, Ill.: Career Publishing, 1972), 246.

3. Carlene Ward, *God Can Handle It for Mother* (Nashville, Tenn.: Brighton Books, 1998), 114.

Chapter 3: Apples of Gold

1. Abigail Van Buren, "Dear Abby," *Dallas Morning News* (10 January 1999), 6F.

2. Glen Van Ekeren, *Speakers Sourcebook II* (Englewood Cliffs, N. J.: Prentice Hall, 1994), 124.

3. Ibid., 123.

4. Evelyn L. Beilenson, comp., *First Aid for a Mother's Soul* (White Plains, N. Y.: Peter Pauper Press, Inc.1998), 52.

Notes

Chapter 4: Great Expectations

1. Summer Sanders, *Champions Are Raised, Not Born* (New York: Random House, Inc., 1999), 5.

2. *Bless Your Heart, Series II* (Eden Prairie, Minn.: Heartland Samplers, Inc., 1990), 3.2.

3. Sanders, *Champions Are Raised, Not Born*, 22.

4. Van Ekeren, *Speakers Sourcebook II*, 174.

5. Donald Clifton, "A Predictive Validity Study of the Basketball Player In-Depth Interview" (The Gallop Organization, 1988).

Chapter 5: The Beauty of a Smile

1. Dale Carnegie, *How to Win Friends & Influence People* (New York: Pocket Books, 1981), 69–70.

2. Michael Collopy, *Works of Love Are Works of Peace* (Fort Collins, Colo.: Ignatius Press, 1996), 123, 125.

Chapter 6: A Positive Mom Is a Praying Mom

1. *God's Little Devotional Book for Moms*, 77.

2. Collopy, *Works of Love Are Works of Peace*, 103.

3. John Blanchard, comp., *More Gathered Gold* (Hertfordshire, England: Evangelical Press, 1986), 233.

4. Ibid., 234.

Chapter 7: Casting Your Cares

1. Van Ekeren, *The Speaker's Sourcebook II*, 399.

2. Ibid.

3. Corrie ten Boom with John and Elizabeth Sherrill, *The Hiding Place* (New York: Bantam Books, 1974), 29.

4. O. Hallesby, translated by Clarence J. Carlsen, "What Is Prayer?" *Intercessor*, Coral Ridge Ministries (November 1990, Volume 1, Number 3), 1.

Chapter 8: Women of Prayer

1. Lindsey O'Connor, *Moms Who Changed the World* (Eugene, Ore.: Harvest House Publishers, 1999), 49–61.

2. *God's Little Devotional Book for Moms*, 231.

3. Blanchard, *More Gathered Gold*, 232.

4. Ralph S. Cushman, *Spiritual Hilltops: A Pocket Prayer Book* (Nashville, Tenn.: Upper Room Press, 1941), 49.

5. Blanchard, *More Gathered Gold*, 232.

Chapter 9: The Ladies Pity Party

1. Van Ekeren, *Speakers Sourcebook II,* 47.

Chapter 10: Attitude of Gratitude

1. Charles R. Swindoll, *Strengthening Your Grip* (Nashville, Tenn.: Word Inc., 1982), 206. All rights reserved. Used by permission of Insight for Living, Anaheim, California 92806.

2. Used with permission of the author.

3. Eleanor H. Porter, *Pollyanna* (Boston, Mass.: Colonial Press, 1920), 43–45.

4. Colleen O'Connor, "Smile, Smile, Smile," *Dallas Morning News,* 25 March 2000, 1G.

Chapter 11: The Challenges of Life

1. Van Ekeren, *Speakers Sourcebook,* 26.

2. Kenneth W. Osbeck, *101 Hymn Stories* (Grand Rapids, Mich.: Kregel Publications, 1982), 145.

3. Ibid., 26.

4. Jack Canfield, Mark Victor Hansen, Jennifer Read Hawthorne, Marci Shimoff, *Chicken Soup for the Mother's Soul* (Deerfield Beach, Fla.: Health Communications, Inc., 1997), 113–14.

Chapter 12: Harmony with Hubby

1. Gary D. Chapman, *The Five Languages of Love: How to Express Heartfelt Commitment to Your Mate* (Northfield Publishers, 1996).

2. James C. Dobson, *Love Must Be Tough: Proven Hope for Families in Crisis* (Nashville, Tenn.: Word, 1996).

Chapter 13: Affirming Friendships

1. Alan Loy McGinnis, *The Friendship Factor* (Minneapolis, Minn.: Augsburg Publishing House, 1979), 25.

2. *The Laurel Instant Quotation Dictionary,* 139.

Chapter 15: Living Lesson Books

1. *The Never Ending Story* (Warner Brothers Family Entertainment, 1984).

2. Van Ekeren, *Speakers Sourcebook II,* 135.

3. Bil Keane, "The Family Circus," *Dallas Morning News,* Sunday, 16 January 2000.

4. Croft M. Pentz, ed., *The Speakers Treasury of 400 Quotable Poems* (Grand Rapids, Mich.: Zondervan Publishing House, 1963), 159.

Chapter 17: Living by the Book

1. From correspondence with author.

2. Josh McDowell, *Right from Wrong* (Dallas, Tex.: Word Publishing, 1994), 12.

3. *God's Little Devotional Book for Moms,* 39.

4. William J. Johnstone, *George Washington the Christian* (Milford, Mich.: Mott Media, 1985), 19.

5. Ibid.

6. W. Herbert Burk, F.D., *Washington's Prayers* (Norristown, Penn.: Published for the Benefit of the Washington Memorial Chapel, 1907), 87–95.

Chapter 18: Legacies in Literature

1. *God's Little Devotional Book for Moms,* 38.

2. William J. Bennett, Chester Finn, and John Cribb, *The Educated Child* (New York: The Free Press, 1999), 534.

3. Linda Karges-Bone, Ed.D., "A New Look at Old Books," *Christian Parenting Today,* July/August 1996, 24.

4. Ibid., 192.

5. Ibid., 193.

Chapter 20: Affirmative Training

1. Dr. Ted Tripp, *Shepherding a Child's Heart* (Wapwallopen, Penn.: Shepherd Press, 1995).

Conclusion: Upward Bound

1. *The Laurel Instant Quotation Dictionary,* 253.

THE
P🌸wer
of A
P☺sitive

W♥man

Karol Ladd

Contents

Power Principle #4: Becoming a Woman of Joy

Power Principle #5: Becoming a Woman of Love

Power Principle #6: Becoming a Woman of Courage

Power Principle #7: Becoming a Woman of Hope

Acknowledgments

Thank you to my precious family, Curt, Grace, and Joy, for your encouragement, love, and support. Thank you to my dad, Garry Kinder. Your positive words and example have been a powerful influence in my life.

Thank you to my dear friends and my sweet sister for your prayers, stories, and advice.

Thank you to Howard Publishing for your continued excellence in producing quality Christian literature.

"Now to Him who is able to keep you from stumbling, and to make you stand in the presence of His glory blameless with great joy, to the only God our Savior, through Jesus Christ our Lord, be glory, majesty, dominion and authority, before all time and now and forever" Jude 24–25 (NASB).

How wonderful is it that nobody need wait a single moment before starting to improve the world?

—Anne Frank

Introduction

The Great Adventure
Living Life As an Expression of God Within

Live a life full of steady enthusiasm.

—Florence Nightingale

Are you a positive woman? By that I mean, do you want to move in a positive direction and make a lasting, positive impact in the lives of the people around you?

Often we think that a positive woman is a perky woman with a perfect life. But I'm going to let you in on a little secret: *I'm not always perky, and my life circumstances are far from perfect.* (I know that's your little secret too. Don't worry; I won't tell anyone.) The good news is we don't have to be perfect, because we have a perfect God who can use even our imperfections in an eternal, powerful, and positive way. We can be positive women simply by choosing to allow God's power and strength to pour through us. We can choose to see God's hand at work in our lives and in the circumstances around us.

Recently I ran across something called "The Ten Commandments for an Unhappy Life." It serves as a humorous reminder of the choices we face every single day: Will we enjoy the gifts and challenges life brings, or will we grumble and be miserable through the process? Will we be women of wonder or women of woe?

The Ten Commandments for an Unhappy Life

1. Thou shalt hold onto bitterness and anger.

2. Thou shalt never get too close to anybody. Keepeth all of thy relationships at surface level.

3. Thou shalt wear a glum expression on thy face at all times.

4. Thou shalt put aside play and shalt inflict upon others that which was once inflicted upon thyself.

5. Thou shalt grumble about the small stuff, forgetting the bigger picture.

6. Thou shalt forget about others' needs, thinking only of your own.

7. Thou shalt hold regular pity parties, inviting others to joinest thou.

8. Thou shalt not take a vacation.

9. Thou shalt expect the worst in all situations, blame and shame everyone around thyself for everything, and dwell on the feebleness, faults, and fears of others.

10. Thou shalt be in control at all times, no matter what.[1]

I don't know about you, but in the great adventure of life, I want to experience joy in the journey—not misery in the muck! I want my life to move in a positive direction. And since you're reading this book, I think you do too.

In the chapters that follow we will explore seven principles that, if applied, can make us positive women—women moving in a positive direction and having a positive impact on our families, our communities, our churches, and our world. These are powerful principles because they are *biblical* principles. In addition to finding delightful quotes, wonderful Bible passages, and motivating messages designed to encourage and strengthen you, you will read true stories of women who have exemplified these principles in their lives. Some stories are from the Bible, while other stories are about famous women from history or the current day. Some are about little-known women who have experienced God's strength in a mighty way and stand as living examples to us all.

Each chapter closes with a Power Point section that allows you to use this book for your own personal growth or for a study with other women in your church or neighborhood. In each Power Point you will find a Bible passage to read and several questions to ponder. Don't miss this opportunity! As great as it is to read a book, I believe it's even better to ponder the implications and reflect on the ideas presented in the text. When I was growing up, one of my favorite Sunday school teachers lived at a unique intersection in Dallas: at the corner of two streets named Pensive and Ponder. I think we should all live at the corner of Pensive and Ponder, figuratively speaking. We need to take the time to ponder and reflect upon God's wonderful words to us.

Each Power Point also includes a suggested Bible verse to place in your heart or memorize. (A simple plan for memorizing scripture is presented in chapter 5.) It also has an action plan to stimulate you to apply and put "feet" on what you have just learned. I'm sure you will find these applications simple yet helpful and even fun. This book is meant to be an energy boost for your spirit. It is a quick read with deep truths. It can be a lifestyle changer, if you'll let it.

Perhaps you're asking, "Can any woman be a positive woman? Can someone who tends to be negative, fearful, or unhappy change her attitude and perspective on life?" Yes! Yes! Yes! Every woman has the potential to be a positive woman, because each of us has the opportunity to invite God to work in our lives. We have the choice to

His divine power has given us everything we need for life and godliness through our knowledge of him who called us by his own glory and goodness. —2 Peter 1:3

273

look to a wonderful heavenly Father and seek his salvation, power, and strength. After all, the qualities of a positive woman are ultimately the qualities of our awesome God. As God works in us and through us, he is able to conform us to his image. And that's the key: It's his work in us, not our own.

The psalmist recognized the positive qualities of God when he declared:

Praise the LORD, O my soul; all my inmost being, praise his holy name. Praise the LORD, O my soul, and forget not all his benefits—who forgives all your sins and heals all your diseases, who redeems your life from the pit and crowns you with love and compassion, who satisfies your desires with good things so that your youth is renewed like the eagle's.

The LORD works righteousness and justice for all the oppressed....The LORD is compassionate and gracious, slow to anger, abounding in love. He will not always accuse, nor will he harbor his anger forever; he does not treat us as our sins deserve or repay us according to our iniquities. For as high as the heavens are above the earth, so great is his love for those who fear him; as far as the east is from the west, so far has he removed our transgressions from us. (Psalm 103:1–12)

Isn't our heavenly Father wonderful? His desire is to love and forgive us, to be gracious to us. He lifts our lives out of the pit of our circumstances and crowns us with love and compassion. He lovingly teaches us how to live according to his righteousness. He doesn't hold grudges. He is slow to anger. He satisfies and renews our spirits.

As God's children, we have a reason to be enthusiastic about life! I love that word, *enthusiasm*. We tend to think of enthusiasm as excitement or passion, but its original meaning is "supernatural inspiration or possession by God." It actually comes from two Greek words, *en theos*—literally, "God within." By definition, then, all Christians should be automatically enthusiastic!

But is that what the people around us see? Can they see our enthusiasm? Can they see God within us?

Given the fear, grief, and turmoil that dominates our world (particularly since the events of September 11) there has never been a more important time for the love of God to shine through positive women. If you and I will choose to live life as an enthusiastic expression of the God who lives within us, we will become beacons that shine forth love, faith, wisdom, prayer, joy, courage, and hope in a world that desperately needs each of these qualities. We will have a powerful, positive impact for Christ in our homes, our communities, and beyond.

Never underestimate the power of a positive woman. And that woman can be you!

Prtrait
OF A
Psitive
W♥man

Light tomorrow with today.

—Elizabeth Barrett Browning

May our Lord Jesus Christ himself and God our Father,
who loved us and by his grace gave us eternal encouragement
and good hope, encourage your hearts and
strengthen you in every good deed and word.

—2 Thessalonians 2:16–17

It's a Girl Thing
Relishing the Unique Qualities of a Woman

I praise you because I am fearfully and wonderfully made;
your works are wonderful, I know that full well.

—Psalm 139:14

Let's play a quick game of Jeopardy. What do the following activities have in common?

- Spending an hour and a half looking at tools in a hardware store.

- Playing thirty-six holes of golf in 103-degree weather.

- Sitting on metal chairs in freezing temperatures watching men beat each other up over a little brown ball.

- Using the remote control to switch to seventeen different stations in less than ten seconds.

- Getting angry when the remote is lost or strategically misplaced.

- Fishing for hours while saying a total of five words the entire time.

If your answer is "What activities do guys typically enjoy?" you're right! Can you believe so many men actually think those activities are fun? I'd rather have my teeth pulled—at least the dentist shoots you full of Novocaine so you can't feel the pain! While it's hard for us to comprehend why anyone would enjoy lying on the frozen ground at the

279

break of dawn to hunt snow geese, men, on the other hand, cannot fathom why women would want to:

- Stroll from one end of a shopping mall to the other in search of the perfect shoes.
- Share favorite recipes over a cup of mocha java.
- Cry at romantic movies.
- Talk for hours about…
- Decorate scrapbooks together until the wee hours of the night.
- Join a garden club, book club, or Bunko group.
- Go to the rest room after dinner in pairs.
- Refresh makeup and hair every three hours.
- Have more than five pairs of black shoes.

I suppose there is a chasm of understanding between the sexes that's just too great to bridge. Even in early childhood the differences between boys and girls are obvious. I'll never forget the time I took my young daughters to see Disney's *Little Mermaid* at the theater. For some unknown reason, the movie projector malfunctioned. The manager came into the auditorium and announced that it would take about fifteen minutes to fix the problem.

As the lights went on, the little girls in the theater sat nicely in their seats and waited patiently for the movie to resume. Not the little boys! They immediately began to fill the aisles—running, playing, and forcing their mothers to chase them. Every child in the aisles was a boy (with the exception of one girl who was being chased by her brother). It was one of those hilarious moments in the observation of human nature—and a glaring example of the innate differences in the behavior and interests of boys and girls. I must admit a thought of gratitude bolted through my mind as I watched some of the frazzled mothers: *Thank you, Lord, for giving me girls!*

The differences, of course, don't end with childhood. In our home my husband, Curt, and I represent two perspectives. Curt's idea of a perfect weeknight evening is eating a home-cooked meal, inviting friends over for dessert, and sitting around talking for hours. My idea of a perfect weeknight evening is eating out at a quiet restaurant; successfully helping the kids with their homework (no griping); then curling up with a good book, a chocolate brownie, and a glass of milk while listening to soothing classical music. (Of course, this second scenario has never actually happened—but I can always dream!)

When it comes to vacations, Curt's ideal adventure would be to charter a sailboat in the Caribbean. We would man the boat along with a hired captain and visit the islands of our choice—each with a golf course on which he would play. My ideal vacation would be on a luxury cruise liner (with large master suites and gourmet food) that would visit five or six islands with the sole purpose of shopping and sunning at each.

Needless to say, Curt and I both have to make a few compromises in our relationship. But our marriage is as strong and as whole as it is today because we blend together our unique qualities and interests. We balance each other out. That's how it is in marriage and in life: God uses the differing gifts, talents, strengths, and weaknesses of men and women to make this world a better place.

I say: Let's celebrate the differences! Let's embrace our uniqueness as women, recognizing that we were created with distinctly feminine characteristics.

Distinctly Feminine

Take a moment to think how you would define a woman. Webster's dictionary defines *woman* as "an adult female person, as distinguished from a girl or a man." I'm sorry, but I think Webster missed a few important distinctions! My definition would include descriptive words such as nurturing, kind, loving, graceful, gracious, intuitive, strong, wise, creative, resourceful, sensitive, caring, courageous, and determined. What words would you add to that definition?

From Eve to Mary to Mother Teresa, God has had a unique plan for women on this earth. He created us with his own definition in mind, using our womanly strengths as well as some of our female flaws to paint an eternal picture.

Consider the beautiful and purposeful creation of the first woman, Eve. In a fascinating passage from Genesis 2, we read: "The LORD God said, 'It is not good for the man to be alone. I will make a helper suitable for him'" (Genesis 2:18). Oddly enough, all the things God had created up to that point had been declared "good." Light, water, atmosphere, vegetation, animals—they were all good. The first man, Adam, communed with God in a perfect garden paradise. Seems as though God could have stopped there. But it was not good that man was alone. God in his wisdom knew that Adam needed a completer, a helper. The world needed a woman's touch.

Verses 21–22 say, "So the LORD God caused the man to fall into a deep sleep; and while he was sleeping, he took one of the man's ribs and closed up the place with flesh. Then the LORD God made a woman from the rib he had taken out of the man, and he brought her to the man." Don't you find it interesting that God didn't form woman from the dust of the ground, as he did man and beast? No, woman was formed from man's side, demonstrating our commonality with men as human beings and yet our unique and separate creation as females.

It is fascinating to note what the Bible says about human beings as opposed to other life forms. Genesis 1:27 tells us mankind was created in God's own image. Male and female alike bear the image and likeness of God. But while you and I were created in the likeness of God, we are not *exactly* like God. Only Christ himself is "the exact representation of his being" (Hebrews 1:3). So how do we humans bear our Creator's likeness? Matthew Henry's *Commentary on the Whole Bible* points out three distinct areas:

The soul. Generally the term *soul* refers to the will, understanding, and active power found within each individual. The soul is the intelligent, immortal spirit within us.

Place and authority. Genesis 1:26 tells us that men and women have dominion or rule over all living things—that we are God's representatives for governing the Earth's lower creatures. That is our role and place of authority in this world. We also have authority over ourselves in that we have been given a free will. We have the right to make choices. What a profound gift from God!

Purity and moral virtue. At first I didn't agree with Matthew Henry on this one. As I read on, however, I began to grasp what he was saying. Before sin entered the world, Adam and Eve saw divine things clearly. Their wills complied readily and universally to the will of God, without reluctance or resistance. The first man and woman were holy and happy as they bore the image of God upon them! It's sad to think about our origin as God's image-bearers and realize the ruin sin has had upon it. Since the Fall we've been corrupt in nature—but thankfully we can put on a new self in Christ.[1]

God formed Eve, the mother of humanity, in his image and according to his perfect design. Like Adam, she had a soul; she was given a place of dominion and authority; and she reflected God's purity and moral virtue. Was she perfect? No; in fact, she was the first to succumb to temptation. But God used both her strengths and her weaknesses for an eternal purpose.

God created each of us in his image as well. Oh that we would value his creation more as we deal with others—and as we deal with ourselves! Let's hold dear the fact that we are wonderfully made by him. And let's relish the heritage we have as specially fashioned creatures designed for a unique plan and purpose in this world.

Created with a Purpose

Within the Bible and throughout history we can read about the women God has used to accomplish his purposes—some in big ways, others in seemingly small ways. All with individual strengths, all with personal weaknesses. Each with a divine purpose. Why didn't God just use men to accomplish his work? Because some purposes required the unique feminine qualities that he placed in women alone.

Let's take a brief carriage ride through history and meet some of the women who exemplified qualities that God used in great and lasting ways.

Courage. According to Edith Deen's *All the Women of the Bible*, Deborah was "the only woman in the Bible who was placed at the height of political power by the common consent of the people."[2] Deborah's courage, like that of Joan of Arc twenty-seven centuries later, was based on her faith in the LORD. She was a counselor, a judge, and a deliverer in time of war. When other leaders were afraid, she led the nation of Israel into battle and on to victory with these words: "Go! This is the day the LORD has given Sisera into your hands. Has not the LORD gone ahead of you?" (Judges 4:14). Deborah's story is told in greater detail when we look at women of courage in chapter 13.

Loyalty. Ruth is the picture of enduring loyalty in unfavorable circumstances. When her Jewish husband died and she was free to go back to her own people, she chose to stay with her mother-in-law, Naomi, and follow the God of Israel. From Ruth we have the oft-quoted statement, "Where you go I will go, and where you stay I will stay. Your people will be my people and your God my God" (Ruth 1:16).

Through her loyalty to Naomi she met Boaz, whom she later married, and had a son, Obed—grandfather of King David and a member of the lineage of Christ!

Beauty. Esther's beauty saved her people! When the king was searching for a new queen, Esther entered the royal beauty contest and won. But Esther had much more than surface beauty; she exhibited strength, courage, patience, wisdom, and faith. When a decree went out that all Israelites would be killed, Esther bravely went before the king, wisely invited him to a series of banquets, and carefully chose her moment to plead their case. Her actions resulted in the saving of the Jewish people, and to this day they celebrate this victory.

Purity of heart. "Do not be afraid, Mary, you have found favor with God," the angel told the woman who would become the mother of Jesus (Luke 1:30). Humble and pure, Mary was highly favored among women as God's chosen vessel to bring his Son into the world. Her response to Gabriel reveals her precious spirit: "I am the Lord's servant. May it be to me as you have said" (Luke 1:38). Her heart was ready to serve God, and she was prepared for the great work he would accomplish through her life. In her song of praise to God, we again see that purity of heart: "My soul glorifies the Lord and my spirit rejoices in God my Savior, for he has been mindful of the humble state of his servant. From now on all generations will call me blessed, for the Mighty One has done great things for me—holy is his name" (Luke 1:46–49).

Organization. As the mother of nineteen children, Susannah Wesley (1669–1742) realized the importance of staying organized. She dedicated her children to God and made a point of spending individual time with each one each day. Her "Thirteen Rules of Child Rearing" are as applicable today as they were over two hundred years ago.[3] Because of her nurturing and caring heart, combined with organization and discipline, her children went on to make an eternal difference in this world. Perhaps you recognize two of their names: John and Charles Wesley.

Creativity. Emily Dickinson (1830–1886) is recognized as one of the greatest poets of the nineteenth century. Peggy Anderson writes of her in *Great Quotes from Great Women,* "Emily Dickinson lived intensely, finding in her books, her garden, and friends the possibilities of rich experience and fulfillment."[4] After Emily's death, over a thousand poems were discovered in her desk. She is estimated to have written a total of more than eighteen hundred poems, several hundred of which are considered to be among the finest ever composed by an American poet. Oddly enough, only a small number were published during her lifetime. Yet Emily's gift remains with us to this day, as she says in her own words: "The poet lights the light and fades away. But the light goes on and on."

Leadership. Born in 1820 as a slave in Maryland, Harriet Tubman escaped to Pennsylvania and to freedom in 1849. She earned enough money to return to the South and led her sister and her two children to freedom. Carrying a long rifle, she continued making trips back and forth from the South to the North, leading an estimated three hundred people to freedom along the secret network of safe houses dubbed the "Underground Railroad." She became known as "Moses" to her people as she led them out of slavery to a better place.

After the Civil War, Harriet opened a home for the aged and raised funds for schools for former slaves. She later worked with her friend Susan B. Anthony in the New England Suffrage Association. The impact of her love, courage, and leadership remains an example for us all.

Resourcefulness. During her high school years, Fannie Farmer (1857–1915) suffered paralysis from a stroke, causing her to discontinue her education. After her recovery she worked as a "mother's helper" and acquired a keen interest in cooking. Resourceful and determined, she went on to study cooking at the Boston Cooking School, where she eventually became the director. She was the first person to institute the use of exact measurements in recipes, thereby guaranteeing more reliable results. In her lifetime she wrote numerous books and opened her own cooking school. Certainly all women can thank Miss Farmer for her lasting contribution to the science of cooking!

Compassion. Clara Barton was known as the "Angel of the Battlefield" during the Civil War. She established several free schools during the war and organized her own band of volunteers to distribute supplies to the battlefields, often driving a four-mule wagon team into the fields herself. After the war she set up a records bureau to help families searching for missing soldiers.

Later Clara founded a military hospital in Europe during the Franco-Prussian War and was decorated with the Iron Cross for her services. It was in Europe that she first learned about the International Red Cross, inspiring her to organize an American branch in 1881. Today more than one million American Red Cross volunteers help millions of people each year.

Nurture. The entire world has been touched by the brilliance of Thomas Alva Edison, born in 1847, to whom is credited the incandescent lamp, phonograph, and microphone, among numerous other inventions. But few people realize the impact his mother made on his life. Although his teachers and classmates considered him a dunce, his mother believed in him to the point of taking him out of school and teaching him herself. Under her tutelage, he was allowed to work on experiments down in the cellar to his heart's content.

Many years later he had this to say about his mother's nurturing spirit: "I did not have my mother long, but she cast over me an influence which has lasted all my life. The good effects of her early training I can never lose. If it had not been for her appreciation and her faith in

God has a history of using the insignificant to accomplish the impossible. —Richard Exley

me at a critical time in my experience, I should never likely have become an inventor. I was always a careless boy, and with a mother of different mental caliber, I should have turned out badly. But her firmness, her sweetness, her goodness were potent powers to keep me in the right path. My mother was the making of me."[5]

Perseverance. Helen Keller showed us how to persevere and overcome great odds. Born in 1880, a severe illness left her unable to see or hear. But through the patient and persistent instruction of her teacher, Anne Sullivan, Helen went on to learn to read, write, and speak. She studied French and Greek at Radcliffe College and graduated in 1904. At the age of twenty-six she published her life story and became a well-known public figure and humanitarian. In her lifetime she lectured in over twenty-five countries and received several awards of great distinction. "It gives me a deep, comforting sense that things seen are temporal and things unseen are eternal."[6] Certainly her incredible accomplishments epitomize human potential in the face of adversity.

Mental fortitude. Marie Curie was a Polish-born French scientist who, along with her husband, Pierre, experimented extensively with uranium radiation. In 1903 the couple shared the Nobel Prize for physics with Henri Becquerel, making Marie the first woman to receive the Nobel Prize. After Pierre's death in 1906, Marie continued her research and succeeded her husband as a professor of physics at the University of Paris. In 1911 she received a second Nobel Prize in chemistry, making her the first person to receive two Nobel Prizes. Not only were her discoveries helpful to mankind, but her example laid the groundwork for women in the field of science.

Determination. Amelia Earhart was the first woman to fly solo across the Atlantic Ocean. She first took up aviation as a hobby, and after a series of record flights, she made a solo transatlantic flight from Harbour Grace, Newfoundland, to Ireland. In 1937 she attempted the first round-the-world flight traveling close to the equator. She took off on July 1 from New Guinea headed toward Howland Island in the Pacific, but her plane vanished. A naval search found nothing, and it was eventually decided that she had been lost at sea. Although her death was a mystery, her courage and determination were unquestioned.

Physical strength. Mildred "Babe" Didrickson Zaharias was named "the greatest woman athlete of the first half of the twentieth century" by the Associated Press in 1950. During her high school years she excelled in basketball, which led to playing sports in the Amateur Athletics Union (AAU). She later took up track and field and again excelled, winning gold medals in javelin and 80-meter hurdles and a silver medal in high jump in the 1932 Olympic Games. Next Babe took up golf, winning an unprecedented seventeen consecutive golf tournaments and becoming the first American to win the Women's British Open. Her success helped to open the door for women athletes in a wide variety of professional sports.[7]

Love. Mother Teresa devoted her life to working with the impoverished people of India. In 1948, through the leading of God, she began the order of the Missionaries of Charity. The sisters of the order serve as nurses and social workers, sharing Christ's love with the poor and the sick. In 1952 Mother Teresa opened the Nirmal Hriday (Pure Heart) Home for Dying Destitutes in Calcutta. She was awarded the Nobel Peace Prize in 1975 and the Presidential Medal of Freedom from the United States in 1985. Her selfless commitment to helping the poor touched nearly eight thousand people in Calcutta alone—not to mention all the rest of us who've been encouraged by her example of selfless, unconditional love.

Encouragement. In the early 1960s, Mary Kay Ash courageously invested her life savings to establish a cosmetics company that ended up revolutionizing the confidence and careers of hundreds of thousands of women. She is best known for her creed: "God first, family second, career third." Her loving encouragement gave the women who joined her company the power to reach their full potential as talented and successful individuals. She gave women hope, encouraged their faith, strengthened their confidence, and changed many lives. You can read more about Mary Kay's story in chapter 4.

Graciousness. It would be impossible to name all of the gracious ladies who have blessed this world with their kindness, hospitality, and sense of honor. Many come to mind, but one stands out in our day: Barbara Bush. As the wife of former President George Bush and mother of current President George W. Bush, her graciousness and steady influence have made an impact on the people of America over recent decades. Whether she is receiving foreign diplomats or reading to schoolchildren, Barbara's positive and gracious spirit continues to inspire us all.

Intuition. Victoria Cross Kelly is the deputy director of the PATH train system, which transports commuters between New York and New Jersey. On the morning of September 11, 2001, just minutes after the first World Trade Center tower was hit by the hijacked airliner, Kelly made the split-second decision to halt all discharge of passengers at the station underneath the Trade Center buildings. By 9:06 A.M. a rescue train had swept through the station one last time, collecting the last of the PATH workers and a homeless man who had to be coaxed onto the car. It was the last train ever to enter the World Trade Center station. Both towers had collapsed by 10:29.

It is estimated that Kelly's keen intuition and quick decision making saved three thousand to five thousand people. She admits that if her intuition had been wrong, "a heck of a lot of people would've been annoyed." But she wasn't wrong—and thousands of people are alive today because of her wise decision.[8]

You're an Original

As I look back on the lives of the women we've listed here, I think, *What a wonderful ride through history!* Our world is a better place because of the unique gifts and talents of such special females. And there are many more names we could add to the list. Untold millions of women have made a positive impact in their lifetimes—some famous, others not so well known. Yet each had a plan and a purpose in this world. Isn't it wonderful to know that God created you and me for a plan and a purpose as well?

Ephesians 2:10 says, "We are God's workmanship, created in Christ Jesus to do good works, which God prepared in advance for us to do." Dear sister, relish the thought that you are God's specially formed workmanship, designed by a perfect Creator and loving Father. You wear a designer label embossed with God's own fingerprint. And you were created to do good works that God has prepared especially for you. May you use the unique gifts, talents, and abilities he has given you to honor him, remembering that you, like me and like the women down through history, are a designer original!

POWER POINT

Read: Luke 8:3; John 20:10–18; Romans 16:1–2; 2 Timothy 1:5. Write down the names of the women mentioned in these passages and tell how God used them in unique ways.

Pray: Wonderful Creator, loving Father, faithful Lord, I praise you for your magnificent character. You are all-wise and all-powerful. Thank you for the wisdom and creativity you used as you fashioned me. Thank you for the unique qualities you have given women in general, and thank you for the characteristics you have specifically given to me. May I honor and glorify you with these gifts, talents, and capabilities. Thank you for the way you have used women throughout the ages. Please use me now to make a positive and eternal impact in this world. In Jesus' name, amen.

Remember: "I praise you because I am fearfully and wonderfully made; your works are wonderful, I know that full well" (Psalm 139:14).

Do: What is unique about you? Name some of the qualities and gifts God has given to you. (Don't say you can't think of anything—we both know there is something special about you!) In what ways can God use your strengths for a greater purpose? Make a list and dream big!

As you do this, consider the fact that God can take a small acorn and make it into a towering tree. And remember, "big" can mean many things. For you "big" may mean leading a company, teaching the Bible to a group of women, or making a difference in the life of one person. What seems small in the world's eyes may be big in the eternal scheme of things.

A Perfect Fit
Discovering Your Source of Power and Strength

Many a humble soul will be amazed to find that the seed
it sowed in weakness, in the dust of daily life,
has blossomed into immortal flowers under the eye of the Lord.

—Harriet Beecher Stowe

When shopping for clothes, I never pay full price. Pantyhose are no exception. After all, name-brand pantyhose are available at discount stores for a fraction of the cost of department stores with only one stipulation: The package is marked "slightly imperfect." Despite that marking, I have never had a problem with quality in the fifteen years I have been buying discounted hose. They have always been perfect for me.

Well, almost always. You know as well as I do that the inevitable was sure to happen—but did it have to happen when I was running late to an important high-society fashion show?

Several months ago I was scheduled to join a friend at Neiman Marcus for a fashion show featuring the best-dressed women in Dallas. In my hurry and fury to get ready, I pulled out my special-purchase pantyhose and immediately became aware that this pair was definitely less than perfect. My first indication was the fact that one leg was five inches longer than the other. Upon further examination, I realized that both legs of the hose were more than four feet long. Being only five-feet three-inches tall from head to toe, I quickly perceived that the legs were much too long for my build. I checked the box to make sure I had bought the right size, and I had. Nevertheless, these pantyhose weren't just too long for me—I think they would have been slightly too long for Andre the Giant! Inspector Number 11 must have been on her coffee break when these hose passed through her station.

"Slightly imperfect" was an understatement. These were uneven, overstretched, obviously imperfect pantyhose. I looked at them and laughed, remembering a time when I heard Florence Littauer talk about personality types. She held up a pair of pantyhose that had been labeled "slightly imperfect." Her pair had three legs! She related the hose to how we often feel slightly imperfect as people.

Would it be too much of a stretch (no pun intended) to say that I can relate to my pair of pantyhose? You see, I often feel overstretched, unbalanced, and obviously imperfect. As a friend, as a mother, as a spouse, in my work, at my church, at board meetings, I often feel as though I don't measure up to people's expectations, whether perceived or real. What about you? Is your package marked "imperfect" too?

The problem is bigger than any of us. Life isn't perfect. Circumstances aren't perfect. And people aren't perfect. But the good news is that God is a perfect fit for our overstretched, out of balance, more-than-slightly imperfect lives. He is able to make up for our imperfections and give us the strength and support we need.

If we want to experience the power of being positive women, we must fill our lives with the perfect power source. Some women believe their source of strength comes from within themselves, and certainly as women we have certain innate abilities; but in our own strength alone we will always fall short. God is our only reliable source of strength and power if we want to accomplish great and mighty things that have eternal value. As the apostle Paul said, "Christ in you" is "the hope of glory" (Colossians 1:27).

It's easy for us to put our hope in ourselves. But the Bible says the Lord delights in those who fear him and put their hope in him. Psalm 147:10–11 tells us, "His pleasure is not in the strength of the horse, nor his delight in the legs of a man; the LORD delights in those who fear him, who put their hope in his unfailing love." Over and over again, the psalmist declares that his own strength comes from the Lord. "The LORD is the stronghold [strength] of my life," he writes in Psalm 27:1 and elsewhere.

As Jesus drew near to his death, he gave his disciples a colorful illustration of God doing his work in and through them. His word picture was of a grapevine, a common plant and an important commodity in the region. Jesus said, "I am the vine; you are the branches. If a man remains in me and I in him, he will bear much fruit; apart from me you can do nothing" (John 15:5).

According to Jesus, our job is not to strive to achieve an abundant and fruitful life in our own strength. Our job is simply to remain in Christ. The words *remain in* mean to "dwell, abide, fellowship, and continue in" him. As we abide in him and he abides in us, he provides the strength, guidance, direction, and ability we need to "bear much fruit." How do we abide in him? By dwelling on his Word, remaining in his love, praying, and practicing his presence throughout the day. In subsequent chapters we will explore many wonderful ways to do each of these things.

Right now we need to ask ourselves: Is God our stronghold, or are we depending on our own strength and power to live our lives? If we want to be positive women, we must look daily to our heavenly Father for strength, support, and direction. He is more than able to work in us and through us, despite our imperfections.

Control Top or Sheer-to-Toe?

"Oh, I'm just a control freak." Have you noticed that more and more women seem to be making that confession? I'm not sure if we're getting better at recognizing and admitting our challenges, or if our hard-driving, Type-A culture is creating more people with control issues.

Of course, the desire to be in control is an age-old problem. Satan himself wanted to be like God, in authority over everything. And then there were the Pharisees. Talk about control freaks! They loaded so many rules and regulations on the Jewish people that Jesus was prompted to speak severely against them. In Matthew 23:4–5 he condemned the Pharisees, saying, "They tie up heavy loads [referring to the rules] and put them on men's shoulders, but they themselves are not willing to lift a finger to move them. Everything they do is done for men to see."

I think most of us want to be in control. But what is it that we want to control, and why do we want to control it? I can answer the first question in two words: *people* and *circumstances.* (That covers quite a bit of territory, don't you think?) Many times we want to make and mold people to fit inside our personal box of expectations. We want to control circumstances so that life will be smooth and easy and safe.

Certainly, we should not allow people to run over us, nor should we allow circumstances to run away with our lives. But neither should we demand to hold everything so tightly. We need to maintain a healthy balance in our lives by releasing those things we were never meant to control in the first place! We need to pry our grimy little hands off of the things that only God can control and look to his strength and power to take care of them.

Taking Matters into Her Own Hands

In the Old Testament, Sarai (later called Sarah) seemed to have a slight control issue. Let's begin her story by taking a brief look at Genesis 15. In a vision God told Abram, Sarai's husband, that he would have a son who would be his heir and that his descendants would be as numerous as the stars in the sky. At this point in the story, God didn't give the exact details on how this would be accomplished; he simply provided a plan with a promise.

By Genesis 16 some time had passed, the promised son had not arrived, and Sarai was itching to take matters into her own hands. From the beginning she'd had a twinge of doubt about her ability to have a baby. Now she told Abram, "The LORD has kept me from having children" (Genesis 16:2)—implying that God had not kept his promise.

We can't be too hard on Sarai. It's probably safe to assume that she had hoped and prayed for a child for years. Now she was far past the normal childbearing years. Her hope had dwindled, and her faith was tender. She had waited so long—and now the situation seemed hopeless. (Been there?) So to solve the problem herself, Sarai offered her maidservant, Hagar, to Abram, expecting Hagar to conceive and bear a child with her husband. It sounds strange to us today, I know, but Sarai was actually carrying out an ancient custom in Assyrian marriage contracts designed to ensure a male heir to a family.

It's so easy for us to turn to cultural, quick-fix solutions to our problems instead of waiting on the Lord! In our hurry-up, fast-track world, we tend to want solutions, and we want them *now*. Have you ever pleaded with God that your husband would change in a certain area, and when immediate changes didn't occur, you took on the job of "holy nudger"? Perhaps you prayed for a situation at work to get better, but when you didn't see quick results, you felt as though God had not heard your cry. Sometimes waiting on the Lord can be the hardest thing to do! But Psalm 27:14 encourages us: "Wait for the LORD; be strong and take heart and wait for the LORD."

Quick solutions rarely bring the best results. (In Sarai's case, the ramifications of her quick-fix decision are still seen in the turmoil in

My grace is sufficient for you, for my power is made perfect in weakness. —2 Corinthians 12:9

☺

the Middle East today.) Immediate gratification can rob us of joys to be received or lessons to be learned from God's deeper, more thorough plan. Remember, God sees the whole picture from a heavenly viewpoint; we only see the narrow situation right before our eyes. Isaiah 55:8–9 reminds us of God's eternal perspective and our own lack of sight: "'For my thoughts are not your thoughts, neither are your ways my ways,' declares the LORD. 'As the heavens are higher than the earth, so are my ways higher than your ways and my thoughts than your thoughts.'" These faith-building words help us recognize that we don't understand everything—but God does.

When faced with a problem, each of us must ask ourselves: Are we willing to trust God's Word and allow his purpose to be worked out in our lives? Or are we going to jump in and try to fix things ourselves? As Isaiah 55 makes clear, God understands our situation much better than we do. We're probably not the best ones to be calling the shots!

Let's rejoin Abram and Sarai and see how God's plan continued to unfold for them. In Genesis 17 God spoke again to Abram, this time telling him specifically that Sarai would have a son and that the covenant promise would be through this son. Interestingly, God also changed Abram's name to Abraham and Sarai's name to Sarah at this point. Both Sarai and Sarah mean "princess." But in announcing Sarah's new name, God added these words: "I will bless her and will surely give you [Abraham] a son by her" (Genesis 17:16)—thus making her name both royal and rich with promise.

In Genesis 18 God assured the couple once again that Sarah would have a son. But watch Sarah's response:

Then the LORD said, "I will surely return to you about this time next year, and Sarah your wife will have a son." Now Sarah was listening at the entrance to the tent, which was behind him. Abraham and Sarah were already old and well advanced in years, and Sarah was past the age of childbearing. So Sarah laughed to herself as she thought, "After I am worn out and my master is old, will I now have this pleasure?"

Then the LORD said to Abraham, "Why did Sarah laugh and say, 'Will I really have a child, now that I am old?' Is there anything too hard for the LORD? I will return to you at the appointed time next year and Sarah will have a son."

Sarah was afraid, so she lied and said, "I did not laugh."

But he said, "Yes, you did laugh." (Genesis 18:10–15)

I have to chuckle a little at the "No I didn't; yes you did" episode, but don't we all have times when we want to hide our shortcomings? Who are we trying to fool? God sees everything, so we might as well confess! In Sarah's case, when God made it clear that his plan was for her to have a baby, she laughed to herself—but God heard her. He recognized her lack of faith, yet loved her through her doubt. "Is anything too hard for the LORD?" he asked in Genesis 18:14, reminding both Abraham and Sarah that with God, nothing is impossible.

The truth is, our need to be in control of a person or a situation is most often a reflection of our lack of faith in God to protect us, lead us, and provide for us in his timing. Are you struggling with doubt? Worried about the future? Perhaps you are having trouble with a relationship. Maybe you feel as though you will never see victory over a sin that has gripped you. Take comfort in the fact that nothing is too hard for God! Trust him with your greatest longings, your deepest needs, and your strongest doubts. He is with you, and he sees far beyond what you see.

Whether God's plan is clear to us or still a bit sketchy, we need to lay down the control panel and let him navigate. But we must not misunderstand what it means to give God control of our lives. It doesn't mean we have no responsibilities or decisions to make. We still must act upon our duties and respond to the opportunities he sets before us. Giving God control doesn't mean that we sit back and do nothing; it means that we move forward in wisdom, let go of the need to control or hurry the process, and trust God to do his divine work.

Fits Like a Glove

One time Corrie ten Boom held up a common, white, ladies' glove to her audience and asked the question, "What can a glove do?" She went on to remind her listeners of the power and influence a woman can have if she relies on God for her strength:

The glove can do nothing. Oh but if my hand is in the glove, it can do many things...cook, play the piano, write. Well, you say that is not the glove, that is the hand in the glove that does it. Yes, that is so. I tell you that we are nothing but gloves. The hand in the glove is the Holy Spirit of God. Can the glove do something if it is very near the hand? No! The glove must be filled with the hand to do the work. That is exactly the same for us: We must be filled with the Holy Spirit to do the work God has for us to do.[1]

Oh, dear friends, we have a powerful God! Is anything too hard for him? And to think that we, as women who have chosen to follow Jesus, have his Spirit living within us! God's Spirit dwells in us, empowering us to live, to walk, and to achieve eternal tasks for his glory. Hear the words of Paul to the Christians in Rome: "But if Christ is in you, your body is dead because of sin, yet your spirit is alive because of righteousness. And if the Spirit of him who raised Jesus from the dead is living in you, he who raised Christ from the dead will also give life to your mortal bodies through his Spirit, who lives in you" (Romans 8:10–11).

Is that not simply amazing? Think about it: The same Spirit of him who raised Christ from the dead dwells within us! Paul was an incredibly powerful and influential apostle, yet he didn't hesitate to say, "For when I am weak, then I am strong" in Christ (2 Corinthians 12:10). He knew that Jesus is the perfect fit for our glove of human weakness, inability, and imperfection.

When I was a counselor at Pine Cove Camp in East Texas, one of my responsibilities was to serve as a lifeguard during the afternoon swimming sessions. In my official training course, I learned that one of the most difficult challenges for a rescuer is to assist swimmers who are struggling and hysterical. When victims are thrashing about in the water and trying desperately to stay afloat, they put the lifeguard in great danger of being pulled under with them. But if they release their struggle and relax in the safe hold of the lifeguard, then the lifeguard's strength can pull them to safety.

I like to picture our release to God in the same way. So often we struggle to solve life's battles in our own strength, and our efforts do nothing but wear us out and pull us under. But when we release our lives to God and trust that he holds us safely in the palm of his hand, we allow his strength and power to see us through.

What exactly does it mean to release our control to God? What does it mean to release our will, our strength, and our power to him? What does it look like on a daily basis? We're not talking about a month-by-month commitment or a year-to-year deal; we're talking about a daily commitment to submit to God's authority. Jesus told his disciples in Luke 9:23–24, "If anyone would come after me, he must deny himself and take up his cross daily and follow me. For whoever wants to save his life will lose it, but whoever loses his life for me will save it." Sounds a lot like the lifeguard situation, doesn't it?

Consider the scenario of two women—I'll call them Tonya and

Susan—each with daughters in kindergarten. Tonya's daughter was one of the younger kids in the class and struggled with several of the basic skills that would be needed for first grade. The teacher recommended that the little girl spend a year in a pre–first-grade class before moving up to the next grade level. Tonya became angry and upset at the idea; she didn't want her daughter to be held back while most of her little friends moved up to first grade.

Tonya never thought to pray about the situation. Instead she argued, complained, and forced the issue with the school administration. With misgivings the principal finally okayed her daughter's move to first grade. Unfortunately, the girl struggled in class the next year and fell behind the other students. She became defeated and discouraged—an attitude that ended up influencing her entire school career.

Meanwhile, Susan was also told that her daughter was not quite ready for first grade. Although Susan was a little surprised and saddened, she listened to what the teacher had to say about her daughter's lag in developmental skills. Over the next few weeks Susan studied the situation and collected pertinent information on child development and success in school. She also began to pray for wisdom and direction, recognizing that God knew exactly what was best for her daughter. She turned over to God any worry or need to control the situation.

In the end Susan decided to put her daughter in the pre–first-grade class for the next school year. Her decision was based on wise counsel, much thought, and faith-filled prayer. The class was, of course, a perfect fit! When her daughter eventually entered the first grade a year later, she was at the top of her class. Her success and sense of accomplishment positively colored the rest of her school experience.

How often do we hold on to an idea of what we think is best rather than resting in the safe care of the Lord? We need to remember that resting in the Lord—giving God the control panel—doesn't mean that we stop doing what it takes to reach our goals. It means that we pray and actively trust God with our goals, our work, and the outcome. It means that as we move forward, we do so believing that he loves us and wants what's best for us. We know he sees a much bigger picture than we ever could.

Jars of Clay

Several years ago we bought a chiminea—a giant clay pot that sits on a stand outdoors. The chiminea has a large hole in the body of the pot and another opening in the top, making it the perfect receptacle in which to burn pinion wood. The wood is not burnt so much for warmth as it is for the wonderful, woodsy aroma it produces. It smells as though we are in Colorado. And since we're in Dallas, that's a treat! The scent can be picked up all over the neighborhood. Many times we will light the wood in the chiminea just before dinner guests arrive, and they consistently comment on the heavenly smell.

The Bible says that you and I are like clay pots. Look with me at 2 Corinthians 4:6–11:

> For God, who said, "Let light shine out of darkness," made his light shine in our hearts to give us the light of the knowledge of the glory of God in the face of Christ. But we have this treasure in jars of clay to show that this all-surpassing power is from God and not from us. We are hard pressed on every side, but not crushed; perplexed, but not in despair; persecuted, but not abandoned; struck down, but not destroyed. We always carry around in our body the death of Jesus, so that the life of Jesus may also be revealed in our body. For we who are alive are always being given over to death for Jesus' sake, so that his life may be revealed in our mortal body.

In Paul's time it was customary to hide personal treasure in clay jars. Because the pots were common and had little beauty or value, they didn't attract attention to themselves or to the precious contents contained therein. What a contrast—treasure in clay pots! Yet that describes us to a *T*. God's all-surpassing power and greatness is placed in common, frail, and unworthy containers known as men and women. Who would have guessed? Paul recognized his weaknesses; yet because of what was inside of him, he was able to move forward powerfully in God's strength. We can too.

Our lives in Christ are like that chiminea I mentioned a moment ago. The scent that permeates the environment, the light that pours forth into the darkness, and the warmth that dispels the cold are the result of the fire within us. God's power takes an unlikely yet willing receptacle and uses it in a mighty way.

Fanny Crosby was a perfect example of a chiminea for God. She was a woman who shined for Christ, allowing God's Spirit to light the world through her, even though her own life was darkened by blindness. Despite her handicap, Fanny wrote an estimated eight thousand gospel songs. Think about that staggering number! Not eighty songs, which would have been quite an accomplishment for anyone. Not eight hundred songs, which would have been a heroic feat. But an overwhelming *eight thousand* songs poured forth from this woman who had a heart for God and a willing hand to write. Given the physical obstacles she faced, we know that this was nothing short of miraculous!

Born into a humble household in Southeast, New York, in 1823, Fanny became blind at six weeks of age due to improper medical treatment. She was educated at the New York School for the Blind and eventually served as a teacher at the school. Her early writing was in secular verse; but through the influence of W. B. Bradbury, a popular church musician of the day, she began writing gospel song lyrics in her early forties, becoming, in her words, "the happiest creature in all the land."

Her gifting and her heart for God were obvious from an early age. When she was eight years old she wrote the following poem:

Oh, what a happy soul am I!
Although I cannot see,
I am resolved that in this world
Contented I will be.
How many blessings I enjoy
That other people don't;
To weep and sigh because I'm blind,
I cannot, and I won't.[2]

Fanny went on to write such well-known hymns as "Blessed Assurance," "All the Way My Savior Leads Me," "Rescue the Perishing," and "Saved by Grace." It has been said that she never wrote the lyrics to a hymn until she had first kneeled in earnest prayer and asked for God's guidance.

In his book *101 Hymn Stories,* Kenneth W. Osbeck notes that "Fanny J. Crosby died at the age of ninety-five. Only eternity will disclose the host of individuals who have been won to a saving faith in Jesus Christ or those whose lives have been spiritually enriched through the texts of her many hymns."[3] On her tombstone is engraved a simple verse: "She hath done what she could." Certainly she was a clay pot who allowed God's power to pour forth through her.

A Motley Crew

St. Augustine said, "Beware of despairing about yourself; you are commanded to put your trust in God, and not in yourself."[4] When I think about the twelve disciples Jesus chose to carry on his kingdom work, I think about what an unlikely group of people they were. Their band included several fishermen, a tax collector, a zealot, and some demanding brothers. They certainly were not trained in the finest schools in the country or prepared for great speaking careers. But God didn't call them to trust in their own abilities. He called them to trust in him. Through his power, direction, and strength, they were able to become Jesus' mouthpieces to spread the good news about the kingdom of God.

If God purposed to use this motley crew to spread the Gospel to the world, what can he do with willing vessels like you and me? The answer has nothing to do with our power and ability—and everything to do with his! What is your source of power and strength? Remember, God's Holy Spirit is at work in your life to accomplish the job he is calling you to do as a positive woman in this world. He's the fire in the pot, the hand in the glove. He's the perfect fit!

POWER POINT

Read: John 6:5–15, the story of Jesus feeding the five thousand. What did the little boy in this passage have to offer? What part did he have in the miracle? What part did God play? Notice how many people were blessed through this boy's willingness combined with God's power. What personal message do you think the disciples received from this experience?

Pray: Dear Lord, Light of the world, I praise you for shining your light through me. I know that I am only a jar of clay in the Potter's hands. Help me to be a willing vessel and not an anxious or controlling woman. Mold me with your powerful touch. Fill me with your wonderful Spirit. Allow your work to be done in my life, using both my strengths and weaknesses for an eternal purpose. I trust you to faithfully lead me because you are my loving heavenly Father. In Jesus' name, amen.

💡 **Remember:** "Is anything too hard for the LORD?" (Genesis 18:14).

☺ **Do:** Set aside thirty minutes to an hour and spend some time alone with God for the specific purpose of releasing your life to him. Ask him to reveal areas where you tend to demand control. Release these areas to him one by one, asking for his power and strength to walk forward with him at the control panel of your life.

Power Principle #1

Becoming A Woman of Faith

Faith does not operate in the realm of the possible.
There is no glory for God in that which is humanly possible.
Faith begins where man's power ends.

—George Mueller

For it is by grace you have been saved, through faith—
and this not from yourselves, it is the gift of God—
not by works, so that no one can boast.

—Ephesians 2:8–9

3

The Race of Life
Finding a Faithful Pace for the Journey

Let us fix our eyes on Jesus, the author and perfecter of our faith,
who for the joy set before him endured the cross, scorning its shame,
and sat down at the right hand of the throne of God.

—Hebrews 12:1–2

You have to wonder about a person who would allow a twelve-foot python snake to roam free in his home. Unfortunately a young man named Grant overlooked the obvious risk, believing that his familiarity with his pet python, Damien, placed him above danger. On October 11, 1996, Grant prepared to feed Damien a chicken, just as he had the week before. Herpetologists suspect that Grant either forgot to wash the smell of the chicken from his hands, or Damien simply desired a larger prey. Whatever the reason, on that fateful day the python decided to wrap himself around Grant.

When a Burmese python is on the brink of a kill, it can move with deadly speed, and rarely can a victim elude its grasp. Grant managed to stagger into the hallway to summon help but soon collapsed in Damien's hold. With great effort the paramedics who arrived were able to uncoil the forty-five-pound, five-inch-thick reptile and hurl it into another room. Grant was rushed to the hospital.

Come to find out, Grant and his brother had been keeping a number of uncaged snakes in their apartment in the Bronx. Their mother had pleaded with them to abandon their hobby, but to no avail. Grant paid dearly for his misplaced faith in Damien the python.[1]

What is faith? According to the writer of Hebrews, faith is "being sure of what we hope for and certain of what we do not see" (Hebrews 11:1). It is a deep conviction—one that is not stagnant or complacent but dynamic in nature. It is an act of believing that overflows from our confidence that something is true or is certain to take place. Going beyond what we can see or touch or feel, we place our faith in something or someone who is worthy of trust.

Grant's problem was that he placed his faith in an unreliable source. Proverbs 13:16 reminds us, "Every prudent man acts out of knowledge, but a fool exposes his folly." Grant's actions were not based on wisdom or prudence but on foolishness. He thought he could trust his python without considering the snake's nature. A python may seem docile at times, but it is—and always will be—a predator that seeks, squeezes, and consumes in order to survive.

Unlike Grant, we must place our faith in a reliable source. But how do we know if something or someone is worthy of our trust? We consider the character (something Grant failed to do when it came to his python). I put my weight on the chair in which I am currently sitting because I have confidence it will hold me up. It is strong and sturdy, it has always held me up before, and I'm sure it won't let me down today. (My computer is another story.) When it comes to sharing my deepest, darkest secrets, I don't spill them to a known gossip but to a loyal friend—someone who has shown herself trustworthy time and time again. I can confidently place my faith in her because her character is proven.

The way we view our world and live our lives is definitely colored by our faith. Do we put our trust in our own abilities and talents? Do we place our confidence in circumstances or fate? Is our hope solely in the goodness of our fellow man? Or do we place our faith in a loving heavenly Father?

The object of our faith is important because that's what floods our lives with purpose. For me, I began to recognize a purpose in my life when I decided to place my faith in Christ. I also began to experience a deep inner peace that only comes from faith in the one true Reliable Source. You may have heard the expression "faith in Christ" before, but do you understand its implications? When we place our faith in Christ, we find both peace and purpose. Let's take a closer look at these two by-products of faith in Jesus.

Peace. "We have peace with God through our Lord Jesus Christ," we read in Romans 5:1. At an early age I learned that God is a perfect and holy God. Man, on the other hand, is sinful and imperfect (no one needed to tell me that part!). Although I was what most people would term a "good little girl," I realized back then that I couldn't earn my way to heaven. The Bible never promises that we get to go through those Pearly Gates if our good deeds outweigh our bad ones. I knew I would never be good enough—but someone else was: Jesus. He was God's perfect gift to mankind. Jesus laid down his life for us as a sacrifice so that, through faith in him, we can have peace with our God.

I will never forget that "aha" moment as a young girl when I first understood that Jesus was more than a baby whose birth we celebrated at Christmas; he was and is the Savior of mankind. At an early age I decided to place my faith in him, praying a prayer something like this:

> Dear Lord, thank you for having mercy on me. I know I am not perfect. I know I can't earn my way to heaven. Thank you for sending your Son, Jesus, to die on the cross as a sacrifice for my sin. I place my faith in him as my Savior. I believe he rose from the dead

Expect great things from God. Attempt great things for God. —William Carey

☺

to give us the hope of eternal life in heaven one day. Thank you, Lord, for your grace toward me through Jesus. In his name I pray, amen.

My prayer was simple but based on faith in a God who loves me and wants to have a relationship with me. No big lightning bolts came out of heaven that day, but I knew I had taken an important step. It was the beginning of a life of faith based on the only reliable source in this universe, God himself. Jesus came to bring peace between God and man, and because I was placing my faith in Christ, that peace was now mine.

Purpose. From that day forward I began to recognize a greater purpose in my life. I wasn't just living for myself. Life was bigger than my circumstances. Finally I understood that I have a God who loves me, who has a plan for my life. My desire became to honor him in everything I do. I realized I don't have to perform or be perfect; I just need to walk in his grace.

Often Scripture refers to the plan or purpose God has for his people. King David said, "Many, O LORD my God, are the wonders you have done. The things you planned for us no one can recount to you" (Psalm 40:5). I haven't always known God's purpose for me at different stages of my life. He doesn't reveal his intentions all at once. But step by step, as I've walked with him, I've found that he faithfully leads me according to his plan.

He Is Worthy of Our Trust

Perhaps there has been a time in your life when you've questioned, "Can God be trusted?" Maybe you've been discouraged after the tragic death of a loved one or a disappointing layoff at work or an unwanted divorce. Perhaps you feel even now that God has left you alone in the pit of life. Your faith has been shaken.

You are not alone. Even John the Baptist experienced a time of questioning as he sat in a prison cell. (You can read about it in Luke 7:18–28.) Earlier John had been the one to boldly declare about Jesus, "Look, the Lamb of God, who takes away the sin of the world!" (John 1:29). But now he was in prison, and his faith was faltering. He sent his disciples to ask Jesus, "Are you the one who was to come, or should we expect someone else?"

John could only see the immediate. Sitting in prison, he thought, *Surely this cannot be God's perfect plan. Maybe I was wrong. Maybe God has left me.* Like us, John couldn't see the big picture; he could only see the present. He didn't completely understand what God was up to.

Understanding God and his ways are one thing; trusting him in faith is another. We may have times when we are unable to understand God's thoughts or discern his plan, but we can still trust him. As our Creator and our loving heavenly Father, he has an eternal plan in mind. He sees the whole picture that you and I only see in part. First Corinthians 13:12 explains, "In the same way, we can see and understand only a little about God now, as if we were peering at his reflection in a poor mirror; but someday we are going to see him in his completeness, face to face. Now all that I know is hazy and blurred, but then I will see everything clearly, just as clearly as God sees into my heart right now" (TLB).

I remember times as a teenager when I didn't understand or like my parents' decisions. Still I knew that I could trust their parental love. My parents were especially careful about the parties I attended in junior high and high school. I was horrified when they insisted on calling the host parents of each party to make sure there would be proper supervision. They gave me a curfew that usually fell some time before the party was completely over. I didn't get my way, I didn't like it, I didn't even understand it at the time; but I knew deep inside that my parents loved me and that in doing what they did, they were looking out for my best interest. Because I knew their character, I knew they were worthy of my trust.

No Need to Guess about God

Fortunately, God didn't leave it up to guesswork when it comes to knowing his character. The Bible reveals quite a bit about God's nature. We see his omniscience and authority in the Creation. We catch a glimpse of his power in his deliverance of his people from the ruthless grip of Pharaoh in Egypt. God's patience is revealed in his treatment of the Israelites in the wilderness and through Israel's cycles of straying from the Lord and then returning to him. God's protection is evident in the story of Daniel in the lions' den. His abundant love for us is shown in the sending of his only Son, Jesus, to die for us. His omnipotence is revealed in the Resurrection. We see his kind provision for us in the sending of his Holy Spirit to dwell within us.

Then there are the numerous statements in the Bible that identify God's character:

- *He is good.* "Give thanks to the LORD, for he good; his love endures forever" (Psalm 118:1).

- *He is compassionate.* "The LORD is compassionate and gracious, slow to anger, abounding in love" (Psalm 103:8).

- *He is just.* "The LORD works righteousness and justice for all the oppressed" (Psalm 103:6).

- *He is our protector.* "God is our refuge and strength, an ever-present help in trouble" (Psalm 46:1).

- *He is our helper.* "You are my help and my deliverer" (Psalm 70:5).

- *He is eternal.* "For this is what the high and lofty One says—he who lives forever, whose name is holy" (Isaiah 57:15).

- *He is all-powerful.* "Ah, Sovereign LORD, you have made the heavens and the earth by your great power and outstretched arm. Nothing is too hard for you" (Jeremiah 32:17).

- *He is everywhere.* "Where can I go from your Spirit? Where can I flee from your presence? If I go up to the heavens, you are there; if I make my bed in the depths, you are there" (Psalm 139:7–8).

- *He is all-knowing.* "For God is greater than our hearts, and he knows everything" (1 John 3:20).

- *He is faithful.* "For great is his love toward us, and the faithfulness of the LORD endures forever" (Psalm 117:2).

- *He is perfect.* "As for God, his way is perfect; the word of the LORD is flawless" (Psalm 18:30).

Of course, I have only begun to touch on the greatness of God's character! Yet even in this short list of some of God's wondrous qualities, we can begin to get the sense that he alone is worthy of our ultimate trust. He alone is the Alpha and Omega, the beginning and the end. He is the one reliable source in whom we can confidently place our faith.

Life with a Purpose

Ten years ago I wrote a book called *Parties with a Purpose.* It's a fun book filled with ideas for creating themed parties for kids. Most people who see the title understand the "parties" part, of course, but the "purpose" part is not so obvious. Along with each party theme, I include a valuable lesson to give a specific purpose to each celebration. For instance, the "Dalmatian Sensation" party includes a brief puppet show. The show's star, Danny the Dalmatian, explains to the little partygoers that just as each Dalmatian dog has its own unique set of spots, so each person has special and unique qualities. Each of us is made by God as a unique creation. Kids and parents alike seem to enjoy the idea of putting on a party with a purpose!

What about *Life with a Purpose*? Could that be the title of your personal book? Women of faith throughout history have been motivated by their faith in God to honor him with their lives. Even when they faced hardships, their faith gave them the hope and perseverance they needed to pursue the purposes God set before them.

Take, for instance, Amy Carmichael, born in 1867 in Northern Ireland. Amy came to know Jesus Christ at an early age and had a keen sense of social concern. When she was seventeen years old she led a Sunday school class for the poor mill girls in Belfast. Her class grew to about five hundred people.

At age twenty-six Amy became a missionary to Japan but returned to Ireland fifteen months later due to illness. The next year she continued her missionary work, this time in South India. She stayed there for fifty-six years until she passed away at the age of eighty-four. Her main concern in India was for the temple slavery of little girls. As a religious rite, children were being dedicated to temple gods and given over to prostitution. Amy rescued many young people from this practice and in 1925 founded the Dohnavur Fellowship, dedicated to saving children in moral danger, training them to serve others, and spreading God's love to the people of India. About nine hundred endangered girls and boys were sheltered through the Dohnavur program.

In 1931 Amy had a serious fall that broke her leg, twisted her spine, and left her an invalid for the rest of her life. Her bedroom and her study became her world. She called this place "the Room of Peace," and it was from this room that she began writing extensively. Her written work has blessed and inspired countless thousands—including Elisabeth Elliot, another woman of faith. One of Amy's books, *If*, made

Faith is inseparable from expectations. Where there is real faith, there is always expectation. —Catherine Booth

a lasting impact on Elisabeth, who wrote: "It was from the pages of this
...book that I, a teenager, began to understand the great message of the
Cross, of what the author called 'Calvary love.'" Elisabeth eventually
wrote Amy's biography, *A Chance to Die.*[2]

What was Amy Carmichael's motivation for leaving her native
homeland, creating a refuge for young people in India, and writing
countless books of insight and inspiration? *Faith.* Faith in a loving God
who had a plan and a purpose for her life. The same faith that led
Elisabeth Elliot to minister to the Ecuadorian Aucas, the tribe that had
slain her missionary husband in the jungle several years earlier. The
same faith that led a woman who was small in stature but big in
heart—we know her as Mother Teresa—to begin a school for poor children in Calcutta. Her communities of Missionaries of Charity have
grown and expanded to spread Christ's love to the sick, needy, and
unwanted in over thirty countries.

"All we do—our prayer, our work, our suffering—is for Jesus,"
Mother Teresa said. "Our life has no other reason or motivation. This is
a point many people do not understand. I serve Jesus twenty-four
hours a day. Whatever I do is for him. And he gives me the strength."[3]

It was faith that led two Baylor University girls to share Christ's
love in predominately Islamic Afghanistan. Heather Mercer and
Dayna Curry were aware of the dangers of ministering in a country
hostile to Christianity, but they chose to step out in faith and follow
what they believed God was calling them to do. It was their faith that
gave them strength through the uncertainty of their three months in
Taliban captivity in late 2001. It was faith that kept the precious
people of Antioch Community Church in Waco, Texas, praying
around the clock for the young women's safety and release. It was
God's mercy and grace that allowed Heather and Dayna, along with six
others, to be set free.

Faith Stands Up When Our World Falls Down

Our faith in God is the anchor that holds us steady through the storms of life. It reminds us that there is an eternal picture and that this life we can see and touch is only temporary. In the introduction to her book *Tramp for the Lord,* Corrie ten Boom quotes a poem by an anonymous author that speaks of solid faith in an unsure world. She introduces the poem by saying, "Faith is like radar which sees through the fog—the reality of things at a distance that the human eye cannot see." Here is the verse:

> My life is but a weaving, between my God and me,
> I do not choose the colors, He worketh steadily,
> Oftimes He weaveth sorrow, and I in foolish pride,
> Forget He sees the upper, and I the underside.
> Not till the loom is silent, and shuttles cease to fly,
> Will God unroll the canvas and explain the reason why.
> The dark threads are as needful in the skillful Weaver's hand,
> As the threads of gold and silver in the pattern He has planned.[4]

Oh, the beauty and the blessing of trusting in our eternal heavenly Father who knows the beginning and the end! He sees the full picture; we only see this side. When the storms of life rock our boat, our faith in God allows us to rest our full weight in his safe and loving arms.

As we saw the awful events of September 11 unfold, we also saw people reaching out in faith to God. Churches were flooded as men and women, young and old began looking for answers, hope, purpose, and salvation. Jim Cymbala, pastor of the Brooklyn Tabernacle in New York City, found his church overflowing in the days following the terrorist attack on the World Trade Center. More than 670 people came to faith in Christ that next Sunday. Pastor Cymbala says there has never been a moment like this in our nation's history when so many people were looking toward faith in God.[5]

Faith Is Essential

How is it that a prostitute from a pagan town could be listed among the great people of the Bible—and named as an ancestor of Christ to boot? The answer is simple: She was a woman with a firm faith in the one true God. The Book of Joshua tells the story of the Israelite spies who entered the town of Jericho and found a place to stay at the home of Rahab the harlot. (We won't ask questions about why or how the men ended up at Rahab's house.) Rahab promised to hide the spies and help them if they would spare her family in the imminent battle between her people and the Israelites. In making the offer, she revealed her motivation in a great statement of faith:

> We have heard how the LORD dried up the water of the Red Sea for you when you came out of Egypt, and what you did to Sihon and Og, the two kings of the Amorites east of the Jordan, whom you completely destroyed. When we heard of it, our hearts melted and everyone's courage failed because of you, for the LORD your God is God in heaven above and on the earth below. Now then, please swear to me by the LORD that you will show kindness to my family, because I have shown kindness to you. (Joshua 2:10–12)

Rahab had heard the stories of the mighty works of the God of Israel. Without a doubt those stories made her tremble, but they also moved her to faith, giving her the confidence to declare that "the Lord your God is God in heaven above and on the earth below." Her faith led her to put her life at risk in order to conceal the Israelite spies and help them escape the city safely. For her faithfulness the spies gave her a scarlet cord to put in her window. The approaching Israelites would see the cord, and Rahab and her family would be kept safe in the battle.

Does this remind you of another time when people were saved by something scarlet? Perhaps you are thinking of the Passover, when the Israelites were instructed to place the blood of a lamb on their doorposts so that the angel of death would pass over their homes. All who were inside, behind the marked doorposts, were safe, while the firstborn children in all unmarked homes were killed.

Both of these Old Testament instances are pictures of salvation through faith in Christ. Today we, too, are saved by something scarlet: our faith in Jesus, who shed his blood for us to save us from "the wages of sin" (Romans 6:23).

We can find Rahab listed in the great "Hall of Faith" of Hebrews 11—right next to such notable patriarchs as Noah, Abraham, and Moses! Hebrews 11:31 tells us, "By faith the prostitute Rahab, because she welcomed the spies, was not killed with those who were disobedient." Rahab is also identified in the direct lineage of Jesus in Matthew 1:5: "Salmon the father of Boaz, whose mother was Rahab...."

In God's eyes, what Rahab had been and what she had done in the past were not as important as her faith. Her faith changed her life. Rahab believed in the one true God, and as she acted on that faith, it saved her both physically and spiritually. If God can take a prostitute living in enemy territory and elevate her to a great woman of faith, what can he do with our scarred and tattered lives?

The writer of Hebrews addresses the essential nature of faith: "And without faith it is impossible to please God, because anyone who comes to him must believe that he exists and that he rewards those who earnestly seek him" (Hebrews 11:6). What about you? Have you taken a step of faith in God? Do you believe God loves you and sent his Son,

Jesus, to save you? Just as the scarlet cord saved Rahab and the Passover blood saved the Israelites' firstborn, so the blood of Christ saves us. Paul said, "Believe in the Lord Jesus, and you will be saved" (Acts 16:31). It's all about faith.

Persevere in the Journey

During my college years I decided to enter a marathon. (Yes—that's 26.2 miles of running!) In my youthful exuberance, I agreed to train with one of my Baylor friends through a rigorous twelve-week program. On the day of the race, I knew I was facing one of the biggest physical challenges of my life. But I was ready. Casting aside my warm-ups and any other weight that could possibly hinder me, I waited at the starting line along with my friend and thousands of other runners. Adrenaline flowed as the gunshot signaled the start of the race.

My friend and I parted after about the fifth mile, but I was not alone. My parents, my sister, and my boyfriend, Curt (now my husband), were all there on the sidelines to cheer me on. They held up signs throughout the race and even joined the race to run with me during some of the tough parts.

It was at about the twenty-second mile that I "hit the wall." Long distance runners are familiar with this phase. It refers to the physical and mental point you reach when you feel as though you can't go one more step. Some people stop running at this point; others give up completely. But most simply persevere through the wall, knowing that the finish line is not far away.

My goal for this race was to finish. It didn't matter to me how long it took; I just wanted to finish. When I hit the wall, all I could do was picture the finish line. I slowed my pace and even walked for a short while, but I kept the finish line foremost in my mind. I knew I would eventually get there. And when I crossed that line, the joy and the sense of accomplishment were overwhelming. The race took me a little over four hours from start to finish, but it was an epoch in my life. I learned through that experience what it means to set a goal, prepare for it, and follow through to the end.

Life is like a marathon—although many times we live it like a sprint. It is a long journey filled with both joys and difficulties. We are bound to hit the wall many times during this race of life. That's why Paul encourages us to "fix our eyes on Jesus, the author and perfecter of our faith" (Hebrews 12:2).

Where is our focus? Is it on the One who is worthy of our faith? Great women of faith have journeyed down this road before us, keeping their eyes steadfastly on Jesus. They were able to stay the course because they cast off the things that entangled them and ran with diligence to the finish line. Like Rahab, Amy Carmichael, Elisabeth Elliot, and Mother Teresa, may you and I run with perseverance the race of life marked out for us!

POWER POINT

Read: The story of Ruth in Ruth 1:1–5, 15–18, and 4:13–22. What great statement of faith did Ruth make? What steps of faith did Ruth take? How was Ruth's faithfulness rewarded?

Pray: Wonderful heavenly Father, I thank you for the peace and the purpose you give to my life. I put my faith in you because you are worthy. Help me to walk in faith, trusting you for the big picture of life. I may not understand all that you do or allow, but I trust your loving grace to see me through every circumstance. Lead me step by step in faith as I follow you. In Jesus' name I pray, amen.

💡 **Remember:** "For it is by grace you have been saved, through faith—and this not from yourselves, it is the gift of God—not by works, so that no one can boast" (Ephesians 2:8–9).

☺ **Do:** When did you first take a step in faith toward God? Write down your story so you can share it with your family and others. If you have never placed your faith and trust in Christ, perhaps this would be a good time to pray a prayer similar to the one I shared in this chapter.

Spiritual Makeover
Faith in Action: Putting on a Whole New Wardrobe

As the body without the spirit is dead,
so faith without deeds is dead.

—James 2:26

In the early eighties (okay, I'm dating myself), several cosmetic lines began a new sales technique that involved identifying a woman's best color scheme. Color consultants draped an array of colorful swatches across a woman's shoulders in order to determine which colors looked best with her natural skin tone. A woman with blond hair, blue eyes, and fair skin was typically identified as a "summer," meaning she looked her best in colors such as pink, purple, and black. A brunette with an olive complexion was most likely a "fall," implying she looked her best in browns, greens, and oranges. Dark hair and fair skin usually marked a "winter" and called for a different color scheme, while still others looked best in a "spring" palette. I had my colors done several times and consistently turned out to be a "summer."

Since I didn't know I was a "summer" until this testing, I had collected a rainbow array of clothes over the years—and not just pinks and purples. Now all the brown, green, yellow, and orange garments in my closet needed to go. I couldn't walk around in "fall" colors if I was a "summer." What a fashion faux pas! From that point on, I determined, I wouldn't be caught dead in brown. Of course, I had to pitch my old makeup colors too. No more blushes with an orange tint; it was pink all the way for me, baby!

We often make changes in our lives according to our beliefs. Some changes are bigger than others. My color makeover was based on my newfound conviction that I was a "summer." The more I learned about seasonal color schemes, the more my wardrobe began to reflect "summer" colors.

When we put our faith in Christ, our lives go through another type of makeover—a *spiritual* makeover. As we become women of faith, our behavior begins to change to reflect our newfound beliefs. Of course, our actions and behavior are not what save us in God's eyes; we are saved by his grace through faith alone (see Ephesians 2:8–9). Our works do not lead to salvation; if they did, we would have reason to be boastful. It is our faith that pleases the Lord (see Hebrews 11:6).

Still, our actions *are* important. Why? Because they are an evidence of our faith.

A Living Example

In the New Testament, James speaks heartily about the connection between faith and works: "What good is it, my brothers, if a man claims to have faith but has no deeds? Can such faith save him? Suppose a brother or sister is without clothes or daily food. If one of you says to him, 'Go, I wish you well; keep warm and well fed,' but does nothing about his physical needs, what good is it? In the same way, faith by itself, if it is not accompanied by action, is dead" (James 2:14–17).

Let's be clear. James is not saying that we please God or make it to heaven by doing good deeds. He is saying that if we have a living faith in Christ, it should be evident in our actions. The "new us" should be reflected in our behavior.

We may be able to quote all the right Bible verses and talk as if we have great faith, but unless that faith is played out in our lives, we have very little evidence that it is real. These are tough words. But as positive women of faith, it is important that we be consistent in what we say and do. My dad has often quoted a poem attributed to Edgar Guest, which speaks to the power of our actions. It's called "Sermons We See":

I'd rather see a sermon than hear one any day.

I'd rather one would walk with me—than merely show the way.

The eye's a better pupil—more willing than the ear,

Fine counsel is confusing, but examples always clear.

And the best of all the people are the ones who live their creed,

For to see the good in action is what everybody needs,

I can soon learn how to do it if you'll let me see it done,

I can watch your hands in action, but your tongue too fast may run.

The lectures you deliver may be very wise and true—

But I'd rather get my lesson by observing what you do.

For I may misunderstand you, and the high advice you give,

But there's no misunderstanding how you act and how you live.[1]

Bible scholars have wrestled for centuries over the proper understanding of faith's relationship to works. C. S. Lewis described this tension when he wrote, "The controversy about faith and works is one that has gone on for a very long time, and it is a highly technical matter. I personally rely on the paradoxical text: 'Work out your own salvation...for it is God that worketh in you.' It looks as if in one sense we do nothing, and in another case we do a...lot. 'Work out your own salvation with fear and trembling,' but you must have it in you before you can work it out."[2]

Certainly we must balance the beauty and wonder of God's grace with the powerful evidence of his grace at work in us. The works we see in our lives are not a result of our own power; they are evidence of God's Spirit working in us. God freely gives us salvation. Will he not also freely give us to the power to live it out?

I love the illustration Jim Cymbala, pastor of the Brooklyn Tabernacle in New York City, provides in his book, *Fresh Power:* "Imagine that my sister, Pat, and her husband, Frank, come over to my house for Christmas, bringing a lovely present for Carol and me. Pat greets me at the front door with a warm hug. 'Here, this is for you!' she exclaims as she hands me a large box wrapped in metallic paper and a fancy bow. 'Merry Christmas! By the way, that'll be $55, please—cash or check. Either one is fine, but I don't take credit cards.'"[3]

It is preposterous to think that someone would give us a gift and then ask us to pay for it. Well, I guess my teenagers do that sometimes. But not God! God freely gives us the gift of his Spirit to work mightily in our lives. The Holy Spirit is God's makeup artist, sent to give us a spiritual makeover—at no charge to us. Ephesians 4:30 says, "And do not grieve the Holy Spirit of God, with whom you were sealed for the day of redemption." May we never be guilty of hindering the Spirit's work!

Cleaning Out the Closet

To say that I revamped my entire wardrobe just because I found out I was a "summer" sounds silly, I know. What can I tell you? I fell victim to a trendy marketing scheme. But not all overhauls are so shallow and short-lived. For example, when I placed my faith in Christ, I had a spiritual makeover of the eternal type. You could say I became a new creation—at least that's how the apostle Paul describes it in 2 Corinthians 5:17: "Therefore, if anyone is in Christ, he is a new creation; the old has gone, the new has come!" How refreshing to begin anew, to start walking in faith, to allow God to change me from the inside out!

What does this "new creation" look like? We find descriptions of our new wardrobe throughout the Bible. In Colossians 3:1–15, Paul talks about cleaning out our closets, so to speak, and putting on new clothes. Let's take a look at his makeover advice:

> Since, then, you have been raised with Christ, set your hearts on things above, where Christ is seated at the right hand of God. Set your minds on things above, not on earthly things. For you died, and your life is now hidden with Christ in God. When Christ, who is your life, appears, then you also will appear with him in glory.
>
> Put to death, therefore, whatever belongs to your earthly nature: sexual immorality, impurity, lust, evil desires and greed, which is idolatry. Because of these, the wrath of God is coming. You used to walk in these ways, in the life you once lived. But now you must rid yourselves of all such things as these: anger, rage, malice, slander, and filthy language from your lips. Do not lie to each other, since you have taken off your old self with its practices and have put on the new self, which is being renewed in knowledge in the image of its Creator....
>
> Therefore, as God's chosen people, holy and dearly loved, clothe yourselves with compassion, kindness, humility, gentleness and patience. Bear with each other and forgive whatever grievances you may have against one another. Forgive as the Lord forgave you. And over all these virtues put on love, which binds them all together in perfect unity.
>
> Let the peace of Christ rule in your hearts, since as members of one body you were called to peace. And be thankful.

Paul covers it all, from our hearts to our minds to our actions. Living a life based on faith in Christ ought to look different than a life lived for self and the here-and-now. This overhaul is a work of God's

If faith produces no works, I see that faith is not a living tree. Thus faith and works together grow; no separate life they e'er can know; they're soul and body, hand and heart; what God hath joined, let no man part. —Hannah More

Spirit, not of our flesh. God, who began this good work in us, has promised he will carry it on to completion (see Philippians 1:6). His Spirit empowers us to live a life of love and forgiveness, and by his Spirit we are able to bear with one another and abide in unity.

Unfortunately, we see very few Christians today who are clothed in these outward signs of an inward faith. Has God's wellspring of power gone dry in our lives? Or are we failing to allow his Spirit to live mightily through us?

Wouldn't It Be Lovely?

If we truly lived in the new clothes Paul describes, wouldn't we be lovely? More than that, wouldn't people be drawn to Christ because we were living such beautiful lives of faith? Could there be a lovelier, more positive woman of faith than one who is clothed with compassion, kindness, humility, gentleness, and patience? Who bears with others and forgives them? Who exudes love and peace? A woman wearing such an outfit would be asked continually where she did her shopping, and the answer would be, "At the feet of Jesus."

Unfortunately, the world rarely sees this type of fashion show when they look at Christians and the church. Instead they see gossip and bickering, disloyalty and bitterness, jealousy and envy. Not very attractive, would you say? Oh friend in faith, if only the new look could start with you and me! Perhaps we could begin to model Christ's love to others and make a real difference in this world. The fruit of God's Spirit in our lives is beautiful. Listen to the description in Galatians 5:19–25:

> The acts of the sinful nature are obvious: sexual immorality, impurity and debauchery; idolatry and witchcraft; hatred, discord, jealousy, fits of rage, selfish ambition, dissensions, factions and envy;

drunkenness, orgies, and the like. I warn you, as I did before, that those who live like this will not inherit the kingdom of God.

But the fruit of the Spirit is love, joy, peace, patience, kindness, goodness, faithfulness, gentleness and self-control. Against such things there is no law. Those who belong to Christ Jesus have crucified the sinful nature with its passions and desires. Since we live by the Spirit, let us keep in step with the Spirit.

As positive women, may we clothe ourselves with the lovely garments of the fruit of the Spirit. May we allow God's Spirit to pour through us and touch this world with Christ's love.

Faith Accessories

Here's a phrase we hear women say quite often: "Oh, I'm just a worrier." We all seem to have anxieties in different areas of life. My mother used to worry about the house always looking clean and perfect. I, on the other hand, worry about the safety of my kids. One of my friends worries about the future. Another friend who is in sales worries about commissions. What do *you* worry about? Worry is an all-too-common thread among women, and we have grown accustomed to it in our lives. But should we?

If faith is truly at work, it leaves little room for worry or fear. An inscription at Hind's Head Inn in Bray, England, says, "Fear knocked at the door. Faith answered. No one was there."[4] Isn't that tremendous? When faith meets fear, worry and doubt disappear. According to George MacDonald, "A perfect faith would lift us absolutely above fear."[5]

How do we grow in our faith to the point that we don't worry? Oddly enough, we can glean our answer from a man in prison. The apostle Paul wrote to the Philippians, "Do not be anxious about anything, but in everything, by prayer and petition, with thanksgiving, present your requests to God. And the peace of God, which transcends all understanding, will guard your hearts and your minds in Christ Jesus" (Philippians 4:6–7). When worry and fear seem to be getting the best of you, pray! Turn your cares over to God through faith in prayer. This is a daily activity, for worries frequently seem to come back and attack us. But Paul tells us we can experience a peace that passes all understanding if we will place our worries in God's hands.

George Mueller was a man of faith. As the founder of numerous orphanages in nineteenth-century England, he depended entirely on God for food and supplies for the orphans under his care. He never asked for a dime in donations but rather, through faith, prayed about every need. God richly blessed Mueller's life of faith, and the orphans never went without. Concerning anxiety, Mueller said, "The beginning of anxiety is the end of faith, and the beginning of true faith is the end of anxiety."[6]

What would our lives look like if they were characterized by less worry and more faith? If we truly trusted God for our future, for our strength, for our direction? If we moved forward in faith instead of worrying about how to make something happen ourselves? Just think about the impact our lives would have if we were to prayerfully live a life of faith day by day. We may never be famous or have an opportunity to influence thousands of people, but if we each walk in faith right where God has placed us, together we can make a positive difference in this world.

Stepping Out in Faith

Faith is stepping forward as God directs, even when we don't know what the outcome will be. It's doing something bigger than ourselves—so big that we are dependent on God and not on our own strength and

Faith does nothing alone—nothing of itself, but everything under God, by God, through God. —William Stoughton

ability. When we step out in faith, God gets the glory, because whatever is accomplished is done by his Spirit at work through us. We can read a roster of heroes and heroines of the faith in Hebrews 11. God accomplished great things through each of these people as they simply stepped out in faith. Take a look at the lineup:

- Verse 7: "By faith Noah, when warned about things not yet seen, in holy fear built an ark to save his family."

- Verse 8: "By faith Abraham, when called to go to a place he would later receive as his inheritance, obeyed and went, even though he did not know where he was going."

- Verse 9: "By faith he made his home in the promised land like a stranger in a foreign country."

- Verse 11: "By faith Abraham, even though he was past age—and Sarah herself was barren—was enabled to become a father because he considered him faithful who had made the promise."

- Verse 17: "By faith Abraham, when God tested him, offered Isaac as a sacrifice."

- Verse 20: "By faith Isaac blessed Jacob and Esau in regard to their future."

- Verse 21: "By faith Jacob, when he was dying, blessed each of Joseph's sons, and worshiped as he leaned on the top of his staff."

- Verse 22: "By faith Joseph, when his end was near, spoke about the exodus of the Israelites from Egypt and gave instructions about his bones."

- Verse 23: "By faith Moses' parents hid him for three months after he was born, because they saw he was no ordinary child, and they were not afraid of the king's edict."

- Verses 24–28: "By faith Moses, when he had grown up, refused to be known as the son of Pharaoh's daughter....By faith he left Egypt, not fearing the king's anger; he persevered because he saw him who is invisible. By faith he kept the Passover and the sprinkling of blood, so that the destroyer of the firstborn would not touch the firstborn of Israel."

- Verse 29: "By faith the people passed through the Red Sea as on dry land."

- Verse 30: "By faith the walls of Jericho fell, after the people had marched around them for seven days."

- Verse 31: "By faith the prostitute Rahab, because she welcomed the spies, was not killed with those who were disobedient."

- Verses 32–35: "What more shall I say? I do not have time to tell about Gideon, Barak, Samson, Jephthah, David, Samuel and the prophets who through faith conquered kingdoms, administered justice, and gained what was promised; who shut the mouths of lions, quenched the fury of the flames, and escaped the edge of the sword; whose weakness was turned to strength; and who became powerful in battle and routed foreign armies. Women received back their dead, raised to life again."

Wow! Do you feel like you have just been on a roller coaster ride through the Old Testament with a park full of faithful followers? Despite all the ups and downs, each person on this ride stayed on the track of faith. Each one received a heavenly blessing—and sometimes an earthly one too.

As each one found out, stepping out in faith is no guarantee of a perfectly smooth ride in this life. In fact, some of the people who stepped out in faith were tortured, jeered, and flogged; others were chained, imprisoned, and stoned (see Hebrews 11:35–39). Clearly, a life of faith is not a life without challenges. But it is a life of victory nonetheless. The writer of Hebrews says of these faithful followers, "the world was not worthy of them" (v. 38). God's plan is bigger than the immediate; it is bigger than what we see or experience in the here and now. Who knows what great work he can and will do with our simple step of faith?

The faithful steps of these Old Testament men and women paved the way for our lives of faith today. Hebrews 11 closes with this statement: "These were all commended for their faith, yet none of them received what had been promised. God had planned something better for us so that only together with us would they be made perfect" (vv. 39–40). We may never see the full blessing of our step of faith until heaven. May we be faithful to hear his call in our lives and take the steps he directs us to take, leaving the results to him. A. W. Pink puts it this way: "Faith is a principle of life by which the Christian lives unto God; a principle of motion, by which he walks to heaven along the highway of holiness; a principle of strength, by which he opposes the flesh, the world, and the devil."[7]

A Modern-Day Woman of Faith

What can happen if we hear God's call and step out in faith? Mary Kay Ash, founder of the Mary Kay Cosmetics company, is a modern-day example of a woman of faith. Her life message was simple: God first, family second, career third. At her funeral, Reverend C. Robert Hasley said, "Mary Kay Ash was one of God's most faithful messengers. She was a saint."[8] Carolyn Dickinson, director of sales development for Mary Kay, Inc., told me this about the company and its founder:

It all began thirty-eight years ago with a dream for all women to fulfill themselves to be what God intended them to be. She stepped up to the plate and made the choice to do what he was telling her to do. Back in the early sixties, a time of injustice for women in the workplace, Mary Kay made the courageous decision to invest her entire life savings of five thousand dollars to follow God's will and change the world through compassion and hope, a lesson from which we can all learn.

Carolyn also told me about a time in 1979 when Mary Kay was interviewed on the popular television show *Sixty Minutes.* She was asked, "Mary Kay, you talk about God being your first priority. Aren't you using God to further your business?" She responded with the perfect answer: "I surely hope not. I hope he is using me." And he certainly did. At the time of her death in November 2001, Mary Kay, Inc., reported revenue of $1.3 billion. But more importantly, through her company, thousands of women's lives had been touched and changed.

Mary Kay once said, "Most people live and die with their music still unplayed. They never dare to try."[9] Certainly Mary Kay Ash dared to step out in faith. She not only acted on her faith in God, she showed her faith in people as well. She encouraged her sales force with the confidence they needed to succeed.

"She taught us well," said Mary Kay's son, Richard Rogers. "Those of us that know her and love her have benefited in our lives from her teachings. Her belief in the beautiful potential inside every human being was a cornerstone, and this became the cornerstone of everyone she touched."[10]

It has been said that Mary Kay Ash gave the women of this world a makeover, offering them the opportunity to join the working world from their own homes. I believe she also offers us a model of a woman who allowed God to give her a spiritual makeover. Her love, kindness, and inspiration—led by God's direction and done in his power—show us what a woman of faith looks like when she puts on her new wardrobe. Her life reminds us to never underestimate what God can do through a willing heart and a step of faith.

Of course, most of the positive women of faith in the world today are women we have never heard of. They are sweet, humble women who walk a life of faith step by step, day by day. They may never achieve fame, but they *are* making a positive difference in the lives of the people around them. They are the faithful prayer warriors at church, the faithful mothers encouraging their children, the faithful employees working heartily as unto the Lord. Whether the results they achieve are big or small, their reward in heaven is profound. And each one can look forward to the day when they are greeted with these words: "Well done, thou good and faithful servant."

POWER POINT

⚙ **Read:** Exodus 1:6 to 2:10, the stories of three women who acted in faith. How did the two Hebrew midwives show their faith in God? In what way did the Levite woman, who is later identified in Scripture as Jochebed (Exodus 6:20), show her faith? What was the result of her faithful actions?

♡ **Pray:** O Giver of Life, thank you for working in my life! Thank you for changing me and making me a new creation in you. In every area of my life, help me to reflect your Spirit living inside of me. I want to honor and glorify you in all I do and say. May my faith be evident as a result of your work in me. In the name of my faithful Savior, Jesus, amen.

♀ **Remember:** "And without faith it is impossible to please God, because anyone who comes to him must believe that he exists and that he rewards those who earnestly seek him" (Hebrews 11:6).

☺ **Do:** Take time to listen to God. Is he telling you to step out in faith in a certain direction? Are you holding back because of fear, anxiety, or lack of self-confidence? Remember, where we are weak, he is strong. Allow God to direct your paths, step out in faith, and watch him work through you.

Power Principle #2

Becoming A Woman of Wisdom

Knowledge comes, but wisdom lingers.

—Alfred, Lord Tennyson

341

For the LORD gives wisdom, and
from his mouth come knowledge and understanding....
For wisdom will enter your heart,
and knowledge will be pleasant to your soul.

—Proverbs 2:6, 10

More Precious Than Rubies
Searching for Wisdom in All the Right Places

It is better to get wisdom than gold.
Gold is another's, wisdom is our own;
gold is for the body and time, wisdom for the soul and eternity.

—Matthew Henry

Wit and wisdom can be found in the oddest places. Bumper stickers, refrigerator magnets, T-shirts, greeting cards, and even decorative pillows tout some of life's best quips. Here are some of my favorites:

- A waist is a terrible thing to mind.

- Anything free is worth what you pay for it.

- Atheism is a nonprophet organization.

- I used to be indecisive; now I'm not so sure.

- My reality check just bounced.

- Everyone is entitled to my opinion.

- It's all about *you,* isn't it?

- Help stamp out and eradicate superfluous redundancy.

- What if there were no hypothetical questions?

- At my age, I've seen it all, done it all, heard it all...I just can't remember it all.

- If I had known being a grandmother was so much fun, I would have done it first!

- *Veni, Vidi, Visa:* I came, I saw, I did a little shopping.

- What if the Hokey Pokey is really what it's all about?

It's fun to discover little gems of wisdom in unexpected places. I'm sure you've discovered a few of your own favorites. I especially liked one T-shirt I saw that pointed to the ultimate source of wisdom. It had a picture of an open Bible and the caption "When all else fails, read the directions." Sometimes reading the directions is our last resort when we're playing a board game or putting together a dollhouse. But when it comes to getting direction in life, we neglect reading our Maker's instructions to our own peril!

As positive women, our search for wisdom ought to take us far beyond gift shop paraphernalia. Certainly T-shirts, bumper stickers, and magnets can offer some fun and frivolous perspectives on life; but when it comes to wisdom, we must pursue a solid base of truth.

Wisdom Defined

Wisdom is a common word used and treasured throughout the ages. But what does it mean to be a woman of wisdom? Webster defines wisdom as "sagacity, discernment or insight." It also calls wisdom "scholarly knowledge or learning." *The New Open Bible* defines wisdom as "knowledge guided by understanding." Putting it all together, we can say that wisdom is a type of application of the knowledge we possess. It is not knowledge in and of itself. I like what Frank M. Garafda says: "The difference between a smart man and a wise man is that a smart man knows what to say, and a wise man knows whether to say it or not."[1]

Solomon, the ancient king of Israel who is widely accepted as one of the wisest people the world has ever known, said, "The fear of the LORD is the beginning of wisdom, and knowledge of the Holy One is understanding" (Proverbs 9:10). In other words, "Do you want wisdom? Then here is the starting point: Fear God."

Stop reading for a moment and ponder the phrase "the fear of the Lord." What does it mean? According to Matthew Henry's commentary, this "fear" is "a reverence of God's majesty and a dread of his wrath." A reverence and awe of God, both in heart and in mind, is where we must begin the process of seeking to be wise. It's the ground floor in the tower of wisdom.

We can see this played out in many ways through life. Our fear of God keeps us from making foolish choices. Take Allison, for example. She is almost guaranteed a big promotion if she simply fudges on some numbers that represent sales quotas for the last quarter. Most likely no one would check the actual accounting. She has been hoping to redecorate her house, and the promotion would give her the income to do it. But Allison fears God and knows that those who seek dishonest gain come to ruin. Even if no one found out about it, God would know. She makes the wise decision to keep the numbers honest.

Wisdom has to do with both lifestyle and discernment. Proverbs 8:13 explains, "To fear the LORD is to hate evil; I [wisdom] hate pride and arrogance, evil behavior and perverse speech." Every day we have choices that confront us. Some are big and some are small, but all of our choices demand wisdom. On what will we base our decisions? A wise person makes decisions based on the understanding that God and his time-honored principles are the only sure foundation for life. A foolish person does not act on the foundation of a reverence for God and instead lives recklessly for selfish gain.

I think about the parable of the wise man who built his house upon a rock. When the rains came down and the floods came up, the house

The greatest good is wisdom. —St. Augustine

☺

345

on the rock stood firm. Meanwhile the foolish man built his house on the sand; when the rains came down and the floods came up, the house on the sand fell. (You can read this parable in Luke 6:46–49.) Jesus told this story to say that if we come to him, hear his words, and do what he says, our lives will be lived on a sure foundation. If we don't—if we fail to respect and honor God's principles—our lives will be shaky and unstable. Leo Tolstoy put it this way: "Each will have to make his own choice: to oppose the will of God, building upon the sands the unstable house of his brief, illusive life, or to join in the eternal, deathless movement of true life in accordance with God's will."[2]

The House of Wisdom

Everyone is invited to dwell in the magnificent house of wisdom. The invitation is found in Proverbs 9:1–10:

Wisdom has built her house; she has hewn out its seven pillars. She has prepared her meat and mixed her wine; she has also set her table. She has sent out her maids, and she calls from the highest point of the city. "Let all who are simple come in here!" she says to those who lack judgment. "Come, eat my food and drink the wine I have mixed. Leave your simple ways and you will live; walk in the way of understanding.…Instruct a wise man and he will be wiser still; teach a righteous man and he will add to his learning. The fear of the LORD is the beginning of wisdom, and knowledge of the Holy One is understanding."

Don't you just love the fact that wisdom is presented in the feminine form in Proverbs? I gladly pointed out that fact to my husband! Lest we become puffed up with pride too quickly, however, it is important to note that *folly* is also presented as a woman in this chapter, and she has an invitation of her own: "The woman Folly is loud; she is undisciplined and without knowledge. She sits at the door of her house, on a seat at the highest point of the city, calling out to those who pass by, who go straight on their way. "'Let all who are simple come in here!' she says to those who lack judgment" (Proverbs 9:13–16).

Two invitations await each of us. Which one will we accept? Wherever we are, whatever our situation, we can choose to go to wisdom's banquet and be a no-show at the other. If we move one step at a time in the right direction, with the fear of the Lord as our foundation, we soon will find ourselves at wisdom's open door. As Benjamin Franklin said, "The Doors of Wisdom are never shut."[3]

The Proper Outfit

Like all banquets, wisdom's banquet requires appropriate attire. Before we visit the house of wisdom, we must first cast off our simple ways and walk in the way of understanding, as Proverbs 9:6 says. In fact, a quick search through the Book of Proverbs identifies a number of the qualities with which we should adorn ourselves:

- *Righteousness.* "Instruct a wise man and he will be wiser still; teach a righteous man and he will add to his learning" (Proverbs 9:9).

- *An obedient heart and quiet tongue.* "The wise in heart accept commands, but a chattering fool comes to ruin" (Proverbs 10:8).

- *A listening ear.* "Now then, my sons, listen to me; blessed are those who keep my ways. Listen to my instruction and be wise; do not ignore it. Blessed is the man who listens to me, watching daily at my doors, waiting at my doorway" (Proverbs 8:32–34).

- *Discernment.* "Wisdom is found on the lips of the discerning" (Proverbs 10:13). "Let the wise listen and add to their learning, and let the discerning get guidance" (Proverbs 1:5).

We need to be properly dressed because, at wisdom's party, we will undoubtedly find ourselves rubbing shoulders with the other guests. Proverbs 8:12 and 8:14 introduce us to a few of wisdom's closest friends. No banquet would be complete without them: "I, wisdom, dwell together with prudence; I possess knowledge and discretion.... Counsel and sound judgment are mine; I have understanding and power."

Prudence. Knowledge. Discretion. Counsel. Sound judgment. Understanding. Power. We find each of these whenever we pursue godly wisdom. In his classic work, *Leviathan,* Thomas Hobbes said, "Knowledge is power." But a truer saying is "Wisdom is power." Wisdom is a great deal more than intellectual awareness. It involves knowledge, yes, but also discretion, sound judgment, and all the rest. Most importantly, wisdom includes a healthy fear of the Lord. When we find wisdom, we become positive women capable of having a powerful impact on our world.

Looking in All the Right Places

Is wisdom an exclusive and snobbish party hostess, or is she kind and available to greet her guests? Lucille Ball once said, "In life, all good things come hard, but wisdom is the hardest to come by."[4] I have to say, Lucy is partly right; wisdom *is* hard to find—unless you know where to look. Proverbs 8:17 says, "I [wisdom] love those who love me, and those who seek me find me." Wisdom is waiting for us to find her. We simply need to look in the right places. Where do we begin?

God's Word. The Bible contains the actual words of our omniscient Creator and loving heavenly Father, making it the perfect starting point. Why in the world would we ignore it? People throughout the ages have looked to the Bible for wisdom. The famous Italian astronomer Galileo once said, "I am inclined to think that the authority of Holy Scripture is intended to convince men of those truths which are necessary for their salvation, which, being far above man's understanding, cannot be made credible by any learning, or any other means than revelation by the Holy Spirit."[5]

Abraham Lincoln was another great man who valued the wisdom of God's Word. He had this to say upon receiving a Bible as a gift: "In regard to this Great Book, I have but to say, I believe the Bible is the best gift God has given to man. All the good Savior gave to the world was communicated through this Book. But for this Book we could not know right from wrong. All things most desirable for man's welfare, here and hereafter, are to be found portrayed in it."[6]

Scripture itself confirms the powerful and credible wisdom found within its pages. The apostle Peter writes, "We have the prophetic word confirmed, which you do well to heed as a light that shines in a dark place....Knowing this first, that no prophecy of Scripture is of any private interpretation, for prophecy never came by the will of man, but holy men of God spoke as they were moved by the Holy Spirit" (2 Peter 1:19–21 NKJV). Timothy says that all Scripture is "God-breathed" (2 Timothy 3:16). That makes the Bible wisdom's most reliable source.

Prayer. James tells us, "If any of you lacks wisdom, he should ask God, who gives generously to all without finding fault, and it will be given to him" (James 1:5). When was the last time you prayed for God to grant you wisdom? According to the Bible, all we have to do is ask, and he will freely give it to us.

I'm reminded of the wonderful request Solomon made of God. In 1 Kings 3:5, God said to Solomon, "Ask for whatever you want me to give you." Solomon could have asked for wealth or fame or honor or even happiness. Instead he asked for a wise and discerning heart to guide his people. God was so pleased with Solomon's request—which he of course fulfilled—that he also granted him riches and honor. Can you imagine the smile that would light a mother's face if her child said to her, "Mom, you are so wise. Can you help me think through this important decision?" I think God smiles like that when we ask for wisdom and discernment to help us along life's way.

Our nation's first president, George Washington, knew the value of seeking God's wisdom and protection on a daily basis. On May 1, 1777, as news finally came that France would be assisting the American troops in the Revolutionary War, he prayed, "And now, Almighty Father, if it is Thy holy will that we shall obtain a place and name among the nations of the earth, grant that we may be enabled to show our gratitude for Thy goodness by our endeavors to fear and obey Thee. Bless us with Thy wisdom in our counsels, success in battle, and let all our victories be tempered with humanity."[7] Obviously Washington was a man of great faith and a great example to us. He knew where to turn for wisdom and strength.

Jeremiah 33:2–3 says, "This is what the LORD says, he who made the earth, the LORD who formed it and established it—the LORD is his name: 'Call to me and I will answer you and tell you great and unsearchable things you do not know.'" Now that's an offer we can't refuse. The God of all creation wants to show us great and mighty things! It almost makes me think of Ed McMahon standing at my door with a million-dollar check from the Publisher's Clearinghouse sweepstakes. There he is, holding out a highly valuable gift in earthly terms, and all I need to do is open the door! God says that all we need to do is call on him, and he will grant us one of the greatest treasures on earth: wisdom.

Wisdom on Tap

Have you seen the new backpack water supply designed for long-distance runners and bikers? It's a half-gallon jug of water that can be strapped to the athlete's back. A long straw runs along the strap, ending

Wisdom is supreme; therefore get wisdom. Though it cost all you have, get understanding. Esteem her, and she will exalt you; embrace her and she will honor you. —Proverbs 4:7–8

near the mouth. It is actually a brilliant invention and a handy way for runners and bikers to have the water resource they need at their disposal. I remember taking long-distance runs with my friends at Baylor University while we were training for a marathon. During the course of a ten-mile run, we needed to drink water. But since we didn't want to carry an extra load in our hands, we depended on local fast food establishments to supply us with a cup of water. We had to break stride to fill up, but water was essential. I think the water backpack is the perfect solution for athletes who want to complete their journeys without interruption.

Did you know there is a kind of "spiritual backpack" we can wear to refresh us along the journey of life? It's called memorizing God's Word. King David said, "I have thought much about your words, and stored them in my heart so that they would hold me back from sin....Nothing is perfect except your words. Oh, how I love them. I think about them all day long. They make me wiser than my enemies, because they are my constant guide" (Psalm 119:11, 96–98 TLB). In my own life, I have found that memorizing Scripture has provided a vital mental resource to help me through difficult times. You have already noticed the memory verses I've included for you in the Power Point sections of each chapter. Let me give you some hints and ideas to help you memorize these verses and others.

Write it. As a former schoolteacher, I know the value of involving as many of the five senses as possible in order to seal ideas, words, and facts in our minds. Once you choose a Scripture verse to place in your heart, write it out several times to begin the sealing process. I suggest using three-by-five index cards. Take the time to write the verse neatly and clearly. Make it easy to read. Write the same verse on three separate cards, and don't forget to include the reference. Say the verse aloud as you write.

Many times I will write a scripture in a creative way to help me identify key words and remember the verse in phrases. Here's an example using Jeremiah 33:3:

> ***Call*** *to me*
> *and I will **answer** you and*
> *Tell you **great** and **unsearchable** things*
> *you do not know.*

You may want to consider using a variety of colors to help you remember key words. The better you can "see" the verse visually in your mind, the easier it will be to remember it. Sometimes I substitute numbers for the words "for" and "to." I also draw pictures to help me memorize. Sometimes silly pictures are the best! I know it sounds funny, but when I memorize a verse that begins with the words "let us," I draw a head of lettuce to help me remember. Our brains tend to remember pictures (especially silly ones) better than they remember words on a page.

See it. Some time ago I purchased three small plastic frames for one dollar apiece at a local craft store. That was easy! Now when I write out a verse, I place the handwritten cards in the frames and set them around the house in places where I am sure to see them. I keep one frame by my kitchen sink, one in the laundry room, and one on my bathroom counter where I do my makeup.

Why not try it? You can have fun decorating the frames with stickers or small objects to add flare and help catch your attention. You can also buy a frame with a magnet on the back for your refrigerator and a smaller-sized frame for your key chain to carry with you in the car. The more you see the verse, the more you will be reminded to practice saying it.

Speak it. Say your verse aloud at least once a day, perhaps just before you brush your teeth in the morning. My husband always repeats his verse before he turns on the radio in his car. When you speak it and hear it, you help to seal it more deeply in your mind. Try to find one opportunity each week to say the verse to someone else, whether in casual conversation or as an exercise with your family at the dinner table or in the car.

Review it. Typically, Sunday is a day of rest from the normal routine and often a day of spiritual reflection. I recommend using this day to choose a new verse, write it on three new index cards, and change out the frames. Place one of the old cards in a "review box." This can be a cute recipe box or decorated file box. (I am a visual person, so everything I do has to be decorated and cute!) Review the verses in your box once a month—perhaps on the first Sunday—as a refresher. Then every January 1, clean out the box, review each card, put a rubber band around the stack, and store it. Yes, I'm talking about memorizing fifty-two Bible verses a year. But with God's help, you can do it!

If you need more motivation, consider this. According to research, brain cells die as we get older. (I didn't really need a scientist to tell me that.) But recent studies show that fewer cells die when the brain is stimulated with new information. So there you have it—memorizing Scripture can help keep our minds young and fresh. What a great additional benefit!

The Wisdom of Friends

Amy and Leslie are heart-friends to me. Every year we step out of the busy schedules of our lives and take a weekend "girls trip" together, usually to a bed-and-breakfast somewhere in Texas. We spend hours laughing, sharing, and counseling. Typically one of us will lay out a problem, and the other two will offer wisdom, advice, and a few new ideas. We love it. We all agree that we come back from our little trips as better women, better mothers, and better wives.

Many times God uses the people in our lives—whether they are friends, mentors, coworkers, or family members—to give us wisdom and guidance. For women, the friendship of other women is a particularly powerful force in life, so much so that I have devoted an entire chapter later in this book (chapter 11) to the topic of friendships. I would be remiss, however, to neglect the importance of friendships in this chapter on wisdom.

Proverbs 13:20 says, "He who walks with the wise grows wise, but a companion of fools suffers harm." The truth is, friends rub off on each other, as another verse in Proverbs illustrates: "As iron sharpens iron, so one man sharpens another" (Proverbs 27:17). If we want to be wise, then it's important for us to walk through life with wise friends. If we choose to walk with foolish friends instead, we're sure to get hurt. How can we know if our friends are wise or foolish? Do a foundation check! Consider: Do they fear God and base their wisdom on a reverence for him?

Sometimes we get counsel from people who are neither friends nor family members but acquaintances or professionals. Whenever we get advice from anyone, we need to consider the source and confirm that the person giving the advice is coming from a foundation of fear and reverence of the Lord and then building on God's truth. The Bible actually gives us a checklist to help us discern whether or not we are receiving wise counsel: "But the wisdom that comes from heaven is first of all pure; then peace-loving, considerate, submissive, full of mercy and good fruit, impartial and sincere" (James 3:17). Wisdom that is none of these things is not wisdom at all.

God's Wisdom vs. Man's Wisdom

There is a vast difference between God's wisdom and man's. In fact, the apostle Paul contrasts them sharply in 1 Corinthians 3:18–19 when he writes, "Do not deceive yourselves. If any one of you thinks he is wise by the standards of this age, he should become a 'fool' so that he may become wise. For the wisdom of this world is foolishness in God's sight. As it is written: 'He catches the wise in their craftiness.'" For example, the world says it's wise to watch out for Number One; God says we must think more highly of others than we do ourselves. The world says it's okay to hold a grudge and make people pay for hurting us; God says we must forgive others and leave any vengeance to him. We need to be sure we're looking for God's wisdom and not simply accepting what the world tells us is wise.

Many people confuse wisdom with knowledge. Earlier in this chapter we said that wisdom includes knowledge, but it is also much more than knowledge. In itself, knowledge is not a bad thing. H. A. Ironside said, "Scripture nowhere condemns the acquisition of knowledge. It is the wisdom of this world, not its knowledge, that is foolishness with God."[8] Wisdom tells us how to apply the knowledge we gain. Knowledge may be taught in the halls of higher learning; wisdom is *caught* as we seek it and abide in the words of our eternal God.

A story is told of a student at Columbia University who was under the impression that the institution assured he would be taught wisdom. He filed a lawsuit for eight thousand dollars based on his claim that the university had failed him in the matter. It is no surprise that the Superior Court dismissed the case, nor that the Appellate Division of the Superior Court ruled the suit had been properly dismissed. Sidney Goldmann, the presiding judge of the three-man appellate court, declared, "These charges were set in a frame of intemperate, if not scurrilous, accusations. We agree with the trial judge that wisdom is not a subject that can be taught, and that no rational person would accept such a claim made by any man or institution."[9]

Walt Whitman spoke well of the contrast between knowledge and wisdom in his *Song of the Open Road:*

Wisdom is not finally tested by the schools,

Wisdom cannot be pass'd from one having it to another not having it,

Wisdom is of the soul, is not susceptible of proof, is its own proof.[10]

There are many benefits to the pursuit of knowledge. The world rewards knowledgeable people with positions of prestige, importance, and many times affluence. But just as there are many rewards for knowledge here on this earth, there are different, more eternal rewards for wisdom. Wisdom produces a blessing that a doctorate degree cannot. Wise Solomon says,

> Blessed is the man who finds wisdom, the man who gains understanding, for she [wisdom] is more profitable than silver and yields better returns than gold. She is more precious than rubies; nothing you desire can compare with her. Long life is in her right hand; in her left hand are riches and honor. Her ways are pleasant ways, and all her paths are peace. She is a tree of life to those who embrace her; those who lay hold of her will be blessed. (Proverbs 3:13–18)

We all have heard the oft-quoted phrase, "Diamonds are a girl's best friend." But for positive women, wisdom is even more valuable. Do you love wisdom? Embrace it. Passionately pursue it from the God of wisdom himself. You will obtain blessings that are lasting and eternal in value. A woman of wisdom is truly adorned with life's greatest jewels.

POWER POINT

Read: The entire chapters of Proverbs 1 and 2. Make a list of the results of rejecting wisdom mentioned in this passage. What are some of the reasons people may choose to reject wisdom? Now make a second list of the benefits of pursuing wisdom. Compare the two lists.

Pray: God of all wisdom, how wonderful it is to go to you for wisdom, direction, and comfort! Thank you for hearing my prayers. As I pursue wisdom, help me to begin at your feet, in fear and awe of you as my wonderful Creator. Help me to grow in wisdom so that I may be a woman of wisdom and a woman of your Word. In the matchless name of Jesus I pray, amen.

Remember: "For the LORD gives wisdom, and from his mouth come knowledge and understanding" (Proverbs 2:6).

Do: Determine to pursue wisdom starting today, and begin by sitting at the feet of the Giver of wisdom, God himself. Decide on a time each day when you will read and meditate on his Word. You may choose a short Bible passage, a few verses, or a longer reading. Whatever you do, commit yourself to pulling up a chair at the banquet table of wisdom and tasting its delicious morsels daily.

6

Winning Wisdom
Becoming a Woman of Direction and Discretion

Before you begin a thing, remind yourself that difficulties and
delays quite impossible to foresee are ahead....
You can only see one thing clearly, and that is your goal.

—Kathleen Norris

Most likely you've been there: sitting in the passenger seat of the car while the driver, a male, searches for your destination for what seems like hours. Whether the guy at the wheel is your dad, your brother, your boyfriend, or your husband, the scenario is still the same. He will never admit that he is lost. Pulling over for directions is totally out of the question, and don't even try to suggest a map! "I know it's around here somewhere. I'm sure we're going in the right direction," he says. I guess it's a male ego thing, but what is so difficult about asking for help after you have been driving aimlessly for forty minutes? Let's face it, we all could use a little help with direction sometimes!

As positive women we want to be purposeful about the direction we are going and the means we use to get there. Aimlessly wandering through life will get us nowhere quickly. But how do we find our direction, our purpose, and our goals in life?

A story is told of Justice Oliver Wendell Holmes who, while traveling on a train, misplaced his ticket. Seeing that Holmes was fumbling through his pockets and belongings with mounting frustration, the conductor tried to put his mind at ease.

"Don't worry about it, Mr. Holmes," he said. "I'm sure you have your ticket somewhere. If you don't find it during the trip, just mail it in to the railroad when you reach your destination."

Holmes appreciated the kind words but was still dismayed about his predicament. He looked the conductor in the eyes and said, "Young man, my problem is not finding my ticket. It's to find out where in the world I'm going.[1]

Certainly we, too, need to have an idea of where we are going in life. Let's consider how we can find direction as we journey down life's pathways.

The Power of a Strategic Plan

Setting goals was part of my life growing up. Every New Year's Day, my dad would encourage my sister and me to take time to consider and prepare a list of our annual goals. Yearly planning was a healthy exercise for me, especially in my high school and college years. I set goals in every area of my life, from grades to body weight to spiritual growth.

My Sunday school teacher Jim Kennedy used to say, "If your target is nothing, you'll end up hitting it every time." The truth is, we need goals—and a plan of action for reaching them. They give us a vision for moving forward in our lives. Paul had this type of focus, as evidenced by what he wrote to the Philippians: "Forgetting what is behind and straining toward what is ahead, I press on toward the goal to win the prize for which God has called me heavenward in Christ Jesus" (Philippians 3:13–14).

Ultimately our goal, like Paul's, is to fulfill God's calling in our lives. As you press toward that goal, consider taking time every January 1 to write out a personal strategic plan for the next year. Your plan should be balanced in four areas: mental, physical, spiritual, and social. Be prayerful as you prepare your plan and listen for God's leading. In each area, set a specific and realistic goal that will move you toward your ultimate goal. Make each goal believable and achievable so you can really commit to it. Make it measurable, too, so you can be sure you're staying on target. Along with each goal, write specific resolutions or steps you will take to meet it.

Let's take a brief look at these four strategic areas.

Mental. Mental goals involve ways to stimulate your brain and stretch your thinking—for example, reading more books or learning a new language or working toward a degree. Whatever goal you choose, it should be measurable. If you decide to read more books, determine how many. Will you commit to reading three books a year, one book a month, a book every two weeks? Write down what is feasible for you and your current lifestyle. Push yourself, but don't discourage yourself by setting an impossible goal.

Physical. In the physical arena, you may want to consider reaching a particular weight range or dress size or cholesterol level. Write down the strategy you intend to use to achieve that goal—say, working out every other day or walking six miles per week. Other physical goals might address sleeping or eating habits. This is a good time to decide when you will make your annual doctor and dentist visits.

Spiritual. When you decide on spiritual goals, you may want to start off broad, then write down specific strategies. Let's say you want to draw closer to God and deepen your prayer life. Your strategy may be to decide on a time you will set aside to pray and meditate on God's Word each day. You may want to add other details, like where you will do this and how long each session will be. How much Scripture will you read each day? Other spiritual strategies could include joining a Bible study, volunteering at church, or meeting with a friend so you can pray together.

Social. In our fast-paced world, if we are not deliberate about getting together with friends, it may never happen. Social goals give us a plan for building relationships. Your goal may be something like "to deepen relationships with the people in my life," or "to develop more good friendships from the acquaintances I know." A specific strategy may be to invite another couple over for dinner or dessert once a month. It may be to meet a friend once a week or go away on a girls' weekend once a year. Other strategies may include hosting two parties a year or writing one note a week to a friend. Personally, I like to identify the relationships that are important to me and set a goal of seeing that person at least once a month for lunch.

Career. If you work outside the home, this additional area is for you. Perhaps you already set annual career goals at work with your staff or management; if not, spend some time praying and thinking through what you want to accomplish in the coming year. It's important that you make the goals dependent on you and not on other people. For instance, you don't want your goal to be "to get a promotion" if that's another person's decision to make. However, you can make it your goal to do everything your job requires plus more in order to put yourself in line for a promotion. Set measurable, short-term goals that will stretch you and encourage you to meet your long-term goals. Beside each goal write down three or four specific strategies you will use to help you obtain it.

As you set goals in these four or five areas, keep in mind that you can't predict the future. Some elements of the coming year are out of your immediate control. Many times, because of people or circumstances, goals have to be rearranged. Stay flexible! I think of a woman I know who had her life in order and her goals set. With both kids in school, she was ready to finish her college degree and begin a career in teaching. Until…unexpected baby number three came along and postponed her perfect plan. Of course, she was thrilled and thankful for her

He holds victory in store for the upright, he is a shield to those whose walk is blameless, for he guards the course of the just and protects the way of his faithful ones. —Proverbs 2:7–8

precious little girl! Her story reminds us that we can go ahead and make our plans; but if God has other plans, we must be flexible enough to joyfully go with God.

Trusting Him to Lead

We may not know what the future holds, but we do know the one who holds the future. Perhaps this is why Solomon tells us that if we want to find direction in life, we must trust God and not depend solely on our own insight. He says in Proverbs 3:5–6, "Trust in the LORD with all your heart and lean not on your own understanding; in all your ways acknowledge him, and he will make your paths straight." Our natural tendency is to direct our own paths according to our own understanding. But this passage says we should defer to the guidance of our omniscient God.

How can we know what is in the road ahead? How can we know what twists and turns life will bring? We can't. But we *can* know that if we trust God wholeheartedly and acknowledge him in all our ways, he will direct our paths.

Joni Eareckson Tada's life has been a journey of trust and dependence on God. As an active teenager, Joni loved life and had great plans for the future—until a diving accident in 1967 left her as a quadriplegic. In despair, she thought that her life was over. Little did she know it was only beginning.

"One of the major turning points in my life was at this time, when I was wrestling against despair and depression at the prospects of living a life of permanent paralysis without use of my hands or legs," she says. "Several good friends helped me grasp the concept of the sovereignty of God and, for me, it was life changing. It helped so much to realize that my accident was really no accident at all. Second Corinthians 4:16–18 took a new and buoyant meaning as I realized that my light and momentary afflictions could achieve for me an eternal weight of glory. The disability became a severe mercy."[2]

God led Joni to start a ministry called Joni and Friends (JAF), which reaches out and ministers to the disabled community around the world. Over the years JAF Ministries has uncovered the hidden needs of people with disabilities and has trained churches in effective outreach and ministry to this special mission field. Joni has served on the National Council on Disability and has received numerous awards and honors over the years for her tireless work on behalf of the disabled. She has authored numerous books and writes for several publications. Her five-minute radio program, "Joni and Friends," is heard daily on more than seven hundred stations.

Certainly God had great plans for Joni's life! The path he set before her may not have been the path she expected to take, but it has been a blessed path nonetheless. "When we reach beyond our comfort zones and embrace the unlikely," Joni says, "people are blessed by the realization that we are all richer when we recognize our poverty, we are strong when we see our weaknesses, and we are recipients of God's grace when we understand our desperate need of him."[3]

In my own life, two Scripture passages have helped me to trust God and embrace his plans for me. They're worth memorizing:

Jeremiah 29:11–13: "For I know the plans I have for you," declares the LORD, "plans to prosper you and not to harm you, plans to give you hope and a future. Then you will call upon me and come and pray to me, and I will listen to you. You will seek me and find me when you seek me with all your heart."

Romans 8:28: And we know that in all things God works for the good of those who love him, who have been called according to his purpose.

The Bible makes clear that our success doesn't lie in having all of the answers about our future; it lies in following God's direction day by day. The famous abolitionist Harriet Tubman revealed the secret of her success when she told her biographer, Sarah H. Bradford, in 1868, "'Twant me, 'twas the LORD. I always told him, 'I trust you. I don't know where to go or what to do, but I expect you to lead me,' and he always did."[4]

The Road Map of Life

Marge Caldwell of Houston, Texas, is a delightful speaker and writer and a wonderful woman of faith and wisdom. During my college years I had the opportunity to hear her speak, and I will never forget one of the stories she told emphasizing the importance of reading God's Word for direction. Here's my version of the story:

Fred and Dottie were a precious newlywed couple living at a navy base in Virginia. You can imagine their dismay when Fred was called into active duty during the Gulf War. In order to console sweet Dottie, Fred promised to write to her as often as possible.

Dottie anxiously waited and was absolutely thrilled when the first letter from Fred arrived in her mailbox. She looked at the envelope, ran her hands over the seal, and pressed it against her heart, knowing that the letter inside was an expression of Fred's love for her. After soaking in the perfect bliss for a while, she placed the envelope on her coffee table so that every time she walked by, she would be reminded of Fred's love.

Soon another letter arrived, and with the same thrill she kissed the envelope, held it close, and admired the handwriting on the address. It was Fred's precious handwriting! She was so happy to have received another letter, she was almost beside herself. Again she placed the envelope on the coffee table, on top of the first. Over the next several weeks, Dottie received additional letters and tenderly placed each one at the top of the mounting stack on her coffee table.

Then the glorious day came when Fred was able to call home. It was a brief call, just long enough for him to tell Dottie that he loved her and to make sure she had been receiving his letters. Dottie was thrilled to hear Fred's voice, and she assured him that indeed she had received all of his letters.

It was then that something peculiar came to light. When Fred asked Dottie if she had taken their car into the shop for an oil change, she replied, "Why no, Fred. I didn't know I was supposed to take the car into the shop."

"But Dottie," Fred said with tinge of frustration, "I told you it needed to be done in the first letter I sent to you. Didn't you read the letter?"

"Why no, Fred, I didn't read the letter," Dottie responded. "It was just so nice that you wrote me. I placed your letter on the coffee table along with the others."

Fred's voice grew more concerned. "You did deposit the check I sent, didn't you?" he asked, to which Dottie replied, "Check?"

Uh-oh. Now Fred was pretty upset, as you can imagine. He had sent numerous detailed letters to his bride, but she hadn't taken the time to read any of them. Dottie was just happy that Fred had written to her and content to keep the envelopes on the coffee table where she could see them every day. Wasn't that enough?

By now you are probably thinking that Dottie is a little nutty. Obviously this is not a true story, but in a way it is. Think about it. We have a wonderful God who has sent us a series of love letters called the Bible. This glorious book is filled with priceless treasures of wisdom as well as vital information and helpful instructions for living an abundant life. Like Dottie, many of us simply set the letters aside on the coffee table and fail to read them. It seems absurd that Dottie didn't read her letters. But isn't it more absurd that we don't read the mail sent to us by our loving heavenly Father?

In our search for direction in life, we have the privilege to turn to the very words of the all-wise Creator of the universe. Psalm 119:105 says, "Your word is a lamp to my feet and a light for my path." The Bible is our flashlight as we journey down the path of life. It leads us and guides us in truth and steers us from false and evil ways. It provides nourishment and strength along the trail. It doesn't tell us what to do in every specific situation, but it does guide us in principle. As 2 Timothy 3:16 says, "All Scripture is God-breathed and is useful for teaching, rebuking, correcting and training in righteousness, so that the man of God may be thoroughly equipped for every good work."

Knowing God's Will

A woman I know, Emily, has become increasingly dissatisfied with her job in recent months. She isn't sure if she should start looking for a new job opportunity—maybe even a whole new line of work—or stay in her current job, even though she doesn't enjoy it anymore. Wouldn't it be nice if she could open up the Bible and find a passage that says, "Emily shall move on to a new job opportunity"? But Scripture doesn't give us exact, specific directions for every decision. Thankfully, our loving heavenly Father gives us the free will to make decisions in life without being micro-managed. What Emily *can* find in the Bible is wisdom to lead her to a wise decision. She can pray, seek wise counsel from someone she trusts, and research all of her options. Then, after weighing her options and determining if any of the choices would go against a biblical principle (for example, would a particular job require her to be dishonest?), she can make her decision confidently.

Sometimes we think that there is only one perfect choice, and we must find it. If we make the wrong decision, we're doomed for life! Granted, certain life decisions do have major consequences and ramifications—like who we will marry and what career path we will take—but most decisions offer several good options. My dad used to say a simple phrase that has always stuck with me: "Make a decision, then make it a right decision." In other words, if you come to a fork in the road, after wise consideration and prayer, start walking down the path that seems the wisest; then make the best of it and leave the results to God. Once you have made a decision, work in a positive way to make it the best decision—without looking back.

People often ask the question, "How do I know if I'm in God's will?" The answer may be simpler than we think. We know we are in God's will if we are living in obedience to his Word. That's it! As we abide in him and he abides in us, our lives will be fruitful, whatever path we choose.

Often the question people are really asking is, "Which road should I take?" If we have a choice between two roads and can be obedient to God's Word on both, then God's answer is this: "I'll be with you down whatever road you choose." Most roads have challenges, twists, turns, joys, and sorrows. Just because we hit a bump or meet a roadblock doesn't mean we made a "wrong" decision—otherwise every character in the Bible went down the "wrong" road! The fact is, as we walk according to God's will, we *will* face challenges. We will have new decisions to make along the way. But as Mary Kay Ash said, "For every failure, there's an alternative course of action. You just have to find it. When you come to a roadblock, take a detour."[5]

Are you seeking direction and don't know which way to turn? Start with the road map of life, the Bible! As you pursue wisdom from above and wise counsel from people you trust, you will find that the steps in front of you become clearer. Take one step at a time. Listen to God's voice as he speaks through his Word, his people, and that still, small voice inside of you that is the Holy Spirit. You may not get the kind of exact answer that would make your decision-making process easy; but you can rest in the assurance that God is with you whatever path you take as you walk in obedience to him.

A Woman of Direction and Discretion

One of my favorite modern American heroines is Elizabeth Dole. A graduate of Duke University and Harvard Law School, Mrs. Dole served five United States presidents in an amazing career dedicated to public service. She became the first female secretary of transportation during the Reagan Administration and was appointed secretary of labor in the first Bush Administration. After completing her cabinet assignments, she became president of the Red Cross, accepting no salary during her first year in order to demonstrate the importance of volunteerism. She left the Red Cross in order to pursue the Republican nomination for president of the United States in 2000. At the time of this writing, she is running for the United States Senate, representing her home state of North Carolina.

Recently I had the opportunity to hear Mrs. Dole speak at a lecture series in Dallas. It was obvious from her speech that she is a woman of vision and direction. She moves forward, taking steps toward new opportunities that allow her to serve the country she so dearly loves. Has she faced discouragement? Yes, but she has experienced many victories as well. She doesn't look back, worrying about whether or not she made the "right" decision; she moves forward, looking toward the goal that lies ahead. She is a wonderful example of a woman of faith, wisdom, and direction.

I'm sure that Elizabeth Dole is also a woman of discretion. I can say that with confidence because discretion and wisdom go hand in hand,

Dost thou love life? Then do not squander time, for that is the stuff life is made of. —Benjamin Franklin

as we see in Proverbs 8:12: "I, wisdom, dwell together with prudence; I possess knowledge and discretion." Proverbs 2:11–12 says, "Discretion will protect you, and understanding will guard you. Wisdom will save you from the ways of wicked men." Discretion can be defined as prudence, or the quality of being careful about what we say or do. It also means the freedom, power, or authority to make decisions and choices using discernment and judgment. A wise woman is always a woman of discretion!

Proverbs paints a not-so-pretty picture of a woman who lacks discretion: "Like a gold ring in a pig's snout is a beautiful woman who shows no discretion" (Proverbs 11:22). What behaviors can we expect from such a woman? The Gold Ring in the Pig's Snout award could be granted for any of the following behaviors:

- gossip

- tearing down others with words

- needless chatter (sharing too much information)

- unkind words

- corrupt communication or foul language

- temper tantrums

- angry outbursts

- adulterous flirting

- overindulgence

- wearing obviously revealing clothing

You can probably think of many more qualifications for this award, but you get the idea. Notice that most of these qualifications tend to deal with words. Unfortunately this can be a dangerous area for women, since we do enjoy talking! As one husband said, "Generally speaking, women are generally speaking." We do tend to use our mouths quite a bit, and with that comes great opportunity for error. James spoke of the power and destructive capability of the tongue in his epistle:

> The tongue is a small part of the body, but it makes great boasts. Consider what a great forest is set on fire by a small spark. The tongue also is a fire, a world of evil among the parts of the body. It corrupts the whole person, sets the whole course of his life on fire, and is itself set on fire by hell....
>
> With the tongue we praise our Lord and Father, and with it we curse men, who have been made in God's likeness. Out of the same mouth come praise and cursing. My brothers, this should not be....
>
> Who is wise and understanding among you? Let him show it by his good life, by deeds done in the humility that comes from wisdom. (James 3:5–6, 9–10, 13)

As women of wisdom, we need to live up to a higher standard, showing our wisdom through our discreet behavior and conversation. Let's determine to use our words for good. Let us not waste them putting people down, when there are so many people we can lift up! Instead, let's be positive women who have a positive influence on the people around us, choosing words and deeds that demonstrate direction, discretion, and the wisdom that comes from God.

POWER POINT

🔘 **Read:** Proverbs 31:10–31. Would you consider the woman in this passage wise? What clue is found in verse 30? List some of the activities and behaviors that indicate she is a woman of wisdom, direction, and discretion.

371

♡ **Pray:** I praise you, Father, for your plans are perfect! You know the way that I should go. Help me to trust you and not simply lean on my own understanding. Help me to acknowledge you in all my ways as you direct my paths. I want to be a woman of wisdom, direction, and discretion, living a life that honors you in both word and deed. In Jesus' name I pray, amen.

♡ **Remember:** "Charm is deceptive, and beauty is fleeting; but a woman who fears the LORD is to be praised" (Proverbs 31:30).

☺ **Do:** Set aside a time to write out a strategic plan for the rest of the year. Remember to seek God's direction. As you set your goals, take some time to reflect on those areas of your life that may need a discretion tune-up. Ask God to help you have victory in these areas.

Power Principle #3

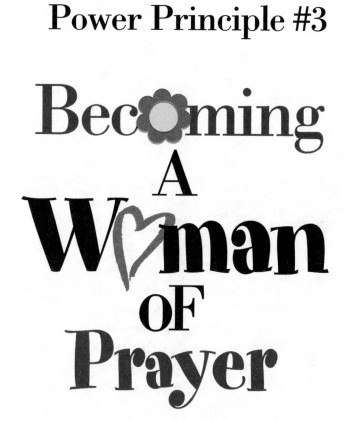

Becoming A Woman OF Prayer

Devote yourselves to prayer, being watchful and thankful.
—Colossians 4:2

I know not by what methods rare,
But this I know: God answers prayer.
I know not if the blessing sought
Will come in just the guise I thought.
I leave my prayer to Him alone
Whose will is wiser than my own.

—Eliza M. Hickok

Extra Baggage
Giving Up a Load We Were Never Meant to Carry

Oh, what peace we often forfeit,
Oh what needless pain we bear,
All because we do not carry,
Everything to God in prayer.

—Joseph Scriven

Recently my sister, Karen, my stepmother, Janet, and I were on our way to Panama City, Florida, to attend the marriage of my cousin David. As we tracked from the airport terminal to our rental car, Janet and I walked briskly with our suitcases rolling along easily behind us. Karen lagged behind carrying her heavy bag. Finally in exhaustion she exclaimed, "I wish I'd brought my bag with rollers!"

Oh, the difference wheels make! Karen was carrying a load that a set of wheels could have borne. What about you and me? Are we struggling to carry our own baggage through life? By baggage I mean the troubles, problems, and challenges that are an inevitable part of human existence. The good news is, we have a God who loves us and wants to help us with our burdens. The same God who parted the Red Sea, who walked on water, and who changed water into wine is ready and willing to be our "wheels." That doesn't mean we can expect a perfect life void of pain; rather, we can rest in the assurance that we have a perfect God who loves us and is with us, whatever challenges life brings.

Don't Give Up

One of my favorite Bible verses is 1 Thessalonians 5:17: "Pray without ceasing" (NKJV). It's a short, sweet reminder that we need to give our cares and burdens to God daily. We need to continually praise him and thank him. We need to be in constant communication with him!

Theologians say this verse can be understood in two ways. I believe that both are correct. One way to "pray without ceasing" is to keep our prayer lives strong and growing. We can do this in part by designating a specific time each day to go to God in prayer with our praises and our cares. (Chapter 8 provides specific and creative ideas for having a daily prayer time.) We need to be diligent to maintain a regular, vibrant prayer life with our glorious Creator.

A second way to understand unceasing prayer is to recognize it as a constant state—a moment-by-moment, living communication with God. Brother Lawrence, who served in the kitchen of a monastery in Paris in the seventeenth century, wrote of the blessings of living in a constant state of devotion and prayer. A simple man with a humble background, his profound writings were compiled in a book called *Practicing the Presence of God,* which is still in print today. Although his job as a kitchen worker was mundane, he determined to live every moment in "the presence of God," transforming his kitchen duties into glorious experiences of heaven. Our lives can be transformed, too, when we know and experience this type of prayer-filled joy in daily living.

Jesus told his disciples a parable to illustrate to them (and to us) that they should always pray and not give up. It is found in Luke 18:2–8:

"In a certain town there was a judge who neither feared God nor cared about men. And there was a widow in that town who kept coming to him with the plea, 'Grant me justice against my adversary.'

"For some time he refused. But finally he said to himself, 'Even though I don't fear God or care about men, yet because this widow keeps bothering me, I will see that she gets justice, so that she won't eventually wear me out with her coming!'"

And the Lord said, "Listen to what the unjust judge says. And will not God bring about justice for his chosen ones, who cry out to him day and night? Will he keep putting them off? I tell you, he will see that they get justice, and quickly."

Jesus wants us to pray. He wants us to come to him continually. Through this parable he compels us to bring our cares, concerns, burdens, and injustices to him. Unlike the judge in the story, God is just and loving, and he is waiting for us with open arms and a listening ear. He stands before us saying, "Come to me, give me your burdens, and find rest for your souls."

Is It Too Much to ASK?

I'm the type that hates to ask anyone for anything. My daughter Joy is the same way. She doesn't even like me to ask someone to give her a ride to a meeting, even when we live on the way to the meeting's location. She just hates to impose. My daughter Grace seems to have the opposite viewpoint. She assumes everyone is willing to help and doesn't mind asking for a favor at all. Her philosophy is, "They can always say no. It never hurts to ask." I suspect the healthiest approach is a balance between the two extremes.

How willing we are to ask for something is often dependent upon the person of whom we're making the request. My street is filled with wonderful, friendly neighbors. The Page family lives just across from us, and they have a daughter, Ashlee, who is in the same grade as Grace. One Friday the girls came home from school with directions for a major science project due the next Wednesday for their freshman biology class. The assignment was to make a detailed model of a living cell with all its basic parts, from mitochondrion to golgi. The only way for the girls to have it finished by Wednesday was to do the bulk of it on Saturday and Sunday.

But that happened to be the weekend I was away on my once-a-year ladies' retreat. I didn't know about the project and couldn't offer any help. Fortunately Ashlee Page invited Grace to come over so they could work on the project together. The Pages have a plentiful amount of craft supplies, and they didn't mind sharing them with Grace when she asked. By the time I arrived home on Sunday afternoon, Grace had spent a good portion of the weekend at the Pages' house, and her project was complete.

On Tuesday night, just before the project was due, Grace went over and asked the Pages if she could use their glue gun one more time. I cringed at the thought of asking one more favor from the Pages, but they were continually gracious. Believe me, I have expressed my gratitude to them many times over!

Grace's experience with the Pages is a good example of a principle that Jesus taught in the Sermon on the Mount. I call it the ASK principle, and it's found in Matthew 7:7–11:

"Ask and it will be given to you; seek and you will find; knock and the door will be opened to you. For everyone who asks receives; he who seeks finds; and to him who knocks, the door will be opened.

"Which of you, if his son asks for bread, will give him a stone? Or if he asks for a fish, will give him a snake? If you then, though you are evil, know how to give good gifts to your children, how much more will your Father in heaven give good gifts to those who ask him!"

There is a limit to human generosity. You and I don't have unlimited resources or the ability to grant every request asked of us. But God's resources and power know no limits. He is able to give abundantly more than we ask or think. What would happen in our lives if we truly applied the ASK principle—if we always remembered to ask, seek, and knock? The Greek present imperative form of the three verbs in this passage indicates that the asking, seeking, and knocking are *continuous* actions. Once again Jesus is talking about persistent prayer. What great things would take place if we prayed persistently and unceasingly to our totally unlimited, loving God?

The point of constant prayer is not so much to see what we can get from God but to build a relationship with him. Ultimately, ASKing is a continuous action of growing closer to God, seeking his ways, and increasing our faith. Let's take a look at each of the three aspects of the ASK principle.

1. "Ask and it will be given to you."

The word *ask* used in this verse suggests a petition made from a lesser entity to a greater one. The same word is found in Ephesians 3:20: "Now to him who is able to do immeasurably more than all we ask or imagine, according to his power that is at work within us." Again we find the word ask in Colossians 1:9: "For this reason, since the day we heard about you, we have not stopped praying for you and asking God to fill you with the knowledge of his will through all spiritual wisdom and understanding."

James used the word *ask* four times in his epistle. In James 1:5–6 we are told to ask for wisdom (as we discussed in the last chapter) and to ask for it without doubting. In James 4:2–3 we find some more instructions: "You do not have, because you do not ask God. When you ask, you do not receive, because you ask with wrong motives, that you may

Cast all your anxiety on him because he cares for you. —1 Peter 5:7

spend what you get on your pleasures." We always need to check our motives when we ask something of God. Is our request being made for selfish gain? This may be one of the reasons we don't receive it.

If our motives are right and we have a living, growing relationship with God, however, we can have confidence whenever we go to him with a request. First John 3:21–22 says, "Dear friends, if our hearts do not condemn us, we have confidence before God and receive from him anything we ask, because we obey his commands and do what pleases him." Later in John's letter we find a passage that uses the word *ask* three more times and reiterates the point: "I write these things to you who believe in the name of the Son of God so that you may know that you have eternal life. This is the confidence we have in approaching God: that if we ask anything according to his will, he hears us. And if we know that he hears us—whatever we ask—we know that we have what we asked of him" (1 John 5:13–15).

Asking of the Lord is an act of faith—one that he encourages us to do. So why are we sometimes hesitant to bring our petitions to him? Is it because we relate asking of God to the awkwardness of imposing on our fellow man? Jesus implores us to ask. Could it be we don't take the time to ask because we live too much in the here and now, always caught up in trying to solve our own problems? Jesus reminds us to ask. Do we feel unworthy, as if we do not deserve to make requests of God? Jesus lovingly tells us to ask.

Dear friend, what do you need to ask of God? Do you need wisdom? What about strength? Perhaps you need a friend. Begin asking. Start now!

2. "Seek and you will find."

The word *seek* is somewhat different than *ask*. It has to do with desiring, endeavoring, or inquiring about something. We can get a better understanding of this word by seeing how it is used in other places in the Bible. For example, Matthew 6:33 tells us to "seek first his kingdom and his righteousness, and all these things [the things we need to live and thrive in this world] will be given to you as well." Similarly, Colossians 3:1–2 tells us to set our hearts and minds "on things above…not on earthly things." In other words, our seeking ought to be geared toward eternal things. If we spend our entire lives seeking worldly riches, beauty, or fame—and that's an easy mode to slip into, since these are things we can see and feel in the here and now—whatever we obtain will be temporal; it will soon fade away. The question we need to ask ourselves is, Are we running this race of life for a temporary reward or an eternal one?

What does it mean to seek eternal things? Actually, there are only a few things that are truly eternal: God, his Word, and the souls of men. Yes, we must earn a living, live in this world, and take care of ourselves; but our real reward comes in investing in the things that won't fade away. Investing in people, drawing near to God, living according to his Word, and sharing it with others: These are activities worth seeking. In 1 Corinthians 3:1–15 Paul tells us that we are building our lives on the foundation of Christ with materials of gold, silver, and costly stones, or with wood, hay, and straw—that is, with things in life that are strong and true and have eternal value, or things that are common and temporal and ultimately flimsy. One day, he says, our works will be tested by fire. If what we have built survives, we will receive our reward.

My friend Carol is a very busy person. Besides working part-time, she volunteers at her kids' school (and with several other organizations) and leads a small-group Bible study. Carol seems to have her priorities straight when it comes to what is worth seeking and what is not. She frequently uses the phrase "hay and stubble" to refer to everything people tend to busy themselves with that is not eternal. Carol lives in a beautifully decorated house, yet she doesn't get frazzled about the details of decorating. Those are hay and stubble issues. Talk to her about the character of her kids, however, and you've got her undivided attention. She is always seeking the best for them and constantly working to enrich them. Why? Because they represent eternal souls. They are more precious than gold in her eyes.

What are you seeking? To what do you devote your heart, mind, soul, and strength? Take a moment to reflect on what you earnestly seek or strive for in life. You may find that you need to readjust your direction. Seek wisely, because you most likely will find what you are seeking!

3. "Knock and the door will be opened to you."

The Gospel of Luke presents another version of Jesus introducing the ASK principle. It is preceded by a parable about a neighbor knocking at a friend's door:

> "Suppose one of you has a friend, and he goes to him at midnight and says, 'Friend, lend me three loaves of bread, because a friend of mine on a journey has come to me, and I have nothing to set before him.'
>
> "Then the one inside answers, 'Don't bother me. The door is already locked, and my children are with me in bed. I can't get up and give you anything.' I tell you, though he will not get up and give him the bread because he is his friend, yet because of the man's boldness he will get up and give him as much as he needs.
>
> "So I say to you: Ask and it will be given to you; seek and you will find; knock and the door will be opened to you." (Luke 11:5–9)

This story is really about you and me knocking on heaven's door. The word *knock* is used figuratively to represent a persistent entreating of God for our needs. If a sinful man is willing to help a friend because

Never, never may we forget that if we would do good to the world, our first duty is to pray! —J. C. Ryle of the friend's persistence, how much more will a loving God hear and reply? The Lord hears our pleas, he knows our needs, and he graciously receives our requests. Isn't it wonderful to know we have a Friend who is always there, ready and anxious to open the door to us?

Of course, *knocking* implies an action on our part—an action that is based on our faith in the One we are petitioning. If we are praying for a job opportunity but take no steps of action to find a job, we are not knocking. If we are praying for a better relationship with our spouse but take no positive steps to build the relationship, we are not knocking. Prayer and action go hand in hand. William Booth, the founder of the Salvation Army, said, "Work as if everything depended upon work, and pray as if everything depended upon prayer."[1] Another man put it this way: "If you want to get to the other side of the lake, you need to get in the boat and start paddling." We can be confident in taking action if we know we are praying according to God's will. The key is to be both diligent in our heartfelt prayers and faithful in our required actions.

Sometimes Wait, Sometimes No

About mid-November every year, I begin pumping my daughters for Christmas present requests. "What do you want? Make a list for me," I tell them. Now that they're teenagers, I can't assume anything; they must tell me exactly what they want. Sometimes we even go shopping together, and they pick out what they want; then I put it away until Christmas. Do they get everything they want? No!

Don't get me wrong; I don't mind their asking. In fact, I want them to put in their requests. So why don't I give them everything they ask for? Two reasons. First, overindulgence is not healthy for a child of any age. Kids must learn to wait for some things; they don't need to have everything they want right *now*. Overindulgence breeds greediness, ingratitude, impatience, and selfishness—traits I don't want to encourage in my kids. After all, the best things in life really do come to those who wait. My girls won't learn this important life lesson if I give them everything they want when they want it.

The second reason I don't grant their every request is because some things are not best for them. I love my kids and want to encourage them to grow into healthy, well-adjusted adults. There have been a few requests they have made over the years that Curt and I knew were not in their best interest, so we simply said "no."

Thankfully our loving heavenly Father doesn't give us everything we ask for either. As one of my favorite authors, C. S. Lewis, said, "If God had granted all the silly prayers I've made in my life, where should I be now?"[2] Imagine for a moment that God did give us everything we requested. Instead of a loving father, he would be a sugar daddy, meeting our every whim or desire. We would become selfish and overindulged. The course of history would be in our hands, because we could change everything with a simple request. People would come to God with only one motive: "I pray, and I get exactly what I want. What a deal!"

Isn't it good that our heavenly Father sometimes says "wait" and sometimes says "no"? Lewis also said, "Prayer is request. The essence of request, as distinct from compulsion, is that it may or may not be granted. And if an infinitely wise Being listens to the requests of finite and foolish creatures, of course He will sometimes grant and sometimes refuse them."[3]

Thankfully, answered prayer doesn't depend on our holiness or goodness. If it did, we might become prideful when God answers us or judgmental of others when their petitions aren't granted. Remember, even Christ in the Garden of Gethsemane got a "no" to his request to "let this cup pass from Me" (Matthew 26:39 NKJV). We must trust

God; he sees the eternal picture while we only see the immediate. Why does God allow a believer to suffer and die, not answering the prayers of numerous petitioners? We can't fully answer questions such as these until we get to the other side. I'm sure those people who have gone on to heaven before us are saying, "Don't worry about me. Don't weep for me. I am in a better place. My suffering was for a greater good, and now I suffer no more."

You Are Coming to a King

The story is told of Alexander the Great, who on one occasion was asked by a courtier for some financial aid. The powerful leader told the courtier to go to the treasurer and ask for whatever amount he wanted. After a little while, the treasurer appeared before Alexander. "The courtier has asked for an enormous amount of money," he reported, "and I'm hesitant to give out such an amount."

"Give him what he asks for," Alexander replied. "He has treated me like a king in his asking, and I shall be like a king in my giving!"

When I first read this story, it was accompanied by the following poem by Walter B. Knight. As positive women, we need to remember these words:

> Thou art coming to a King,
> Large petitions with thee bring;
> For His grace and power are such,
> None can ever ask too much![4]

Many years ago there was a card on the wall of a cotton factory that read, "If your threads get tangled, send for the foreman." One day a new worker discovered that her threads had become tangled. She tried to disentangle them herself but succeeded only in making the tangle worse. Finally she sent for the foreman. When he came and looked over the situation, he asked her, "You have been doing this yourself?"

"Yes," she replied.

"But why didn't you send for me, as the instructions said?"

"I did my best," she meagerly replied.

"No, you did not," the foreman firmly stated. "Remember that doing your best is sending for me."[5]

When our lives get tangled, we are doing *our* best when we take our needs before our great Creator. Our first step is never to try to fix things ourselves; it's to go to God in prayer and seek his guidance, direction, and help. We may never know the full impact of our prayers this side of heaven. But we do know this: God wants us to ASK—and then trust him for the answer.

We can be confident that prayer changes things, because God changes things. Never underestimate the power and lasting influence of a positive woman's prayers!

POWER POINT

⚙ **Read:** 2 Chronicles 7:14 and Mark 1:35. As we come humbly before God, seeking his face, what does the passage in 2 Chronicles say he will do? What does the passage in Mark tell you about Jesus? If the Son of God made it a priority to pray, what should we do?

♡ **Pray:** I praise you, loving and kind heavenly Father, for hearing my prayers. Thank you for encouraging me to ask of you. It is overwhelming to think that you invite simple little me to come to you, the high King of heaven. I humbly draw before your throne of grace. In faith I reach out to you, offering my love, my obedience, and my requests. Thank you for answering my prayers in the way you know is best for me. In Christ's holy name I pray, amen.

💡 **Remember:** "Ask and it will be given to you; seek and you will find; knock and the door will be opened to you. For everyone who asks receives; he who seeks finds; and to him who knocks, the door will be opened" (Matthew 7:7–8).

☺ **Do:** Apply the ASK principle in your life starting today. Put small, motivating signs around your home that say, "Remember to ASK." Begin each day with prayer; then in every situation that day, before fretting or becoming discouraged, pray and ask for God's help and direction. Make this a moment-by-moment practice, walking hand in hand with God throughout the day.

A Simple Guide to Effective Prayer

Praying for Family, Friends, and the World

The prayer of a righteous man is powerful and effective.

—James 5:16

Sir Isaac Newton, famous discoverer of the law of universal gravitation, was gifted as a mathematician, scientist, and philosopher. He formulated the three laws of motion, advanced the discipline of dynamics, and helped develop the study of calculus. He laid the foundation for the law of energy conservation and constructed the first reflecting telescope. His profound intellect never diminished his deep faith, however. In fact, using the telescope as an illustration, he gave us a beautiful picture of prayer: "I can take my telescope and look millions and millions of miles into space; but I can lay my telescope aside, go into my room and shut the door, get down on my knees in earnest prayer, and I see more of heaven and get closer to God than I can when assisted by all the telescopes and material agencies on earth."[1]

Isn't it wonderful to realize that the God of the universe is close at hand? We don't have to travel to distant lands or the deepest regions of space to find our great and mighty Creator. As Newton said, it's in earnest prayer that we see heaven and get close to God.

There is no secret scientific formula for prayer. Prayer is simple. It is a humble coming to God with a heart of praise, thankfulness, and need. In the last chapter we said that the main purpose of prayer is not to get God to give us things, but rather to grow with him in a deeper, more intimate relationship. I like how Hank Hanegraaff puts it in his book *The Prayer of Jesus:* "For Christians, prayer should be its own reward. Prayer is not a magic formula to get things from God. Communing with God in prayer is itself the prize."[2]

Prayer is not for show or for the applause of men, but for intimacy with the Father. I think of the story of the little girl who was saying her nightly prayers with her mother sitting next to her on the bed. The young girl's lips were moving, her expression was earnest, but the mother could barely make out what she was saying. When the little girl said, "Amen," her mother commented, "Honey, I didn't hear a word you said." Her daughter answered, "That's okay, I wasn't talking to you anyway."[3] Our prayers are very real, meaningful conversations between meager mankind and our glorious God. Aren't you overwhelmed at the thought of it?

In this chapter I want to deal with the nitty-gritty of prayer—the how, when, what, and where of prayer. Let's begin with the question "How do we learn to pray?"

Lord, Teach Us to Pray

The disciples asked Jesus this very question. One day, after Jesus had finished praying in a certain place, one of the disciples said to him, "Lord, teach us to pray." Matthew 6:9–13 gives us Jesus' response:

"This then, is how you should pray:
'Our Father in heaven,
hallowed be your name,
your kingdom come,
your will be done

on earth as it is in heaven.
Give us today our daily bread.
Forgive us our debts,
>   as we also have forgiven our debtors.
And lead us not into temptation,
but deliver us from the evil one.'"

Jesus gave this model for prayer to his disciples and to us. How wonderful to learn the principles of prayer from Jesus himself! Just as in school we have the three R's (reading, writing, and arithmetic), so in this prayer we see three R's emerging: recognize who he is; remember what he has done; request according to his will. Let's take a brief look at each of these prayer principles in light of Jesus' example prayer.

Recognize who he is. Jesus began his prayer with the words, "Our Father in heaven, hallowed be your name." This statement makes very clear to whom we pray. We pray to God, our Father in heaven—not to angels or people who have gone before us. The phrase "in heaven" reminds us of God's glory and majesty. Psalm 103:19 says, "The LORD has established his throne in heaven, and his kingdom rules over all." For believers, this throne is a throne of grace. Because of Jesus' death on the cross, we have ready access to God's presence in heaven.

The term *hallowed* means holy, set apart, sanctified. When we come to God in prayer, we not only recognize that he is our loving Father in heaven, but also that his name is holy, pure, powerful. It is a name to be respected and revered. His name provides a place of safety for us, as we read in Proverbs 18:10: "The name of the LORD is a strong tower; the righteous run to it and are safe." Do you find safe refuge in him through prayer? Run to the strong tower of his holy name and find peace!

Remember what he has done. Once we reflect and begin to recognize the greatness of God, our hearts overflow with thankfulness for what he has done. Surely he is at work in big and small ways in our lives! One person put it this way: "God's giving deserves our thanksgiving." Vincent de Paul said, "We should spend as much time in thanking God for his benefits as we do in asking him for them."[4] I don't know about you but I'm a little convicted by that statement. If we spent more time in gratitude and less time in grumbling, I wonder how different our world would be.

Paul says we should "give thanks in all circumstances, for this is God's will for you in Christ Jesus" (1 Thessalonians 5:18). Thanking God for the good things in our lives is easy. Thanking him for the challenges—now that's a different story! But we have much to be thankful for, even when life is difficult. We can begin by thanking God that he is with us in our circumstances. We may not like the situation, but we can thank him for his strength and his help to make it through. As positive women, let's determine today to spend more time thanking God and reflecting on his work in our lives. I have a feeling we'll begin to see a difference in our attitude toward life as well.

Request according to his will. Jesus' model prayer goes on to present several petitions before the Lord. This section begins, however, by deferring to God's will. How do we know we are praying according to God's will? By praying according to his Word. George Mueller, the great prayer warrior of England, always consulted Scripture before petitioning God. At times he spent days searching the Scriptures before asking God for a request, because he wanted to be sure that his prayer request was in the will of God.

Madame Jeanne Guyon, born in France in 1648, was a humble yet positive woman of prayer. At the age of fifteen she married an invalid who was twenty-three years her senior. He was a rather difficult man; yet throughout her unhappy marriage, she found respite in her devo-

Satan trembles when he sees the weakest saint upon his knees. —William Cowper ☺

tional life. Later Jeanne lived in a convent under royal order for a year. She was eventually imprisoned in Vincennes because her religious beliefs differed from the established church. She spent almost twenty-five years of her life in confinement, and many of her books were written during that period.

Madame Guyon's writings compel readers to experience God at a deeper level. In her book *Experiencing the Depths of Jesus Christ* (sometimes titled *A Short and Very Easy Method of Prayer*), she talks about a wonderful way to pray. She writes, "'Praying the Scripture' is a unique way of dealing with the Scripture; it involves both reading and prayer. Turn to the Scripture; choose some passage that is simple and fairly practical. Next, come to the Lord. Come quietly and humbly. There, before him, read a small portion of the passage of Scripture you have opened to. Be careful as you read. Take in fully, gently, and carefully what you are reading. Taste it and digest it as you read."[5]

I love that descriptive phrase "Taste it and digest it." It reminds me of Psalm 34:8, which says, "Taste and see that the Lord is good; blessed is the man who takes refuge in him." If we know that the LORD is good, we will be more likely to trust him and submit our will to his. Jesus said, "If you remain in me and my words remain in you, ask whatever you wish, and it will be given you" (John 15:7). As we taste and digest God's Word, we come to know God's will, and we are better able to pray according to it.

Prayer Requests

We can learn a lot from looking at the specific petitions in Jesus' model prayer. When we pray, "Give us this day our daily bread," for example, we are acknowledging that God is the supplier of our daily needs. How easy it is for us to look ahead and worry about tomorrow! But God wants us to trust him and look to him for provision day by day.

When we pray, "Forgive us our debts as we forgive our debtors," we are recognizing the significant role of forgiveness in a believer's life. Forgiveness is a very important concept to God. Certainly the Bible teaches about it often (see Matthew 18:21–35; 2 Corinthians 2:10; Ephesians 4:32; Colossians 3:13). We ought to value forgiveness highly as well. Why should we forgive? Because we have no right to hold something over another person when God has forgiven us our entire debt of sin. We must not let unforgiveness ruin our lives! (We will talk more about forgiving others in chapter 11.)

When we pray, "Do not lead us into temptation, but deliver us from the evil one," we are asking God not only to steer us away from temptations but also to give us the strength to stand against them. The Old Testament character Jabez prayed a similar prayer when he asked "that Your hand would be with me, and that You would keep me from evil, that I may not cause pain!" (1 Chronicles 4:10 NKJV). Do we sincerely pray that God will lead us away from temptation, or do we dabble near temptation, forgetting to ask for God's help? May our daily cry be for God's leading and deliverance!

Jesus closes his sample prayer with another acknowledgment of who God is and how great he is: "For yours is the kingdom and the power and the glory forever." When we pray these or similar words, we are making a statement of faith. We are confirming that we believe God can do all things, including answering our prayers. We are making a profound statement that erupts from a heart of faith. Let's make it our daily proclamation!

For Whom Do We Pray?

Mrs. B lives next door. She is a kind, lovely lady with grown children whose life has taken several significant and difficult turns in the last few years. Her husband left her, she was diagnosed with cancer, and she requires regular chemotherapy treatments. Several gracious women in our neighborhood who also have grown children have joined together to take turns driving Mrs. B to the hospital and back. What a beautiful picture of compassion as her neighbors surround her with love!

Wondering what I could do for Mrs. B, I asked her son if I could bring meals. He told me his mother felt sick to her stomach so often that she probably wouldn't be able to eat much food. Visiting time was limited because her energy was zapped, and she spent much of the day resting. With that option out, it occurred to me that I could be a messenger of encouragement to Mrs. B by sending her notes, books, and gifts. And I could give her an even greater gift: I could faithfully pray for her.

It is easy to think that prayer is a small thing to do for someone, when in fact it is the most powerful and positive thing we can do for another human being. We should never downplay its value. J. C. Ryle said, "Never, never may we forget that if we would do good to the world, our first duty is to pray!" Have you wondered what you could do for the families of the victims of September 11? Pray that they know God's love and strength and that they feel his arms of comfort around them. Are you concerned about the burn patient you know in the ICU? Pray for God's help and healing, both physical and emotional. Have you tried to help a friend in a troubled marriage, to no avail? Pray for God to work in ways you can't even imagine. Always do what you can to help others, but make sure your prayers are included in your help.

Remembering to pray for everyone in our lives and for everyone who is in need may seem like a monumental task. I have found it helpful to break down my prayer requests by praying for certain people or groups of people on certain days of the week. Of course there are people I pray for every single day, such as the members of my family.

I pray every day for immediate needs. But here's how I schedule prayer time for the other people I want to pray for on a regular basis:

- Sunday—Pray for preachers, missionaries, and others in ministry

- Monday—Pray for my extended family, sister, in-laws, and cousins

- Tuesday—Pray for America, the president, and other national leaders

- Wednesday—Pray for world leaders and people in different lands

- Thursday—Pray for those who are sick, hurting, and suffering, both near and abroad

- Friday—Pray for friends, their families, their marriages, and their needs

- Saturday—Pray for the surrounding community, civic leaders, and teachers

You may want to make up your own schedule, one that covers all of the prayer bases that are important to you. Many resources are available to help you pray for different groups or needs. Zondervan's *Operation World: The Day by Day Guide to Praying for the World* by Patrick Johnstone is a book that provides information about every country in the world and how you can pray specifically for the people of each nation. At www.Roaring-Lambs.org you can find a prayer guide for praying for the governors and leaders of each state in our nation week by week. In *The Power of a Positive Mom,* I included a list of specific and scriptural areas of prayer for your family. But remember, the best resource of all is God's Holy Spirit within you, as Romans 8:26 says: "In the same way, the Spirit helps us in our weakness. We do not know what we ought to pray for, but the Spirit himself intercedes for us with groans that words cannot express." God knows the names and the needs, even if you don't. Your part is to be faithful to pray.

Finding the Best Time to Pray

You may be like me. If I don't put something down on my schedule, it won't happen. That's why it's important for me to place prayer on my daily docket of activities. If I do not deliberately set aside a time for prayer, the day will fly by, and my prayer time will disappear as well.

Jesus purposefully went out early in the morning and prayed, as Mark 1:35 notes. Certainly we can pray throughout the day, here and there, and we should. But it is also important to plan a deliberate meeting with God. The great Martin Luther once said, "I am so busy now that I find if I did not spend two or three hours each day in prayer, I could not get through the day. If I should neglect prayer but a single day, I should lose a great deal of the fire of faith."[6] Okay, okay. Maybe you and I can't pray two or three hours a day. But you get Luther's point!

When is the best time to pray during the day? The psalmist said, "In the morning, O LORD, you hear my voice; in the morning I lay my requests before you and wait in expectation" (Psalm 5:3). There are a number of good reasons to meet God in the morning. Nevertheless each of us should determine what time is best for our own schedules. I personally love getting up early in the morning before anyone else in the house is awake. I grab my cup of coffee and enjoy those quiet moments with my loving heavenly Father. How wonderful it is to enjoy the sunrise with its Maker!

Morning offers me the opportunity to lay my cares before the Lord; then I don't have to worry about them during the day. I ask the Lord to order my day from the very start, so I will be able to use my time to the fullest. I also ask God to make me aware of people's needs and direct my steps so I can be a vessel of his love and care. I find that meeting God in the morning gives me an eternal perspective on the circumstances that occur throughout the day.

You are never so high as when you are on your knees. —Jean Hodges

397

Where's Your Secret Spot?

My giant dog, Bear, has a favorite spot in the house. The full-length windows in our living room at the front of the house offer the perfect guard post for our Great Pyrenees. This oversized white ball of fluff rests at his spot throughout the day, laying his head on the window sill and peering out at the neighborhood. All is right with the world when Bear is in his spot! Do you have a spot—a favorite place to read the paper or a beloved book? Having a spot for prayer is a good idea too. A solitary place, similar to the kind to which Jesus often withdrew. A place where you can be alone to converse with God. Keep a Bible, a blank journal, and a pen at your spot so you'll have them ready, and use the prayer journal to write your thoughts, praises, and requests to God.

Think of this spot as your special meeting place with God, just as you may have a special restaurant or coffee shop or park bench to meet your best friend. Your prayer spot may be a couch near the window, a small room away from the hustle and bustle of home life, or even a large closet. It may be helpful to inform other family members that when you are in this spot, there is an invisible "do not disturb" sign; this is your time alone with God.

In my high school years I began to recognize my need for solitude in prayer, so I used my walk-in closet as my prayer place. My parents knew if they couldn't find me anywhere else, I could possibly be in there. Using a closet for prayer may sound silly, but it is actually biblical! In the Sermon on the Mount, Jesus addresses the importance of praying in secret: "But you, when you pray, go into your inner room [*closet* in the King James Version], close your door and pray to your Father who is in secret, and your Father who sees what is done in secret will reward you" (Matthew 6:6 NASB).

My friend Carol Regehr recognized her need for a special time alone with God and wanted an "inner room" in which to pray. She finally found the perfect spot: a space between two unused clothing racks in her master bedroom closet. Understand, Carol lives in Texas, where everything is big—and that includes most closets. Carol's closet had just the perfect amount of unused space, so she hung white lace curtains on the metal rods and turned it into her sacred spot to meet with the Lord.

Wanting to put a desk and chair in her inner room, she began praying that God would lead her to the perfect little desk. Her husband assured her she'd never find a desk small enough to fit in the closet area, but Carol persisted in prayer and hunting. One day she happened to walk by an antique store, and guess what she saw in the window? The perfect desk! Her husband even came to the store with measuring tape to be quite sure of the dimensions. It truly was a perfect fit—and a gift from God. Carol says her prayer time in her special, homemade prayer closet is the secret to her peaceful and joyful life.

Of course with prayer, the place is not as important as the heart. No matter where our special place is, we must come with an open heart and a listening ear. Prayer is not just a time to read out our list of requests and be done with it, like a visit to Santa Claus at the mall. We need to listen too. Can you imagine meeting with a dear friend every day and never giving your friend a chance to say anything? A good relationship is based on communication from both parties.

How does God speak to us? Perhaps through a passage of Scripture he leads us to in the Bible. Perhaps through a still, small voice as we sit quietly before him. As we commune with God, we truly begin to abide in him. Our relationship becomes rich and full. We become less worrisome and more faithful. The time we spend with him will be evident in our peace and joy.

Hannah Whitall Smith lived a life of joy in the Lord. She is the author of *The Christian's Secret of a Happy Life,* a book that has sold more than three million copies since it was first published in 1870. It is considered one of the great classics in Christian literature. According to Hannah, the secret to a happy life is to trust completely in the promises of God's Word. She shares this story concerning prayer:

> The story was of a poor woman who had been carried triumphantly through a life of unusual sorrow. She was giving the history of her life to a kind visitor on one occasion, and at the close, the visitor said feelingly, "I do not see how you could bear so much sorrow!"
>
> "I did not bear it," was the quick reply; "the Lord bore it for me."
>
> "Yes," said the visitor, "that is the right way. We must take our troubles to the Lord."
>
> (The poor woman replied) "We must do more than that; we must leave them there. Most people take their burdens to him, but they bring them away with them again, and are just as worried and unhappy as ever, but I take mine and I leave them with him, and come away and forget them. I do this over and over, until at last I just forget I have any worries."[7]

Do you want to live a happier, more joyful Christian life? Learn to give your worries to God in prayer. To make it easier, consider trying something I first learned to do in high school. Make a small "prayer box." A simple shoebox will do, and you can decorate it if you like. Then, when you have a care or worry, write out a prayer to God about that concern on a small piece of paper. Place the paper in the prayer box and leave it there as a physical reminder that you have given the matter over to God, and you are not to worry about it yourself.

Of course, as we discussed earlier in chapter 7, it's important to be persistent in prayer. But persistence based on trust and faith in God's ability to answer us is not the same as worrying. When we offer a concern to God, it is no longer ours. The issue and its resolution are now in his hands—and we can rest in the assurance that he is big enough to handle any care that comes our way.

Oh the joy of releasing all our worries to him! A positive woman is one who knows this secret of a happy Christian life. Let's commit ourselves to becoming women of faithful, daily prayer, and watch how our lives—and the lives of those around us—fill up with the peace and joy of God.

POWER POINT

⚙ **Read:** Psalm 116. What reason does the psalmist have to be elated? Have you ever been overflowing with joy as you've seen God work in your life? Did you share your gratitude with God and with others? Will you do as David did and share the thrill of answered prayer in the future?

♥ **Pray:** Wonderful Lord, loving heavenly Father, thank you for allowing me to bring my burdens to you each day. How marvelous you are to listen to my requests! I confess that I often try to carry too many burdens and worries on my own. Help me to give these cares over to you on a daily basis. Help me to be faithful to meet with you and enjoy the sweet fellowship of your love, your Word, and your presence. In Jesus' loving name, amen.

💡 **Remember:** "Enter his gates with thanksgiving and his courts with praise; give thanks to him and praise his name. For the LORD is good and his love endures forever; his faithfulness continues through all generations" (Psalm 100:4–5).

☺ **Do:** Decide today on a time and a place where you will meet with the Lord in prayer. Begin the time by reading Scripture and praising God, thanking him for his care. Then share your needs with him. Take time to listen to him too.

Power Principle #4

Becoming A Woman of Joy

For the joy of the LORD is your strength.

—Nehemiah 8:10

Joy is not a luxury or a mere accessory in the Christian life.
It is the sign that we are really living in God's wonderful love,
and that love satisfies us.

—Andrew Murray

9

Experiencing Joy
Finding Bright Skies in a Dark World

Christianity is the most encouraging, the most joyous,
the least repressive of all the religions of mankind.
While it has its sorrows and stern disciplines,
the end of it is a resurrection, not a burial—a festival, not a funeral.

—L. P. Jacks

What makes you happy? Your answer to that question may fluctuate throughout life. When I was a teenager, my list of things that made me happy went something like this:

- A trip to Six Flags Amusement Park with my best friend

- An *A* in chemistry

- Giggling with friends at a slumber party

- A phone call from a certain boy

- A smile of approval from my mother and/or dad

- Going to the mall with my sister

- A fun date

- Playing with my dog Fritz

- Eating a Fletcher's Corny Dog at the Texas State Fair

- Going to the movies

- Going on a chapel choir tour

Now that I'm forty-something, my happiness list looks a little different. Here's the current list:

- A cup of hot tea and a good book on a rainy day
- Lunch with friends (and of course, still giggling)
- A smile from my husband
- Quality time with my daughters doing what they want to do
- A date with my husband at a quiet restaurant
- A Caribbean cruise with family and friends
- Prayer time with my girlfriends
- Writing for hours at a time
- Going to the movies with another couple, and dessert afterward
- Watching my kids perform in athletics or on stage
- Snuggling up with my husband
- Hugging my kids
- Long family walks

What does your happiness list look like? You may want to take a moment to write it out. It's actually fun to reflect on happy moments and think about what really makes you feel warm and fuzzy. The interesting thing about happiness is that it is a *dependent* quality. It depends on people and circumstances. If things are nice and pleasant and people are kind, then we'll be happy. If events don't run smoothly or people are rude, then happiness seems to flutter away. Happiness is nice, but it's temporary. Here today, gone tomorrow.

Joy is something different altogether. Joy is a constant. It's not dependent on circumstances or people but rather on a heart issue. Happiness is external; joy is internal. Joy can be tucked deep in the heart, even in difficult circumstances. We have a tendency to hope that joy will come to us, and we often pursue a variety of pleasures to get it—from shopping to eating to extramarital affairs. But if we are looking for pleasure and hoping to find joy, we are wasting our time. Joy dwells within and cannot be secured with outward things.

Where Is Joy?

In the Bible *joy* is used as both a noun and a verb. The noun *joy* means "delight or gladness." We see it used in Acts 2:28: "You have made known to me the paths of life; you will fill me with joy in your presence." We find *joy* in the verb form in Habakkuk 3:18: "Yet I will rejoice in the LORD, I will joy in the God of my salvation" (NKJV). I am actually overwhelmed at the number of verses that speak about joy in the Bible. In my exhaustive concordance I found more than 180 verses mentioning joy. I'm exhausted just counting them!

If God speaks so much about joy, then why don't more Christians experience it? Like a "Where's Waldo" picture, picking out a joyful Christian in certain groups of believers can be hard. It shouldn't be that way! As women of faith, our joy can and should be evident. I wonder what the effect would be on the unbelieving world if they could see the evidence of joy in our lives on a daily basis. The German philosopher Friedrich Nietzsche said scornfully about Christians of his day, "I would believe in their salvation if they looked a little more like people who have been saved."[1] Ouch, that hurts! Surely those of us who have tasted God's abundant love, his everlasting forgiveness, and his glorious mercy ought to be radiating an overwhelming joy!

What does joy look like? Is it a glowing expression and a delightful smile? It can be. But while our facial expressions are certainly one way we express the joy in our hearts, there are times in our lives when we may have joy without a smile. Then, evidence of our joy may be found in our words. Words of kindness, gratitude, and praise represent a joyful heart, while words of gossip, grumbling, and complaining reflect quite the opposite. Joy may also be evident in our actions. Joy spreads encouragement and hope; it delights in the Lord and his work; it is glad when his righteousness wins out.

The opposite of joy is not necessarily sorrow, for we can be sorrowful over a situation yet still have a deep, abiding joy. No, the opposite of joy is the state of being restless, discouraged, hopeless, and discontent. I'd rather be joyful, wouldn't you? The fact is, a positive woman is a joyful woman, and a joyful woman has a powerful effect on the people around her. Joy is a magnet that draws people to God's love, hope, and forgiveness.

Got Joy?

Don't you just love the advertisements from the dairy industry showing various distinguished celebrities with more than enough evidence on their faces to prove they have been drinking milk? The dairy farmers are hoping these ads will make us want to drink more milk from their favorite source, the cow. Hey, if Mr. Celebrity loves milk, then I want to drink it, too! The caption always reads, "Got milk?"

I have a different caption for Christians: "Got joy?" In other words, is the evidence of joy obvious in our lives? What kind of advertisements are we? Are people drawn to God because of our joy? What is the source of our joy? To answer that last question, let's take a quick "joy jog" through the Bible and see what the Scriptures reveal about the source of a believer's joy:

- Psalm 35:9: "Then my soul will rejoice in the LORD and delight in his salvation."

- Psalm 43:4: "Then will I go to the altar of God, to God, my joy and my delight."

The deepest wishes of the heart find expression in secret prayer. —George E. Rees

- Isaiah 61:10: "I delight greatly in the LORD; my soul rejoices in my God. For he has clothed me with garments of salvation and arrayed me in a robe of righteousness."

- Luke 1:46–47: "And Mary said: 'My soul glorifies the Lord and my spirit rejoices in God my Savior.'"

- John 15:11: "I have told you this so that my joy may be in you and that your joy may be complete.

- Romans 5:11: "Not only is this so, but we also rejoice in God through our Lord Jesus Christ, through whom we have now received reconciliation."

- Philippians 4:4: "Rejoice in the Lord always. I will say it again: Rejoice!"

Did you notice that joy is closely connected to salvation? Christians have a joy and delight that unbelievers cannot experience. It is the joy of knowing that our sins are forgiven and our lives are made new through God's gift of his Son, Jesus. We ought to sing along with the psalmist (who looked to God for his salvation), "But I trust in your unfailing love; my heart rejoices in your salvation. I will sing to the LORD, for he has been good to me" (Psalm 13:5). He has been good to us! *Rejoice!*

Even now God is at work in our lives through the Holy Spirit, producing "fruit" such as love, joy, peace, patience, kindness, goodness, faithfulness, gentleness, and self-control (Galatians 5:22–23). Do we strive and work for this fruit? No, the fruit is the work of the Holy Spirit. Jesus tells us that if we abide in him and he abides in us, then we will bear much fruit; but without him we can do nothing (see John 15:4). So the question arises: If joy is something we receive from the Lord, do we have any responsibility in obtaining it?

Yes, joy is a gift from God, but we must make the decision to experience it. Paul instructed the believers at Thessalonica, "Be joyful always" (1 Thessalonians 5:16), implying that joy is an act of will. In numerous letters Paul tells his readers to rejoice. God gives us joy, and we must act upon it.

Think of it this way. Imagine that a large, colorful package is delivered to your door. The courier tells you the box is filled with wonderful gifts that will bless you and everyone around you. You bring it inside and set it in the middle of the living room. You plan to open it, but you figure you will wait until your life is a little better, a little more settled, with fewer problems. So there the package sits, waiting to be opened. It's your gift; it belongs to you, but you're just not ready to open it. "Life's too busy," you say. Or perhaps you say, "There are people in my life right now who hurt me or make me angry. When they go away, I'll open the package." Or, "My job makes me miserable. I'll open the box when I find the perfect job." Or, "I don't feel well. When I am out of this physical pain, I'll open it." So the present sits unopened.

Many of us fail to unwrap the box, and we use a variety of excuses in our defense. "My childhood was miserable, so I can't experience joy." "My husband is awful, so I can't rejoice in the Lord." To one degree or another, we all need to go through and weed out our excuses by confessing our unforgiveness toward others. By releasing the bitterness that has crowded out any hope of joy. By recognizing that no one is perfect, including us. By relinquishing the hurt and pain we've grown strangely accustomed to. By applying God's healing salve of forgiveness.

Let's choose joy instead of bitterness. The people who anger us or the circumstances that annoy us should not darken the joy within us. Jesus prepared his disciples for his coming death by telling them, "Now is your time of grief, but I will see you again and you will rejoice [speaking of his resurrection], and no one will take away your joy" (John 16:22). Remember, no one can take away the joy we have in Christ!

That's assuming, of course, we have opened the package. What will we find inside? The promise of eternal life, for one thing. Can you imagine how joyless life would be if we didn't have the hope of spending eternity with God? Also inside are other amazing gifts such as forgiveness, freedom from guilt, salvation, and the right to become "children of God" (John 1:12). Each of these and more have been prepared for us by our loving heavenly Father. Joy is born as we accept his gift and grow in our relationship with him. Joy erupts as we enjoy his presence and follow his will. Joy overflows as we serve others and allow God's love to pour through us.

All this joy is available, just waiting to be accessed! Let's choose to open the gift of joy and watch the blessings flow out. Joy is one of those gifts that keeps on giving. When we open the gift of joy in our hearts, it will always overflow to those around us.

*Son*shine behind the Clouds

Please understand that Paul's instruction to "rejoice always" does not diminish the necessity of mourning or grieving. There are times in each of our lives when we face pain, disappointment, and loss, whether great or small. The death of a loved one, the suffering of an innocent child, the pain of divorce—these are reasons for deep sadness and sorrow, and rightly so. We must cry. Just as we should rejoice with those who rejoice, we must weep with those who weep (see Romans 12:15). Having joy doesn't negate grief. Real joy, after all, is not a surface-type happiness. Joy and sorrow *can* coexist.

You may be asking, "But where is the joy when life gets difficult? If it's there, why can't I see it?" Think about the sky on a stormy day.

Although the clouds cover up the sun, the sun is still there. It hasn't left and gone to another solar system. We can't see it, but it is there; it's just hidden. The good news is that as the clouds break up—and they always do—the sunshine returns to full view. In difficult times our joy may not be visible on the outside, but it's still there on the inside. It hasn't left.

Joy is more than a feeling; it is a deep peace, blended together with a solid hope that God has not left us. Joy is a delight in knowing there will be a better day. Can we have joy as our companion even when the road gets bumpy? Absolutely. James made a shocking contrast when he wrote, "Consider it pure joy, my brothers, whenever you face trials of many kinds, because you know that the testing of your faith develops perseverance. Perseverance must finish its work so that you may be mature and complete, not lacking anything" (James 1:2–4).

Many examples throughout history attest to the presence of joy even in the midst of sorrow. In my own life, I grieved when my mother, Barbara Kinder, was tragically killed at age fifty-five. My father, my sister, my husband, and my kids were shocked and saddened beyond belief. Yet we all experienced a peaceful joy knowing that Mom was in heaven with the Lord. I can't explain it. It wasn't a joy with a happy face; it was a peace deep within our hearts. We knew that we knew that God loves our family, and he had his loving arms wrapped around us. This kind of joy doesn't come from just knowing about God. It comes from experiencing him in our lives.

Kathleen is a woman who has experienced "*Son*shine"—the joy of the Lord—in the midst of dark circumstances. Most likely you will never see her on television or read about her in the newspaper; but like many heroes of the faith who will have great rewards in heaven, she has lived a humble life here on earth. Her granddaughter, Lisa Flagg, shares this account of her life:

In 1939, when she was twenty-eight years of age, Kathleen's husband left her and her five children who ranged in age from two to ten. Living in East Texas with no money and meager job opportunities, her future and that of her children looked very bleak. The first work she could find was in the fields at local farms. Soon she found a job cooking meals for the little community school in their area.

Rather than despair and give in to bitterness, she accepted her lot and moved forward. She never gave in to self-pity. The family endured years of true poverty, often having only a little food of the simplest kind. She kept the family together and raised all five children to responsible adulthood. A testimony to her success is the closeness of our family to this day. Growing up I never heard her complain about her circumstances in those early years or speak ill of the husband who left her to endure such hardship. That kind of life makes an impact!

Whenever we ask about that long and awful period in her life, she responds with unselfconscious frankness: "I didn't have a choice. I had five children to care for, and I was too busy doing what I could to dwell on how things could be or should be." But my grandmother did have a choice. She could have chosen despair and self-pity, which only drains initiative and will. I'm thankful she chose to face her problems and deal with them. She always reminds us that she "prayed a lot" and trusted that God was in control and could see them through.

Because of her faith, courage, and positive attitude, my grandmother has been a very strong influence in my life. If I ever find myself overwhelmed by difficult circumstances or seem to be slipping into self-pity during a hardship or unpleasant time, I think of my grandmother and say to myself, "I have it easy! Look at what Nannie endured and survived"—and I am revived![2]

If you obey my commands, you will remain in my love, just as I have obeyed my Father's commands and remain in his love. I have told you this so that my joy may be in you and that your joy may be complete. —John 15:10–11

Kathleen is a testimony to God's strength, peace, and joy—not a giddy, schoolgirl-type of joy, but the type of joy that runs deep within the soul. The type of joy that looks beyond the problems and sees God in the solution. The type of joy that is spoken of in Hebrews 12:2: "Let us fix our eyes on Jesus, the author and perfecter of our faith, who for the joy set before him endured the cross, scorning its shame, and sat down at the right hand of the throne of God."

Greater Joy Up Yonder

As positive women and believers in Christ, we can look forward to an even greater joy: the joy of seeing Jesus face to face one day. We may find ourselves in a difficult situation or feel like we've been handed a terrible lot in life, but as Christians we can always look forward to the joy down the road. A day will come when all sorrow and pain will cease. Psalm 30:5 says, "Weeping may remain for a night, but rejoicing comes in the morning." D. L. Moody put it this way: "This is the land of sin and death and tears...but up yonder is unceasing joy!"[3] We take joy in the anticipation of that great day!

The story is told of a Christian lady who frequently visited an old, bedridden saint who always seemed to be cheerful despite her circumstances. This visitor had a wealthy friend who also professed to be a believer but was constantly looking at the dark side of things. Thinking it would do her glum friend good, she brought her on the next visit to the old woman's fifth-story apartment.

Climbing the stairs, the two friends reached the first story of the building. At that point the rich lady held her dress high off the ground and said, "How dark and filthy it is!"

"It's better higher up," said her friend.

They got to the next story, which was no better than the first. The rich lady complained again, but her friend replied, "It's better higher up."

At last they got to the fifth story. When they entered the sickroom, the rich woman saw a lovely carpet on the floor, flowering plants on the window sill, and birds singing from the roof outside. There they found the bedridden woman—one of those saints God is polishing for a greater kingdom—beaming with joy.

"It must be very hard for you to lie here," the wealthy woman said.

The sweet saint simply smiled and said, "It's better higher up."[4]

Truly one of these ladies was very rich indeed! She was rich with an eternal joy, because her mind and heart looked forward to a better day. It's so easy to sweat the small stuff and groan over our immediate cares and concerns; but as we turn our sights heavenward, we gain a whole new perspective. In this life we are going to have happy times and sad times. But at all times, we can be positive, joyful women because we have our heavenly Father's assurance: "It's better higher up."

POWER POINT

Read: Luke 10:38–42. Which of the two women in this passage seemed to experience joy? Describe Martha's main focus and then describe Mary's main focus. Which description fits you best?

Pray: Glorious heavenly Father, you are the Giver of joy. I praise you for the joy of my salvation. Oh, how wonderful to know that I am forgiven! I praise you for the joy that is set before me as I look heavenward. Thank you for the joy your Spirit produces in me. Forgive me for covering up or hiding my joy at times when I should allow it to shine forth. Help me to share this joy with others. I rejoice in you, my Lord, my Redeemer. In the abundant name of Jesus I pray, amen.

Remember: "You have made known to me the paths of life; you will fill me with joy in your presence" (Acts 2:28).

Do: Write out a "happy list"—a list of things you enjoy doing. Now write out a "joy list" naming the reasons you have to rejoice in the

Lord. Compare the two lists. Do they look different from each other? Generally, the things that make you happy are based on temporary enjoyments, while your reasons for joy are based on things that are eternal. Take a moment to thank God for the gift of joy he brings, and ask him to help you open that gift in your daily life.

10

My Life As a Three-Ring Circus
Enjoying a Life in Balance

I will rejoice in the LORD, I will be joyful in God my Savior. The Sovereign LORD is my strength; he makes my feet like the feet of a deer, he enables me to go on the heights.

—Habakkuk 3:18–19

When is the last time you visited the circus? For me, it was about ten years ago when my daughters were preschoolers. Although my girls didn't fully grasp the degree of heroism involved in the incredible feats, the adults in the audience ooh-ed and ahh-ed throughout the entire program. The circus is definitely one of the "greatest shows on earth"! My only complaint that day was that too much was going on at once. While the acrobats flew through the air in ring one, the tigers performed in the center ring, and the human cannonball was sent into flight in the third. I wish I could have concentrated on everything all at once, but my little brain was overwhelmed.

Unfortunately my life is like a three-ring circus most of the time. What about yours? I often feel like a circus clown trying to juggle five different responsibilities at home while jumping through hoops in my work and scurrying around town running errands and taking my kids to activities. But I don't want to be like the clown on stage with a fake smile painted on his face; I want to have a very real smile on mine. Is it possible in the midst of a fast-paced, circuslike life to experience a deep and lasting joy?

In the previous chapter we said that joy is a constant that's not dependent on outward circumstances. Rather, it's an inner strength, contentment, and peace based on our relationship with the Lord. No one can rob us of our joy, even though difficult situations or painful circumstances can seem to cloud its radiance. We may not have control over some of these circumstances. But in many cases, we can make choices. This chapter is all about making the right choices to ensure that we experience the joy of a balanced life.

The Storm Clouds of Overactivity

Cumulus clouds (those large, puffy ones) are actually named from a Latin word that means "heap." Ironically, the heap of activities we tend to pile on our calendars can be the very thing that cloud-covers our joy.

Although we think of "activity overload" as a current cultural problem, it has age-old roots. Marcus Aurelius, the second-century Roman emperor and philosopher, had this to say about busy schedules: "'If thou wouldst know contentment, let thy deeds be few,' said the sage. Better still, limit them strictly to such as are essential, and to such as in a social being reason demands, and as it demands. This brings the contentment that comes of doing a few things and doing them well."[1] Apparently we are not the first generation to experience overloaded schedules! Human beings always have had and always will have twenty-four hours in each day. It's up to us to make wise choices as to how we will fill that time.

When I was a young girl, my family went out to eat every Sunday after church. And every Sunday, my mother gave me the same advice: "Karol, don't put more on your tray than you can eat." I think I could write a book titled, *Life Lessons Learned at Luby's*! My mother's words can apply to activities as well: "Don't put more on your schedule than you can handle." Like Luby's, life can offer a myriad of good opportunities. That's the problem!

We live in a society in which wonderful opportunities are offered to us on a silver platter each day. Hobbies, family time, sports, career, shopping, school, church, volunteer work—from a plethora of possible activities, we must continually decide what to do and what not to do. For mothers, the list is even bigger, because our kids' activities become our activities, too, as we drive them to and from practices and attend performances.

Solomon said in Ecclesiastes 3:1, "There is a time for everything, and season for every activity under heaven." It's important for us to realize that there is a time and place for everything—and that time may not be right now. We don't have to do everything this year or this season. How do we make wise choices?

A good formula to follow is encompassed in the acronym PDA. If you're up on technology, you know that a PDA is a "personal digital assistant"—a small, hand-held computer that keeps track of schedules, addresses, phone numbers, and so much more. For our purposes, however, PDA stands for "pray, determine, ask." Let's take a look at each of these components.

Pray. When you are confronted with a decision about adding a particular activity or interest to add to your schedule, ask for God's direction. Many times I've found that God will lead me down a certain road or steer me away from a particular situation when I ask for his guidance. He knows my capabilities and he knows the future, so I defer to his leadership first.

Determine. Determine if the activity has value in your life (or the life of your child). Will it build character? Will it help you reach a long-term goal? Will it take an inordinate amount of time away from family?

Does it allow you to use your gifts and talents? Determine the time commitment and duration of the activity. And finally, determine your motive. Are you choosing to take on a responsibility because of pride—because it will put you in the spotlight or bring you accolades? Are you doing it because everyone else is doing it? Are you being directed by selfish ambition? Many times as we pray about these issues, God will help us see more clearly what our motive really is.

Ask. Have you found, as I have, that whenever someone asks you to take on a leadership or volunteer role, the task inevitably takes about twice as much time as you were told it would? To avoid this problem, ask other people who have done this activity about the time commitment it really takes. Ask them to give you a clearer picture of what's really involved. Ask specific questions about time requirements and other expectations. Keep in mind, however, that each of us is wired a little differently; what frazzled one woman may be an easy job for another. A task that is a piece of cake for an organized person may be overwhelming to someone else who is organizationally challenged.

Another little word that is important to remember is "no." Get comfortable saying it! It may seem ironic, but "no" can be one of the most positive words you can have in your vocabulary when it comes to your schedule. Know your limits. Recognize that you will gain much more respect from doing a few things well than from doing a myriad of activities halfheartedly. It's true that we need to be stretched sometimes and take on an added responsibility that requires a step of faith (as we learned in chapter 4), but such a decision must be made with prayer and care. Count the cost and talk to your heavenly Activity Director. If God is the one doing the stretching, you'll grow stronger in the process. If he's not, you're sure to pop like a rubber band!

Cultivate more joy by arranging your life so that more joy will be likely. —Georgia Witkin

The Balance Beam of Life

My daughter Joy (perfect name for this chapter, don't you think?) has been taking gymnastics for over five years. When she first started, she could barely walk across the balance beam without falling off; but as she progressed, she learned to accomplish a cartwheel on the beam. Recently she mastered a back handspring on the beam. I am absolutely amazed whenever I watch her do this feat! After years of practice, she now completes her routine with ease and rarely falls off the beam. She has learned how to balance herself.

We, too, can learn how to balance ourselves—not necessarily on a balance beam, but in our lives and schedules. Just as Joy developed balance through hours of practice, excellent coaching, and a few falls along the way, we can achieve balance in life through maturity, good advice, and experience.

By maturity I mean the years of growth that develop wisdom in us. One of the blessings of aging (yes, there are some benefits) is that it teaches us to take our time, pray, and make wise, seasoned choices for ourselves and our families. As we mature, we develop greater balance. We also become more balanced as we listen to the wise advice of significant, trusted people in our lives. Did you know that in the business world, some people actually make a living as "life coaches" for others, helping their clients develop goals and maintain a balanced perspective? We may not want to hire a life coach, but we can certainly benefit from a little coaching through life by wise friends, family members, and counselors. The people who know us best can help us look at our schedules and commitments and offer insight into how we can achieve a healthy equilibrium.

When it comes to balance, though, experience is often our best teacher. Through our successes and our mistakes, we begin to learn what does and does not work in our lives. Personally, I can look back and recall times when I was overcommitted or engaged in responsibilities that played to my weaknesses instead of my strengths. In each of these cases I learned to make changes, adjust myself, and find the proper balance. Experience has taught me a great deal about when to say "yes" and when to say "no" to additional activities or responsibilities.

The Perfect Balance

What does it take to live a life of balance? We can find the answer by looking at Jesus and the perfect, balanced life he lived. We read in Luke 2:52 that "Jesus grew in wisdom and stature, and in favor with God and men." That statement identifies four areas of growth and development that are necessary for balanced living. We must pursue them intentionally if we want to follow Jesus' example in our own lives. Let's look at them individually.

Wisdom. I know we have covered the topic of wisdom earlier in this book, but here I want to emphasize the importance of wisdom in maintaining a balance in life. It is through wisdom that we make proper decisions about our schedules. Through wisdom we find opportunities to serve and to get involved in the work that God is doing all around us. A wonderful saying is attributed to German poet Wolfgang von Goethe's mother: "How many joys are crushed underfoot because people look up at the sky and disregard what is at their feet."[2] Wisdom gives us eyes to see the joy that's right there waiting be discovered. If we pursue wisdom, we're certain to find joy in the process.

Stature. Stature relates to the physical side of our well-being, which definitely plays an important role in healthy, balanced living. Physical health is closely connected to emotional health; it's much harder to keep our emotions in balance when our bodies are sick or in pain. A regular exercise routine can be an important key to healthy stature. The obvious physical benefits are a trimmer look and stronger muscle tone, but the emotional benefits are just as real as the physical ones. Studies now show that exercise releases endorphins—neurochemicals in the brain that help head off depression, reduce anxiety, and boost energy.

How do you choose the workout or exercise routine that is right for you? It's important to consider your age, your natural physical abilities, and your overall health. With some sports, like swimming or jogging, you may have to start out slowly and build up to a more demanding workout. It is also crucial to consider your own personal enjoyment. If you hate to run, you probably won't be motivated to get out and jog on a regular basis. Walking may be a better choice; it's considered one of the best exercises for women over forty. Remember to consult your doctor before you start any new exercise program.

You may find it helpful to enlist a workout buddy to make the exercise time more enjoyable and to hold you accountable. My husband and I walk each morning together. I must admit there are mornings I don't want to get out of bed, stretch out, and walk for several miles; but knowing that my husband is expecting me to join him helps me get moving. We have a wonderful time talking along the way (actually, I do 85 percent of the talking, but he's a great listener).

Proper nutrition is another important key to functioning at our peak, both mentally and physically. As we choose to eat a healthy diet of whole grains, lean proteins, fruits, and vegetables, we begin to look better and feel better. In his recent book *Food and Love,* Dr. Gary Smalley points to an amazing connection between what we eat and how we relate to other people. Smalley specifically identifies four categories of food that tend to harm our emotional and physical health: white or refined sugar, white or refined flour, hydrogenated oils or animal fat, and chemically laden foods.[3] In our society of abundant fast and processed foods, we need to ask ourselves, "Am I eating healthy? Am I giving my body the energy and nutrition it needs?"

Sleep is also an important factor that impacts our physical and emotional well-being. I know one thing about myself: a tired Karol is not necessarily a nice Karol. Perhaps you've noticed that about yourself too. Yet many of us fill our calendars with all kinds of activities and fail to schedule enough time for proper sleep. Studies show that most adults need eight hours of rest in order to function at their best. Of course, we all know people who seem to require fewer hours; but personally, I can't relate to those who say they can get by on four hours of sleep night after night. We need to give attention to the amount of sound sleep we're getting and adapt our schedules if necessary to make sure we're getting enough. And if on occasion we have a short or restless night, the best thing we can do for ourselves is try to catch a late-afternoon power nap to help us make it through the rest of the day. Ultimately, hearty, healthy sleep can be just the catalyst we need for a happier, more energetic life!

Favor with God. The word *favor* reflects a type of grace in a person or on the part of a giver. In Luke 1:30 we read that Mary, the mother of Jesus, found favor with God. Acts 7:46 says that King David enjoyed God's favor. Unlike salvation by grace, which is a free gift from God that cannot be earned, favor is something that can be deserved or gained. Jesus himself tells us how in John 15:10–14:

> "If you obey my commands, you will remain in my love, just as I have obeyed my Father's commands and remain in his love. I have told you this so that my joy may be in you and that your joy may be complete. My command is this: Love each other as I have loved you. Greater love has no one than this, that he lay down his life for his friends. You are my friends if you do what I command."

We experience the favor of God when we walk in obedience to Christ. The result, Scripture says, is great joy. Sin or disobedience to God, on the other hand, is like a dark cloud that covers our joy. Are there any dark clouds in your life? Do you struggle with a gossiping or backbiting tongue, with bitterness or jealousy, with impure thoughts? Take a few moments right now and ask God to reveal areas of sin in your life that you need to confess. Then ask him to help you turn from them. There is sorrow in our sin, but great joy in a life of obedience!

I want to be perfectly clear: Our eternal destiny is not in question; that's sealed from the moment we step out in faith and trust Christ. As Christians we cannot fall out of grace with God. However, we can draw closer to him as a friend and experience his favor and joy as we walk in his ways. With God's favor, our lives are in balance; without his favor, we tend to be off-kilter.

Favor with mankind. How we relate to others certainly has an effect on the balance and joy reflected in our lives. Jesus spoke often about our relationships with one another. In fact, when someone asked him to name the two greatest commandments, Jesus responded, "'Love the Lord your God with all your heart and with all your soul and with all your mind.' This is the first and greatest commandment. And the second is like it: 'Love your neighbor as yourself'" (Matthew 22:37–39). That's "favor with God and men" in a nutshell! The next chapter is devoted entirely to relationships, but I mention them here because we need to recognize their vital role in healthy, balanced living. As Thomas Aquinas said, "There is nothing on this earth more to be prized than true friendship."[4]

Growing in favor with mankind does not imply that we are to become people pleasers, frantically running around trying to make everyone happy. We must distinguish between the thoughtfulness involved in serving others, which is healthy, and the giving in to people's thoughtless demands, which can be unhealthy. Jesus himself said that not everyone is going to be supportive of us. Matthew 5:11–12 records his words: "Blessed are you when people insult you, persecute you and falsely say all kinds of evil against you because of me. Rejoice and be glad, because great is your reward in heaven, for in the same way they persecuted the prophets who were before you."

There you have it! Because we are followers of Christ, people are not always going to like us. We shouldn't be caught off guard by that. The same kinds of people didn't like the prophets down through the ages. But what should our response be? Jesus tells us to rejoice (there's that *joy* word again) because we can look forward to a heavenly reward. Of course, we're not to go around looking for trouble or causing disagreements. But if people choose to dislike us or even persecute us for following Christ, we shouldn't let it get us down. We can still live a peaceful, balanced life, growing in favor with God and man, if we heed Solomon's general life principle: "When a man's ways are pleasing to the LORD, he makes even his enemies live at peace with him" (Proverbs 16:7).

As positive women we need to focus on developing these four areas of a life in balance: wisdom, stature, favor with God, and favor with mankind. All four are important. Think of them as the four legs of a chair; if one is missing, balance is difficult to maintain. If we work on our relationship with God, for example, but neglect our fellow man, we hide God's light to the world. If we pursue wisdom but fail to maintain our physical well-being, our lives lack the energy to share what we have learned. If we focus on our physical beauty to the detriment of the other areas, our existence is shallow and futile. But by growing in these four areas together, our lives will be in healthy balance and God's joy will shine through us, lighting up a darkened world.

Hormonal Storms

I want to mention one other area that can affect a woman's sense of balance and joy. Perhaps you have noticed there are times during a typical month when you get a run in your hose or forget your lipstick, and you think to yourself, *Oh well.* Then there are other times during the month when the same simple annoyances cause you to completely lose your composure with your spouse, your kids, or your coworkers. The difference comes down to that lovely feminine predicament known as *fluctuating hormones.*

We cannot overlook the part that hormones play in our physical and emotional well-being. In her book *Women and Stress,* Jean Lush likens the cycle of a woman's hormones to the cycle of seasons in a year. Here's a brief summary of what she shares at length in her book. Keep in mind that the symptoms may vary somewhat from month to month:

The *spring phase* starts with the blood flow of the menstrual cycle and is dominated by the hormone estrogen. A woman feels bright, positive, outgoing, energetic, and well coordinated during this time. Little threatens her, and her relationship with her husband and kids is delightful.

The *summer phase* can be described as peaceful, happy, affirming, and creative. The woman is able to accomplish much, but she is a little less assertive. Estrogen continues to dominate, and she feels generally pleased with life.

The *midsummer phase* is the short period in which ovulation occurs. The woman feels euphoric, motherly, peaceful, sensual, and integrative. She loves her husband and kids, who can do no wrong. These feelings are influenced by the production of progesterone.

The *fall phase* begins after ovulation, and now the woman begins

Joy is the echo of God's life within us. —Joseph Marmion

to slowly lose energy. Slight depression or the doldrums set in, and she becomes less enthusiastic. Her husband and children don't seem quite so lovable, and her confidence is droopy. Hormone fluctuations during this phase play a part in the unpleasant symptoms.

The *winter phase* occurs in the fourth week of the menstrual month. The woman turns into the "winter witch" as she experiences depression, fatigue, outbursts of emotion (she'll cry over anything), outbursts of temper, frustration, loss of self-control, suspicious or irrational thoughts, low self-esteem, and absent-mindedness. The good news is that the menstrual flow is only a few days away at that point, and she can look forward to feeling much better soon![5]

We should never use our hormones as an excuse for rude or unkind behavior. At the same time, we need to understand our monthly cycle in order to understand ourselves better. Basically, we need to be in harmony with our hormones and recognize when they may be a factor in our attitudes and actions. For instance, when I sense I'm in the winter phase, I know it's not the best time to have a discussion with my husband about a sensitive issue. If I'm feeling annoyed by a salesclerk, I ask myself, *Is the problem really with that person, or is it something going on inside of me?* If I'm in the fall or winter phase and I feel overwhelmed with responsibilities, I know I need to put off making major decisions about my schedule until I move into a more confident phase.

Each of us must pay attention to our own cycles and recognize when our hormones may be affecting us. At certain times it may be wise to talk to a doctor about hormone replacement therapy to bring our hormones into balance. If we understand our hormones and stay alert to their regular fluctuations, we can maintain our balance and our joy through all the seasons.

The Beauty of Joy

A balanced life is a joyful life, and a joyful life is a beautiful life. The true beauty of a positive woman is not simply external, but rather the reflection of the fountain of joy overflowing from her heart. It can be seen in the glow in her eyes, the warmth of her smile, and the kindness of her words.

Our culture is obsessed with outward beauty. You and I shouldn't be. Recently a friend e-mailed me the following comforting facts that have been circulating on the Web. I can't vouch for their complete accuracy, but they seem on target to me:

- There are three billion women who don't look like supermodels and only eighty who do.

- The photos of models in magazines are airbrushed because the models are not perfect.

- If Barbie were a real woman, she'd have to walk on all fours due to her proportions.

- The average woman weighs 144 pounds and wears between a size 12 and 14.

- A 1995 study found that three minutes spent looking at a fashion magazine caused 70 percent of women to feel depressed, guilty, and shameful.

- Twenty years ago models weighed 8 percent less than the average woman. Today they weigh 23 percent less.

As positive women, let's put our focus on developing the true beauty I describe in the following poem:

True Beauty

A woman's beauty does not rest
On her chains of gold or designer dress.
Her beauty is that gentle glow
Which from the heart does clearly grow.
Kindness, peace, hope, and love,
These are the jewels from above.
A smile of joy adorns her face
Founded upon God's true grace.

Jesus said, "You are the light of the world. A city on a hill cannot be hidden. Neither do people light a lamp and put it under a bowl. Instead they put it on its stand, and it gives light to everyone in the house" (Matthew 5:14–15). Let's not allow anything—person, circumstance, or hormone—to cloud our joy. Instead, let's make wise choices every day so that God's joy will shine brightly through us to all of the world.

POWER POINT

Read: The story of two joyful women in Luke 1:39–55. What was the source of the joy these women experienced? How did they express their joy? Were the circumstances in their lives perfect? How were these women an encouragement to each other?

Pray: Oh wise and wonderful God, how joyful I become whenever I turn my eyes toward you and recognize your loving kindness and grace! Forgive me for the times I've been too busy to enjoy the sweet fellowship that comes from spending time with you. Help me to balance my time and my life wisely and carefully. Make me aware of choices I've made that tend to cover up my joy, and show me how to set things right so that my joy will overflow once again. What an awesome

God you are—for you truly want me to experience joy! Thank you! In Jesus' name, amen.

💡 **Remember:** "I will rejoice in the LORD, I will be joyful in God my Savior. The Sovereign LORD is my strength; he makes my feet like the feet of a deer, he enables me to go on the heights" (Habakkuk 3:18–19).

☺ **Do:** On a blank piece of paper, draw a simple picture of the sky, including a large sun and several big, puffy clouds. On the sun write, "The joy of the Lord." Add several words describing what this phrase means to you. On the clouds list those areas in your life that tend to hide the joy that's inside you. Then pray and ask God to help you diminish these clouds so that his joy can shine through you to others.

Power Principle #5

Becoming A Woman of Love

😊

A woman who loves always has success.

—Vicki Baum

Dear friends, let us love one another,
for love comes from God.

—1 John 4:7

11

Friendships in the Fast Lane
Maintaining Quality Relationships in a Hurried World

I think that God will never send
A gift so precious as a friend.

—Rosalie Carter

My golden retriever, Honey, is a faithful friend. Every time I walk in the door, he runs and greets me with a wagging tail and what seems to be a big smile on his reddish-brown face. He follows me through the house during the day, from the laundry room to the study to the bedroom and, of course, to the kitchen. At night he lays on the floor by my bed as if to say, "Don't worry, I love you and I'm here to protect you." He's hopelessly loyal. He absolutely loves his walks yet is forgiving when I can't take him. Wouldn't it be delightful if people were as easy to get along with as dogs?

The reality is that people-to-people relationships are a little more work. They can be demanding and complex at times. They require patience, love, forgiveness, and even sacrifice from us. Perhaps you are thinking right now, *Maybe I'll forget friendships and just get a dog!* Yes, pets are great, but they can't replace people in importance in our lives. Remember the Garden of Eden? We learned in chapter 1 that it was not good for Adam to be alone; he needed a human companion. We were created to be relational beings. Solomon recognized the significance of relationships when he wrote, "As iron sharpens iron, so one man sharpens another" (Proverbs 27:17). In Ecclesiastes 4:9–10 he reflected further, "Two are better than one, because they have a good return for their work: If one falls down, his friend can help him up. But pity the man who falls and has no one to help him up!"

Jesus affirmed the high priority of loving and relating to others when he said, "This is my command: Love each other" (John 15:17). He modeled this in his life on earth by surrounding himself with a group of disciples whom he taught, encouraged, and loved. When he prayed in the Garden of Gethsemane, anticipating his death on the cross, he specifically asked Peter, James, and John to stay close to him. Even Jesus wanted close friends around when things got tough.

Peter tells us to "love one another deeply, from the heart" (1 Peter 1:22). Paul encourages us to be "devoted to one another in brotherly love" (Romans 12:10). John speaks forthrightly, "We love because he first loved us. If anyone says, 'I love God,' yet hates his brother, he is a liar. For anyone who does not love his brother, whom he has seen, cannot love God, whom he has not seen. And he has given us this command: Whoever loves God must also love his brother" (1 John 4:19–21).

Clearly the Bible places a high priority on how we relate to one another. So why is it that so many of us struggle to maintain deep and abiding relationships?

Cultural Roadblocks on the Friendship Freeway

Part of the problem is that we live in a hurry-up, get-it-now society. Everything is fast, from food to photos to FedEx. Friendships, on the other hand, take time and nurturing to grow.

Not only is our culture programmed for fast, it is also programmed for busy. When someone asks, "So, what do you do?" we proudly rattle off a long list of the activities we're involved in—careers, family responsibilities, community service, hobbies, and interests. "Oh, I spend time working on my relationships" is not a phrase we typically add to the mix.

Dr. Alan Loy McGinnis, in his best-selling book *The Friendship Factor,* writes, "Why is there such a shortage of friendship? One simple reason: We do not devote ourselves sufficiently to it. If our relationships are the most valuable commodity we can own in this world, one would expect that everyone everywhere would assign friendship highest priority. But for many, it does not even figure in their list of goals. They apparently assume that love will 'just happen.'" He goes on to say, "Significant relationships come to those who assign them enough importance to cultivate them."[1]

The question is, how do we make relationships a priority? How do we cultivate friendships? Is it simply a matter of scheduling our time differently? If the key to relationships were as simple as time management, we could take some lessons on how to use a Palm Pilot and get better relationships with a few keystrokes. Right? No, you and I both know people who have great organizational skills yet lack friendships. We know others who are highly disorganized yet manage to maintain meaningful relationships. Scaling back our activities so we have more time for friendships may be a good idea, but it's not the whole answer. We all know people who are involved in few activities but still long for deeper connections with friends.

So what is the key to quality relationships? I believe it goes back to something our grandmothers told us: "If you want to have friends, you must show yourself friendly." To have good friends, we must be good friends.

Seven Qualities of a Good Friend

After years of speaking to women's groups on the topic of friendship, I have discovered a pattern of characteristics that women typically appreciate in other people. Here are the top seven relationship ingredients that have surfaced over the years. I encourage you to consider these qualities in light of your current friendships and, if you are married, in light of your relationship with your spouse. (They're great building blocks for marriage.) These are qualities to internalize in your own life in order to become a better friend. You can also use them as a measure to consider (not judge) potential friendships in the future.

1. Take a genuine interest in others.

Dale Carnegie, author of *How to Win Friends and Influence People,* said, "You can make more friends in two months by becoming interested in other people than you can in two years by trying to get people interested in you."[2] As we listen to others and show an interest in what is important to them, we begin to truly love and understand them. Every person has an invisible sign around his or her neck that reads, "I want to feel important." Everyone has something to offer this world. We need to search for it, find it, and bring it to the surface.

I've found that scheduling an "Others Hour" is a good way to make time to be attentive to others. What is an Others Hour? It's a sixty-minute period we reserve on our schedules each week in order to focus solely on our friends and their needs. I know for me, if something is not on the calendar, it typically doesn't happen. An Others Hour is a time when we can write a note or make a call or deliver a gift or do a favor. It's a time when we can pray for a certain friend in need. Try it. Who knows? You may find your Others Hour multiplies throughout the week!

2. Be a giver, not a taker.

Ask not what your friends can give to you but rather what you can give to your friends. (Sound familiar? Sorry, John, for reworking your quote.) What can we give to others? How about a smile, a hug, a kind word, a listening ear, help with an errand, a prayer, an encouraging note, a meal? We can come up with many things to give others if we are willing to be attentive to their needs. (Hint, hint: To know someone's needs, you must take a genuine interest in the person first.) Giving may take time. It may take us out of our way. But giving and self-sacrifice are part of the definition of love. I like this little poem by John Oxenham:

Art thou lonely, O my brother?
Share thy little with another.
Stretch a hand to one unfriended,
And thy loneliness is ended.[3]

3. Be loyal.

Loyalty is a rare commodity in today's world, but it's an absolute requirement in true and abiding friendships. When we are loyal to one friend, we prove ourselves worthy of many.

One way we show our loyalty is through our words—or lack thereof. In fact, a key to being loyal is keeping a tight rein on our tongues. If we're loyal, we won't tear a friend down behind her back or share her personal story without her permission. It's easy to gossip or pass judgment; it's much harder to keep silent. I like what Marsh Sinetar said: "When you find yourself judging someone, silently say to yourself, 'They are doing the best they can right now.' Then mentally forgive yourself for judging."[4] As positive women, we need to make sure our tongues are used for good and not evil. We should be builders with our words, not demolishers.

Jealousy, envy, and a range of other negative emotions can keep us from being loyal. But true loyalty overcomes all of them. I think of the beautiful Old Testament story about the friendship between Jonathan and David. Jonathan had reason to be jealous of his friend, David. Jonathan was King Saul's son and in line to succeed his father to the throne, but God anointed David to be the next king instead. At the same time, David easily could have been angry with Jonathan. Jonathan's father, the king, chased David out of the country and tried to kill him. Yet these two men pledged their loyalty in friendship and never wavered from it. Eventually Jonathan saved David's life, and David continued to show his loyalty to his friend by watching out for Jonathan's son.

Jealousy, envy, bitterness, and anger are all sisters in sin and killers of loyalty in relationships. But if we continually take these emotions to God and ask for his help in overcoming them, we can remain loyal to our friends through the thick and thin of life.

4. Be a positive person.

The most consistent comment I hear about what people want in friendships is this: "I want a friend I can laugh with." We all want friends we can enjoy! People who consistently bring us down with their problems and complaints are generally not the ones we want to pal around with for any length of time. Of course, sometimes a friend will go through a difficult time, and we need to be ready and willing to hold a hand and provide a listening ear. But a friend in need is different than a habitual whiner. We want our friendships to be positive and uplifting— and that means we must be positive, uplifting friends ourselves.

It has been said that there are two kinds of people: those who brighten the room when they enter, and those who brighten the room when they leave. Let's make sure we're brightening our friendships with our presence. Positive women demonstrate an attitude and a spirit that sees God at work in all of life and encourages others to see him too. They are generous with praise, with smiles, and with love, remembering what Francis Bacon said: "Friendship doubles joys and halves griefs."[5]

5. Appreciate the differences in others.

Variety is the spice of life. I'm so glad that when I walk into an ice cream store, vanilla isn't the only option! I'm glad, too, that God created people with a variety of personalities, talents, and interests. Each one of us is a unique creation. Mixed together we blend to form the body of Christ.

So why is it that, instead of appreciating our differences, we tend to despise them or become jealous of them? Apparently this was as much a challenge in the early church as it is today. Paul wrote in 1 Corinthians 12:18–25:

> But in fact God has arranged the parts in the body, every one of them just as he wanted them to be. If they were all one part, where would the body be? As it is, there are many parts, but one body.
>
> The eye cannot say to the hand, "I don't need you!" And the head cannot say to the feet, "I don't need you!" On the contrary, those parts of the body that seem to be weaker are indispensable, and the parts that we think are less honorable we treat with special honor....But God has combined the members of the body and has given greater honor to the parts that lacked it, so that there should be no division in the body, but that its parts should have equal concern for each other.

Along with a variety of personalities come a variety of faults. I am the creative type and love to spend hours writing and brainstorming, but I am a little scatterbrained when it comes to details and being on time. Of course I need to work on my faults, but I also need understanding friends who will bear with me (see Colossians 3:13). At the same time, I need to overlook my friends' faults in other areas. An old Turkish proverb states, "Whoever seeks a friend without a fault remains without one."[6] The truth is, we will never find a perfect friend here on this earth (except Jesus). So let's appreciate our differences, both the good and the bad.

6. Build on common interests.

What is it that brings friends together in the first place? There is usually something that draws us to others—a common hobby, a sport, a Bible study, a volunteer project, a children's activity. My friend Karen and I got to know each other as our daughters grew to be friends at school. Our friendship developed as we took our kids to activities together and talked and planned over the phone. We go to the same church, which gives us another common bond. Karen and her husband, Dick, organize many of the mission opportunities at the church, so Curt and I join them occasionally to help feed the homeless. Since our husbands enjoy hunting and golfing together, we build on their common interests as well.

In our busy society, it can be difficult to create times to get together with people. But if we take advantage of the common activities and interests we have with others, we can fit the time for friendship into our schedules. If you and a friend both like to exercise, work out together. If you both like to read, go to the bookstore together to pick out your next selection, grab some coffee, and talk about the last book you read. If your kids are your common interest, consider getting together on a regular basis to pray for them. The point is to allow your common interests to draw you together.

Married couples need to practice this too. Many couples tend to get focused on (and frustrated with) their differences, while overlooking the common interests that brought them together in the first place.

When that happens they need to go back to basics and begin to build again on their common interests, overlooking each other's faults and appreciating the different qualities they bring into the marriage. Marriages seem to be made in heaven when they start, but they most assuredly need to be maintained and continually tended here on earth. Mignon McLaughlin puts it this way, "A successful marriage requires falling in love many times, always with the same person."[7]

7. Be open, honest, and real.

The word *hypocrite* originally described actors on a stage who covered their faces with masks to conceal their real identities. Today the word describes people who pretend to be something they're not. True friendship cannot be built on false images. We must be true to ourselves. We may think we have to present a faultless picture of ourselves to the rest of the world, but why? No one wants to be friends with someone who is perfect! We simply need to be our best selves and allow people to know the real us.

Of course, being open and honest doesn't mean spilling our guts to everyone. As we already know, loyalty is a rare commodity; when we find it, we know we have a friend we can trust—someone with whom we can share openly about our deepest issues and feelings. George Washington offered some wise words about friendship when he said, "Be courteous to all, but intimate with few; and let those few be well tried before you give them your confidence. True friendship is a plant of slow growth and must undergo and withstand the shocks of adversity before it is entitled to the appellation."[8]

Growing Deeper

Have you noticed that there are certain levels of friendships in life? Not every friend is your best friend. Rather, we have what I call different *circles* of friends. Think of three concentric circles (for all you nonmath majors, think of three circles of different sizes, one inside another inside another). The outer circle represents the large pool of acquaintances we have. These are friends that we know, but not well. We may have fifty to 150 acquaintances, depending on our personalities and the kinds of activities we're involved in. In this outer circle, conversations stay pretty much at surface level:

"How are you doing?"

"Okay, I guess. I've been a little tired lately."

"Oh, me too. I hope you get some rest."

"Thanks. Good to see you."

"Yeah, see you later. Bye."

From within our pool of acquaintances comes the next circle of friends, people we would call "good friends." These are kindred spirits with whom we "click." In fact, a good friendship forms from that "Aha" moment when we first realize we have something in common and begin walking in the same direction side by side. That's what the word *companion* actually means—two people walking in the same direction.

With good friends we tend to reveal ourselves on a deeper level. We share opinions, concerns, facts, and interests. We set aside time for good friends, whether that means meeting them for lunch or simply calling them on the phone. We may have five to twenty-five good friends at different times in our lives.

Finally, from within the garden of good friends grows the wonderful flower that is a best friend, a soul mate, a true heart-to-heart companion. These are the people in our inner circle. They're the lifetime friends with whom we can pick up right where we left off, even when we haven't talked for months. Soul mates share not only opinions and beliefs, but hopes and dreams, struggles and challenges. They enrich one another. We can count ourselves fortunate if we have three or four best friends over a lifetime.

Terry Ann is this type of friend to me. We met during our freshman year at Baylor and soon realized that not only did our personalities mesh, but we also had similar family backgrounds. Tat, as I called her, became my dearest college friend. We were roommates for three years at school and were in each other's weddings. Although we don't see each other often now, we still are able to share our hearts whenever we talk because we have a real depth of friendship between us.

Typically this type of inner-circle friendship doesn't happen overnight but rather over time and through much nurturing and growth. Terry Ann and my sweet friend Beth are two of the soul mates God has given me in my life. My husband, Curt, is another one. A spouse should definitely fit into the soul mate category of friendship. Unfortunately in many marriages, partners have relegated one another to the perimeter circle. If you've done this, invite your spouse back to the inner circle and begin applying the seven principles of friendship to your marriage relationship. You'll be glad you did.

How do we develop friendships that move from acquaintance to good friend and perhaps to soul mate? We begin our friendship circles by making relationships a priority. We apply the seven qualities of a good friend to our own lives, and we ask God to direct us to those people with whom we can connect. Is the goal to see who can have the most friends? No. In fact, when it comes to friendship, quality is more important than quantity. It's difficult to juggle a large number of friends and do it well. Proverbs 18:24 reminds us, "A man of many companions may come to ruin." Quality relationships take time, investment, and yes, self-sacrifice—which is why maintaining meaningful relationships may mean having fewer of them.

Difficult People

Unfortunately, some people we meet don't fit easily into even the outer circles of our lives. We all know them: people who are a little hard to get along with, who perhaps agitate us or annoy us in some way. People who seem to drain us of our emotional strength. As long as there are imperfect people in this world, there will be difficult people in our lives. We may see them at work, in the neighborhood, at a Bible study, or at the places we volunteer. They may be family members. What should we do about them? We can't stick our heads in the sand and pretend they're not there. Ignoring them is not necessarily the most loving approach. Instead, we need to have a plan for dealing with the difficult people who cross our paths at various times. Any effective plan will include the following four R's:

1. Release the need to change the person.

Often our energy is zapped by difficult people because we take on the responsibility of changing them ourselves. We need to take a deep breath and realize that unless people want to change, we cannot force change on them. You and I don't have the ability to make drastic changes in the personalities or habits of others. We can help and assist and at certain times confront, but then we must leave the results up to them and to God.

2. Recognize strengths.

Every person on earth has both positive and negative qualities. "Build on the strengths and manage around the weaknesses," my dad always says. We need to look for the good qualities in others and encourage them to nurture and develop those qualities. If we help people devote more time to their positive strengths, possibly some of the negatives will diminish.

3. Require boundaries.

Many times we dread being around difficult people because they tend to steal our time and energy or demand our attention in some way. We need to determine a limit on how much we can do or give, express it, and stick to it. For example, if a coworker continues to take up time with chitchat or gossip, we can say, "I only have five minutes to talk right now, then I need to get back to my project." Or, "I don't feel comfortable talking about Susie or listening to stories about her, so let's avoid that subject." Self-discipline may be needed to stick to the boundaries we set, but limits will make a difficult relationship much more enjoyable in the long run.

4. Reflect on God's love and forgiveness.

Whenever I think about the myriad of times that God has forgiven me, I find it hard to hold something over someone else. We need to continually extend God's love and forgiveness to the difficult people in our lives. That may mean helping someone turn from sin or a destructive lifestyle. It undoubtedly means praying for them and asking God to work in their lives. We may not be able to change someone, but with God all things are possible. Change is his work, not ours; if we do our part to love and forgive, he will take it from there.

Choose Wisely

Certain friends will come and go throughout life. Other friends will be our friends for life. Such is the cycle of acquaintances and friends, and the fact that some friends move in and out of our lives over the years shouldn't discourage us. When it comes to choosing companions and soul mates, however, we should choose wisely, because these are the people who will have the most significant and long-lasting influence on us. Curt and I tell our teenaged daughters to choose their

A good deed is never lost; he who sows courtesy reaps friendship and he who plants kindness gathers love. —St. Basil

447

friends carefully, because they will become like the people they hang around. Paul recognized this when he told the Corinthians, "Bad company corrupts good character" (1 Corinthians 15:33). Another oft-quoted statement from Volney Streamer goes like this: "We inherit our relatives and our features and may not escape them; but we can select our clothing and our friends, and let us be careful that both fit us."[9]

In my backyard I have several beautiful rosebushes that I enjoy tending. I try to make sure they have adequate water during the hot summer months, add rose food to their soil twice a year, and keep them pruned every week. My love, care, and attention definitely help to nourish them and encourage their growth. But as much as I would like to take all the credit for their beauty, I must admit there are times when I'm not as attentive to my precious plants as I should be. Yet the roses still seem to flourish in spite of me.

In life, friendships are like roses. They need care and attention to grow. They can be nurtured, but they can't be forced. Sometimes they flourish, not because of anything we do, but because there is an invisible hand—the touch of God—at work in the relationship. As positive women, let us tend our friendship gardens with kindness, forgiveness, and love. And let's open our eyes to the friendships all around us that are just waiting to bloom.

POWER POINT

⚙ **Read:** Matthew 27:55–56, 61 and 28:1–10. What circumstances brought the women in this passage together? Describe the grief and the joy they experienced with one another. What level of friendship do you think these women had with one another? How do you think their friendship developed? Can you name a friend in your life who is most like a "Mary" to you?

♥ **Pray:** I praise you, Father, for you are the truest of friends! Not only have you told us how to love in your Word, you've shown us how to love through your Son's example here on earth. Thank you! Help me now to share that kind of love with others and be a reflection of your love in all my relationships. Help me to be a good friend to the people who are precious to me. May all my friendships honor you, my dearest and closest Friend. In Jesus' name, amen.

♀ **Remember:** "Be devoted to one another in brotherly love. Honor one another above yourselves" (Romans 12:10).

☺ **Do:** On a large piece of paper, draw the three concentric circles mentioned in this chapter. In the outer circle write the names of acquaintances currently in your life. (Don't belabor this; just write the names of the ones who come to your mind first. You don't have to list all two hundred of them.) In the next circle write the names of those people you consider good friends. Finally, in the inner circle write the names of your soul mates or best friends.

Using your drawing as a guide, pray for your friends, and pray for your friendships. Ask God to direct you to a person who may eventually move to the next circle. Decide on some deliberate steps you will take to deepen that friendship—for example, make a phone call, write a note, or set a lunch date.

Creative Compassion
Loving Heartily in a Hurting World

I am a little pencil in the hand of a writing God who is sending a love letter to the world.

—Mother Teresa

Over half a century ago, the *Chicago Daily News* reported a fascinating story under the title, "Love Working Miracles for Mentally Ill in Kansas." The article centered on the amazing success rate of the Topeka State Hospital in returning eight of every ten new mentally ill patients to useful and productive lives outside the facility. Observers throughout the country wanted to know, "What's their secret?" In fact, the hospital's success did not come from electroshock therapy, surgery, group counseling, drugs, or any of the conventional treatments for mental disorders. These played a part, but the real secret was contained in a single word: love.

Dr. Karl Menninger of the famed brother/psychiatrist team explained, "The doctor doesn't cure by any specific treatment. You cure by atmosphere, by attitude, by sympathetic understanding on the part of everyone in the hospital." He went on to say, "By our words and deeds at the hospital, we must gently persuade them that society is worth coming back to. There is none of the professional-staff jealousy that poisons so many institutions. Everyone is on the

451

team. The hospital attendants' opinion is as readily considered as a nurse's or social worker's."[1]

It's easy to talk about love or even to say loving words; but as Dr. Menninger discovered, what people really need is to see love in action. Love in action boosts people to greater heights of development and growth than words or good intentions alone. Can you imagine what would happen if positive women everywhere began putting the power of Christ's love into action on a daily basis? We'd make a lasting and positive difference in this world!

What Love Looks Like

What does real love in action look like? Jesus gave us the perfect picture in his story of the Good Samaritan. A legal expert had just questioned Jesus about the great commandment, "Love your neighbor as yourself." "Who is my neighbor?" the expert wanted to know. Jesus responded immediately with this profound illustration.

"A Jewish man was traveling on a trip from Jerusalem to Jericho, and he was attacked by bandits. They stripped him of his clothes and money, beat him up, and left him half dead beside the road.

"By chance a Jewish priest came along; but when he saw the man lying there, he crossed to the other side of the road and passed him by. A Temple assistant walked over and looked at him lying there, but he also passed by on the other side.

"Then a despised Samaritan came along, and when he saw the man, he felt deep pity. Kneeling beside him, the Samaritan soothed his wounds with medicine and bandaged them. Then he put the man on his own donkey and took him to an inn, where he took care of him. The next day he handed the innkeeper two pieces of silver and told him to take care of the man. 'If his bill runs higher

than that,' he said, 'I'll pay the difference the next time I am here.'"
(Luke 10:30–35 NLT)

Truly this Samaritan man showed love in action. The fact that the Jewish people despised the Samaritan people makes the story even more profound. True love crosses over the lines of racism or stereotyping. It stretches beyond the convenient or the comfortable.

Mother Teresa is a twentieth-century example of someone who put love in action. She founded the Order of the Missionaries of Charity, and her selfless commitment to serving the poor in Calcutta, India, saved the lives of nearly eight thousand people. In 1979 she was awarded the Nobel Peace Prize for her compassion and devotion to the destitute. She humbly poured out Christ's love to everyone she touched, believing that acts of love begin in the small things we do for others. She said, "We can do no great things—only small things with great love."[2]

Everyday Illustrations

We can learn from Mother Teresa's example as well as her words. While love in action can mean opening a home for the impoverished in India or building an orphanage in Guatemala, it can also mean volunteering at a local hospital or helping to organize cans at a local food bank. It can mean taking a meal to a new mother or tutoring a child at the elementary school down the street. Each of these actions is important, and each is needed. Every act of love, great or small, noticed or unnoticed, makes a positive impact in the world. Even if no one sees the love and kindness we show to others, God sees, and he knows that we are obeying his command to love our neighbor.

Let me share with you some stories of a few modern-day "Samaritans." You probably haven't heard of any of these people. They're not famous, but they're sincere. They lead full and busy

Dear children, let us not love with words or tongue but with actions and in truth. —1 John 3:18

lives, just like you and me. I pray that their stories encourage and inspire you.

Feeding the homeless. Rip Parker rarely misses a day. Every weekday, every weekend, Rip drives his van packed with sandwiches and water to feed the homeless men and women in downtown Dallas. Cheryl Reinhart, a loving mother and nurse practitioner, joyfully serves with Rip once a month. She also volunteers at least once a week at the Dallas Life Foundation (a homeless shelter), helping to give medical exams to the homeless. Cheryl has known her share of heartache; her teenage son was tragically killed in a car accident. Yet she offers help, love, and hope to others, saying, "We are all put on the earth for something beyond ourselves."

... "And if anyone gives even a cup of cold water to one of these little ones because he is my disciple, I tell you the truth, he will certainly not lose his reward" (Matthew 10:42).

Adopting girls. Lance and Carol Wagers realized their life was in for a change, but they didn't realize how big the change would be. In their early fifties and after twenty-nine years of running a huge cheerleading company, they felt God call them into semiretirement. Since they had no children, they felt their life was an open book, and they were excited to see what story God would write on the rest of their lives.

On a mission trip down the Amazon River in Brazil, they encountered a poor family with nine children. Before they left the family's village, the mother came to Lance and Carol and asked if they would take her two youngest daughters back to the United States with them. She had been praying for years for a Christian family to adopt her daughters, then ten and eleven years old. She wanted the girls to get away from their difficult environment and have an opportunity for a better life. Hearing very clearly God's call to them, the Wagers obeyed. They eventually adopted Leni and Loraine and became an instant family with teenagers.

... *"Religion that God our Father accepts as pure and faultless is this: to look after orphans and widows in their distress and to keep oneself from being polluted by the world" (James 1:27).*

Visiting those in prison. "Nothing can prepare you perfectly for ministry to death row inmates," says army major Kathryn Cox. Kathryn has been ministering to inmates on "The Row" and their families since 1986. While her undergraduate degrees in psychology and journalism and her master's degree in criminal justice are helpful as she coordinates Bible correspondence courses for thirty thousand inmates through the army's Texas division, she believes God developed a strong spirit of compassion and understanding in her for this special ministry. She says that everything she has witnessed through her ministry "attests mightily to a salvation that can penetrate any locked door."[3]

... *"Come, you who are blessed by my Father; take your inheritance, the kingdom prepared for you since the creation of the world. For I was hungry and you gave me something to eat, I was thirsty and you gave me something to drink, I was a stranger and you invited me in, I needed clothes and you clothed me, I was sick and you looked after me, I was in prison and you came to visit me" (Matthew 25:34–36).*

Reaching children with HIV. Beth Dykhuizen loves children. As the mother of four, she is devoted to serving her family and raising her kids to be fine Christian young people. Early on, Beth learned how painful it is to see innocent children suffer. Her own son, Kurt, was born with Goldenhar Syndrome, which meant he had numerous birth defects and required over eighteen surgeries. Watching her son go through these physical challenges drew Beth's heart to other hurting children.

"People used to tell me that I am very sensitive to other people's needs," Beth says. "But it made me think, what am I doing with it? I finally realized that the sensitivity was not beneficial unless I acted upon it. When I would see suffering in this world, I would question why God would allow it. But then I realized that God had made me to reach out, touch the suffering, and show them his love."

As a member of her church's missions committee, Beth sought out ministries in need of volunteers and came across an organization that helps children and their families impacted by HIV. Beth knew immediately that this was where she wanted to serve. She started taking care of the babies—loving them, feeding them, and changing their diapers. Her daughter Connie began to help too. Because her own son had such loving support at her home, her heart went out to those children who did not have such comfort.

... *"I tell you the truth, whatever you did for one of the least of these brothers of mine, you did for me" (Matthew 25:40).*

Teaching generations. Jan Gilliland earned her Masters of Divinity from Southwestern Baptist Theological Seminary at a time when few women pursued advanced degrees. She planned to go away to the mission field but found her mission was in her own home. Having successfully raised four children, she now pours her talents into the lives of her grandchildren and the community around her. Every summer she organizes a Cuzzins Camp for her grandchildren who are five years of age and up. The camp creatively centers on a different biblical theme each year, giving Jan the opportunity to pour God's Word into generation after generation. Her daughter Leslie says this about her: "Mom is always doing something for someone else. I remember hitting the 'sophomore slump' at Baylor. She listened patiently and then asked me, 'What are you doing for other people?' That truly is the theme of her life."

... *"Do nothing out of selfish ambition or vain conceit, but in humility consider others better than yourselves. Each of you should look not only to your own interests, but also to the interests of others" (Philippians 2:3–4).*

Showing mercy to many. Probably one of the most compassionate people I know is Karen McFarland. Her life is a picture of devotion to

God and commitment to serve others with his love. A wonderful mother, she serves at her kids' school. She faithfully feeds the homeless once a month. She organizes mission opportunities at our church, so that many willing hearts can reach out to the community in Christ's love. She opens her home for friends, family, meetings, and gatherings. Karen also cares for her elderly mother-in-law, who lives in a retirement community nearby. Karen is a blessing to others not only for her acts of kindness, but also for her mind of mercy that is always thinking of others.

... *"Let this mind be in you which was also in Christ Jesus, who, being in the form of God, did not consider it robbery to be equal with God, but made Himself of no reputation, taking the form of a bondservant, and coming in the likeness of men" (Philippians 2:5–7 NKJV).*

God has a gift he wants to give to the world through each of us, and that gift is love. But as we can see from these examples, love has many faces. It displays itself uniquely in and through each individual life. Colossians 3:12 tells us, "Since God chose you to be the holy people whom he loves, you must clothe yourselves with tenderhearted mercy, kindness, humility, gentleness, and patience" (NLT). The form each of these pieces of God's wardrobe takes will be different on different individuals. But one thing is constant: When we clothe ourselves with these things, God's love becomes visible to everyone around us.

The Law of Kindness

Have you noticed that some people seem to have a gift for loving others? Romans 12:6–8 tells us that God has given each of us gifts in certain areas. "Service" and "kindness" are two of the gifts in the list. Obviously, many of the women mentioned in this chapter have gifts of service or kindness. Other women may have different gifts, such as teaching or administration or encouragement. But even when kindness is not our predominant gift, it still should be a quality that is evident in our lives. Love and kindness are two of the fruits of the work of the Holy Spirit (see Galatians 5:22–23). Love should always be a central theme in the life of a follower of Christ.

First John 4:7–8 says, "Dear friends, let us love one another, for love comes from God. Everyone who loves has been born of God and knows God. Whoever does not love does not know God, because God is love." Christians ought to be the most loving people in the world. Unfortunately, that's not always the case. From backbiting to gossip to harassing people who don't know Christ, our negative behavior can speak volumes. But when the people around us experience true kindness and love through the Holy Spirit at work in us, they begin to get a picture of Christ's abiding love. According to Proverbs 31:26, a positive woman exhibits the "law of kindness with her tongue" (NKJV). Could others say that about us? Do kindness and love control our words and actions?

Of course, love is not always warm and fuzzy. Sometimes love means encouraging someone to become a better person. At times the most compassionate thing we can do is to confront a friend or loved one and then offer a step up—a lift to help the person move forward in a positive direction. In such cases, kindness should be coupled with wisdom as we speak the truth in love.

A friend of mine (I'll call her Susan) uses the following formula for encouraging people to experience health and wholeness when they've been caught in a destructive lifestyle. She actually formulated these principles when her daughter's friend began to make unwise relationship choices and needed direction and help. Susan told her daughter to talk to her friend and follow these three steps:

People don't care how much you know, until they know how much you care…about them. —Zig Ziglar

1. *Revelation.* Say, "Here's what you are doing." In this case, Susan's daughter helped her friend recognize her destructive behavior.

2. *Reaction.* Say, "Here's what could happen." The daughter pointed out the consequences of her friend's behavior.

3. *Road to success.* Say, "Here's a better way." The daughter offered tips on how to be a positive friend.

Susan will be the first to tell you that these principles must be delivered in kindness and love. Furthermore, we'd be wise to remember that advice is best offered when it is requested or desired; otherwise we may be wasting our time. As we learned in the last chapter, any change, reaction, or result is in God's hands; our responsibility is simply to love.

Jesus is our example when it comes to "speaking the truth in love" (Ephesians 4:15) and helping others choose a more positive direction in life. He showed us love by showing us a better way. In his Sermon on the Mount, he gave us a loving and beautiful picture of how to enjoy a happy life. The word *blessed* in this passage comes from the same Greek root (*makarios*) as the word *happy*:

> Blessed are the poor in spirit, for theirs is the kingdom of heaven.
> Blessed are those who mourn, for they will be comforted.
> Blessed are the meek, for they will inherit the earth.
> Blessed are those who hunger and thirst for righteousness, for they will be filled.
> Blessed are the merciful, for they will be shown mercy.
> Blessed are the pure in heart, for they will see God.
> Blessed are the peacemakers, for they will be called sons of God.
> Blessed are those who are persecuted because of righteousness, for theirs is the kingdom of heaven. (Matthew 5:3–10)

Compassion is a feeling of sorrow for the sufferings or troubles of others, along with an urge to help. Jesus showed his love and compassion toward us by encouraging us to leave behind our dark, empty lives and experience a life that's abundant, happy, and blessed. Because God loves us, he taught us how to live!

Taking Action

In God's vocabulary, love is an action word. Paul describes true love in 1 Corinthians 13:4–7: "Love is patient, love is kind. It does not envy, it does not boast, it is not proud. It is not rude, it is not self-seeking, it is not easily angered, it keeps no record of wrongs. Love does not delight in evil but rejoices with the truth. It always protects, always trusts, always hopes, always perseveres."

You and I can't deliver this kind of love in our own strength. But if we allow ourselves to be open vessels in God's hands, God's love can pour through us to others. John reminds us, "This is how we know what love is: Jesus Christ laid down his life for us. And we ought to lay down our lives for our brothers" (1 John 3:16). God demonstrated his own great love for us in that while we were still sinful people, he sent his Son, Jesus, to die for us (see Romans 5:8). Now we can love too— because the God of love lives inside of us.

Several years ago I began collecting golf hats from the various cities and restaurants our family visits on vacations. One of my favorites is from the Hard Rock Café. It's black and white, and it sports a simple logo on the back that says, "Love all; serve all." What a great motto! As positive women, we should wear that motto continually on our hearts and minds every day. Jesus showed us what it means to love all and serve all. May this be our creed as we shine brightly in our world for him!

POWER POINT

⚙ **Read:** The story of Dorcas (also know as Tabitha) in Acts 9:36–43. What was Dorcas known for in her community? Why was there such an outpouring of grief when she died? What great miracle occurred in this story, and how did it affect others? Do you know someone who is like Dorcas?

♥ **Pray:** Oh, compassionate heavenly Father, may my life be a reflection of your love! I know that I am able to love only because you have loved me so abundantly. Help me now to love others as you have loved me. I thank you that your love is complete in kindness, compassion, service, and truth. May it overflow to all the people in my life! Help me to be a vessel you can use to show your love and compassion to the world. In Christ's loving name, amen.

💡 **Remember:** "Finally, all of you, live in harmony with one another; be sympathetic, love as brothers, be compassionate and humble" (1 Peter 3:8).

☺ **Do:** Pray and ask God to direct you to one area of service or ministry through which you can show his love to others. It may be something you do once a week, once a month, or sporadically throughout the year. Ask God to open up an opportunity that will best utilize your unique gifts and talents. Then decide today to actively pursue that opportunity to show his compassion to the people around you.

Power Principle #6

Becoming A Woman of Courage

*Courage is not simply one of the virtues,
but the form of every virtue at the testing point.*

—C. S. Lewis

Have I not commanded you? Be strong and courageous.
Do not be terrified; do not be discouraged,
for the LORD your God will be with you wherever you go.

—Joshua 1:9

13

High Heels on a Dirt Road
Walking with Courage down the Road of Life

Leadership is capitalizing on a God-given window of opportunity when it is presented. Not tepidly. Not timidly. But boldly, by jumping into the fray with both feet and a determination to change your world with your ideas and your proposals.

—Michelle Easton

In 1998 Michelle Toholsky felt that God was leading her to create a quality fashion magazine with a Christian emphasis. She launched out on this monumental project with little capital but loads of courage. If God was guiding her to do this magazine, she figured, he would provide a way. She didn't know important people; she didn't have the background, knowledge, or experience to create this magazine; she simply knew God was with her and leading her. Michelle says she grew up in a family that exhibited this type of courage based on their faith in God.

"When you truly believe God has no limits, you have the courage to move forward," says Michelle. "It's when we get our eyes on our circumstances and our own limitations that we begin to sink, as Peter did when he was walking on the water."

The first issue of *Shine* magazine leaped off the presses in 1999. Sheila Walsh graced the cover, the photographer worked at his own cost, and the writers contributed articles without compensation. There were fifty subscribers, and the printer agreed to print 150 issues to distribute to bookstores around the nation.

Those who hope in the LORD will renew their strength. They will soar on wings like eagles; they will run and not grow weary, they will walk and not be faint. —Isaiah 40:31

Michelle experienced struggles along the way, but God always provided the funds for her to keep going. By January 2002 *Shine* had reached a distribution of 60,000, and the numbers keep growing.

"If we wait until things are perfect, we will never accomplish anything," Michelle told me. "For me, stepping out in courage meant stepping into God's work. I wasn't afraid of failing, because I knew if I fell, I would fall right into his arms."

Michelle Toholsky is a picture of a woman of courage—courage coupled with faith in a God who is bigger than any circumstance. The road she took wasn't easy; it had its twists, turns, and potholes. But her courage and faith saw her through.

As Michelle discovered, faith in an all-powerful God goes hand in hand with courage. When we choose to move courageously ahead, we are actually putting our faith into action. It was courageous faith that led David to fight Goliath when no one else would step up to the plate. It was courageous faith that inspired Joan of Arc to lead French troops into battle, thus turning the tide of the Hundred Years War. Courageous faith motivated Harriet Tubman to lead Southern slaves to freedom through the Underground Railroad. Courageous faith inspired Corrie Ten Boom to hide Jewish people in her home during World War II; after she was caught, it helped her survive life in a Nazi death camp.

Courage takes us out of our comfort zones and into magnificent places we could never reach on our own. When we step out in faith, we choose to depend on God—and not ourselves—for both direction and strength for the journey. Over and over in the Old Testament, God told his people, "Be strong and of good courage," as he led them forward to the Promised Land. "Oh, love the Lord, all of you who are his people," the psalmist wrote, "for the Lord protects those who are loyal to him, but harshly punishes all who haughtily reject him. So cheer up! Take courage if you are depending on the Lord" (Psalm 31:23–24 TLB).

Taking a Step of Courage

One of my favorite Bible stories is the epic tale of Deborah found in the fourth chapter of the Book of Judges. She was a true hero—the only woman named in the Bible who was placed in high political leadership by the consent of the people. She served the Israelites in many ways, first as a counselor, then as a judge, and finally as their leader in battle. How did she rise to such prominence in a male-dominated society? Through her faith. She trusted God implicitly, and through this trust, courage was born.

At the time this story begins, the Israelites had been cruelly oppressed by the pagan king of Canaan for twenty years. Now they cried out to God for help. Deborah, who was holding court under a palm tree and advising people in disputed matters, heard this cry and sent for a man named Barak. She relayed a message from God: Barak was to take ten thousand men with him to Mount Tabor. When they arrived, God would lure Sisera, the commander of the Canaanite troops, along with his men and nine hundred iron chariots, to the Kishon River. There Barak would easily defeat them.

Barak's response to Deborah was slightly wimpy: "If you go with me, I will go; but if you don't go with me, I won't go" (Judges 4:8).

So Deborah agreed to go to the battlefield. "But because of the way you are going about this," she told Barak, "the honor will not be yours, for the LORD will hand Sisera over to a woman" (v. 9).

Sure enough, when the Israelites reached Mount Tabor, Sisera gathered his army and chariots at the Kishon River. Deborah told Barak, "Go! This is the day the LORD has given Sisera into your hands. Has not the LORD gone ahead of you?" (verse 14). So Barak advanced, and with the Lord's help, the Israelites easily routed Sisera and his army.

"Has not the Lord gone ahead of you?" What a profound statement by a courageous woman of faith! Deborah didn't focus on the nine hundred iron chariots (which had the Israelites shaking in their boots); she saw a powerful God who had directed them to move forward.

Is God directing you to move forward? What enemies are hindering you—fear, doubt, worry? Like Deborah, be strong and of good courage. Has not the Lord gone ahead of you? Is he not able to do all things? If he is guiding you, he will provide for you!

Against the Odds

Courage can take many forms. Think of Marie Curie (you read her story briefly in chapter 1), who wrote in her journal, "I felt the impossibility of going on." She penned these words on the day her husband, who was also her coworker, died in a tragic accident involving a horse-drawn wagon. Yet Marie *did* go on to achieve great advancements in the study of uranium. Think of Rosa Parks, who courageously stayed in her seat on a bus rather than relinquishing it to a white man, thus making an historical breakthrough against social injustice. Think of Wilma Rudolph, who, after a series of childhood illnesses, lost the use of her left leg. Doctors told her she would never walk, but Wilma courageously pushed beyond her limitations and learned not only to walk but to run. She became the first American woman to win three gold medals in track and field in a single Olympiad.[1]

A woman's courage is displayed when she must face great odds—whether she chooses the circumstances or they choose her. My friend Leslie didn't choose the challenges she has faced in the past two years of her life. After an accident in which their car rolled over and was totaled, Leslie and her daughter Amanda suffered minor injuries. Not long after that, Leslie's mother went into the hospital with intestinal problems and passed away after several weeks of complications. Just recently Leslie's other daughter, Natalie, was rushed to the hospital in critical condition after a go-cart accident. Because of severe liver damage, Natalie spent a week in the hospital followed by a long period of recovery at home. Suffice it to say, Leslie and her husband, Roger, have grown tremendously in courage and strength over this period.

Where did they find the courage to face each new challenge? Leslie and Roger will tell you they didn't feel particularly courageous ahead of time; rather, the courage to go on arrived just at their moment of need. They say it came from the Lord—and from the people he brought to their side to encourage and help them. It came from the knowledge that their loving, all-wise God was with them and would be with them, whatever happened.

That's where our courage as Christians comes from. We know that no matter how a situation turns out, God will be there to help us and see us through. What did Jesus say to his disciples when he told them to go out and change the world with the gospel message? "And surely I am with you always, to the very end of the age" (Matthew 28:20).

My dad has always said, "The greatest motivational statement ever uttered is, 'God is with you.'" Not that we have a guarantee of success or a guarantee that everything will turn out the way we want it to; no, we simply have a guarantee that God is with us.

In Deuteronomy 31:6 we read these words of Moses, spoken to the Israelites as they progressed toward the Promised Land: "Be strong and courageous. Do not be afraid or terrified because of them [the enemy armies], for the LORD your God goes with you: he will never leave you nor forsake you." Let's take hold of that message for today. The Lord our God goes with us. He will not leave us or forsake us. Take courage!

"Let's Roll"

Todd Beamer was one of the passengers aboard United Flight 93 on September 11, 2001. As the people on the flight became increasingly aware of the fate the terrorists had planned for them, Todd and some of the others made a plan to fight back. After quietly praying the Lord's Prayer with a telephone operator and passing on a message to his family that he loved them, he dropped his cell phone and said, "Let's roll." Along with several other passengers, Todd bravely overpowered the hijackers, and the plane ended up crashing in an empty field in Pennsylvania rather than into a crowded building in Washington, D.C. Todd and the others gave their lives to save many more.

Afterward Lisa Beamer, Todd's widow, chose courage instead of defeat in response to the news of her husband's death. Seven months pregnant, Lisa left her hometown of Cranbury, New Jersey, and boarded the same flight from Newark to San Francisco that her husband had taken six weeks earlier. In doing so, she set an example of strength and courage for an entire grieving nation. The trip was not only symbolic but purposeful. She met with Todd's former business associates and launched the Todd M. Beamer Foundation, an organization intended to provide health insurance, mental health support, and financial-planning services for the twenty-two children who lost parents on Flight 93.

On November 10, 2001, Lisa addressed twenty thousand women gathered at a Women of Faith conference in Philadelphia. She said, "If my choice is to live in fear or to live in hope, I've chosen to live in hope."[2] Recently she gave birth to a healthy baby girl—even as her story of courage continues to give birth to strength and hope in the hearts of those who hear it. Who can know the countless lives that Lisa and Todd Beamer have touched through their separate examples of courage?

The Courage to Stand for What Is Right

There are many stories of courage throughout American history—courage in times of war, courage during natural disasters, and courage in standing up for convictions. Susan B. Anthony's life is one example. Susan was born in 1820. When she was eighteen years old, she took a job as a teacher to help alleviate her family's desperate financial situation. For fifteen years she taught in both public and private schools, never making more than three dollars a week (with one of those dollars going for boarding). When she discovered that male teachers made three times what she did, she became concerned about the inequalities in men's and women's salaries.

That concern went on the back burner when Susan decided to devote her time and energy to the temperance movement. Before long she became discouraged by the limited role women were allowed to have in the established movement, however, so she helped start the Woman's State Temperance Society in New York. From 1856 to 1861, Susan turned her attention to the antislavery movement before finally picking up the cause that had originally caught her attention. She committed her later years to the women's suffrage movement, helping to organize the National Woman's Suffrage Alliance in 1904.

Susan's road was not easy. She endured physical discomfort, name-calling, and disrespect, but she courageously pressed on for what she believed was right. It took courage and conviction for her to stand up for her belief in the equality of women before God. She always remembered the words of her precious Quaker father: "Tolerate not evil against humanity. And when thee is powerless to do anything else, speak with vigor."[3] Certainly Susan lived up to her father's words.

There are times when we must have the courage to stand up for our

My job is to take care of the possible and trust God with the impossible. —Ruth Bell Graham convictions, even when very few are standing with us. Some of us are called to be active and speak out like Susan B. Anthony, while others are called to quietly hold strong like Rosa Parks. Whenever and however we take a stand, we must do it prayerfully and with wisdom. And we must do it with love and kindness, as we discussed in the last chapter.

When my daughters were in their early years of grade school, they were invited to join a girls organization that was quite popular not only in our school but around the nation. I was hesitant, however. I'd read not long before that the organization had started to veer away from some of the standards our family valued. Several other mothers had the same concern, I soon discovered.

Instead of fighting the established national organization, a few of us decided to start our own after-school club for girls. We named it "Sonshine Girls." The meetings would teach character and values in a clublike environment, using biblical standards as the guide. Each month the girls would go on a field trip to put into action the character quality they'd learned. Well, Sonshine Girls took us all by storm. We had sixty-four girls at the first meeting! The idea spread, and today Sonshine Girls can be found in schools and homeschool groups around the nation.

It took courage to start. We were beginning from scratch with no curriculum, no funds, and no assurance of support. We were also going against the grain of the established organization, and that rubbed some powerful women the wrong way. We were called divisive and self-righteous, even though we were only following our convictions in a creative and loving way.

Quite honestly, I was both surprised and hurt by many of the reactions we received. There were times when I felt discouraged and fearful about moving forward with Sonshine Girls. The task seemed overwhelming—and I didn't like the opposition. I wanted to quit. Then one day I opened my Bible, searching for encouragement. My eyes fell immediately on Joshua 1:9: "Be strong and of good courage; do not be afraid, nor be dismayed, for the LORD your God is with you wherever you go" (NKJV).

This passage filled me with such hope and courage that I immediately called my Sonshine Girl coworker and shared it with her. With great excitement she told me that God had just led her to Deuteronomy 31:6, which says nearly the same thing: "Be strong and courageous. Do not be afraid or terrified…for the LORD your God goes with you." Amazing! God gave both of us this same message from his Word to remind us to stand tall. He was saying to us, "Don't be afraid to do what I have put in your heart to do. I'm in this with you." Because we continued to go forward with courage, many girls (and their moms) have now been blessed through Sonshine Girls.

My Help Comes from the Lord

Do you feel courageous? Neither do I! The truth is, we may not know we have the courage to face a challenge until that challenge comes. In ourselves we are weak; we are clothed in human frailties. But God promises us that when we are weak, *he* is strong. Courage is his work in us. Paul said this about one of his own challenges:

> Three times I pleaded with the Lord to take it away from me. But he said to me, "My grace is sufficient for you, for my power is made perfect in weakness." Therefore I will boast all the more gladly about my weaknesses, so that Christ's power may rest on me. That is why, for Christ's sake, I delight in weaknesses, in insults, in hardships, in persecutions, in difficulties. For when I am weak, then I am strong. (2 Corinthians 12:8–10)

Like Paul, you and I are weak. But also like Paul, we can find our strength, our courage, and our help in the Lord. Whatever circumstances we face, we don't have to despair. God is sufficient to see us through all the challenges at hand.

Anne Peters is a talented poet and a dear Christian. God has done a miraculous work in her life, bringing her through a childhood filled with struggle and abuse. Today she is a positive woman—and a courageous one. Our chapter closes with one of her many poems about courage.

If Courage Could Be Mine

I asked you one day Father
If courage could be mine
You told me to be patient
All virtues come with time.

I looked for her in trials
I looked for her in pain
For it was hard to see her
When comfort came again.

Never did I notice
Until the years went by
That courage had been watching
When tears did cloud my eyes.

She came upon a whisper
And held my hand in hers
Slowly she did lift me
To take away my fears.

She woke my heart up slowly
Or I would turn away

Too frightened by the picture
Of the love God gave away.

I felt my spirit growing
No fear or shadows fell
Courage was beneath me
My faith the deepest well.

I asked you one day Father
If courage could be mine
You said that it was with me
And had been for all time.

POWER POINT

⚙ **Read:** Judges 4 and 5, the story of two brave women and a song of praise. What evidence do you have that Deborah's courage was based on her faith in God? Although she was a courageous leader and hero, to whom did she give honor? Think back to a time in your life when you demonstrated courage. Where did your courage come from, and who received the credit?

♡ **Pray:** Lord, you are my rock and my refuge. You are a very present help in time of need. Thank you for promising that you will never leave me nor forsake me. Thank you that although I may not always understand your ways, I can always depend on your faithfulness. You are worthy of my trust. Help me to have the courage to boldly step out in faith, following your direction. May my life, my actions, and my courage ultimately bring glory to you. In Jesus' name, amen.

♡ **Remember:** "Be strong and courageous. Do not be afraid or terrified because of them, for the LORD your God goes with you; he will never leave you nor forsake you" (Deuteronomy 31:6).

☺ **Do:** Think of one or two people you know (or know about) who need courage right now. Pray for them, asking that they would feel God's presence and strength. When you're done, write a letter of encouragement to let them know you are praying for them.

Next, think of an area in your own life in which you need courage. Take your concern before the Lord in prayer. Ask him to strengthen your heart and sear into your memory the greatest motivational statement of all time: "God is with you."

14

Facing Fears
Finding the Courage to Move Forward

Courage is not the absence of fear;
rather it is the ability to take action in the face of fear.

—Nancy Anderson

My friend Pam came over to my house recently for our regular prayer time. Usually a group of five moms, all with teenage daughters, meet together every Wednesday to pray. On this particular Wednesday, however, Pam and I were the only ones who could make it, so we began talking about the fact that both of us have daughters who are about to get their driver's licenses. Pam's voice became serious as she told me that a family she knew had just been through the grievous loss of one of their daughters in a car accident. Instantly I felt a surge of fear pump through my body. *How will Grace survive in the brutal Dallas traffic?* I thought. *What if she doesn't see a stop sign? What if she looks away for just a moment to adjust the radio?* Anything is possible, Pam and I agreed. We both stared at each other with fear in our eyes.

What could we do to protect our sweet daughters? Keep them from driving until they turned thirty-five? Bar all other traffic from the highways so that only our daughters could drive on them? As much as Pam and I liked these options, we knew they weren't realistic. There was really only one thing we could do: face our fears, move forward, and pray for God's protection over our loved ones.

Fear tends to grip all of us in different areas and at different times in our lives. When we allow it to get the upper hand, it captures us in its net and keeps us from experiencing the abundant and fulfilling life God intends for us. "Where fear is," the philosopher Seneca said, "happiness is not."[1]

The story is told of an old farmer who was sitting on the steps of his rickety shack when a stranger approached. Trying to initiate conversation, the stranger asked, "How's your wheat coming along?"

"Didn't plant none," the farmer replied.

"Really?" said the stranger. "I thought this was good wheat country."

"I was afraid it would rain," the farmer said.

"How is your corn crop?" the stranger persisted.

"Ain't got none. Afraid of corn blight."

"Well, sir, how are your potatoes?"

"Didn't plant no potatoes either. Afraid of the potato bugs."

"Well, then, what in the world did you plant?" the exasperated stranger asked.

"Nothin'," said the farmer. "I just played it safe."[2]

Oh, the stifling effect fear can have on our lives! The farmer's story reminds me of the parable Jesus told about the wealthy man who entrusted his servants with the care of his property when he went away on a journey. To one servant he gave five talents (a talent was a measure of money in Jesus' day); to another servant he gave two talents, and to another, one. The servant with five talents went out immediately and put his master's money to work earning five more talents. The servant with two talents also gained two more. But the servant with one talent dug a hole in the ground and hid his money.

When the master returned, he was pleased with the two servants who had invested their talents wisely. He said to each of them, "Well done, good and faithful servant! You have been faithful with a few things; I will put you in charge of many things. Come and share your master's happiness!" (Matthew 25:21, 23). But the third servant didn't receive such a high compliment:

> "Then the man who had received the one talent came. 'Master,' he said, 'I knew that you are a hard man, harvesting where you have not sown and gathering where you have not scattered seed. So I was afraid and went out and hid your talent in the ground. See, here is what belongs to you.'
>
> "His master replied, 'You wicked, lazy servant!...Take the talent from him and give it to the one who has the ten talents. For every-one who has will be given more, and he will have an abundance. Whoever does not have, even what he has will be taken from him.'" (Matthew 25:24–29)

Why did the third servant hide his talent? He said it himself: "I was afraid." You see, fear paralyzes us. It keeps us from moving for-ward in life and making full use of the gifts and talents God has given us. In my line of work, I meet many potential authors. Some are tal-ented writers, but they do not submit their work to publishers because they are afraid of rejection. Fear keeps them from taking that next step forward.

Jesus told us plainly that we should let our lights shine, not cover them under a basket or bushel (Matthew 5:14–16). Yet like the third servant, we often hide our talents because that's the safe and comfort-able thing to do. And in the process, we miss out on hearing God say, "Well done, good and faithful servant." As positive women, we need to throw off those baskets! We need to face our fears, move ahead, and let our lights shine brightly for Christ in this dark world.

Fear Not!

God does not want us to live our lives in fear. As part of my research for this chapter, I decided to find out how many times the phrase, "Fear not," is proclaimed by God in the Old and New Testaments. Pulling out my analytical concordance of the Bible, I started counting, but the task quickly proved quite daunting. While I was still in the early books of the Old Testament, I decided to stop and pay one of my research assistants (my daughter Grace who needs to earn gas money for the car) to count the rest for me. She came up with approximately seventy-five.

As that number attests, God frequently and continually comforted his people with the words, "Fear not." They're the words God said to Abraham as he began his journey of faith to the Promised Land. They're the words the angel used when he visited Mary and declared she would be the mother of the Son of God. And they're the words spoken by God and his messengers to many other people in between.

Today God is saying these very same words to you and me. Romans 8:15 says, "For you did not receive a spirit that makes you a slave again to fear, but you received the Spirit of sonship. And by him we cry, '*Abba*, Father.'" Hebrews 13:6 adds, "So we say with confidence, 'The Lord is my helper; I will not be afraid. What can man do to me?'"

The only thing the Bible tells us to fear is God himself. This is not the shaking-in-your-boots, panicky, trembling kind of fear, but rather a reverence, awe, and respect for who God is and what he can do. It's a healthy fear—the kind of fear we talked about in chapter 5 when we said, "The fear of the Lord is the beginning of wisdom." Only as we fear God in this reverential way can we walk in wisdom and confidence throughout our lives.

But fear—the unhealthy kind—can be subtle. Often it creeps into our hearts undetected, quietly sets up camp, and then slowly immobilizes us in a certain area. We don't know we've been infiltrated until we suddenly realize we can't move forward in a particular part of our lives. Facing that fear is like waging war against an entrenched enemy. Victory is possible, however, if we follow this four-part battle plan:

1. Recognize the enemy.

In any type of warfare, the first step is to identify the enemy. Theologian A. W. Tozer said, "Fear is of the flesh and panic is of the devil."[3] We know from 2 Timothy 1:7 that fear is not from God. Rather, it is from Satan, who uses it as a weapon to "steal and kill and destroy" our faith, our joy, and our effectiveness as Christians (John 10:10).

Some fears grip our entire being; others give us only a twinge of worry now and then. However they manifest, they need to be identified specifically. Ask God to reveal areas in your life where fear has sneaked in and made a home for itself. Are you afraid for your family's safety? Are you afraid your spouse or your friends will abandon you? Are you afraid you may lose your job? Are you afraid of the future? Some fears are irrational, while others are based on a high probability of truth. Many are somewhere in between. At this stage, don't dwell on your fears; simply identify them. Recognize them for what they are and whom they're from. What are the ways these fears keep you in bondage?

Do keep one important fact in mind: Sometimes the enemy can look bigger than he really is. In chapter 10, for example, we said that hormone fluctuations during our monthly cycles can cause us to feel particularly fearful or suspicious. Certain medications that affect chemical levels in the brain can also make us more susceptible to fearful thinking. Then there's depression, which goes hand in hand with fear. Take a look at your physical health and circumstances and see if any of

So do not fear, for I am with you; do not be dismayed, for I am your God. I will strengthen you and help you; I will uphold you with my righteous right hand. —Isaiah 41:10

these factors may be inducing or magnifying fear—particularly irrational fear—in your life. Talk to your doctor about them. Fear is a big enough adversary without hormones, medicines, or the chemicals in our brains inflating it to larger-than-life size.

2. Realize that some things are out of your control.

Once you look your fear in the face, you need to make a realistic determination: What, if anything, can you do about it? If you're worried about theft, for example, you can purchase a home security system or put new locks on your windows and doors. These are things that are within your control. You don't have to go overboard; just take wise precautions.

Some things are not within your control, however, no matter how many precautions you take. That's the case with my daughter's driving. I can make sure Grace gets the best instruction available, and I can set rules and curfews intended for her safety. But an element of hazard will always exist whenever she gets behind the wheel. That's something I have no control over.

The truth is, our world can be a dangerous place, and anything is possible. In most areas of life, we don't have complete control—whether we're talking about job security, a spouse's faithfulness, or an airplane ride. We can be wise and realistic and do what we can do, but sometimes what happens next is out of our hands.

3. Relinquish control to God and rest in him.

After you have taken wise precautions, you need to relinquish control over the circumstances to God and rest in his loving care. You and I have no guarantee that the next moment will be free from tragedy. We only know that God will not leave us, whatever comes our way, and that he is working all things together for good. All things may not seem good at the time, but we can rest in the assurance that God is lovingly working in our lives and in our world in bigger ways than we can imagine.

You may be wondering, *If God is with me, then why doesn't he prevent bad things from happening to me and my loved ones?* Certainly, it's hard to comprehend human suffering. We may never understand why some things happen this side of the Pearly Gates. For now we only know that God is with us. He doesn't guarantee that our lives will be pain free; he simply promises to hold us and care for us through the challenges of life. Because he is a God of redemption, we can trust him to take circumstances that seem hopeless and infuse them with hope.

4. Renounce the fear.

Often little fears tend to creep back into our heads, gripping us and stifling us all over again. We need to be ready for this eventuality with prayer and God's Word. When you recognize fear knocking at the door of your mind, answer it with faith in God, saying, "Although I can't control the outcome of this situation, I know God will be with me. Nothing is too difficult for him." Pray, "Lord, help me to have strength for this moment. I trust you and rest in your loving care. Keep me from fear and worry, because I know they don't come from you." Finally, memorize one or more Bible verses that give you courage and strength, and speak them aloud when you're afraid. (You can start with the Bible verse in the Power Point section, or choose one of the other verses from this chapter.)

Putting On Our Armor

Not only is there a strategy for battling fear; God has provided us with protective armor for the fight. This armor is spiritual, because the battle is against a spiritual enemy. Read Ephesians 6:10–18 along with me:

> Finally, be strong in the Lord and in his mighty power. Put on the full armor of God so that you can take your stand against the devil's schemes. For our struggle is not against flesh and blood, but against the rulers, against the authorities, against the powers of this dark world and against the spiritual forces of evil in the heavenly realms. Therefore put on the full armor of God, so that when the day of evil comes, you may be able to stand your ground, and after you have done everything, to stand. Stand firm then, with the belt of truth buckled around your waist, with the breastplate of righteousness in place, and with your feet fitted with the readiness that comes from the gospel of peace. In addition to all this, take up the shield of faith, with which you can extinguish all the flaming arrows of the evil one. Take the helmet of salvation and the sword of the Spirit, which is the word of God. And pray in the Spirit on all occasions with all kinds of prayers and requests. With this in mind, be alert and always keep on praying for all the saints.

When Paul delivered this message, he was addressing Christians who were facing persecution for their faith—a very real and present danger in those days. No doubt many of the Ephesian believers were struggling with fear. But God spoke these words through Paul to strengthen and encourage the Ephesians, and by extension, to strengthen and encourage us in our own spiritual battles. I like to use the words of this passage as a prayer for myself and for my family members, asking God to equip us with his armor for our daily battles and help us to stand firm against the enemy. Let's take a brief look at each piece of our spiritual battle gear.

The belt of truth. In Bible times the belt was an important part of a soldier's armor, because it was used to hold battle tools. For us, the belt of truth is vital because it holds the one tool we can use to overcome Satan's lies. The Bible says that Satan is "a liar and the father of lies." Sometimes his lies sound true, and they tend to instill fear. But believers have the truth of God's Word—and God's truth always flushes out and defeats the enemy's deceit.

The breastplate of righteousness. The purpose of the breastplate in ancient armor was to guard the heart of the soldier. Satan often attacks us by appealing to our hearts, the seat of our emotions. If we pursue God's righteousness and apply his pure principles of life, however, our hearts will be protected, and Satan cannot to lead us astray.

Feet fitted with the readiness that comes from the gospel of peace. Some soldiers in the Roman army of Jesus' day had spikes in the bottom of their shoes to help them stand their ground. For our own protection, our feet and our very lives should be firmly planted in the gospel message of Jesus Christ—the good news of who he is and what he has done for us. We need to be ready at all times to share that good news and never hesitate to tell others about the peace that comes from having a relationship with God through his Son, Jesus.

The shield of faith. The shield was used to protect the soldier from the attack of the enemy's weapons. Our faith in God is the shield that withstands the flaming arrows of our enemy, Satan. He hurls temptations, fears, lies, and destruction toward us, but our unswerving faith in a loving, all-powerful God is an impenetrable defense.

The helmet of salvation. The helmet was worn to protect the soldier's head—his most vital area besides the heart. Satan tries to use our minds as a destructive force, filling us with fearful doubts and temptations. He particularly wants us to doubt God's salvation and love for us.

We protect our minds with the assurance of salvation that comes from God's Word.

The sword of the Spirit, which is the word of God. This is the only tool used for the offensive battle mentioned in this passage. Jesus used the Word of God as a sword to cut down each one of Satan's temptations in the wilderness (Matthew 4:1–11). We, too, can respond to Satan's lies and schemes with the weapon of God's Word, which is always true. That's why it's important for us not only to study the Bible, but also to memorize Scripture verses that we can call upon in the midst of battle.

Paul encourages us to use every part of our spiritual armor in order to resist Satan's attacks and stand firm in God. Notice that he tells us to pray at all times and in all situations. In spiritual warfare, we need to stay alert and persist in our prayers for ourselves, our families, and Christians everywhere. In fact, when we face our fears, this is a good battle cry: "Stay alert, and keep praying!" We stay alert by taking wise and realistic precautions when it is within our power to do so. We also stay alert by recognizing that our enemy, Satan, "prowls around like a roaring lion looking for someone to devour" (1 Peter 5:8). Knowing this, we pray for God's protection and power and place our challenges and fears in our heavenly Father's loving hands. Then we stand firm, resisting the temptation to let fear set up camp in our hearts or minds.

Our Deliverer

In the last chapter I mentioned my friend Leslie, whose daughter suffered a critical and life-threatening liver injury in a go-cart accident. Leslie says that while she doesn't understand why God allowed this accident to happen (or why he allowed any of the other tragedies she has faced in the last two years), she did feel God's complete comfort and strength in the midst of it. She says she literally felt a warm blanket

No passion so effectually robs the mind of all its powers of acting and reasoning as fear. —Edmund Burke

of God's love covering her throughout the entire ordeal, from the ICU to her daughter's long recovery at home.

Asking God, "Why?" is not necessarily wrong, as long as we realize that we may not get an answer. As Job recognized (you can read his story in the book of the Bible that bears his name), we finite human beings can't begin to understand all of the ways of our great, all-knowing Creator. We can only rest in the fact that our awesome and powerful God is able to bear us up through the storms of life. Psalm 34:17–19 says, "The righteous cry out, and the LORD hears them; he delivers them from all their troubles. The LORD is close to the brokenhearted and saves those who are crushed in spirit. A righteous man may have many troubles, but the LORD delivers him from them all." Does this verse promise we'll have no troubles in life? No, it promises that God will deliver us in the midst of them.

What about my friend Lynn, who lost her daughter to leukemia? Did God deliver her family from their troubles? If you were to ask Lynn if God was there when she faced the biggest fear any parent could face—the loss of a child—she would tell you, "Yes, God delivered us. He held us all in his loving hands, especially when he ushered our daughter into his kingdom." None of us knows what the future holds, but we do know the one who holds the future—and he's the same one who holds us right now. We can trust him, even when we don't understand everything that's going on around us.

In Matthew 6:25–27 Jesus says, "Do not worry about your life, what you will eat or drink; or about your body, what you will wear.... Who of you by worrying can add a single hour to his life?" The number of days of our lives on earth (and those of our children, spouse, and friends) is in God's hands, not ours. Our worries and fears can't add a single hour to even one day! Instead of useless worrying, we need to spend our time listening for the voice of God as he continually tells us,

"Do not fear; do not worry. I am the Good Shepherd who tenderly watches over his flock. I have my eye on you." Whatever fears we may face in life, we can trust him to be with us and to deliver us.

"I'm Taking Off My Skis"

My friend Dana affectionately uses the words, "I'm taking off my skis," with her dad whenever she is facing a tough challenge and needs encouragement and strength. I'll let her tell you in her own words where that phrase originated:

One of the most valuable lessons I have learned in life occurred on a ski slope when I was about twelve years old. It had been a long day and I was tired, wet, and cold. My feet were killing me, and I had fallen more than my fair share of times. As my dad and I glided along an easy path, we came to an opening. I was relieved, thinking that I was just minutes away from a warm fire, dry socks, and a soft sofa. But then I saw that there was one last price to be paid for my comfort: There between me and the bottom of the mountain was one more slope. I don't remember its level of difficulty, but in my mind it was a dreaded black diamond. It had more moguls than Moses would care to part, and I could imagine the imprint of my behind on each one of them.

That was it! I wasn't about to tackle any more hills that day, so I came up with a plan to solve the problem: I would simply take off my skis and walk down. My dad had already started skiing down the hill but stopped and looked back to see if I was coming. I called out, "I'm taking off my skis and walking down."

"No you're not," he replied firmly.

"But dad, I'm tired, and I can't make it," I pleaded.

"C'mon, just follow me," he said confidently.

My dad is the kind of person that when he told you to do something, you didn't stop to think about it; you just did it. With tears streaming down my face, I began the descent. Side to side we went. When I fell, he stopped and waited, and then we slowly continued on. It wasn't easy and I fell many times, but I made it down that hill. The funny thing is that when I looked at it from the bottom, it didn't seem as big or as difficult as it did from the top.

I've had many more hills to conquer since then, and sometimes they seem overwhelming. But I know that my heavenly Father is waiting for me just ahead, saying, "C'mon, follow me." It may not be easy, and I may fall, but he will be there to pick me up and encourage me.

Now whenever I am fearful of something or feel like quitting, I call my dad and say, "I'm taking off my skis." He faithfully reminds me that God is there, and he will get me down the mountain.[4]

What about you, dear sister? What scary slopes are you looking down that seem too difficult to tackle? What fears have paralyzed you, convincing you that you have neither the faith nor the strength to make it to safety and comfort? Remember your heavenly Father is right there with you. If you will trust yourself to his wise guidance and loving care, he will help you make it down that mountain of fear and into the valley of peace, joy, and abundant life.

God is with you, positive woman of faith! Fear not!

POWER POINT

⚙ **Read:** The entire book of Esther. (It's not that long, and it's definitely an interesting story about a woman who faced her fear.) Describe the real and present danger that threatened the Israelite nation. What wise and courageous preventative steps did Esther take? Who did she depend upon for the ultimate outcome of the situation?

♡ **Pray:** Glorious King of heaven, you are worthy of praise and honor. You are always upholding me with your righteous right hand. Thank you for reminding me continually in your Word to not be afraid, because you are with me. What comfort I have in you! Help me to face the fears in my life that stifle me and keep me from moving forward in faith. I relinquish them to you and ask that you would replace them with your peace. Help me to fear not! I love you, Lord. In Jesus' name I pray, amen.

♀ **Remember:** "God is our refuge and strength, an ever-present help in trouble. Therefore we will not fear" (Psalm 46:1–2).

☺ **Do:** Take a few moments to identify areas in your life that are currently stifled by fear. What reasonable actions or precautions can you take to help reduce your concerns? In prayer, deliver to God those factors that are out of your control. Relinquish them to his hands, trusting him for the outcome.

Every morning, make a conscious effort to "put on" the armor of God. Stay alert, and refuse to allow fearful thoughts to set up camp in your mind or heart.

Power Principle #7

Becoming A Woman of Hope

Optimism is the faith that leads to achievement.
Nothing can be done without hope or confidence.

—Helen Keller

Put your hope in the LORD,
for with the LORD is unfailing love
and with him is full redemption.

—Psalm 130:7

15

Stop Whining and Start Smiling
Wearing the Bright Glasses of Hope

Behind the cloud the starlight lurks,
Through showers the sunbeams fall;
For God, who loveth all His works,
Has left His hope with all!

—John Greenleaf Whittier

The funeral of former Soviet leader Leonid Brezhnev would not seem to be a likely place to find hope, yet a glimmer of hope was there. The story is told of Brezhnev's widow, who stood by his coffin until just before it was closed. As the soldiers touched the lid, she reached down and made the sign of the cross on her husband's chest—an obvious act of civil disobedience in this stronghold of atheistic power. In this one act, Brezhnev's wife provided a courageous and beautiful picture of hope. Clearly, she hoped for life beyond the grave. She hoped for mercy. She hoped for salvation. And she based this hope on a man who died on a cross two thousand years ago.[1]

The message of the Bible is a message of hope. Hope is not simply a sense of expectation, because you can expect good things or bad things to happen. No, hope is a yearning for something wonderful to happen; it is a looking forward to the best. This is the kind of hope we have as Christians based on our faith in Christ. We have the anticipation of eternal life with Christ in our heavenly home, despite whatever challenges and difficulties we experience in our life on earth. We have the expectation that all things will work together for our good if we

493

love God and are called according to his purpose (see Romans 8:28). We have the hopefulness of knowing that God is at work in our lives through the sad moments as well as the happy ones. First Peter 1:3–7 describes the vibrant hope believers are meant to experience:

> Praise be to the God and Father of our Lord Jesus Christ! In his great mercy he has given us new birth into a living hope through the resurrection of Jesus Christ from the dead, and into an inheritance that can never perish, spoil or fade—kept in heaven for you, who through faith are shielded by God's power until the coming of the salvation that is ready to be revealed in the last time. In this you greatly rejoice, though now for a little while you may have had to suffer grief in all kinds of trials. These have come so that your faith—of greater worth than gold, which perishes even though refined by fire—may be proved genuine and may result in praise, glory and honor when Jesus Christ is revealed.

Yes, we have a living hope—a hope that is in God and his salvation through his son, Jesus. It's a hope that cannot be taken away from us. Even when a loved one dies, we grieve, but not as those who have no hope; for we know we will see that person again one day. How hopeless life must seem to those who have no understanding of our great and loving God, who has an ultimate plan for this world and for our lives! And how joyless! The words *hope* and *joy* are often found together in Scripture for good reason. Romans 5:1–2 spells out why Christians can rejoice in hope: "Since we have been justified through faith, we have peace with God through our Lord Jesus Christ, through whom we have gained access by faith into this grace in which we now stand. And we rejoice in the hope of the glory of God."

Christians ought to be the most optimistic people in the world. After all, we are the ones who have the one true hope! But believers can

Be joyful in hope, patient in affliction, faithful in prayer. —Romans 12:12

fall into the trap of hoping in the here and now, in what can be seen and felt, just like everyone else. Many people put their hope in wealth or fame or perfect circumstances, expecting these things to bring them life and joy and strength. But in his letter to Timothy, Paul warns against hoping in such things: "Command those who are rich in this present world not to be arrogant nor to put their hope in wealth, which is so uncertain, but to put their hope in God, who richly provides us with everything for our enjoyment" (1 Timothy 6:17). Hope is only as good as the one in whom it is placed. We can be confident in our hope when our hope is in the Lord.

Another story of hope set in the former Soviet Union is told of Alexander Solzhenitsyn, a Soviet political prisoner around the middle of the twentieth century. Forced to work twelve-hour days of hard labor while existing on a meager diet, Solzhenitsyn was on the verge of giving up all hope. He was starving and gravely ill, and the doctors were predicting his death. One afternoon, as he was shoveling sand in the hot sun, he simply stopped working. He knew the guards would beat him severely, but he just couldn't go on. It was then that he saw a fellow Christian prisoner cautiously moving toward him. The man quickly drew a cross in the sand with his cane and then erased it. In that brave gesture of love and encouragement, all the hope of the Gospel flooded Solzhenitsyn's soul. That hope helped him endure that difficult day as well as the months and years of prison life that followed.[2]

The hope of the cross is powerful. It is the hope that Christ paid the price for our salvation. It is the hope that Christ rose from the dead and that the same power that raised him from the dead is at work in our lives. We can rejoice in this hope, and we can rest in it. As the writer of Hebrews said, "We have this hope as an anchor for the soul, firm and secure" (Hebrews 6:19).

Give Up Grumbling

You would think the Israelites would have been an optimistic group of people. The God of the universe had miraculously delivered them from Egyptian slavery. They were headed toward the Promised Land with not only their freedom, but also the riches of Egypt—an extra parting gift from God. You would think they would have easily put their hope in the Lord and his provision, but they didn't. Instead, they got caught up in their own temporary discomforts and difficulties. Granted, the tents in the wilderness were no Ritz Carlton. But incredible satisfaction and joy were just ahead, waiting for them just over the Jordan. Sadly, the Israelites chose to whine and complain about their circumstances rather than trust God and put their hope in his promises.

How did God feel about their pessimistic complaining? Numbers 11:1 says, "Now the people complained about their hardships in the hearing of the LORD, and when he heard them his anger was aroused." God was not happy about their grumbling because it exposed their lack of faith. It was destructive, killing their hope and interfering with God's plan to bless them.

What about us? Are we much different from the whining Israelites? What do we tend to grumble and whine about in our temporary journey here on earth? No doubt God feels the same way about our grumbling as he did the Israelites'. Paul tells us in Philippians 2:14 to "do all things without grumbling" (NASB). Yet most of us tend to ignore this guideline and chatter on and on about our problems.

Grumbling is an unproductive use of our time, words, and energy. When we whine and complain, we encourage doubt instead of faith. We take our eyes off of the hope we have in God and place them on immediate issues and temporary things. Of course there may be times when we see something that is wrong and need to take action to make a positive change, but we can do this without grumbling.

Romans 12:12 gives us a remedy for grumbling: "Be joyful in hope, patient in affliction, faithful in prayer." Next time you feel a whine or complaint coming on, take a dose of Romans 12:12 instead! It may seem silly, but I recommend putting an empty medicine bottle on the kitchen counter with a label that reads:

Rx: Grumble Squelchers

Reduces symptoms of whining, complaining, and fretting.
Take at first sign of bellyaching.

Write out Romans 12:12 on a strip of paper and put it inside the bottle. Then when you feel like grumbling, pop the top and follow the directions:

1. Be joyful in hope. This means that we take pleasure and find joy in our expectation that God is mightily at work in our lives. We know that our future is bright as we look forward to a heavenly home.

2. Be patient in affliction. Because we have hope in God, we can be patient when life gets difficult. We know that our present circumstances are only temporary; they *will* pass. According to James 1:2–4, we can even be joyful when we face trials and struggles, because they test our faith and develop perseverance—a quality that's necessary if we're going to become mature, complete, and positive women of faith.

3. Be faithful in prayer. We can't avoid all pain and difficulty in life, but we can allow these things to mature us as we persevere in joyful hope and faithful prayer. As we deliver our dilemmas and defeats to God in daily prayer, he is faithful to give us wisdom, direction, comfort, and strength. Imagine what would happen if you and I decided to spend more time praying and less time grumbling and complaining. We would become much more positive, joyful, and hopeful people, and everyone around us would clamor to know the one in whom we place our hope.

She Wore Bright Glasses

I'm sure you know the story of Helen Keller. Born in 1880, she contracted a severe illness in infancy that left her in a dark world void of sound and sight. Unable to communicate, she became an angry and frustrated child—until hope came into her life in the form of a teacher named Anne Sullivan. Helen learned to read, write, and speak through Anne's patient and loving instruction. Eventually she graduated cum laude from Radcliffe College, published her life story, and became a well-known and much-honored public figure.

Helen Keller's life represents one of the most extraordinary stories of hope, courage, and perseverance in American history. She may have worn dark glasses in public; but in her spirit and attitude, she clearly wore bright glasses that focused her sights on life's potential rather than life's difficulties. Through these glasses she saw opportunity instead of defeat, hope instead of despair. How is it possible to be hopeful in the face of such immense challenges? Here's the key in Helen's own words: "Keep your face to the sunshine and you cannot see the shadows."[3]

Like Helen, we have a choice as to which "attitude glasses" we will put on each day. Despite our circumstances, we can choose to don the bright glasses of hope, which see God's hand at work in our lives; or we can choose the dark glasses of despair, which only see our immediate troubles. If we wear these dark glasses long enough, we will become hopeless, angry, and bitter people—chronic whiners and grumblers. It's a daily choice. Will we focus on God and his provision, or will we focus on our handicap—whether it's a serious illness, a difficult spouse, an unpleasant work environment, a dysfunctional family, a broken down car? Are we willing to look beyond the handicap and see the possibilities?

God didn't take away Helen's handicaps; he accomplished great things through them. He didn't take away Paul's unnamed handicap, even though Paul asked God three times to remove it. Instead, Paul learned that God's grace was sufficient for him to survive and even thrive in spite of his challenge (2 Corinthians 12:7–10). Our difficulties may not go away, either, but that doesn't mean God is not with us. He is able to work in us and through us, no matter what struggles we face.

And therein lies our hope. Hope goes beyond what we see and feel in the here and now. Romans 8:24–25 says, "Hope that is seen is no hope at all. Who hopes for what he already has? But if we hope for what we do not yet have, we wait for it patiently." Have hope in God! His work in us is not finished. As one person put it, "Hope is putting faith to work when doubting would be easier.[4]"

It's All in Your Perspective

Here's a little poem about a frog with a hope-filled perspective:

Two frogs fell into a deep cream bowl,
One was quite an optimistic soul;
But the other took the gloomy view,
"We shall drown," he cried, without ado.
So with a last despairing cry,
He flung up his legs and he said, "Goodbye."
Quoth the other frog with a merry grin,
"I can't get out, but I won't give in.
I'll just swim till my strength is spent,
Then will I die the more content."
Bravely he swam till it would seem
His struggles began to churn the cream.
On the top of the butter at last he stopped,

And out of the bowl he gaily hopped.

What of the moral? 'Tis easily found:

If you can't hop out, keep swimming round.[5]

When it comes to hope, perspective is everything! One frog lost hope and died in a bowl of cream; the other hoped for the best, did what he could, and ended up climbing out of his troubles. Hope kept him going—and it keeps us going too. With a bright outlook and an eternal perspective, we can see past the small stuff. We can keep ourselves from getting weighed down in the cream of life.

I think about a woman I know who has a marvelous singing voice. Unfortunately, she continually wrings her hands in defeat, telling herself, "I'll never be a singer. No one will help me get the big break I need. I don't have connections in the industry. I think I'll quit." She's lost in the cream. Hope says, "There are opportunities all around you to use your talent. Yes, the audiences are small and the stages are not lighted, but you still can be a blessing to many people." Hope says, "God has a plan for your life. If you will step through the open doors that are in front of you and keep your eyes on the Lord, he will lead you to greater heights than you could even imagine."

When we lose hope, we sink. But even then God is there to lift us up; we just have to reach out for his hand. Matthew 14:22–33 tells the story of Jesus walking across the water to meet his disciples, who were in a boat on a lake in the middle of a storm. When Peter saw Jesus, he boldly called out, "Lord, if it's you, tell me to come to you on the water." Jesus replied, "Come." So Peter stepped out of the boat and started walking—that is, until he noticed the raging wind and crashing waves around him. Becoming afraid, he immediately started to sink. But before he went all the way under, he managed to cry out, "Lord, save me!" Jesus responded by reaching out his hand and pulling Peter to safety. "You of little faith, why did you doubt?" he said to his very wet disciple.

Peter started out with his hope in the Lord. He didn't hesitate to get out of the boat when Jesus said, "Come." But then Peter got his focus off of Jesus and onto the wind and the waves—and he sank. Been there? It's so easy to lose perspective. Life's difficulties and challenges perplex us and distract us on every side, pulling our focus away from the Lord and the hope we have in him. Like Peter, when we take our eyes off of Jesus and put them on our circumstances, we begin sinking into despair. But also like Peter, when we reach out in hope to the one who loves us and has the power to save us, we experience miracles!

Keep Smiling

I love Emily Dickinson's words about hope: "Hope is the thing with feathers that perches in the soul and sings the tune without words and never stops at all."[6] When we have hope within us, it overflows like a fountain to those around us. It lifts people's spirits like a never-ending song, inspiring them to hope too.

How do we share hope? We'll talk about this more in the next chapter, but what I want to emphasize here is that it's not difficult. Sometimes it takes little more than a smile. Proverbs 15:13 tells us, "A happy heart makes the face cheerful." As women of hope, we ought to have joyful, hopeful hearts. We have reason to smile! We can smile at today, because we know that a greater day is coming. We can smile at the future, because we know the one who holds the future. A smile is like a gift of hope we offer to others. It speaks a thousand words, saying, "It will be okay. There is a better day ahead. God is with us."

Abraham Lincoln said, "I have found that most people are about as happy as they make up their minds to be."[7] The question is, how happy do you want to be? Will you choose today to put on the glasses of hope

As God is the author of our salvation, so Christ is the embodiment of our hope. —Geoffrey B. Wilson

☺

in God, or will you wear the glasses of gloom in circumstances? Will you smile more and grumble less, or will it be the other way around?

In the August 5, 2001, issue of *Parade* magazine, a small article appeared about a Texas-based group called the Secret Society of Happy People. The article noted that happy people generally aren't invited to tell their stories on TV talk shows, even though studies have proven that a positive outlook can lead to a longer life. The Society of Happy People declared August to be "Admit You Are Happy Month." Their hope was that the month of good cheer would rub off on people, and everyone would spend less time thinking and talking about what makes them miserable.

As women of hope, we should declare every day "Admit You Are Hopeful Day." The psalmist said, "Why are you downcast, O my soul? Why so disturbed within me? Put your hope in God, for I will yet praise him, my Savior and my God" (Psalm 43:5). You and I have reason to put away doom and gloom and be glad: God, through Christ, has given us a living and lasting hope. As Thomas Manton said, "What an excellent ground of hope and confidence we have when we reflect upon these three things in prayer: the Father's love, the Son's merit, and the Spirit's power!"[8] Let's make a daily choice to share that hope with the world.

POWER POINT

Read: The story of the Shunammite woman's hope in 2 Kings 4:8–37. What positive qualities do you see in this woman? What did she do when it seemed as though all hope was gone for her son? Notice that she told no one about her son's death; instead, she went straight to the prophet of God. What can be learned from her example?

Pray: God of hope, I praise you for your Word and your power, which give me hope for the journey of life. Thank you for my greatest hope: that I will live with you one day in glory. Renew my hope, and help me to keep an eternal perspective. Today and every day, help me to choose an attitude of hope rather than an attitude of gloom or despair. Teach me to be joyful in hope, patient in affliction, and faithful in prayer. In Christ's name, amen.

💡 **Remember:** "Be joyful in hope, patient in affliction, faithful in prayer" (Romans 12:12).

☺ **Do:** Write out a statement of hope. Make it a personal reminder of hope, based on God's truth. It may sound something like this:

> My hope is based on the fact that God loves me and sent his Son, Jesus, to die on the cross as a payment for my sins. He rose again, giving me hope for eternal life. I have hope for each day because I know that God is working all things in my life together for good, as Romans 8:28 promises to those who love God and are called according to his purpose.

Place your statement of hope in your Bible and refer to it whenever you need to be reminded to get your eyes off of your immediate circumstances and back onto Jesus.

16

Delicious Morsels
Serving Up a Hearty Portion of
Hope and Encouragement

*Believe that your tender, loving thoughts and wishes for good have
power to help the struggling souls of earth to rise higher.*

—Ella Wheeler-Wilcox

Abigail Van Buren occasionally shares stories of "random
acts of kindness" sent in by readers of her popular column,
"Dear Abby." Recently she printed a letter from a woman from
Long Island who was reflecting on a visit she made some time ago to
Albuquerque, New Mexico. The purpose of the woman's trip was to be
alone and finally accept the fact that her husband had died. This was
her first vacation without him. As she sat by herself in a lovely restaurant, she noticed a corner table being prepared near hers, complete with
a fresh flower arrangement and champagne bucket. Soon a couple was
escorted to the table. She recognized the man immediately as a famous
personality. She tried not to glance at the couple too often as she sat
nearby, alone and forlorn.

To her surprise, a server approached her and said, "The couple at
the corner table would like to send a glass of champagne to you." When
he asked if that would be all right, she graciously accepted. Then,
catching the couple's attention, she lifted her glass appreciatively and
toasted them on their special occasion.

The famous gentleman leaned toward her and said, "It's not a special occasion, just a celebration of life—to the good times ahead."

In her letter to "Dear Abby," the woman said that whenever she feels blue, she reflects on that special couple and their "celebration of life." Abby commented, "People who are happy are usually inclined to spread the joy."[1]

That couple in New Mexico offered a glimmer of hope to a needy soul that night. Sending the glass of champagne was a small act of kindness on their part, but it was a lasting gift to this woman who shared her story with Abby nearly ten years later. We, too, have baskets full of hope that we can share with the world around us. Like the little boy who offered up to Jesus his five loaves and two fish, God can take our simple gifts of hope and multiply them many times over in the lives of others. Never underestimate the power of your words and actions to provide hope to your family, your friends, and everyone around you!

Handing Out Hope

The most satisfying moments in life are those in which we encourage other people to go on to greater heights. When we hand out hope to those we hold dear, we often get to participate in their renewed dreams and become a part of their significant life experiences. When we give hope to those we don't know so well, we may never know the long-term effect; but like the couple in New Mexico, we get to experience the immediate joy of watching the light of hope go on in someone else's eyes.

How do we effectively encourage someone along life's pathway? How do we hand out hope? The answer begins with simple steps—small acts of encouragement and kindness, based on our recognition of the other person's great value and worth in God's eyes. Because every one of us has been uniquely created by God, each person has worth just waiting to be discovered. It may be simple; it may not be newsworthy;

506

but each person has something to offer; each person has a contribution to make to this world.

We can encourage that God-given potential to bloom and grow by looking deep inside a person and drawing out the good things we see planted there. When we do this, we water that life with hope. We especially need to keep an eye out for those lasting qualities that rarely fade or diminish, like love, joy, peace, patience, kindness, goodness, faithfulness, gentleness, and self-control. These are qualities that God develops through the work of his Holy Spirit, and they are ones we particularly want to encourage in others.

Teachers, managers, bosses, coaches, and especially mothers have opportunities built in to their daily tasks to encourage potential and inspire hope. Baseball legend Reggie Jackson describes an uplifting manager this way: "A great manager has a knack for making ballplayers think they are better than they think they are. He forces you to have a good opinion of yourself. He lets you know he believes in you. He makes you get more out of yourself. And once you learn how good you really are, you never settle for playing anything less than your very best."[2]

Wouldn't it be wonderful if we, as positive women, regularly gave this kind of encouragement and hope to the people around us? If we always looked for and drew out the good qualities, abilities, and talents in others? What a blessing it would be to hear people say, "That Karol Ladd, she has a knack for making people think they are better than they are. She forces them to have a good opinion about themselves. Yes, she lets people know she believes in them!" Our world would be a better place if we took the time and made the effort to help others recognize their worth. As Goethe said, "Treat people as if they were what they should be, and you help them become what they are capable of becoming."[3]

Apples of Gold

"A word aptly spoken is like apples of gold in settings of silver," says Solomon in Proverbs 25:11. According to the Bible, words are both valuable and powerful. They can be lovely and life-giving, or they can be sour and destructive. They can be the tools by which we build a future, encourage a dream, or unleash great potential; or they can be the weapons by which we destroy a reputation, diminish a self-image, or quench an inner fire. If you think back, you can probably remember times when words spoken by others either empowered you or discouraged you. As positive women, we need to be life-givers with our words!

I remember the first time my husband heard me speak to a large group of men and women. I had spoken on this particular topic many times before, but I was extremely nervous at the thought of Curt being there. What if I told a joke that flopped? What if I went completely blank? What if the material was dry? When the talk was over, I would have to live my life—for better or for worse—with a member of the audience! (Did I mention that Curt is very blunt and doesn't mind speaking the truth in love, even if it hurts?) Fortunately the talk went well, and people laughed in all the right places. Curt darted up to me afterward and said, "You were fantastic! I knew you were good, but I didn't know you were this good!" He believed in me! His words of strength gave me hope and encouragement to carry on. They still ring in my mind to this day.

When was the last time you delivered a healthy dose of encouragement to another person? Words of hope can be delivered in many forms. Not long ago I noticed that I was continually on my teenage daughter's case for every little issue. (She noticed it too.) Knowing how powerful words are, and realizing that I was nitpicking her over some pretty unimportant things, I determined to change. First, I decided to only concern myself with what was really important and relax about the small stuff. Second, I decided to make sure I gave her words of hope every day.

I already had the habit of telling her "I love you" several times a day. Now I began telling her at other times, "Grace, I believe in you." "Grace, God has a wonderful plan for your life." "Grace, God is going to bless you and use your gifts and talents." I began giving my other daughter similar words of hope: "Joy, you have a kind and tender servant's heart that is such a blessing to me and to others." "Joy, it's beautiful to see how God's love shines through you." "Joy, God is working in mighty ways in your life." Over time I began to see courage, discipline, and a renewed zest for life rising in both my girls.

Years ago a song hit the charts with the lyric, "Accentuate the positive, eliminate the negative." I've found that as I focus on the positive qualities of the people around me and feed them words of encouragement, their best qualities tend to develop and grow. In the process their negative qualities tend to take care of themselves and diminish in prominence. Dishing out delicious morsels of hope to my family strengthens them greatly—and brings me great pleasure. Encouraging words help my kids and my husband rise to their potential, and they give me a lift too!

Of course, words of hope and encouragement don't always have to be verbal. Sometimes I find it easier to write a note of encouragement to a friend than to pick up the phone and call. That's okay. The written word is powerful! I have a file at my house that I've labeled, "Encouraging Words." In it I place the kind, supportive, and meaningful notes and letters I receive from people. Some are from friends; others are from people who have heard me speak or who've read my books. Their words of encouragement are a source of great strength and hope to me. Even in the process of writing this book, I received several letters from readers of my previous book, *The Power of a Positive Mom*. Their

May the God of hope fill you with all joy and peace as you trust in him, so that you may overflow with hope by the power of the Holy Spirit. —Romans 15:13

☺

notes were an inspiration, particularly at those times (every writer has them!) when I felt dry or discouraged. These letters spurred me on to complete the task that was before me. You hold the end result in your hands!

Hope Floats

A few years ago actress Sandra Bullock starred in a movie by Twentieth Century Fox titled *Hope Floats.* The film begins with Sandra's character being invited to appear on a sleazy talk show where, in front of a national television audience, she finds out that her husband is having an affair with her best friend. Distraught and broken, she decides to take her young daughter and move back to her mother's house in her old hometown. There, in the small, quaint town of Smithville, she starts to work through her grief and begins to see glimmers of hope in her life. Her family and friends stand with her, encourage her, and let her know they believe in her through this process. They shower her with hope. It takes time, it's not easy, it doesn't happen the way she planned; but eventually hope wins out, and Sandra's character finds the peace and joy she is searching for.

Most of the people we know and love are not likely to have their lives turned upside down by a revelation on national television, but they will have their share of difficulties and challenges. We need to tell them: There is hope! Hope for a better day. Hope for eternal life. Hope that God can take even the bad experiences and somehow use them for good. As we sit alongside a hurting or struggling person, sometimes the only thing we can give them to hold on to is the fact that God is with them, and he loves them. He will give them strength moment by moment. And as they persevere, trusting in him, they will become better, stronger, and more positive people.

The following poem by an anonymous author says it well:

The Hard Way

For every hill I've had to climb,

For every stone that bruised my feet,

For all the blood and sweat and grime,

For blinding storms and burning heat,

My heart sings but a grateful song—

These were the things that made me strong![4]

Many times I have used science experiments to demonstrate lessons in my talks to women. One *egg*cellent *egg*speriment comes from—you guessed it—the egg. Did you know that you can make an egg float? Try this: Place an egg in a bowl of water. It slowly sinks to the bottom, right? Now take the egg out of the bowl for a moment, add salt to the water, and gently stir. *Voila,* you have salt water. And because salt water has a greater density than plain water, the egg will now float when you place it back in the bowl.

Jesus told his followers they were "the salt of the earth" (Matthew 5:13). Salt has many wonderful qualities. In our *egg*speriment we saw that it can buoy up a sinking egg—much like our message of hope can lift a sinking soul. Salt also seasons and preserves. Paul tells us in Colossians 4:6, "Let your conversation be always full of grace, seasoned with salt, so that you may know how to answer everyone." Our words to others can be powerful, life-giving, and uplifting tools in God's hands. When they are full of his grace and truth, hope floats!

Beautiful Feet

My dear friend Beth is a positive woman and a true encouragement to me. We laugh together about many things. One time, as we were bantering back and forth about the qualities we have that we could brag about, Beth said that one of her finer qualities was that she had great-looking feet!

We agreed this wasn't the kind of information she'd want to put on her application for Woman of the Year; but to this day, we laugh about her outstanding physical quality. She does have lovely toes!

Did you know that the Bible talks about people with beautiful feet? Yes, you and I can have beautiful feet too. (Watch out, Beth!) Isaiah 52:7 says, "How beautiful on the mountains are the feet of those who bring good news, who proclaim peace, who bring good tidings, who proclaim salvation, who say to Zion, 'Your God reigns!'" Paul quotes this passage in his letter to the Romans, speaking about the power of our words in sharing the gospel message:

> That if you confess with your mouth, "Jesus is Lord," and believe in your heart that God raised him from the dead, you will be saved. For it is with your heart that you believe and are justified, and it is with your mouth that you confess and are saved. As the Scripture says, "Anyone who trusts in him will never be put to shame." For there is no difference between Jew and Gentile—the same Lord is Lord of all and richly blesses all who call on him, for, "everyone who calls on the name of the Lord will be saved."
>
> How, then, can they call on the one they have not believed in? And how can they believe in the one of whom they have not heard? And how can they hear without someone preaching to them? And how can they preach unless they are sent? As it is written, "How beautiful are the feet of those who bring good news!" (Romans 10:9–15)

The greatest hope we can deliver to another person is the hope we have in God through Christ Jesus. When we share the Gospel, our words become a message of peace to those who are restless, a message of love to those who are angry, and a message of hope to those who are hopeless. We offer them healing and wholeness as we share the good news that they, too, can be reconciled to God through faith in his Son, Jesus. Peter tell us, "Always be prepared to give an answer to everyone who asks you to give the reason for the hope that you have" (1 Peter 3:15). If we ask God to open our eyes to see the myriad of opportunities we have to share the reason for our hope, and if we then open our mouths to speak that truth in love, we will have beautiful feet (metaphorically speaking, of course). Why should Beth be the only one?

A Charlie Brown Perspective

Over the years my friend Peni has sent me a variety of fun e-mails. One recent one was a two-part quiz that I found particularly interesting. She prefaced the e-mail by saying that I didn't need to actually answer the questions; I just needed to read the quiz through to get the point. It was purportedly developed by Charles Schulz, the creator of the comic strip "Peanuts." Here it is:

1. Name the five wealthiest people in the world.

2. Name the last five Heisman Trophy winners.

3. Name the last five winners of the Miss America contest.

4. Name ten people who have won the Nobel or Pulitzer Prize.

5. Name the last half-dozen Academy Award winners for best actor and actress.

6. Name the last decade's worth of World Series winners.

How did you do? Probably about as badly as I did! Now see how you do on this second part:

1. List a few teachers who aided your journey through school.

2. Name three friends who have helped you through a difficult time.

3. Name five people who have taught you something worthwhile.

4. Think of a few people who have made you feel appreciated and special.

5. Think of five people you enjoy spending time with.

6. Name half a dozen heroes whose stories have inspired you.

That was quite a bit easier, wasn't it? That's because the people who make the biggest difference in our lives are not necessarily the ones who have achieved fame or fortune or worldly success; they're the ones who care—the ones who give us hope and encouragement to reach our highest potential.

You and I don't have to be celebrities or national heroes to have a positive impact on others. We only need to offer encouragement through our caring smiles, our loving touches, our words of hope—and even our supportive cheers. Recently my daughters and I volunteered at a local swimming competition for the Special Olympics. I think the participants in these unique competitions are possibly the most delightful people I have ever met. They are eager, joyful, innocent, and loving individuals who have an amazing knack for rising above their physical and mental challenges. In these races, no one loses!

When we arrived at the Special Olympics that morning, the director of the volunteers instructed us to go to the edge of the pool, help the participants out of the water after each race, and then chaperone them to the awards ceremony. But when we got to the pool, we saw that many volunteers were already helping in that capacity. Someone directed us further, "Stand at the top of a lane and cheer the swimmer on." So Joy, Grace, and I took our positions at different lanes and began to cheer.

Have you noticed that it's hard to cheer and cry tears of joy at the same time? Over and over my eyes welled up as I was moved by the

The word which God has written on the brow of every man is Hope. —Victor Hugo

514

courage of the contestants. I could only imagine that for many of them, it had taken every ounce of courage they could muster to get into the water initially, much less learn to swim and eventually compete. All had disabilities to one degree or another; some had to be lowered into the water from their wheelchairs. Every stroke took intense energy and strength, yet they bravely completed their laps without complaint. The smiles of joy that beamed from their faces brought tears of joy to mine.

For three and a half hours, the girls and I cheered our hearts out! We hugged these wonderful Olympians and didn't mind at all getting soaked with each embrace. When we left that day, we knew we were not the same people. We saw life from a new perspective now. What had seemed like major challenges in our lives looked rather minor in this new light. The dilemma of which high school homecoming dress to buy paled in comparison to the struggle of an Olympian deciding which shoe went on the right foot.

Our day at the Special Olympics taught us that we could press on courageously in spite of difficulties. It taught us we could finish our course without complaining. After all, we really had very little to complain about! It also taught us that a cheerleader's role is just as important as a scorekeeper's—maybe even more so. My daughters and I brought hope to the pool that day in the form of hugs and cheers. We left with a new and hopeful outlook on life, delivered by the examples of these special competitors.

Remember, we don't need to be famous. We don't need to be rich. We don't need to wait for our lives to be trouble free before we begin to encourage other people in theirs. Right now, right where we are, we can begin to dole out delicious morsels of encouragement and hope to our families, our friends, and everyone around us. When we do—when we get our eyes off of ourselves and pour our lives out to others in words and actions and cheers that inspire hope—we can't help but become more hopeful too. And that's when we become truly positive women.

POWER POINT

Read: Mark 5:25–34, the story of a woman's desperate hope. How long had this woman been ill? What measures had she tried to get better, to no avail? Did she give up hope? What did her hope lead her to do? The Greek word for *healed* in verse 34 actually means "saved." Knowing this, how is this story meaningful to you?

Pray: I praise you wonderful Lord, for you are truly good. Thank you for bringing your *Son*shine into my life. Thank you for the radiant glow on my face that only comes from you. I want to share those rays of hope with the world around me! Help me to bring hope and encouragement to others through my words and actions, and help me to lead them to you, the source of all hope. In Jesus' wonderful name, amen.

Remember: "Put your hope in the LORD, for with the LORD is unfailing love and with him is full redemption" (Psalm 130:7).

Do: Make a conscious decision to feed delicious morsels of hope and encouragement to your family and close friends every day. Make a list of specific ways you can do this for each person. Then prayerfully ask God to show you someone outside your close circle of friends to whom you can be an encouragement with words or actions of hope. Remember to pray for that person daily.

Conclusion

Press On!
Making a Powerful Difference

*We have learned that power is a positive force
if it is used for positive purposes.*

—Elizabeth Dole

Beth Anne DeCiantis was determined to qualify for the marathon in the 1992 U.S. Olympic Trials. In order to qualify, a female runner had to complete the 26.2-mile course in less than two hours and forty-five minutes. Beth started the race strong, but she began having trouble around the twenty-third mile. She reached the final straightaway with just two minutes left to qualify. With only two hundred yards to the finish line, the unthinkable happened: She stumbled and fell. She stayed down for twenty seconds in a bit of a daze with the crowd yelling, "Get up!" The clock was still ticking, and she had just a minute left.

Beth staggered to her feet and slowly began walking. But just five yards short of the finish line and with ten seconds to go, she fell again. With dogged determination she began to crawl, while the crowd cheered her on. She finally crossed the finish line on her hands and knees. Her time? Two hours, forty-four minutes, and fifty-seven seconds.[1]

When the race got tough, Beth Anne DeCiantis persisted. How easy it would have been for her to give up! She had every opportunity

517

to quit, but she didn't. She pressed on in spite of the pain and struggle and reached her goal.

There are times in all of our lives when we want to throw in the towel and say, "Forget it! This is too hard! I want to quit!" We make mistakes, people do things to hurt us, tragedies happen, sadness prevails. We wonder if we can or should go on. Dear sister, press on! As Beth Anne DeCiantis did, as Helen Keller did, as Harriet Tubman did, as Sarah and Esther and Ruth and Mary did, so can we. We only have to live our lives one step at a time. Perseverance is the key to reaching the finish line.

I am reminded of the story of the great missionary William Carey. When Carey began thinking of traveling to India as a pioneer missionary, his father felt it necessary to point out that he had no academic qualifications to prepare him for the task. Carey responded, "I can plod."[2] In many cases the ones who accomplish lasting results for the kingdom and for the good of mankind are not those who can get things done quickly and easily, but rather the plodders who persist through thick and thin. Plod on!

An Unquenchable Spirit

History is replete with the stories of plodders. Although we may not be aware of all the challenges that were involved, many success stories are really stories of people who had persistence and an unquenchable spirit—people who were absolutely determined to reach their goal. You are probably familiar with the following people, but did you know:

- Dr. Seuss's first children's book was rejected by twenty-three publishers.

- The Coca-Cola Company sold only four hundred Cokes in its first year of business.

- In his first three years in the automobile business, Henry Ford went bankrupt twice.

- Robert Frost's poetry was rejected by the poetry editor of the *Atlantic Monthly* in 1902 with a letter saying, "Our magazine has no room for your vigorous verse."

- Michael Jordan was cut from his high school basketball team.

- In 1905 the University of Bern rejected Albert Einstein's Ph.D. dissertation, saying that it was irrelevant and fanciful.

- Joan Benoit underwent knee surgery seventeen days before the U.S. Olympic Trials for the marathon. She not only made the team; she came home with the gold medal.

- Vince Lombardi was forty-seven when he finally became a head coach in the NFL.[3]

What do all of these people have in common? They pressed on! Though they faced discouragement, they did not lose heart. As Christians, we of all people should not give in to discouragement. Paul explains, "Therefore we do not lose heart. Though outwardly we are wasting away, yet inwardly we are being renewed day by day. For our light and momentary troubles are achieving for us an eternal glory that far outweighs them all. So we fix our eyes not on what is seen, but on what is unseen. For what is seen is temporary, but what is unseen is eternal" (2 Corinthians 4:16–18). In other words, we need to keep our eyes on the big, eternal picture and stop sweating the small stuff!

Persisting with Enthusiasm

In 1964 J. V. Cerney wrote a book entitled *How to Develop a Million-Dollar Personality.* In it he described the physiological benefits

Never, never, never give up. —Winston Churchill

:-)

of having enthusiasm in life. Here is his "top ten" list, so to speak, of reasons to be enthusiastic:

1. Aids digestion.

2. Improves metabolism.

3. Relieves tension.

4. Improves muscle function.

5. Stimulates circulation.

6. Steps up endocrine action (hormones).

7. Stabilizes the blood pressure.

8. Stimulates a dynamo of energy.

9. Provides a feeling of euphoria (well-being).

10. Establishes reserve power for periods when you are feeling low.[4]

Wow! Did you have any idea enthusiasm was so beneficial to our bodies? But its benefits don't stop there. Enthusiasm plays a big part in what you and I are able to achieve in this world. A survey was given to a group of self-made millionaires, asking them to list and rate the qualities that had contributed to their success. The final tally looked like this:

Ability ....5 percent
Knowledge ....5 percent
Discipline ....10 percent
Attitude ....40 percent
Enthusiasm ....40 percent[5]

Sometimes we can increase our abilities or our knowledge with outside input, but discipline, attitude, and enthusiasm can only come from within. Of course, we all have days when we just don't feel bubbly, springy, or lively. That's okay. In the introduction to this book, I mentioned that the word *enthusiasm* comes from the Greek words *en theos,* meaning "God within." Enthusiasm is not so much an outward quality as it is an inward desire, based on the assurance we have that God is with us and his Holy Spirit is in us. For positive women of faith, enthusiasm is more than its modern definition of an intense or eager interest. Rather, it is a deep longing and persistent desire to use the gifts and talents God has placed in us, knowing that he will give us the strength and power to express them in a positive way that will bless others and glorify him.

Ralph Waldo Emerson said, "Enthusiasm is one of the most powerful engines of success. When you do a thing, do it with your might. Put your whole soul into it. Stamp it with your own personality. Be active, be energetic, be enthusiastic and faithful, and you will accomplish your object."[6] Paul puts it another way, "Work hard and cheerfully at whatever you do, as though you were working for the Lord rather than for people" (Colossians 3:23 NLT).

Each day we can choose whether or not to be enthusiastic in our lives. As the author of several party books, I speak to women quite often on the topic of parties and entertainment. But as I noted in my last book, *The Power of a Positive Mom,* one huge party goes on every day all around the world, and we have a standing invitation: the Ladies Pity Party. Don't accept! Instead of focusing on our problems and circumstances and feeling sorry for ourselves, let's choose to be grateful for God's goodness and hopeful and enthusiastic about the future, knowing that God is with us. He is at work in us at this very moment, and he has great plans in store.

Choose to Move Forward

We all have regrets. We've all made mistakes. We all have all sinned. It's easy to beat ourselves up mentally, telling ourselves that we are foolish, or failures, or not capable or deserving of moving on in life. Yes, God hates sin because he knows how it can ravage our lives. But he doesn't hate us. God is a forgiving God. He is a God of new beginnings. His love and forgiveness can give us the courage to turn from our sin and begin moving again in a positive direction.

The Bible is all about moving forward and not looking back. Paul, who had persecuted Christians in his younger days and had much to regret, said he was forgetting those things that were behind him and moving forward to what was ahead (Philippians 3:12–14). Wallowing in regret is never healthy. We may have remorse or grief over sin for a time, and rightly so; but ultimately we must leave it behind and move on in forgiveness and newness of life.

We can find motivation to move on in the story of the woman who was caught in adultery and brought before Jesus for judgment. Her accusers were the so-called righteous Pharisees, who wanted to trick Jesus in the process of punishing the woman for her sin. The Law of Moses said that a woman caught in adultery must be stoned. Would Jesus go along with that law or get himself into trouble by breaking it? Jesus responded to their challenge by bending down to the ground and writing in the sand with his finger—perhaps writing out the personal sins of the accusers, as some scholars suggest. The story continues:

> When they kept on questioning him, he straightened up and said to them, "If any one of you is without sin, let him be the first to throw a stone at her." Again he stooped down and wrote on the ground.
>
> At this, those who heard began to go away one at a time, the older ones first, until only Jesus was left, with the woman still standing there. Jesus straightened up and asked her, "Woman, where are they? Has no one condemned you?"

Therefore, my beloved brethren, be steadfast, immovable, always abounding in the work of the Lord, knowing that your toil is not in vain in the Lord. —1 Corinthians 15:58 NASB

"No one, sir," she said.

"Then neither do I condemn you," Jesus declared. "Go now and leave your life of sin." (John 8:7–11)

Let's be quite clear: Jesus was not condoning adultery. He spoke strongly against it on other occasions (see Matthew 5:27–30 and 19:18). Rather, his message to this woman was to stop sinning and move on. Is there sin that needs to be dealt with in your life? Stop reading right now and take those sins before the Father, confessing them and asking for his forgiveness. Ask him to give you the strength to turn from them and to stay turned from them. You can do this confidently, knowing that God is faithful and just to forgive you of your sins and cleanse you from all unrighteousness (see 1 John 1:9). Now go and sin no more!

Satan, our enemy, is an accuser. He would love to disarm our enthusiasm and thwart our potential in life by bombarding us with guilt and regret. When we find ourselves being attacked with debilitating thoughts, we need to put on our armor (as we learned in chapter 14). We need to hold up our shield of faith, knowing that Jesus took care of our sins on the cross, and we are forgiven completely.

Of course, we shouldn't be fooled into thinking that because God is a forgiving God, sin is no big deal. Sin has consequences. God forgives us, but he doesn't take away all the inevitable trouble that our own bad choices set in motion. Thankfully, though, he loves us enough to be with us even through the difficulties we bring upon ourselves.

Living in Contentment

An important part of moving forward in our lives is learning to be content. Living in contentment doesn't imply that we are stagnant and dull, sticking with the status quo. No, contentment is a quality of the heart that can be found in many of the movers and shakers of our world. It is certainly a quality we want to have as positive women. A content woman is one who accepts the people and the circumstances around her and makes the best of her situation. She has an inner peace, leaving to God those things she cannot change and making a difference where she can. Paul spoke of his own contentment in Philippians 4:11–13: "I have learned to be content whatever the circumstances. I know what it is to be in need, and I know what it is to have plenty. I have learned the secret of being content in any and every situation, whether well fed or hungry, whether living in plenty or in want. I can do everything through him who gives me strength."

Perhaps you have heard or even memorized another common version of that last verse: "I can do all things through Christ who strengthens me" (NKJV). Often Philippians 4:13 is used as a motivational, catchall phrase to imply that we can accomplish anything we set our minds to with God's help. But did you realize that Paul was talking about contentment here? Philippians 4:13 was the key to his contented state.

Can we say the same? Is our contentment found in our relationship with Christ, the one who gives us strength to make it through the various circumstances in our lives? Or do we hang our happiness and contentment on the "if onlys" of life:

- If only I had a better job.
- If only my husband were kind and sensitive.
- If only he worked harder.
- If only I had a bigger house.
- If only my kitchen were updated.
- If only I didn't have this boss.

- If only my childhood hadn't been so bad.

- If only someone would believe in me!

What is the "if only" that is keeping you from being content? Counter that "if only" thinking with a new phrase: "but God can." Pray about your situation, change what ought to be or can be changed, and relinquish everything else to God. Desire contentment as one of the highest virtues.

Paul was undoubtedly one of the greatest "go-getters" in all of Christendom. He was a positive apostle, always encouraging, always teaching, always building new communities of believers. He preached and traveled widely, often finding himself in difficult, even life-threatening circumstances. Yet wherever God led him, he was content in his spirit, and his heart was constantly motivated to press on. Even when he was thrown in prison, he didn't become defeated or discontented. Instead he did what he could do to further the Gospel and encourage the early churches. Many of the letters we have in the New Testament today were written by Paul from a prison cell, including the letter to the Philippians that talks about contentment!

What prison cell are you living in right now? What circumstances are threatening to hold you down and keep you from moving on in your walk with God? Be careful; a discontented spirit will only lead to bitterness, anger, and frustration and will keep you from going forward into the abundant life God has planned for you. What if Paul had sat in his prison cell, feeling sorry for himself and saying, "This is not fair. I shouldn't be here. My ministry is over"? We wouldn't have the benefit of some of the greatest teaching in the Bible! Can you be content and allow God to work through you, too, despite the difficulties you face?

Conclusion

It's Your Choice

As positive women we must make positive choices every day. My hope is that this book has encouraged you to do just that. I pray that you will:

- choose to have faith instead of doubt

- choose to search for wisdom instead of wandering aimlessly in life

- choose to pray instead of worrying and fretting

- choose to experience joy instead of bitterness

- choose to love instead of hate

- choose to live courageously instead of in fear

- choose to have hope instead of despair

- choose to live enthusiastically, knowing that God has a purpose and a plan for your life, and he will empower you to live it out

Press on! Move ahead victoriously on the pathway that God has set before you, despite the inevitable bumps and potholes. Don't waste time complaining about what's wrong, what you don't have, or what other people are doing or thinking. Celebrate what's right in your life. Enjoy what you do have. And most importantly, enjoy being with the people who are dear to you.

As a positive woman, you can be a beacon of light shining in a dark world. You can be a vessel of God's love and joy and forgiveness and hope in a world badly in need of each of these things. Never underestimate the powerful impact you can have on your family, your friends, and the world around you. After all, the power of a positive woman is not your power; it's God's.

POWER POINT

⚙ **Read:** Acts 18:2, 18, 24–26; also Romans 16:3–4 and 1 Corinthians 16:19. What part did Priscilla play in the early church? What gifts did she seem to have? Which of the seven principles of a positive woman do you see at work in her life? Do you think her actions had an eternal impact?

♡ **Pray:** Lord, you are a wonderful and loving heavenly Father! You forgive my sins and heal my diseases. You redeem my life from the pit and crown me with love and compassion. You renew my strength like the eagle's. I love you, Lord! Help me to continue moving forward in my walk with you. Tenderly teach me and guide me along the way, and help me to make positive choices each day. Help me to press on for your glory until the day I meet you face to face. In Jesus' name, amen.

💡 **Remember:** "Work hard and cheerfully at whatever you do, as though you were working for the Lord rather than for people" (Colossians 3:23 NLT).

☺ **Do:** Thumb back through this book and highlight or paper clip pages and passages that were particularly meaningful to you. Review the memory verses at the end of each chapter and determine to apply them to your life from this day forward.

Notes

Introduction: The Great Adventure

1. Adapted from Edward Rowell and Bonnie Steffen, *Humor for Preaching and Teaching* (Grand Rapids, Mich.: Baker Books, 1996), 176.

Chapter 1: It's a Girl Thing

1. Adapted from Matthew Henry, *Commentary on the Whole Bible* (Peabody, Mass.: Hendrickson Publishers, Inc., 1991), 6.

2. Edith Deen, *All the Women of the Bible* (Edison, N.J.: Castle Books, 1955), 69.

3. J. C. Webster and K. Davis, ed., *A Celebration of Women* (Southlake, Tex.: Watercolor Books, 2001), 171.

4. Peggy Anderson, *Great Quotes from Great Women* (Lombard, Ill.: Celebrating Excellence Publishing, 1992), 62.

5. Mabel Bartlett and Sophia Baker, *Mothers—Makers of Men* (New York: Exposition Press, 1952), 92.

6. Anderson, *Great Quotes from Great Women,* 11.

7. Gail Rolka, *One Hundred Women Who Shaped World History* (San Meteo, Calif.: Bluewood Books, 1994), 97.

8. Robert Schwaneberg, "Stop the Trains!" *Reader's Digest* (December 2001), 67.

Notes

Chapter 2: A Perfect Fit

1. Webster and Davis, *A Celebration of Women,* 146.

2. Kenneth W. Osbeck, *101 Hymn Stories* (Grand Rapids, Mich.: Kregel Publications, 1982), 167.

3. Ibid., 43–44.

4. Frank S. Mead, ed., *12,000 Religious Quotations* (Grand Rapids, Mich.: Baker Book House, 1998), 448.

Chapter 3: The Race of Life

1. Wendy Northcutt, *The Darwin Awards* (New York: Dutton, 2000), 27.

2. Richard J. Foster and Emilie Griffin, ed., *Spiritual Classics* (New York: HarperCollins, 2000), 360.

3. Michael Collopy, *Works of Love Are Works of Peace* (Fort Collins, Colo.: Ignatius Press, 1996), 98.

4. Corrie ten Boom with Jamie Buckingham, *Tramp for the Lord* (Old Tappan, N.J.: Revell Company, 1974), 12.

5. "At Home Live with Chuck and Jenny," *Family Network, Inc.* (Sept. 26, 2001).

Chapter 4: Spiritual Makeover

1. Croft M. Pentz, ed., *The Speaker's Treasury of Four Hundred Quotable Poems* (Grand Rapids, Mich.: Zondervan Publishing House, 1963), 159.

2. Walter Hooper, ed., *God in the Dock* (Grand Rapids, Mich.: Eerdmans, 1970), 55.

3. Jim Cymbala, *Fresh Power* (Grand Rapids, Mich.: Zondervan Publishing, 2001), 200.

4. Mead, *12,000 Religious Quotations,* 134.

5. Ibid., 135.

6. Ibid., 135.

7. John Blanchard, *More Gathered Gold* (Hertfordshire, England: Evangel Press, 1986), 94.

8. Joe Simnacher, *Dallas Morning News,* Thursday, November 29, 2001, A33, 39.

9. Anderson, *Great Quotes by Great Women,* 99.

10. Simnacher, *Dallas Morning News,* A33, 39.

Chapter 5: More Precious Than Rubies

1. Roy B. Zuck, *The Speaker's Quote Book* (Grand Rapids, Mich.: Kregel Publications, 1997), 411.

2. Michael Caputo, *God Seen through the Eyes of the Greatest Minds* (West Monroe, La.: Howard Publishing, 2000), 165.

3. Gorton Carruth and Eugene Ehrlich, *American Quotations* (New York: Gramercy Books, 1988), 599.

4. Angela Beasley, *Minutes from the Great Women's Coffee Club* (Nashville: Walnut Grove Press, 1997), 97.

5. William J. Federer, *America's God and Country* (Coppell, Tex.: Fame Publishing, 1994), 255.

6. Stephen Abbott Northrop, D.D., *A Cloud of Witnesses* (Portland, Oreg.: American Heritage Ministries, 1987), 285.

7. Ibid., 484.

8. Zuck, *The Speaker's Quote Book,* 411.

9. Ibid.

10. *The Pocket Book of Quotations* (New York: Pocket Books, Inc., 1942), 437.

Chapter 6: Winning Wisdom

1. Glenn Van Ekeren, *Speaker's Sourcebook II* (Englewood Cliffs, N.J.: Prentice Hall, 1994), 176–177.

2. Helen Kooiman Hosier, *One Hundred Christian Women Who Changed the Twentieth Century* (Grand Rapids, Mich.: Fleming H. Revell, 2000), 238–241.

3. Ibid.

4. John Bartlett, *Barlett's Familiar Quotations* (Boston: Little, Brown and Company, 1855, 1980), 593.

5. Anderson, *Great Quotes by Great Women,* 99.

Chapter 7: Extra Baggage

1. Blanchard, *More Gathered Gold,* 227.

2. C. S. Lewis, *Letter to Malcolm: Chiefly on Prayer* (New York: Harcourt Brace Javanovich, 1964), 28.

3. C. S. Lewis, *The World's Last Night and Other Essays* (New York: Harcourt Brace Javanovich, 1960), 4–5.

4. Walter B. Knight, *Knight's Master Book of Four Thousand Illustrations* (Grand Rapids, Mich.: Eerdmans Publishing, 1956), 492.

5. Ibid., 485.

Chapter 8: A Simple Guide to Effective Prayer

1. Knight, *Four Thousand Illustrations,* 485.

2. Hank Hanegraaff, *The Prayer of Jesus* (Nashville: Word Publishing, 2001), 10.

3. Rowell and Steffen, *Humor for Preaching and Teaching,* 135.

4. Blanchard, *More Gathered Gold,* 318.

5. Richard J. Foster and James Bryan Smith, *Devotional Classics* (San Francisco: HarperCollins, 1993), 320.

6. Knight, *Four Thousand Illustrations,* 489.

7. *More of God's Words of Life for Women* (Grand Rapids, Mich.: Zondervan Gifts, 2000), 207.

Chapter 9: Experiencing Joy

1. Zuck, *The Speaker's Quote Book,* 215.

2. Used by permission of the author.

3. Edward K. Rowell ed., *Quotes and Idea Starters for Preaching and Teaching* (Grand Rapids, Mich.: Baker Book House, 1996), 92.

4. Knight, *Four Thousand Illustrations,* 347.

Chapter 10: My Life As a Three-Ring Circus

1. *The Secrets of Joy, A Treasury of Wisdom* (Philadelphia: Running Press, 1995), 23.

2. Ibid., 18.

3. Gary Smalley, *Food and Love* (Wheaton, Ill.: Tyndale House Publishers, 2001), 41.

4. John Cook, *The Book of Positive Quotations* (Minneapolis: Fairview Press, 1997), 89.

5. Adapted from Jean Lush, *Women and Stress* (Grand Rapids, Mich.: Fleming H. Revell, 1992), 109–112.

Chapter 11: Friendships in the Fast Lane

1. Alan Loy McGinnis, *The Friendship Factor* (Minneapolis: Augsburg Publishing House, 1979), 25–26.

2. Dale Carnegie, *How to Win Friends and Influence People* (New York: Pocket Books, 1936), 54.

3. Lewis C. Henry, ed., *Five Thousand Quotations for All Occasions* (Garden City, N.Y.: DoubleDay, 1945), 120.

4. Angela B. Freeman, *One Hundred Years of Women's Wisdom* (Nashville: Walnut Grove Press, 1999), 59.

5. Zuck, *The Speaker's Quote Book,* 158.

6. Louise Bachelder, ed., *A Selection on Friendship* (White Plains, N.Y.: Peter Pauper Press, Inc., 1966), 58.

7. *God's Little Devotional Book for Couples* (Tulsa: Honor Books, 1995), 118.

8. Bachelder, *A Selection on Friendship,* 1.

9. Ibid., 25.

Chapter 12: Creative Compassion

1. Knight, *Four Thousand Illustrations,* 395.

2. Anderson, *Great Quotes from Great Women,* 19.

3. Webster and Davis, *A Celebration of Women,* 191.

Chapter 13: High Heels on a Dirt Road

1. K. Golden and B. Findlen, *Remarkable Women of the Twentieth Century* (New York: Friedman Publishing Group, 1998), 20.

2. D. Heyman, "Women of the Year," *US Weekly* (December 10, 2001), 55.

3. Hosier, *One Hundred Christian Women,* 198.

Chapter 14: Facing Fears

1. Blanchard, *More Gathered Gold,* 102.

2. Zuck, *The Speaker's Quote Book,* 151. Adapted from a story by A. L. Kirpatrick.

3. Blanchard, *More Gathered Gold,* 102.

4. Used by permission from Dana Crawford, Dallas, Texas.

Notes

Chapter 15: Stop Whining and Start Smiling

1. Gary Thomas, *Christianity Today,* December 3, 1994. Reprinted in *Fresh Illustrations for Preaching and Teaching,* Edward K. Rowell, ed. (Grand Rapids, Mich.: Baker Book House, 1997), 117.

2. Zuck, *The Speaker's Quote Book,* 199.

3. Anderson, *Great Quotes from Great Women,* 11.

4. Cook, *Positive Quotations,* 285.

5. Knight, *Four Thousand Illustrations,* 471.

6. Cook, *Positive Quotations,* 288.

7. *The Secrets of Joy,* 111.

8. Blanchard, *More Gathered Gold,* 156.

Chapter 16: Delicious Morsels

1. Abigail Van Buren, "Dear Abby," *Universal Press Syndicate,* October 13, 2001.

2. Cook, *Positive Quotations,* 271.

3. *The Power of Hope* (New York: Inspirational Press, 1976), 141.

4. Cook, *Positive Quotations,* 272.

Conclusion: Press On!

1. Edward K. Rowell, ed., *Fresh Illustrations for Preaching and Teaching* (Grand Rapids, Mich.: Baker Book House, 1997), 156.

2. Knight, *Four Thousand Illustrations,* 474.

3. Van Ekeren, *Speaker's Sourcebook II,* 279–280.

4. Jennifer McKnight-Trontz, *Yes You Can* (San Francisco: Chronicle Books, 2000), 22.

5. Zuck, *The Speaker's Quote Book,* 131.

6. Ibid.